The Definitive QUEEN'S PARK RANGERS F.C.

A statistical history to 1996

Statistics by Gordon Macey
Production by Tony Brown

Volume 6 in a series of club histories
The Association of Football Statisticians

First published in Great Britain by Tony Brown, on behalf of the Association of Football Statisticians, 22 Bretons, Basildon, Essex SS15 5BY.

Other volumes in this series are:

and clubs under consideration for future volumes include Scunthorpe United, Aldershot, Hartlepool United, Torquay United and Luton Town

ISBN 1 899468 06 4

QUEEN'S PARK RANGERS F.C.

Contents

FOREWORD by Chris Wright

I cannot profess to have been a QPR supporter all my life as I was born on a farm in Lincolnshire in the mid 1940s when the local team, Grimsby Town, were, I believe, still in the top half of the First Division of the old Football League. However, they quickly graduated through to the Third Division and I can distinctly remember seeing QPR playing there in the 1950s.

It was not until I relocated from Manchester to London in the late 1960s that I started going to Loftus Road and not until 1970 that I became a fully fledged Rangers supporter. This of course meant that QPR's glory years of the 1970s, 1980s and early 1990s are the ones with which I am most familiar, in particular Dave Sexton's great team of the mid-1970s from Parkes to Givens and including Bowles and Francis. I vividly remember the occasion when we cheered the lads off the pitch on a Saturday afternoon, knowing that if Liverpool slipped up to relegated Wolves in their last game, we would be crowned champions of the First Division. I also remember listening to the Wolves v. Liverpool game from my office in Los Angeles over the telephone until it became clear that Liverpool were winning 3-1 and we would finish Runners-up.

Since then, I have seen managers came and go, players come and go but always with the same QPR distinctive brand of football. Whatever anyone says about football academies at other London clubs, it bas always been QPR in recent times that have been the epitome of a club which manages to play attractive football regardless of the result and now I am Chairman, this is a tradition I feel most strongly should be perpetuated.

QPR has a distinct place in the fabric of London football and it is on this foundation that we wish to build a successful and prosperous future for Rangers well into the next Century.

Chris Wright
September 1996

AUTHOR'S NOTES

I was bitten by the Ranger's bug as early as November 1961, when I saw my first professional match at White City Stadium, the occasion being the FA Cup first round tie against Newport County. Ever since then I have been a committed follower and have shared the usual ups and downs a club has. During my time the 'highs' have included the 1966/67 'Double' Season, followed by the first promotion to the top division and (of course) the 'Championship' season of 1975/76. The 'lows' include all relegation seasons, with the most single disappointing match being the Milk Cup Final against Oxford United in April 1986. However, overall looking back the balance is still on the 'profit' side, despite the relegation of last season, 1995/96.

I have always been interested in collecting and collating statistics on the club and had great satisfaction in producing the 'Complete Record' book a few years ago. There have been a number of challenges in trying to compile a complete set of line-ups, etc. for a club that, back in the pre-WW2 days, were not covered very well by the national press. The local papers have on several occasions been the only source of information. This book not only continues the QPR story from my last one, but also includes all corrections and omissions that have been identified by keen-eyed readers. Also as this book has been compiled entirely on a PC using Excel spreadsheets, and with Tony's superior skill and ability with Excel, it has enabled a through cross-checking of the statistics for total appearance and goals scored. I now hope that with the use of technology the 'gremlins' are an extinct race!

With age my wife hoped that my interest would wane, but luckily for me my three children have all shown a strong interest in Rangers so I will just have to keep going to the matches! In my role as the Club's Official Historian I have had correspondence with a large number of people from all around the world which has proved to be very interesting. There seems to be a link that all people who have ever been connected with the club keep, even passing that interest on through their children and grand-children. This 'family' atmosphere is one of Ranger's best assets which I hope the club never loses.

Here's hoping that with the new owner/manager combination Rangers have a successful season and regain their deserved top-flight league position in the shortest possible time.

Gordon Macey
September 1996

PRODUCER'S NOTE

Those of us with a few grey hairs will remember the (then) Third Division club upsetting all the odds in 1967 with a victory at Wembley in the League Cup final. The club have been blessed with some outstanding footballers over the last 30 years, which always made Loftus Road a pleasurable place to visit.....except perhaps during the years of the "artificial surface"! Rangers were the first club to lay down such a surface, in 1981.

Gordon's 1993 book on the club, published by Breedon Books, is now out of print and difficult to find at a sensible price in secondhand bookshops. It is still well worth searching out in your local library and in my view is one of the best books of its type. Though simpler in concept, the book you are reading now brings the QPR story up to date and seeks to correct the (few) errors in the earlier volume.

Gordon's efforts on his computer, and his prompt answers to my many questions despite the pressures of business life, made work on the book much easier. My thanks go as usual to the regular contributors to these books, Brian Tabner (attendances), and Michael Joyce and Leigh Edwards (players). Special thanks to the Chairman, for finding the time to write a foreword without having had an opportunity to see the proofs. Otherwise, he would have found some of those old Grimsby Town v. QPR meetings, in the Second Division up to 1950/51 and in the Third Division from 1959/60!

Tony Brown
September 1996

Season 1920/21. Back row, left; Draper. Second row; Marsden, Donald, Ashford, Grant, McGovern, Baldock, unknown, Watts, Birch, Chandler, John, Grimsdell. Third row; Price, Manning, Wingrove, Cane, Mitchell, Smith, Gregory, Middlemiss, O'Brien, Hill. Front; Two unknowns, Faulkner, Blackman, Pidgeon, unknown.

1934/35: Back; Jones, Barrie, March, Hammond, Crawford, Watson, Ridley, Dutton, Blake, Blackman. Centre; D Richards (trainer), Bartlett, Russell, Abel, Beecham, Langford, Allen, Mason, Reid, Ashman, Famer, J Eggleton (assistant trainer). Front; Emmerson, McCarthy, Devine, Mr. CH Bates (director), Mr. CW Fielding (chairman), Mr. MT O'Brien (secretary manager), Mr. AE Pearsall (vice chairman), Goodier

1949/50: Back; Heath, Parkinson, Woodward, Allen, Reay, Wardle. Front; Pointon, Ramscar, Hatton, Hudson, Pattison.

1962/63, last year at White City Stadium. Back; Large, Drinkwater, Williams, F Smith, Ingham. Centre; Baker, Anderson, Keen, Rutter, Barber, Collins. Front; McClelland, Bedford, Bentley, Evans, Towers, Lazarus.

QUEEN'S PARK RANGERS RECORDS PAGE

PLAYERS:

Most Appearances   Tony Ingham 555 (514 League, 30 FA Cup, 4 League Cup, 7 others)
           Ian Gillard 484 (408+36+32+8)
           Dave Clement 476 (407+29+34+6)
           Peter Angell 457 (417+27+6+7)

Most Goals   George Goddard 186 (174+12)
           Brian Bedford 180 (161+13+6)

Most League Goals in a Season George Goddard 37, 1929/30

Most International Appearances Alan McDonald 43 (Northern Ireland)

THE CLUB:

Honours   Southern League Champions 1907/08, 1911/12
           League Cup Winners 1966/67

Best League performance   2nd in Division One 1976/76
Best F.A. Cup performance   Beaten finalists 1981/982
Most League points   67, Division 3 1966/67 (2 points for a win)
           85, Division 2 1982/83 (3 points for a win)

Most League goals   111, Division 3, 1961/62
Most League wins in a season 26, 1947/48, 1966/67, 1982/83
Best League win   8-0 v. Merthyr Town, 9/3/1929
Best League away win   7-1 v. Mansfield Town, 24/9/1966
Best F.A. Cup win   8-1 v. Bristol Rovers (a) 27/11/1937
Best League Cup win   8-1 v. Crewe Alexandra 3/101983
Best League run undefeated 20, from 3/12/1966 and 11/3/1972
Undefeated League games, home 25, from 2/12/1972
Undefeated League games, away 17, from 10/9/1966
Best run of League wins   8, from 7/11/1931
Best run of home League wins 11, from 26/12/1972
Longest run of League draws 6, from 14/12/1957

INTRODUCTION TO THE STATISTICS PAGES

The season by season grids show the results of games in the Football League, the F.A. Cup, the Football League Cup, and other first team competitions. The results of the 1939/40 season are not included since the League competition was abandoned at the outbreak of World War Two. However, details of these games can be found in a later section.

Home games are identified by the opponents name in upper case, away games by the use of lower case. Queen's Park Rangers' score is always given first. Attendances for League games are taken from the official Football League records since 1925/26; before that, estimated attendances based on newspaper reports have to be used.

Substitutes have the numbers 12, 13 and 14. 12 is used if only one substitute appeared (no matter what number was on the player's shirt). 14 is used for the second substitute until 1994/95 unless he was a goalkeeper. In 1995/96, 13 is used for the second substitute, 14 for the third. The players who were substituted are underlined. Squad numbers are ignored, and numbers approximating to their playing position used instead.

A full player list is provided for every player who made a League appearance. Date and place of birth are shown, where known, and the year of death. Players with the same name are given a (1) or (2) after their name to avoid confusion. The next two columns, "seasons played", act as an index to the season by season grids. The years shown are the "first year" of the season; for example, 1971 is season 1971/72. The two columns show the season in which the player made his League debut; and the final season that he played. However, if he only played in one season, the second column is blank. An entry of "1995" in the second column does not imply that the player has left the club, but means that he appeared in this "final season" of the book.

Note that some players also made F.A. Cup appearances before 1921 and in 1945/46. If a player also made a League appearance his F.A. Cup appearances and goals from these seasons are included in the list.

Previous and next clubs show where he was transferred from, and the club he moved to. Non league club information is included when known.

The appearance columns have separate totals for the League, F.A. Cup, Football League Cup and miscellaneous tournaments. In Queen's Park Rangers' case, the latter category includes the EUFA Cup, the Charity Cup, the Division 3 (South) Cup, the Southern Professional Floodlight Cup, the Mercantile Credit Centenary Trophy and the Full Members' Cup (the latter played under a variety of sponsors' names). "Goals scored" are also shown under the four headings.

If a player has had more than one spell at the club, a consolidated set of appearance and goals are shown on the first line. Subsequent lines show the seasons involved in his return, and his new pair of previous and next clubs.

A full record of meetings against all other League clubs is included. Some clubs have played in the League under different names, but the totals are consolidated under the present day name in this table. Other pages show the club's record in the F.A. Cup in non League seasons and the list of managers.

QUEEN'S PARK RANGERS IN NON LEAGUE SEASONS

Queen's Park Rangers was formed in 1886 by the merger of two local youth club teams in West London, St. Jude's Institute and Christchurch Rangers. Both of these clubs had started playing in 1882. Members had to pay an annual subscription of 7/6d (now 37p). The club joined the West London League in 1891/92 and played in local cup competitions. The F.A. Cup was entered for the first time in 1895/96.

The club turned professional in 1898 and joined the Southern League in 1899. In common with many other Southern League clubs, they played simultaneously in the Western League, winning it in 1905/06. Twice champions of the Southern League, the club then met the champions of the Football League to play for the Charity Shield.

Southern League:

	p	w	d	l	f	a	pts	
1899/00	28	12	2	14	49	57	26	8th
1900/01	28	11	4	13	43	48	26	8th
1901/02	30	8	7	15	34	56	23	12th
1902/03	30	11	6	13	34	42	28	9th
1903/04	34	15	11	8	53	37	41	5th
1904/05	34	14	8	12	51	46	36	7th
1905/06	34	12	7	15	58	44	31	13th
1906/07	38	11	10	17	47	55	32	18th
1907/08	38	21	9	8	82	57	51	1st
1908/09	40	12	12	16	52	50	36	15th
1909/10	42	10	13	10	56	47	51	3rd
1010/11	38	13	14	11	52	41	40	6th
1911/12	38	21	11	6	59	35	53	1st
1912/13	38	18	10	10	46	35	46	4th
1913/14	38	16	9	13	45	43	41	8th
1914/15	38	13	12	13	55	56	38	12th
1919/20	42	18	10	14	62	50	46	6th

Western League:

	p	w	d	l	f	a	pts	
1900/01	16	7	4	5	39	25	18	4th
1901/02	16	5	1	10	17	43	11	8th
1902/03	16	6	2	8	18	31	14	7th
1903/04	16	5	5	6	15	21	15	6th
1904/05	20	6	3	11	27	45	15	11th
1905/06	20	11	4	5	33	27	26	1st
1906/07	10	5	1	4	17	11	11	2nd
1907/08	12	5	1	6	20	23	11	5th
1908/09	12	6	1	5	28	24	13	2nd

Division One to 1905/06, Division One A from 1906/07

1920/21   3rd in Division 3(S)

#	Date	Opponent	Score	Scorers	Att	Ashford HE	Baldock JWN	Birch J	Blackman FE	Chandler ACH	Clayton HL	Donald DM	Faulkner R	Gould HL	Grant GM	Gregory J	Grimsdell EF	Hill LG	John R	McGovern T	Manning JT	Marsden B	Middlemiss H	Mitchell AP	O'Brien MT	Price E	Smith JW	Watts TF	Wingrove J
1	Aug 28	WATFORD	1-2	Birch	20000			8	2				7		5	10				4			11		6	1	9		3
2	Sep 2	NORTHAMPTON T	1-2	Birch	14000			8	2				7		5	10				4			11		6	1	9		3
3	4	Watford	2-0	Birch 2	9000			8	2				7		4	10	3	1					11	5	6		9		
4	6	Northampton Town	3-0	Gregory, Smith, Middlemiss	6000			8	2				7		4	10	3	1					11	5	6		9		
5	11	READING	2-0	Gregory, Smith	15000			8	2				7		4	10	3	1					11	5	6		9		
6	18	Reading	0-0		9000			8	2				7		4	10	3	1					11	5	6		9		
7	25	LUTON TOWN	4-1	Birch 2, Gregory (p), Mitchell	20000			8	2				7		4	10	3	1					11	5	6		9		
8	Oct 2	Luton Town	1-2	Birch	10000			8	2				7		4	10	3	1					11	5	6		9		
9	9	SOUTHEND UNITED	2-0	Smith, Dorsett (og)	20000			8	2				7		4	10	3	1					11	5	6		9		
10	16	Southend United	0-1		8000		6	8	2				7		4	10	3	1					11	5			9		
11	23	Swansea Town	3-1	Gregory, Birch, Manning	16000			8	2			11	7		4	6	3	1			10			5			9		
12	30	SWANSEA TOWN	1-1	Manning	20000			8	2			11	7		4	6	3	1			10			5			9		
13	Nov 6	Southampton	2-2	Manning, Gregory	15000			8	2			11	7		5	6	3	1	4		10						9		
14	13	SOUTHAMPTON	0-0		20000			8	2			11	7		4	6	3	1			10			5			9		
15	20	Grimsby Town	1-2	Smith	8000				2			11	7		4	10	3	1			8			5	6		9		
16	27	GRIMSBY TOWN	2-0	Smith, Gregory	10000			8	2				7		4	10	3	1					11	5	6		9		
17	Dec 4	Brighton & Hove Albion	1-2	Gregory	9000			8	2				7		4	10	3	1					11	5	6		9		
18	11	BRIGHTON & HOVE ALB	4-0	Smith 3, Birch	7000			8	2						4	10	3	1			7		11	5	6		9		
19	18	CRYSTAL PALACE	3-0	Birch 2, Gregory	18000			8							4	10	3	1			7		11	5	6		9		2
20	25	Brentford	2-0	Smith 2	20000			8							6	10	3	1			7		11	5	4		9		2
21	27	BRENTFORD	1-0	Birch	25000			8							4	10		1			7	2	11	5	6		9		3
22	Jan 1	Crystal Palace	0-0		20000			8		10					4	11		1			7			5	6		9	3	2
23	15	Merthyr Town	1-3	Birch	15000			8		9					4	11	3	1			7			5	6		10		2
24	22	MERTHYR TOWN	4-2	Gregory, Manning, Birch (p), Smith	9000			8		9					5	11		1	4		7				6		10	3	2
25	Feb 5	Norwich City	0-2		9000				2	9			7		4	11	3	1			8			5	6		10		
26	12	Plymouth Argyle	0-1		14000	6		8	2			11			4	10		1			7			5			9		3
27	17	NORWICH CITY	2-0	Gregory, Birch	4000			8	3			11			4	10		1			7			5	6		9		2
28	26	Exeter City	1-0	Smith	10000	6						11	7		4	10		1			8	2		5			9		3
29	Mar 5	EXETER CITY	2-1	Gregory 2	15000							11	7		4	10		1			8	2		5	6		9		3
30	12	Millwall	0-0		25000	6						11	7		4	10		1			8	2		5			9		3
31	17	PLYMOUTH ARGYLE	4-0	Smith 2, Clayton, Gregory	8000	6					8	11	7		4	10		1				2		5			9		3
32	19	MILLWALL	0-0		20000	6					8	11	7		4	10		1				2		5			9		3
33	25	Bristol Rovers	0-3		15000						8	11	7		4	10		1				2		5	6		9		3
34	26	NEWPORT COUNTY	2-0	Mitchell, Smith	10000					10		11	7	1	4						8	2		5	6		9		3
35	28	BRISTOL ROVERS	2-1	Mitchell, Smith	15000					10		11	7	1	4						8	2		5	6		9		3
36	Apr 2	Newport County	3-1	Smith, Chandler, Manning	15000					8		11	7		4						10	2		5	6	1	9		3
37	9	GILLINGHAM	0-1		10000					8		11	7		4	10						2		5	6	1	9		3
38	16	Gillingham	2-1	Gregory, Smith	8000					8		11	7		4	10						2		5	6	1	9		3
39	23	SWINDON TOWN	1-0	Chandler	12000				3	8		11	7		4	10						2		5	6	1	9		
40	30	Swindon Town	1-0	Gregory	7000					8		11	7		4	10						2		5	6	1	9		3
41	May 2	PORTSMOUTH	0-0		5000					8		11	7		4	10		1				2		5	6		9		3
42	7	Portsmouth	0-0		13000					8		11	7		4	10		1				2		5	6		9		3
		Apps				5	1	25	22	12	3	22	33	2	42	39	20	32	2	2	22	16	16	35	36	7	42	2	24
		Goals						15		2	1					15					5		1	3			18		

One own goal

F.A. Cup

#	Date	Opponent	Score	Scorers	Att	Birch J	Blackman FE	Chandler ACH	Grant GM	Gregory J	Grimsdell EF	Hill LG	Manning JT	Mitchell AP	O'Brien MT	Smith JW	Wingrove J
R1	Jan 8	ARSENAL	2-0	Chandler, O'Brien	20000	8		10	4	11	3	1	7	5	6	9	2
R2	29	Burnley	2-4	Smith, Birch	41007	8	2	9	4	11		1	7	5	6	10	3

		P	W	D	L	F	A	W	D	L	F	A	Pts
1	Crystal Palace	42	15	4	2	45	17	9	7	5	25	17	59
2	Southampton	42	14	5	2	46	10	5	11	5	18	18	54
3	QUEEN'S PARK RGS.	42	14	4	3	38	11	8	5	8	23	21	53
4	Swindon Town	42	14	5	2	51	17	7	5	9	22	32	52
5	Swansea Town	42	9	10	2	32	19	9	5	7	24	26	51
6	Watford	42	14	4	3	40	15	6	4	11	19	29	48
7	Millwall	42	11	5	5	25	8	7	6	8	17	22	47
8	Merthyr Town	42	13	5	3	46	20	2	10	9	14	29	45
9	Luton Town	42	14	6	1	51	15	2	6	13	10	41	44
10	Bristol Rovers	42	15	3	3	51	22	3	4	14	17	35	43
11	Plymouth Argyle	42	10	7	4	25	13	1	14	6	10	21	43
12	Portsmouth	42	10	8	3	28	14	2	7	12	18	34	39
13	Grimsby Town	42	12	5	4	32	16	3	4	14	17	43	39
14	Northampton Town	42	11	4	6	32	23	4	4	13	27	52	38
15	Newport County	42	8	5	8	20	23	6	4	11	23	41	37
16	Norwich City	42	9	10	2	31	14	1	6	14	13	39	36
17	Southend United	42	13	2	6	32	20	1	6	14	12	41	36
18	Brighton & Hove A.	42	11	6	4	28	20	3	2	16	14	41	36
19	Exeter City	42	9	7	5	27	15	1	8	12	12	39	35
20	Reading	42	8	4	9	28	22	4	3	14	16	37	31
21	Brentford	42	7	9	5	27	23	2	3	16	15	44	30
22	Gillingham	42	6	9	6	19	24	2	3	16	15	50	28

1921/22   5th in Division 3(S)

#		Date	Match	Result	Scorers	Att.	Ashford HE	Bailey S	Bain K	Birch J	Blackman FE	Bradshaw JH	Burnham J	Chandler ACH	Clayton HL	Edgley HH	Faulkner R	Grant GM	Gregory J	Hill LG	John R	Knight FC	Lock H	Marsden B	O'Brien MT	Ramsey AP	Reed A	Smith JW	Thompson C	Vigrass J
1	Aug	27	SWINDON TOWN	0-0		18000				8	3			9		7		4	10	1				2	6	11	5			
2		29	Newport County	1-0	Birch	10000				8	3			9		7			10	1			4	2	6	11	5			
3	Sep	3	Swindon Town	0-2		10000				8	3			9		7			10	1			4	2	6	11	5			
4		5	NEWPORT COUNTY	2-1	Birch, Smith	7000				8	3						?		10	1			4	2	6	11	5	9		
5		10	Norwich City	0-0		9000					3			8					10	1			4	2	6	11	5	9		
6		17	NORWICH CITY	2-0	Gregory, Smith (p)	15000					3				10	11	7	4	8	1				2	6		5	9		
7		24	Reading	1-0	Gregory	12000					3		7		10	11		4	8	1				2	6		5	9		
8	Oct	1	READING	1-1	Birch	16000				8	3		7			11		4	10	1				2	6		5	9		
9		8	Bristol Rovers	1-1	Smith	16000				8	3		7			11		4	10	1				2	6		5	9		
10		15	BRISTOL ROVERS	1-2	O'Brien	10000				8	3		7			11		4	10	1				2	6		5	9		
11		22	Brentford	1-5	Birch	16000				8	3			9	10	11	7	4		1				2	6		5			
12		29	BRENTFORD	1-1	Smith	15000	6			8	3		7			11			10	1			4				5	9	2	
13	Nov	5	Aberdare Athletic	2-4	Birch, Gregory	12000				8	3					11	7	4	10	1				2	5		6	9		
14		12	ABERDARE ATHLETIC	1-0	Knight	12000			3	8	2					11	7	4	10		9	1					6	5		
15		19	Brighton & Hove Albion	1-2	Faulkner	9000			3	8	2					11	7	4	10		9	1					6	5		
16		26	BRIGHTON & HOVE ALB	3-0	O'Brien, Birch 2	12000			3	8			6	10			7	4	11					1	2		5	9		
17	Dec	3	Watford	2-2	Gregory, Birch	8000			3	8			6	10			7	4	11					1	2		5	9		
18		10	WATFORD	1-1	Birch	8000			3	8			6	10			7	4	11					1	2		5	9		
19		17	Charlton Athletic	1-1	Chandler	12000			3	8			6	10			7	4	11					1	2		5	9		
20		24	CHARLTON ATHLETIC	3-1	O'Brien, Smith, Chandler	12000			3	8			6	10		7		4	11	1				2			5	9		
21		26	SOUTHAMPTON	2-2	Birch, Chandler	18000			3	8			6	10		7		4	11	1				2			5	9		
22		27	Southampton	1-1	Birch	20940				8	3		6	10		7			11	1				2			5	9		
23		31	NORTHAMPTON T	4-0	Birch 2, Smith 2	10000			3	8	2		6	10		7		4	11	1							5	9		
24	Jan	14	Northampton Town	0-1		6000			3	8	2		6	10		7		4		1						11	5	9		
25		21	GILLINGHAM	1-0	Chandler	5000			3	8			6	10		7		4	11	1				2			5	9		
26		28	Gillingham	2-1	Smith 2	10000				8	3		6	10		7		4	11	1				2			5	9		
27	Feb	4	MILLWALL	6-1	Edgley, Smith, Grant, Birch, Chandler 2	6000				8	3		6	10		7		4	11	1				2			5	9		
28		11	Millwall	0-0		22000			3	8			6	10		7		4	11	1				2			5	9		
29		18	EXETER CITY	2-1	Chandler, Gregory	10000			3	8			6	10		7		4	11	1				2			5	9		
30		25	Exeter City	1-0	Edgley	7000			3	8			6	10		7		4	11	1				2			5	9		
31	Mar	4	SWANSEA TOWN	1-0	Birch	5000			3	8			6	10		7		4	11	1				2			5	9		
32		11	Swansea Town	0-1		10000			3	8			6	10		7		4	11	1				2			5	9		
33		18	Southend United	2-1	Edgley, Birch	7000			3	8			6	10		7		4	11	1				2			5	9		
34		25	SOUTHEND UNITED	1-0	Edgley	12000			3	8			6	10		7			11	1			4	2			5	9		
35	Apr	1	Portsmouth	0-1		8000			3	8			6	10		7			11	1			4	2			5	9		
36		8	PORTSMOUTH	1-1	Chandler	10000	6		3	8		5		10		7			11	1			4	2				9		
37		14	LUTON TOWN	1-0	Gregory	11000	6		3	8		5		9		11	7		10	1			4	2						
38		15	Merthyr Town	0-2		4000	6		3	8		5				11	7		10	1			4	2				9		
39		17	Luton Town	1-3	Birch	16000	6		3	8		5				11	7		10	1			4	2				9		
40		22	MERTHYR TOWN	0-0		4000			3	8		5		9		11	7		10	1			4	2						6
41		29	Plymouth Argyle	0-4		19000			3				5	9		11	7	4	10	1				2				8		6
42	May	6	PLYMOUTH ARGYLE	2-0	Eastwood (og), Edgley	18000			3	8			5	9		11	7		10	1			4	2						6
			Apps				5	1	25	38	20	5	27	30	3	36	17	27	40	36	13	2	6	37	30	6	21	33	1	3
			Goals							17				8		5	1	1	6			1			3			10		

One own goal

F.A. Cup

		Date	Match	Result	Scorers	Att.	Ashford HE	Bailey S	Bain K	Birch J	Blackman FE	Bradshaw JH	Burnham J	Chandler ACH	Clayton HL	Edgley HH	Faulkner R	Grant GM	Gregory J	Hill LG	John R	Knight FC	Lock H	Marsden B	O'Brien MT	Ramsey AP	Reed A	Smith JW	Thompson C	Vigrass J
R1	Jan	7	Arsenal	0-0		31000			3	9			6	11		8	7			1			4	2			5	10		
rep		11	ARSENAL	1-2	Smith	21411			3	8			6	10		11	7	4		1				2			5	9		

		P	W	D	L	F	A	W	D	L	F	A	Pts
1	Southampton	42	14	7	0	50	8	9	8	4	18	13	61
2	Plymouth Argyle	42	17	4	0	43	4	8	7	6	20	20	61
3	Portsmouth	42	13	5	3	38	18	5	12	4	24	21	53
4	Luton Town	42	16	2	3	47	9	6	6	9	17	26	52
5	QUEEN'S PARK RGS.	42	13	7	1	36	12	5	6	10	17	32	49
6	Swindon Town	42	10	7	4	40	21	6	6	9	32	39	45
7	Watford	42	9	9	3	34	21	4	9	8	20	27	44
8	Aberdare Ath.	42	11	6	4	38	18	6	4	11	19	33	44
9	Brentford	42	15	2	4	41	17	1	9	11	11	26	43
10	Swansea Town	42	11	8	2	40	19	2	7	12	10	28	41
11	Merthyr Town	42	14	2	5	33	15	3	4	14	12	41	40
12	Millwall	42	6	13	2	22	10	4	5	12	16	32	38
13	Reading	42	10	5	6	28	15	4	5	12	12	32	38
14	Bristol Rovers	42	8	8	5	32	24	6	2	13	20	43	38
15	Norwich City	42	8	10	3	29	17	4	3	14	21	45	37
16	Charlton Athletic	42	10	6	5	28	19	3	5	13	15	37	37
17	Northampton Town	42	13	5	3	30	17	0	8	13	17	54	37
18	Gillingham	42	11	4	6	36	20	3	4	14	11	40	36
19	Brighton & Hove A.	42	9	6	6	33	19	4	3	14	12	32	35
20	Newport County	42	8	7	6	22	18	3	5	13	22	43	34
21	Exeter City	42	7	5	9	22	29	4	7	10	16	30	34
22	Southend United	42	7	5	9	23	23	1	6	14	11	51	27

1922/23 — 11th in Division 3(S)

#	Date	Opponent	Score	Scorers	Att	Bain K	Birch J	Burnham J	Butler E	Chandler ACH	Davis AG	Edgley HH	Gardner W	Gregory C	Gregory J	Grimsdell EF	Hart E	Hill LG	John R	Lane HW	Leach JM	Marsden B	Parker RR	Rance CS	Vigrass J	Watson E	Watts TF
1	Aug 26	WATFORD	1-2	Birch	20000	3	8	5		10				11		4		1			6	2	9				
2	28	Norwich City	1-1	Davis	10000	3	8			9	10	7		11			6	1	4			2			5		
3	Sep 2	Watford	3-0	Chandler 2, Davis	10000	3	8			9	10	7		11			6	1	4			2			5		
4	4	NORWICH CITY	2-0	C Gregory, Birch	8000	3	8			9	10	7		11			6	1	4			2			5		
5	9	GILLINGHAM	2-1	Birch 2	9000	3	8			9	10	7		11			6	1	4			2			5		
6	11	Brentford	3-1	Parker 2(1p), Birch	15000		8			10		7		11	6			1	4			3	9		5	2	
7	16	Gillingham	1-0	Birch (p)	8000		8			10		7		11	6	3		1	4				9		5	2	
8	23	BRIGHTON & HOVE ALB	0-0		12000	3	8			10		7		11	6			1	4			2	9		5		
9	30	Brighton & Hove Albion	0-2		11000	3	8			10		7		11	6			1	4			2	9		5		
10	Oct 7	SWINDON TOWN	0-2		12000	3	8		7	9	10			11	6	2		1	4						5		
11	14	Swindon Town	0-1		8000	3	8		7	10				11	6			1	4				9		5	2	
12	21	CHARLTON ATHLETIC	1-2	Birch	11000	3	8			10		7		11	6			1	4			2	9		5		
13	28	Charlton Athletic	1-1	Birch	10000	3	8		6	10	9	7		11				1	4			2			5		
14	Nov 4	Aberdare Athletic	0-0		7000	3	8			9	10	7		11				1	4	6		2			5		
15	11	ABERDARE ATHLETIC	4-1	Davis 3, Hart	8000	3	8			9	10	7		11			6	1	4			2			5		
16	18	Newport County	0-1		8000	3	8			9	10	7		11				1	4	6		2			5		
17	25	NEWPORT COUNTY	1-1	Hart	9000	3	8			9	10	7		11			6	1	4			2			5		
18	Dec 9	BRENTFORD	1-1	Marsden (p)	19000	3	8			6	9	7		11	10			1				2			5		4
19	16	BRISTOL CITY	1-2	Marsden (p)	12000	3			7	10	8			11	6			1	4			2	9		5		
20	23	Bristol City	2-3	Davis 2	15000	3			7	10	8			11	6			1				2	9	4	5		
21	25	LUTON TOWN	4-0	Parker 2, Birch 2	16000	3	8		7	10				11	6			1	4			2	9		5		
22	26	Luton Town	0-1		11000	3	8		7	10	9			11	6			1				2		4	5		
23	30	PORTSMOUTH	0-1		9000	3	8		7	10				11	6			1				2	9	4	5		
24	Jan 6	Portsmouth	1-1	Parker	12000	3			7	10	8			11	6			1	4			2	9		5		
25	20	MILLWALL	2-3	Parker, Davis	10000	3			7	10	8			11	6			1	4			2	9		5		
26	27	Millwall	0-0		20000	3		6	7	10	8			11				1	4				9		5	2	
27	Feb 10	Plymouth Argyle	0-2		11000	3			7	10	8			11	6			1	4			2	9		5		
28	17	BRISTOL ROVERS	3-1	Parker, Davis, Chandler	9000	3			7	11	10				8		6	1	4			2	9		5		
29	Mar 3	READING	1-0	Davis	10000	3			7	10	8			11	6			1	4			2	9		5		
30	15	PLYMOUTH ARGYLE	2-3	Birch, Parker	4000	3			7	10	8			11	6			1	4			2	9		5		
31	17	Southend United	0-2		6630				7	10	8		9		6			1	4			3			5	2	
32	21	Reading	0-0		4000	3			7	10	8			11	6			1	4			2	9		5		
33	24	SOUTHEND UNITED	1-0	Davis	8000				7	10	8			11	6			1	4			2	9		5		3
34	26	Bristol Rovers	3-1	Parker, Chandler, Davis	18000				7	10	8			11	6			1	4			2	9		5		3
35	30	SWANSEA TOWN	2-1	Davis, Chandler	18000	3			7	10	8			11	6			1	4			2	9		5		
36	31	Merthyr Town	1-0	Parker	5000	3			7	10	8			11	6			1	4			2	9		5		
37	Apr 2	Swansea Town	0-3		23000				7		8			11	10	3	6	1	4			2	9		5		
38	7	MERTHYR TOWN	1-1	Vigrass	8000	3			7		8	4	10	11	6			1				2	9		5		
39	14	Exeter City	2-1	Parker 2	6000	3			7		8	4	10	11	6			1					9		5	2	
40	21	EXETER CITY	2-0	Parker 2	6000	3	10		7		8	4		11	6			1				2	9		5		
41	28	Northampton Town	2-4	Parker 2	7000	3	8	6	7	10		4		11				1					9		5	2	
42	May 5	NORTHAMPTON T	3-2	Chandler, Edgley, Williams (og)	9000	3	8			9	10	7		11	6			1	4			2			5		
		Apps				36	32	4	21	36	35	33	2	24	33	2	5	42	33	5	1	34	28	13	33	8	2
		Goals					11			6	13	1		1			2					2	16		1		

One own goal

F.A. Cup

Rd	Date	Opponent	Score	Scorers	Att	Bain K	Birch J	Burnham J	Butler E	Chandler ACH	Davis AG	Edgley HH	Gardner W	Gregory C	Gregory J	Grimsdell EF	Hart E	Hill LG	John R	Lane HW	Leach JM	Marsden B	Parker RR	Rance CS	Vigrass J	Watson E	Watts TF
R1	Jan 13	CRYSTAL PALACE	1-0	Gregory	18030	3			7	10	8			11	6			1	4			2	9		5		
R2	Feb 3	Wigan Borough	4-2	Parker 2, Chandler, Birch	23454	3	8			11	10	7			6			1	4			2	9		5		
R3	24	SOUTH SHIELDS	3-0	Parker 2, Gregory	15099	3			7	10	8			11	6			1	4			2	9		5		
R4	Mar 10	SHEFFIELD UNITED	0-1		20000	3			7	10	8			11	6			1	4			2	9		5		

Final table

		P	W	D	L	F	A	W	D	L	F	A	Pts
1	Bristol City	42	16	4	1	43	13	8	7	6	23	27	59
2	Plymouth Argyle	42	18	3	0	47	6	5	4	12	14	23	53
3	Swansea Town	42	13	6	2	46	14	9	3	9	32	31	53
4	Brighton & Hove A.	42	15	3	3	39	13	5	8	8	13	21	51
5	Luton Town	42	14	4	3	47	18	7	3	11	21	31	49
6	Millwall	42	9	10	2	27	13	5	8	8	18	27	46
7	Portsmouth	42	10	5	6	34	20	9	3	9	24	32	46
8	Northampton Town	42	13	6	2	40	17	4	5	12	14	27	45
9	Swindon Town	42	14	4	3	41	17	3	7	11	21	39	45
10	Watford	42	10	6	5	35	23	7	4	10	22	31	44
11	QUEEN'S PARK RGS.	42	10	4	7	34	24	6	6	9	20	25	42
12	Charlton Athletic	42	11	6	4	33	14	3	8	10	22	37	42
13	Bristol Rovers	42	7	9	5	25	19	6	7	8	10	17	42
14	Brentford	42	9	4	8	27	23	4	8	9	14	28	38
15	Southend United	42	10	6	5	35	18	2	7	12	14	36	37
16	Gillingham	42	13	4	4	38	18	2	3	16	13	41	37
17	Merthyr Town	42	10	4	7	27	17	1	10	10	12	31	36
18	Norwich City	42	8	7	6	29	26	5	3	13	22	45	36
19	Reading	42	9	8	4	24	15	1	6	14	12	40	34
20	Exeter City	42	10	4	7	27	18	3	3	15	20	66	33
21	Aberdare Ath.	42	6	8	7	25	23	3	3	15	17	47	29
22	Newport County	42	8	6	7	28	21	0	5	16	12	49	27

1923/24 Bottom of Division 3(S)

#	Date	Opponent	Score	Scorers	Att	Abbott SW	Bain K	Benson GH	Birch J	Butler E	Cameron J	Davis AG	Dobinson H	Drabble F	Field WH	Goodman WR	Hart G	Hill LG	Hurst W	John R	Johnson HE	Keen JF	Knowles F	Marsden B	Oxley RL	Parker RR	Pierce W	Robinson JW	Vigrass J	Waller W	Waugh LS	Wood AB
1	Aug 25	BRENTFORD	1-0	Parker	18000		3	11	8		6	10						1		4		7		2		9			5			
2	27	Bristol Rovers	1-2	Parker	8000		3	11	8		6	10						1		4		7		2		9			5			
3	Sep 1	Brentford	1-0	Birch	12000		3	11	8		6	10						1		4		7		2		9			5			
4	5	BRISTOL ROVERS	1-2	Davis	8000		3	11	8		6	10						1		4		7		2		9			5			
5	8	Swindon Town	0-0		6000		3	11			6	10						1		4		7		2	8	9			5			
6	12	NEWPORT COUNTY	0-3		5000		3		8	11	6	9						1		4		7		2	10				5			
7	15	SWINDON TOWN	2-2	Birch, Davis	6000		3		8	11	6	9						1		4		7		2	10				5			
8	22	Watford	2-0	Birch, Davis	8218		3		8	11	6	9						1		4		7		2	10				5			
9	29	WATFORD	2-1	Birch, Marsden (p)	6000		3		8	11	6	9						1		4		7		2	10				5			
10	Oct 6	Swansea Town	0-2		18000	5		11	8		6	10						1		4		7		2		9		3				
11	13	SWANSEA TOWN	2-2	Davis, Marsden (p)	12000	5	3	11			6	10						1		4		7		2	8	9						
12	20	Northampton Town	0-3		8994	5	3	11	8		6	10	9					1		4		7		2								
13	27	NORTHAMPTON T	3-2	Davis 2, Robinson	9000				8		6	9					4	1				11		2	7			3	10		5	
14	Nov 3	Gillingham	0-0		9000	3			4		6	8						1				11		2	7		9		10		5	
15	10	GILLINGHAM	1-1	Davis	9000	3		11	4			8					6	1				7		2		9			10		5	
16	Dec 1	PLYMOUTH ARGYLE	3-2	Parker, Birch, Davis	8000		3	11	4			8						1			6	7		2		9			10		5	
17	8	Plymouth Argyle	0-2		8000	3		11	4			7						1			6	8		2		9			10		5	
18	15	MERTHYR TOWN	3-0	Parker 2, Marsden (p)	7000			11	4			8						1			6	7		2		9		3	5			10
19	22	Merthyr Town	0-2		2000			11	4			8						1			6	7		2		9		3	5			10
20	25	CHARLTON ATHLETIC	0-0		15000			11	4			8						1			6	7		2		9		3	5			10
21	26	Charlton Athletic	0-3		10000			11	4			8						1			6	7		2		9		3	5			10
22	29	PORTSMOUTH	0-2		8000		2	11	4			8						1			6	7				9		3	5			10
23	Jan 1	Newport County	1-2	Parker	6000	3	2	11	4			8						1			6	7				9			5			10
24	5	Portsmouth	0-7		11085	3	2		8		4	9						1			6	7					11		5			
25	19	BRIGHTON & HOVE ALB	1-0	Parker	4000		2		8	11	6	10			1					4					7	9	3		5			
26	26	Brighton & Hove Albion	0-3		8000		2		8	11	6	9			1					4					7		3		5			10
27	Feb 2	LUTON TOWN	0-2		9000		2		4	11	6	10			1				8			7				9	3		5			
28	9	Luton Town	0-2		6000		2			11			8					1		4		7				9	3		5			10
29	16	READING	1-4	Birch	6000		2		8	11	6							1		4	10	7				9	3		5			
30	23	Reading	0-4		10000		2		7	11								1		4	10		5			9	3		6			8
31	Mar 1	BOURNEMOUTH	0-1		8000		3			11	6			1			4				8	7	5			9	2			10		
32	8	Bournemouth	1-3	Johnson	5000		3		8	7	6			1			4				9		5			11	2			10		
33	15	Millwall	0-3		25000	2	3		8	7								1		4	10		5			11	9		6			
34	22	MILLWALL	1-1	Parker	15000		3		8									1		4	10		5			11	9	2	6			7
35	29	Aberdare Athletic	1-1	Birch	5000		3		8									1		4	10		5			11	9	2	6			7
36	Apr 5	ABERDARE ATHLETIC	3-0	Parker 2, Johnson	6000		3		8									1		4	10		5			11	9	2	6			7
37	12	Southend United	2-4	Parker, Birch	5000		3		8									1		4	10		5			11	9	2	6			7
38	18	NORWICH CITY	2-1	Parker (p), Johnson	10000		3		8							11		1		4	10		5			9	2		6			7
39	19	SOUTHEND UNITED	0-0		8000	3			8		6							1		4	10	11	5			9	2					7
40	21	Norwich City	0-5		12000	3			8									1		4	10	11	5			9	2		6			7
41	26	Exeter City	0-3		5000	3			8									1		4	10	11	5			9	2		6			7
42	May 3	EXETER CITY	2-0	Parker 2	6000		3				6							1	8	4	10		5			9	2					7
		Apps				12	30	17	37	13	24	27	2	2	3	1	4	37	2	36	14	31	13	21	18	33	24	5	30	2	5	19
		Goals							8			8									3			3		14		1				

F.A. Cup

| R1 | Jan 12 | NOTTS COUNTY | 1-2 | Davis | 15000 | | 2 | | 8 | 11 | 6 | 10 | | | | | | 1 | | 4 | | 7 | | | | 9 | 3 | | 5 | | | |

	P	W	D	L	F	A	W	D	L	F	A	Pts
1 Portsmouth	42	15	3	3	57	11	9	8	4	30	19	59
2 Plymouth Argyle	42	13	6	2	46	15	10	3	8	24	19	55
3 Millwall	42	17	3	1	45	11	5	7	9	19	27	54
4 Swansea Town	42	18	2	1	39	10	4	6	11	21	38	52
5 Brighton & Hove A.	42	16	4	1	56	12	5	5	11	12	25	51
6 Swindon Town	42	14	5	2	38	11	3	8	10	20	33	47
7 Luton Town	42	11	7	3	35	19	5	7	9	15	25	46
8 Northampton Town	42	14	3	4	40	15	3	8	10	24	32	45
9 Bristol Rovers	42	11	7	3	34	15	4	6	11	18	31	43
10 Newport County	42	15	2	4	39	15	2	5	14	17	49	43
11 Norwich City	42	13	5	3	45	18	3	3	15	15	41	40
12 Aberdare Ath.	42	9	9	3	35	18	3	5	13	10	40	38
13 Merthyr Town	42	11	8	2	33	19	0	8	13	12	46	38
14 Charlton Athletic	42	8	7	6	26	20	3	8	10	12	25	37
15 Gillingham	42	11	6	4	27	15	1	7	13	16	43	37
16 Exeter City	42	14	3	4	33	17	1	4	16	4	35	37
17 Brentford	42	9	8	4	33	21	5	0	16	21	50	36
18 Reading	42	12	2	7	35	20	1	7	13	16	37	35
19 Southend United	42	11	7	3	35	19	1	3	17	18	65	34
20 Watford	42	8	8	5	35	18	1	7	13	10	36	33
21 Bournemouth	42	6	8	7	19	19	5	3	13	21	46	33
22 QUEEN'S PARK RGS.	42	9	6	6	28	26	2	3	16	9	51	31

1924/25 19th in Division 3(S)

#	Date	Opponent	Score	Scorers	Att	Birch J	Bolam RC	Brown C	Brown HA	Dand R	Evans WB	Fenwick H	Field WH	Ford E	Harris GT	Hart G	Hill LG	Hurst W	John R	Johnson HE	Knowles F	Lillie J	Marsden B	Moore J	Myers EC	Ogley W	Pierce W	Pigg W	Sweetman SC	Symes HC	Thompson J	Wicks JR	Wood AB	Young W
1	Aug 30	Newport County	0-0		10000			7	9					11			1		4	10	5	3	2	8		6								
2	Sep 3	WATFORD	0-0		9000			7	9					11			1		4	10	5	3	2	8		6								
3	6	BRISTOL ROVERS	1-2	H Brown	12000			7	9					11			1		4	10	5	3	2	8		6								
4	10	Watford	0-1		6000	8		7	9					11	6		1		4		5		2	10		3								
5	13	Exeter City	3-1	H Brown, Moore, Crompton (og)	6000	8		7	9					11	6		1		4		5		2	10		3								
6	17	Southend United	0-1		8000	8		7	9					11	6		1		4		5		2	10		3								
7	20	SWANSEA TOWN	0-0		9000	8		7	9		2		1	11	6				4		5			10		3								
8	24	Plymouth Argyle	0-1		5000	8		7	9		2		1	11	6				4		5			10		3								
9	27	Reading	1-2	Hart	1000	8		7	9		2		1	11	6	10			4		5					3								
10	Oct 4	MERTHYR TOWN	1-1	Birch	7000	8		7	9		2	4		11	6	10	1				5					3								
11	11	Brentford	1-0	H Brown	8000	8		7	9			4		11	6		1			10	5		2			3								
12	18	Charlton Athletic	0-2		5000	8		7	9			4		11	6		1			10	5		2			3								
13	25	MILLWALL	0-0		12000	8		7	9			4		11	6		1			10	5		2			3								
14	Nov 1	Luton Town	0-3		4000	8		7				4		11	6		1				5		2	10		3								9
15	8	GILLINGHAM	1-1	Marsden (p)	9000			7						11	6				4	9	5		2	10	8	3						1		
16	15	Swindon Town	3-5	Myers 2, Johnson	7000			7						11	6				4	9	5		2	10	8	3						1		
17	22	BRIGHTON & HOVE ALB	2-0	Johnson 2	9000	8		7					1	11	6				4	9	5		2	10		3								
18	Dec 6	BRISTOL CITY	3-0	Moore 2, Johnson	6000	11		7					1		6				4	9	5		2	10	8	3								
19	20	ABERDARE ATHLETIC	4-1	Birch 2, Johnson, Myers	9000	8		7			5		1		6				4	9			2	10	11	3								
20	25	NORWICH CITY	1-2	Ogley	6000	8		7			5	4	1	11	6					9			2	10		3								
21	26	Norwich City	0-5		12000	8		7	4		5		1	11	6					9			2	10		3								
22	27	NEWPORT COUNTY	4-3	Ford 2, Johnson, Moore	4000	8		7			5		1	11	6				4	9			2	10		3								
23	Jan 17	EXETER CITY	1-4	Moore	10000	8		7					1	11	6					9	5		2	10		3				4				
24	24	Swansea Town	0-2		6000	8		7					1	11	6				4	9	5		2	10		3								
25	31	READING	1-0	Johnson	6000	8		7					1	11	6				4	9	5		2	10							3			
26	Feb 7	Merthyr Town	3-2	Johnson 2, Ford	5000	8		7					1	11					4	9			2	10	6	3			5					
27	14	BRENTFORD	1-0	C Brown	10000	8		7					1	11					4	9				10	6	3	2		5					
28	21	CHARLTON ATHLETIC	0-0		10000	8		7					1	11					4	9				10	6	3	2		5					
29	28	Millwall	0-3		16000	8		7					1	11					4	9				10	6	3	2		5					
30	Mar 7	LUTON TOWN	2-1	Hurst 2	7000	8		7				3	1	11				9						10			2	6	5		4			
31	14	Gillingham	0-1		6000	8		7				3	1	11				9						10			2	6	5		4			
32	18	Bristol Rovers	0-3		5000			7				3	1	11				9						10	8		2		5	6	4			
33	21	BOURNEMOUTH	0-2		7000			7				3	1	11				9						10			2		5	6	4		8	
34	28	Brighton & Hove Albion	0-5		7000	8		7				3	1	11				9						10			2		5	6	4			
35	Apr 4	PLYMOUTH ARGYLE	0-1		11000	8	7					3	1	11				9						10			2		5	6	4			
36	11	Bristol City	0-5		9000	8	7					3	1	11				9						10			2		5	6	4			
37	13	NORTHAMPTON T	2-0	Johnson, Birch	8000	8		7			5		1	11					4	9				10			2			6	3			
38	14	Northampton Town	0-1		8000	8		7			5		1	11					4	9				10			2			6	3			
39	18	SWINDON TOWN	1-0	Pierce (p)	9000	8		7			5		1	11					4	9				10			2			6	3			
40	22	Bournemouth	2-0	Hurst, John	8000	8		7			5		1	11				9	4					10			2			6	3			
41	25	Aberdare Athletic	1-1	Birch	4000	8		7			5		1	11				9	4					10			2			6	3			
42	May 2	SOUTHEND UNITED	3-1	Birch, Ogley (p), Hurst	7000	8		7			5		1	11				9	4					10		3	2			6				
		Apps				36	2	40	13	1	17	19	22	37	24	2	15	8	21	27	22	3	18	26	17	36	22	2	8	8	9	5	1	1
		Goals				6		1	3					3		1		4	1	10			1	5	3	2	1							

One own goal

F.A. Cup

Round	Date	Opponent	Score	Scorers	Att	Birch J	Brown C	Field WH	Ford E	Harris GT	John R	Johnson HE	Knowles F	Myers EC	Ogley W	Marsden B	Symes HC
Q5	Nov 29	CLAPTON	4-4	Myers 4	5000	8	7	1	11	6	4	9	5	10	3	2	
rep	Dec 4	Clapton	2-0	Birch 2	4700	8	7	1	11	6	4	9	5	10	3	2	
Q6	13	CHARLTON ATHLETIC	1-1	Myers (p)	13000	8	7	1	11	6	4	9	5	10	3	2	
rep	18	Charlton Athletic	2-1	Myers, Birch	5000	8	7	1	11	6	4	9	5	10	3	2	
R1	Jan 10	STOCKPORT COUNTY	1-3	Myers	19640	8	7	1	11	6		9	5	10	3	2	4

Final Division 3(S) Table

		P	W	D	L	F	A	W	D	L	F	A	Pts
1	Swansea Town	42	17	4	0	51	12	6	7	8	17	23	57
2	Plymouth Argyle	42	17	3	1	55	12	6	7	8	22	26	56
3	Bristol City	42	14	5	2	40	10	8	4	9	20	31	53
4	Swindon Town	42	17	2	2	51	13	3	9	9	15	25	51
5	Millwall	42	12	5	4	35	14	6	8	7	23	24	49
6	Newport County	42	13	6	2	35	12	7	3	11	27	30	49
7	Exeter City	42	13	4	4	37	19	6	5	10	22	29	47
8	Brighton & Hove A.	42	14	3	4	43	17	5	5	11	16	28	46
9	Northampton Town	42	12	3	6	34	18	8	3	10	17	26	46
10	Southend United	42	14	1	6	34	18	5	4	12	17	43	43
11	Watford	42	12	3	6	22	20	5	6	10	16	27	43
12	Norwich City	42	10	8	3	39	18	4	5	12	14	33	41
13	Gillingham	42	11	8	2	25	11	2	6	13	10	33	40
14	Reading	42	9	6	6	28	15	5	4	12	9	32	38
15	Charlton Athletic	42	12	6	3	31	13	1	6	14	15	35	38
16	Luton Town	42	9	10	2	34	15	1	7	13	15	42	37
17	Bristol Rovers	42	10	5	6	26	13	2	8	11	16	36	37
18	Aberdare Ath.	42	13	4	4	40	21	1	5	15	14	46	37
19	QUEEN'S PARK RGS.	42	10	6	5	28	19	4	2	15	14	44	36
20	Bournemouth	42	8	6	7	20	17	5	2	14	20	41	34
21	Brentford	42	8	7	6	28	26	1	0	20	10	65	25
22	Merthyr Town	42	8	3	10	24	27	0	2	19	11	50	21

1925/26   Bottom of Division 3(S)

#	Date		Opponent	Score	Scorers	Att	Barr W	Birch J	Brown C	Burgess D	Cable TH	Campbell CJ	Edwards JH	Field WH	Ford E	Harris GT	Hebden GHR	Hirst H	John R	Johnson HE	Kerr A	Middleton J	Paterson J	Pierce W	Pigg W	Plunkett AETB	Richmond H	Rowe AJ	Smith SR	Spotiswood J	Sweetman SC	Symes HC	Thompson J	Whitehead WT	Young W
1	Aug 29		Gillingham	0-3		7612			7	10		9				6	1			4		8		2			3	5		11					
2	Sep 3		READING	1-2	Campbell	9313			7	10		9				6	1			4		8		2			3	5		11					
3		5	MERTHYR TOWN	1-1	Spotiswood	8284	8		7			9				6	1			4		10					3	5		11		2			
4		9	Reading	1-2	Burgess	8754	5	8	7	9						6	1			4		10					3			11		2			
5		12	Newport County	1-4	Burgess	8834		8	7	9				1		6				4		10					3	5		11		2			
6		19	LUTON TOWN	1-0	Johnson	5198	8								7		1			4	9	10		2	6		3	5		11					
7		23	Exeter City	0-3		5034	10								11		1			4	9	8		2	6		3	5		7					
8		26	Brentford	2-1	Johnson, Birch	9719		8	7	10							1			4	9			2	6		3			11				5	
9	Oct 3		Bristol Rovers	0-5		7110		8	7	10							1			4	9			2	6		3			11				5	
10		8	EXETER CITY	0-0		4154		8	7								1				10	4		2	6	9				11		3	5		
11		10	SWINDON TOWN	1-1	Middleton	9877			7		8				11		1	4			9	10		2	6							3	5		
12		17	WATFORD	2-0	Whitehurst, Middleton	10711			7						11		1		4	10		8		2	6							3	5	9	
13		24	Brighton & Hove Albion	1-2	Middleton	8816			7						11		1		4	10		8		2	6							3	5	9	
14		31	BRISTOL CITY	0-2		8494			7	10					11		1		4			8		2	6							3	5	9	
15	Nov 7		Crystal Palace	0-1		11829			7	10					11		1		4					2	6							3	8	9	
16		21	Norwich City	1-1	Whitehead	6258		7		10					11		1	4	5					2	6							3	8	9	
17	Dec 5		Plymouth Argyle	1-3	Whitehead	11287		7		10					11		1	4	5					2	6							3	8	9	
18		19	Northampton Town	2-3	Spotiswood, Burgess	5495			7	10							1	4	5					2	6					11		3	8	9	
19		25	CHARLTON ATHLETIC	2-2	Burgess, C Brown	8747			7	10	5					9	1	4						2	6					11		3	8		
20		26	Charlton Athletic	1-1	Burgess	11745			7	10	5		1			9		4						2	6					11		3		8	
21		28	MILLWALL	3-0	Cable 2, Whitehead	8000			7	10	5		1	11	9			4						2	6							3		8	
22	Jan 2		GILLINGHAM	0-1		7287			7	10			1	11	9				5	4				2	6							3		8	
23		16	Merthyr Town	0-1		4378				10					11		1		5	4		7	8	2	6							3		9	
24		23	NEWPORT COUNTY	0-2		6385			7	10							1		5	4			8	2	6					11		3		9	
25		30	Luton Town	0-4		6750			7	10	5						1	6	4	9			8	2		3				11					
26	Feb 6		BRENTFORD	1-1	Burgess	13085		7		10					11	6	1	5	4				8	2		3								9	
27		13	BRISTOL ROVERS	2-1	Ford (p), C Brown	6975			7	10					11	6	1	5	4				8	2		3								9	
28		20	Swindon Town	0-2		6063			7	10					11	6	1	5	4				8	2		3								9	
29		25	ABERDARE ATHLETIC	1-3	Burgess	4385			7	10					11	6	1	5	4				8	2		3									
30		27	Watford	1-3	Young	6578			7	10					11	6	1					5	9									2	3	4	8
31	Mar 4		SOUTHEND UNITED	2-2	Patterson, Young	3377				10	5						1	4				6	9							11		2	3	7	8
32		6	BRIGHTON & HOVE ALB	0-2		8799				10	5						1	4				6	9	3						11		2		7	8
33		13	Bristol City	1-3	Patterson	12193			7	10	5						1	4				6	9	3						11		2			8
34		20	CRYSTAL PALACE	1-3	Burgess	8389			7	10							1	4			9	6	8	3			5			11		2			
35		27	Millwall	0-3		12862			7	10							1	4			9	6	8	3			5			11		2			
36	Apr 2		BOURNEMOUTH	2-2	Whitehead, Patterson	7065					5	7					1	4				6	10	3						11		2		9	8
37		3	NORWICH CITY	0-1		6006					5	7					1	4				6	10	3						11		2		9	8
38		5	Bournemouth	1-4	Rowe	5576	10				5	7					1	4				6					3	11				2		9	8
39		10	Southend United	1-2	Middleton	6398		7		8	5						1	4				6	10	3					11			2		9	
40		17	PLYMOUTH ARGYLE	0-4		9338		7		8	5						1	4				6	10	3					11			2		9	
41		24	Aberdare Athletic	0-1		3526		7		8	5							4				6	10					11	1			2	3	9	
42	May 1		NORTHAMPTON T	3-2	Birch 2, Middleton	4586		7		8					11			4				6	10	3			5			1		2		9	
			Apps				2	15	27	32	13	4	3	4	18	14	36	26	26	9	2	26	19	35	19	15	10	4	2	22	16	18	13	24	7
			Goals					3	2	8	2	1			1					2		5	3					1		2				5	2

Played in game 29: SH Murdin (at 9).

F.A. Cup

	Date		Opponent	Score	Scorers	Att	Barr W	Birch J	Brown C	Burgess D	Cable TH	Campbell CJ	Edwards JH	Field WH	Ford E	Harris GT	Hebden GHR	Hirst H	John R	Johnson HE	Kerr A	Middleton J	Paterson J	Pierce W	Pigg W	Plunkett AETB	Richmond H	Rowe AJ	Smith SR	Spotiswood J	Sweetman SC	Symes HC	Thompson J	Whitehead WT	Young W
R1	Nov 28		Gravesend & Northfleet	2-2	Birch 2	5165		7		10					11		1	5	4					2	6							3	8	9	
rep	Dec 2		GRAVESEND & N'FLEET	2-0	Birch 2	6000		7		10					11		1	5	4					2	6							3	8	9	
R2		12	CHARLTON ATHLETIC	1-1	Hirst	11000		7		10					11		1	5	4					2	6							3	8	9	
rep		17	Charlton Athletic	0-1		7246	8	7		10					11		1	5	4					2	6							3		9	

1926/27 — 14th in Division 3(S)

League Match Results

No	Month	Date	Opponent	Result	Scorers	Att.
1	Aug	28	Crystal Palace	1-2	Varco	18261
2	Sep	1	Gillingham	2-2	Lofthouse, Wilcox	6208
3		4	COVENTRY CITY	1-1	Lofthouse	13699
4		11	Brentford	2-4	Patterson, Goddard	17380
5		18	Charlton Athletic	0-2		9189
6		20	Aberdare Athletic	2-0	Goddard 2	1864
7		25	BRISTOL CITY	1-2	Middleton	11921
8		30	ABERDARE ATHLETIC	3-0	Goddard, Lofthouse, Brophy (og)	5898
9	Oct	2	Bournemouth	2-6	Young (p), Goddard	6342
10		9	PLYMOUTH ARGYLE	4-2	Lofthouse 2, Middleton, Goddard	12699
11		16	BRISTOL ROVERS	2-2	Burgess, Goddard	11225
12		23	Millwall	1-2	Middleton	14803
13		30	NORTHAMPTON T	4-2	Lofthouse 2, Goddard, McAlister	10058
14	Nov	6	Brighton & Hove Albion	1-4	Goddard	10875
15		13	NORWICH CITY	4-0	Goddard 2, Lofthouse, Vargo	2954
16		20	Luton Town	0-2		5075
17	Dec	4	Merthyr Town	0-4		2330
18		11	Plymouth Argyle	0-2		10947
19		18	Swindon Town	2-6	Goddard 2	6706
20		25	WATFORD	2-4	Young, Mustard	11893
21		27	Watford	2-1	Charlesworth, Lofthouse	13004
22	Jan	1	GILLINGHAM	1-1	Goddard	7714
23		8	SOUTHEND UNITED	3-2	Charlesworth, Middleton, Goddard	6726
24		15	CRYSTAL PALACE	0-2		11506
25		22	Coventry City	0-1		8187
26	Feb	5	CHARLTON ATHLETIC	2-1	Goddard 2	8744
27		12	Bristol City	0-1		12029
28		19	BOURNEMOUTH	1-1	Lofthouse	6678
29		24	EXETER CITY	1-1	Lofthouse	2283
30	Mar	5	Bristol Rovers	1-4	Wilcox	4222
31		12	MILLWALL	1-1	Goddard	14730
32		19	Northampton Town	0-1		5369
33		26	BRIGHTON & HOVE ALB	2-2	Mustard, Lofthouse	8401
34	Apr	2	Norwich City	1-0	Lofthouse	10973
35		9	LUTON TOWN	1-0	Goddard	4484
36		15	Newport County	2-0	Goddard, Virgo	5938
37		16	Southend United	3-0	Charlesworth, Swan, Goddard	7813
38		18	NEWPORT COUNTY	2-0	Goddard, Young (p)	9057
39		23	MERTHYR TOWN	5-1	Young 2(2p), Varco, Patterson, Goddard	8406
40		30	Exeter City	2-0	Lofthouse, Patterson	5952
41	May	5	BRENTFORD	1-1	Hawley	11355
42		7	SWINDON TOWN	0-1		10158

Appearances and Goals

Player	Apps	Goals
Bowers AGW	1	
Burgess D	14	1
Cable TH	5	
Charlesworth GW	23	3
Collier JC	20	
Cunningham J	19	
Drew WA	1	
Eggleton JAE	12	
Goddard G	38	23
Gough CWM	19	
Hamilton JE	10	
Hawley FW	22	1
Hebden GHR	23	
Hooper H	16	
Lofthouse J	42	14
McAlister W	26	1
Middleton J	28	4
Mustard J	14	2
Paterson J	15	3
Pierce W	19	
Salt H	5	
Swan J	14	1
Sweetman SC	18	
Varco PS	16	4
Waterall A	2	
Wilcox JC	9	2
Young J	31	5

One own goal

F.A. Cup

Did not enter

Division 3 (South) Final Table

		P	W	D	L	F	A	W	D	L	F	A	Pts
1	Bristol City	42	19	1	1	71	24	8	7	6	33	30	62
2	Plymouth Argyle	42	17	4	0	52	14	8	6	7	43	47	60
3	Millwall	42	16	2	3	55	19	7	8	6	34	32	56
4	Brighton & Hove A.	42	15	4	2	61	24	6	7	8	18	26	53
5	Swindon Town	42	16	3	2	64	31	5	6	10	36	54	51
6	Crystal Palace	42	12	6	3	57	33	6	3	12	27	48	45
7	Bournemouth	42	13	2	6	49	24	5	6	10	29	42	44
8	Luton Town	42	12	9	0	48	19	3	5	13	20	47	44
9	Newport County	42	15	4	2	40	20	4	2	15	17	51	44
10	Bristol Rovers	42	12	4	5	46	28	4	5	12	32	52	41
11	Brentford	42	10	9	2	46	20	3	5	13	24	41	40
12	Exeter City	42	14	4	3	46	18	1	6	14	30	55	40
13	Charlton Athletic	42	13	5	3	44	22	3	3	15	16	39	40
14	QUEEN'S PARK RGS.	42	9	8	4	41	27	6	1	14	24	44	39
15	Coventry City	42	11	4	6	44	33	4	3	14	27	53	37
16	Norwich City	42	10	5	6	41	25	2	6	13	18	46	35
17	Merthyr Town	42	11	5	5	42	25	2	4	15	21	55	35
18	Northampton Town	42	13	4	4	36	23	2	1	18	23	64	35
19	Southend United	42	12	3	6	44	25	2	3	16	20	52	34
20	Gillingham	42	10	5	6	36	26	1	5	15	18	46	32
21	Watford	42	9	6	6	36	27	3	2	16	21	60	32
22	Aberdare Ath.	42	8	2	11	38	48	1	5	15	24	53	25

1927/28   10th in Division 3(S)

No	Date		Opponent	Score	Scorers	Att	Beats E	Burns JC	Collier JC	Coward WC	Crompton N	Cunningham J	Duthie JF	Eggleton JAE	Gilhooley M	Goddard G	Hawley FW	Johnson JH	Kellard T	Lofthouse J	Mustard J	Neil A	Paterson J	Pierce W	Roberts J	Rounce GA	Stephenson J	Swan J	Sweetman SC	Turner W	Woodward JH	Young J
1	Aug	27	NEWPORT COUNTY	4-2	Goddard 2(1p), Lofthouse, Swan	15489			4			1			5	9				11		8						7	10	2	6	3
2	Sep	1	GILLINGHAM	3-3	Goddard 2, Lofthouse	9241			4			1			5	9				11		8						7	10	2	6	3
3		3	Swindon Town	2-0	Swan, Johnson	9659			4			1			5			9		11		8		3				7	10	2	6	
4		7	Gillingham	2-1	Johnson, Neil	5499			4			1			5			9		11		8		3				7	10	2	6	
5		10	BRENTFORD	2-3	Lofthouse 2	18826			4			1				9	5			11		8		3				7	10	2	6	
6		17	WATFORD	2-1	Swan, Goddard	13950			4			1				9	5			11		8		3				7	10	2	6	
7		21	Bournemouth	2-1	Lofthouse, Goddard	4440			4			1				9	5			11		8		3				7	10	2	6	
8		24	Charlton Athletic	0-1		12823			4			1					5	9		11		8		3				7	10	2	6	
9	Oct	1	BRISTOL ROVERS	4-2	Goddard 3, Collier	8448			4			1				9	5			11		8						7	10	2	6	3
10		8	Plymouth Argyle	0-3		12343			4			1				9	5			11		8							10	2	6	3
11		15	MERTHYR TOWN	0-0		11406			4			1				9	5			11	7	8		3					10	2	6	
12		22	Crystal Palace	1-1	Lofthouse	7115			4			1	10	5		9				11	7	8		3						2	6	
13		29	MILLWALL	0-1		16960			4			1	10	5		9				11	7	8		3						2	6	
14	Nov	5	Luton Town	1-0	Goddard	7695			4			1		5		9		10			7	8		3		11				2	6	
15		12	EXETER CITY	0-1		8291			4			1		5		9		10		7		8		3		11				2	6	
16		19	Torquay United	0-1		2235			4			1	10	5		9				11		8					7			2	6	3
17	Dec	3	Northampton Town	0-1		9737						1	4	5		9		10		11	7	8		2						6		3
18		17	Brighton & Hove Albion	3-1	Goddard 2, Lofthouse	5835						1	4	5		9				11	8	10		2			7			6		3
19		24	BOURNEMOUTH	2-0	Goddard, Mustard	6260						1	4	5		9				11	8	10		2			7			6		3
20		27	Coventry City	0-0		8975						1	4	5		9				11	8	10		2			7			6		3
21	Jan	7	SWINDON TOWN	0-1		9981						1	4	5		9				11	8	10		2			7			6		3
22		14	SOUTHEND UNITED	3-2	Burns, Mustard, Young (p)	7294		8				1		5		9		10		11	7	4		2						6		3
23		21	Brentford	3-0	Goddard 2, Burns	10430		8				1		5		9		10		11	7	4		2						6		3
24		28	Watford	3-3	Lofthouse 2, Goddard	5597		8				1		5		9		10		11	7	4		2						6		3
25	Feb	4	CHARLTON ATHLETIC	3-3	Goddard 2, Burns	10830		8				1		5		9		10		11	7	4		2						6		3
26		11	Bristol Rovers	4-0	Goddard 2, Johnson, Lofthouse	6862		8				1		5		9		10		11	7	4		2						6		3
27		18	PLYMOUTH ARGYLE	0-1		17377		8				1		5		9		10		11	7	4		2						6		3
28		25	Merthyr Town	4-0	Goddard 3, Rounce	2869						1		5		9				11	7	4		2		8		10		6		3
29	Mar	3	CRYSTAL PALACE	2-0	Swan, Goddard	16468						1		5		9				11	7	4		2		8		10		6		3
30		10	Millwall	1-6	Beats	18689	9	8				1		5						11	7	4		2				10		6		3
31		17	LUTON TOWN	3-2	Johnson, Burns, Lofthouse	11217		8					6	5				9		11		4		2		10	7		1			3
32		24	Exeter City	0-4		5657		8						5		9				11		4		2		10	7		1	6		3
33		31	TORQUAY UNITED	2-3	Coward, Rounce	5839		8		7		1		5		9				11		4		2		10				6		3
34	Apr	6	Newport County	6-1	*See below	5918		8		7		1		5		9				11		4		2		10				6		3
35		7	Southend United	0-7		8126		8		7		1		5		9				11		4		2		10				6		3
36		9	WALSALL	1-1	Young (p)	8082		8		7		1		5		9				11		4		2		10				6		3
37		10	Walsall	2-2	Lofthouse, Rounce	6419		8		7		1		5		9				11		4		2		10				6		3
38		14	NORTHAMPTON T	0-4		8399		8		7		1		5		9						4		2	11	10				6		3
39		21	Norwich City	1-3	Johnson	4867						1	6	5				9			8	4		2	11	10	7					3
40		26	COVENTRY CITY	1-5	Rounce	4095				7		1	6	5				9			8	4		2	11	10						3
41		28	BRIGHTON & HOVE ALB	5-0	Johnson 2, Rounce, Lofthouse, Young(p)	5394		8				1		5				9		11	7	4		2		10				6		3
42	May	3	NORWICH CITY	0-0		4691		8			5		6			9		10		11		4		2			7		1			3
			Apps				1	16	16	7	1	36	11	26	9	33	7	17	1	38	23	41	2	38	4	13	18	14	16	38	6	30
			Goals				1	5	1	2						26		7		13	2	1				6		4				4

Scorers in game 34: Goddard 2, Burns, Young (p), Coward, Rounce.

F.A. Cup

	Date		Opponent	Score	Scorers	Att	Beats E	Burns JC	Collier JC	Coward WC	Crompton N	Cunningham J	Duthie JF	Eggleton JAE	Gilhooley M	Goddard G	Hawley FW	Johnson JH	Kellard T	Lofthouse J	Mustard J	Neil A	Paterson J	Pierce W	Roberts J	Rounce GA	Stephenson J	Swan J	Sweetman SC	Turner W	Woodward JH	Young J
R1	Nov	30	ALDERSHOT	1-2	Johnson	4000			4			1		5		9		10		11	7	8		2						6		3

		P	W	D	L	F	A	W	D	L	F	A	Pts
1	Millwall	42	19	2	0	87	15	11	3	7	40	35	65
2	Northampton Town	42	17	3	1	67	23	6	6	9	35	41	55
3	Plymouth Argyle	42	17	2	2	60	19	6	5	10	25	35	53
4	Brighton & Hove A.	42	14	4	3	51	24	5	6	10	30	45	48
5	Crystal Palace	42	15	3	3	46	23	3	9	9	33	49	48
6	Swindon Town	42	12	6	3	60	26	7	3	11	30	43	47
7	Southend United	42	14	2	5	48	19	6	4	11	32	45	46
8	Exeter City	42	11	6	4	49	27	6	6	9	21	33	46
9	Newport County	42	12	5	4	52	38	6	4	11	29	46	45
10	QUEEN'S PARK RGS.	42	8	5	8	37	35	9	4	8	35	36	43
11	Charlton Athletic	42	12	5	4	34	27	3	8	10	26	43	43
12	Brentford	42	12	4	5	49	30	4	4	13	27	44	40
13	Luton Town	42	13	5	3	56	27	3	2	16	38	60	39
14	Bournemouth	42	12	6	3	44	24	1	6	14	28	55	38
15	Watford	42	10	5	6	42	34	4	5	12	26	44	38
16	Gillingham	42	10	3	8	33	26	3	8	10	29	55	37
17	Norwich City	42	9	8	4	41	26	1	8	12	25	44	36
18	Walsall	42	9	6	6	52	35	3	3	15	23	66	33
19	Bristol Rovers	42	11	3	7	41	36	3	1	17	26	57	32
20	Coventry City	42	5	8	8	40	36	6	1	14	27	60	31
21	Merthyr Town	42	7	6	8	38	40	2	7	12	15	51	31
22	Torquay United	42	4	10	7	27	36	4	4	13	26	67	30

1928/29   6th in Division 3(S)

#	Date	Opponent	Score	Scorers	Att	Armstrong JH	Burns JC	Cockburn WO	Coward WC	Cunningham J	Eggleton JAE	Foster CJ	Goddard G	Johnson JH	Kellard T	McNab JS	Neil A	Nixon T	Pierce W	Price LP	Rogers A	Rounce GA	Smith SC	Sweetman SC	Thompson O	Vallence H	Whatmore EL	Woodward JH	Young J
1	Aug 25	Torquay United	4-3	Goddard 3, Burns	7357		8	5	7	1			9			4	6			11				2			10		3
2	30	NEWPORT COUNTY	0-0		9920		8	5	7	1			9			4	6			11				2			10		3
3	Sep 1	GILLINGHAM	1-0	Coward	12969		8	5	7	1			9			4				11		10		2	6				3
4	6	Newport County	0-0		5293			5	7	1			9	10		4					8	11		2	6				3
5	8	Plymouth Argyle	2-1	Goddard 2	10303		8	5	7	1			9			4						10	11	2	6				3
6	15	FULHAM	2-1	Young (p), Goddard	21805		8	5	7	1			9			4						10	11	2	6				3
7	22	Brentford	1-1	Smith	20783		8	5	7	1			9			4						10	11	2	6				3
8	29	Bristol Rovers	1-1	Goddard	8928		8	5	7	1			9			4	6					10	11	2					3
9	Oct 6	WATFORD	3-2	Goddard, McNab, Coward	18263		8	5	7	1			9			4	6					10	11	2					3
10	13	Walsall	1-3	Rounce	7441		8	5	7	1			9			4	6					10	11	2					3
11	20	BOURNEMOUTH	0-0		11815			5	7	1		8	9			4	6					11		2			10		3
12	27	Merthyr Town	2-1	Rounce (p), Goddard	2446		8	5	7	1			9			4	6					10	11	2					3
13	Nov 3	SOUTHEND UNITED	3-1	Burns, Rounce, Goddard	12701		8	5	7	1			9			4	6					10	11	2					3
14	10	Exeter City	1-1	Burns	4483	4	8	5	7	1			9					3				10	11	2	6				
15	17	BRIGHTON & HOVE ALB	3-2	Young, Rounce, Goddard	11065		8	5	7				9			4	6					10	11	2				1	3
16	Dec 1	CHARLTON ATHLETIC	2-2	Goddard 2	10491		8	5	7				9			4						10	11	2	6			1	3
17	8	Northampton Town	2-4	Goddard 2	10124		8	5	7	1			9			4						10	11	2	6				3
18	15	COVENTRY CITY	3-1	Rogers 2, Goddard	8201		8	5	7	1			9			4					10		11	2	6				3
19	22	Luton Town	2-3	Goddard 2	9112		8	5	7	1			9			4					10		11	2	6				3
20	25	SWINDON TOWN	4-2	Rogers, Burns, Goddard, Kellard	14962		8	5		1			9		7	4					10		11	2	6				3
21	26	Swindon Town	1-2	Dickenson (og)	9392		8			1		5	9		7	4					10		11	2	6				3
22	29	TORQUAY UNITED	5-1	Goddard 3, Burns, Oxley (og)	11471		8			1		5	9		7	4					10		11	2	6				3
23	Jan 5	Gillingham	0-0		4493		8	5	7	1			9			4					10		11	2	6				3
24	19	PLYMOUTH ARGYLE	2-0	Burns, McNab	17913		8	5	7	1			9			4					10		11	2	6				3
25	26	Fulham	0-5		26743		8	5	7	1			9			4					10		11	2	6				3
26	Feb 2	BRENTFORD	2-2	Coward, Herod (og)	10590		8	5	7	1			9			4					10			2	6		11		3
27	9	BRISTOL ROVERS	0-3		10736			5	7	1			9			4					10		8	2	6		11		3
28	16	Watford	1-4	Rogers	7185			5	7	1			9			4	6				10		8	2			11		3
29	23	WALSALL	2-2	Goddard, Young (p)	8762			5	7	1			9			4	6				10			2		8	11		3
30	Mar 2	Bournemouth	3-2	Haywood (og), Rounce, Goddard	5045		8	5	7	1			9			4	6	3				10		2			11		
31	9	MERTHYR TOWN	8-0	Goddard 4, Burns 3, Rounce	11611		8		7	1			9			4	6	5	3			10		2			11		
32	16	Southend United	3-0	Burns 2, Goddard	6259		8		7	1			9			4	6	5	3			10		2			11		
33	23	EXETER CITY	1-0	Goddard	12294		8		7	1			9			4	6	5	3			10		2			11		
34	29	Crystal Palace	4-1	Goddard 3, Coward	33160		8	5	7	1	6		9			4			3			10		2			11		
35	30	Brighton & Hove Albion	1-2	Pierce	9413		8	5	7	1	6		9			4			3			10		2			11		
36	Apr 1	CRYSTAL PALACE	1-1	Goddard	19341		8	5	7	1	6		9			4			3			10		2			11		
37	6	NORWICH CITY	3-0	Coward 2, Rounce	12961		8	5	7	1	6		9			4			3			10		2			11		
38	13	Charlton Athletic	2-2	Coward, Rounce	17258		8	5	7				9			4	6		3			10	11	2				1	
39	20	NORTHAMPTON T	4-1	Rounce, Goddard. Burns, Whatmore	21916		8	5	7	1			9			4	6	3				10		2			11		
40	22	Norwich City	1-3	Goddard	7670		8	5	7			4	9				6		3			10		2			11	1	
41	27	Coventry City	0-0		11698		8	5	7	1			9			4	6		3			10		2			11		
42	May 4	LUTON TOWN	1-1	Goddard	13449		8	5	7	1			9			4	6		3			10		2			11		
	Apps					1	37	35	39	38	4	3	42	1	4	32	29	5	12	3	11	28	24	42	18	1	21	4	28
	Goals						12		7				37		1	2			1		4	9	1				1		3

Four own goals

F.A. Cup

R	Date	Opponent	Score	Scorers	Att	Armstrong JH	Burns JC	Cockburn WO	Coward WC	Cunningham J	Eggleton JAE	Foster CJ	Goddard G	Johnson JH	Kellard T	McNab JS	Neil A	Nixon T	Pierce W	Price LP	Rogers A	Rounce GA	Smith SC	Sweetman SC	Thompson O	Vallence H	Whatmore EL	Woodward JH	Young J
R1	Nov 24	Guildford City	2-4	Goddard, Burns	10000		8	5	7				9			4	6					10	11	2				1	3

	P	W	D	L	F	A	W	D	L	F	A	Pts
1 Charlton Athletic	42	14	5	2	51	22	9	3	9	35	38	54
2 Crystal Palace	42	14	2	5	40	25	9	6	6	41	42	54
3 Northampton Town	42	14	6	1	68	23	6	6	9	28	34	52
4 Plymouth Argyle	42	14	6	1	51	13	6	6	9	32	38	52
5 Fulham	42	14	3	4	60	31	7	7	7	41	40	52
6 QUEEN'S PARK RGS.	42	13	7	1	50	22	6	7	8	32	39	52
7 Luton Town	42	16	3	2	64	28	3	8	10	25	45	49
8 Watford	42	15	3	3	55	31	4	7	10	24	43	48
9 Bournemouth	42	14	4	3	54	31	5	5	11	30	46	47
10 Swindon Town	42	12	5	4	48	27	3	8	10	27	45	43
11 Coventry City	42	9	6	6	35	23	5	8	8	27	34	42
12 Southend United	42	10	7	4	44	27	5	4	12	36	48	41
13 Brentford	42	11	4	6	34	21	3	6	12	22	39	38
14 Walsall	42	11	7	3	47	25	2	5	14	26	54	38
15 Brighton & Hove A.	42	14	2	5	39	28	2	4	15	19	48	38
16 Newport County	42	8	6	7	37	28	5	3	13	32	58	35
17 Norwich City	42	12	3	6	49	29	2	3	16	20	52	34
18 Torquay United	42	10	3	8	46	36	4	3	14	20	48	34
19 Bristol Rovers	42	9	6	6	39	28	4	1	16	21	51	33
20 Merthyr Town	42	11	6	4	42	28	0	2	19	13	75	30
21 Exeter City	42	7	6	8	49	40	2	5	14	18	48	29
22 Gillingham	42	7	8	6	22	24	3	1	17	21	59	29

#	Date	Opponent	Score	Scorers	Att	Armstrong JH	Burns JC	Cockburn WO	Coward WC	Cunningham J	Evans C	Foster CJ	Goddard G	Gretton T	Harris B	Hebden GHR	Howe HG	McNab JS	Moffatt H	Neil A	Nixon T	Pickett TR	Pierce W	Pollard R	Rogers A	Rounce GA	Whatmore EL	Wiles GH	Wiles HS	Yates J	Young H
1	Aug 31	Crystal Palace	1-1	H Wiles	20268			5	1				9	3				4	7	6			2			10			8		11
2	Sep 5	WALSALL	2-2	Goddard, Moffat	8539			5	1				9					4	7	6			2			10		3	8		11
3	7	GILLINGHAM	2-1	Goddard, Moffat	11875		8		1				9					4	7	6	5		2			10		3			11
4	9	Walsall	0-4		5579				1		4		9						7		5		2			10		3	8	6	11
5	14	Northampton Town	1-2	Rounce	12876			5	1				9					4	7	6			3	2		8	10				11
6	16	FULHAM	0-0		12491			5	1				9					4	7	6			3	2		8	10				11
7	21	EXETER CITY	2-0	Young, Rounce	11071			5	1				9					4	7	6			3	2		8	10				11
8	28	Southend United	0-1		10867			5	1				9					4	7	6			3	2		8	10				11
9	Oct 5	LUTON TOWN	1-0	Goddard	12273		8	5	1				9					4	7	6			3	2		10					11
10	12	Bournemouth	0-0		8371		8	5	1				9					4	7	6			3	2		10					11
11	19	CLAPTON ORIENT	1-1	Rounce	14130		8	5	7	1			9				11	4		6			3	2		10					
12	26	Coventry City	3-2	Howe 2, Goddard	13477		8	5	7	1			9				11	4		6			3	2		10					
13	Nov 2	WATFORD	0-0		12774	6	8	5	7	1			9				11	4					3	2		10					
14	9	Newport County	5-4	Goddard, H Wiles 3, Rounce	3527		8	5	7	1			9				11	4					3	2		10	6		8		
15	16	TORQUAY UNITED	1-1	Fowler og	2360	6	8	5	7				9				11	4				1	3	2		10			10		
16	Dec 7	Swindon Town	2-2	Coward, Howe	3954		8	5	7			1					11	4		6			3	2		10			9		
17	21	Bristol Rovers	1-4	Goddard	6539		8	5	7	1			9				11			4			3	2	10		6				
18	25	Norwich City	0-3		11163		8	5	7	1			9				11	4					3	2		10					
19	26	NORWICH CITY	3-2	Goddard 3	13530		8	5	7	1			9				11	4					3	2		10					
20	28	CRYSTAL PALACE	4-1	Rounce 2 (1p), Burns, Goddard	12709		8	5	7	1			9				11	4					3	2		10					
21	Jan 4	Gillingham	1-3	Goddard	5961		8	5	7	1			9				11	4					3	2		10					
22	18	NORTHAMPTON T	0-2		11696		8	5	1				9					4	7	6			3	2		10					11
23	25	Exeter City	2-0	Moffat, Goddard	5653		8	5	1				9					4	7	6			3	2		10					11
24	Feb 1	SOUTHEND UNITED	2-5	Rounce, Goddard	8187			5			8		9			1		4	7	6			3	2		10					11
25	8	Luton Town	1-2	Goddard	7049	5	8						9	1	3				7	4			2			10				6	11
26	15	BOURNEMOUTH	3-1	Coward, Goddard 2 (1p)	9464	5			7				9	1	3		11			4			2			10			8	6	
27	22	Clapton Orient	4-2	Goddard, Rounce 2 (1p)	12816	5	8		7				9	1	3		11			4			2			10				6	
28	Mar 1	COVENTRY CITY	3-1	Armstrong, Howe 2	17903	5	8		7	1			9		3		11			4			2			10				6	
29	3	Merthyr Town	4-1	H Wiles, Goddard 3	963	5			7	1			9		3		11			4			2			10			8	6	
30	8	Watford	1-1	Bresford (og)	11577	5	8		7	1			9		3		11			4			2			10				6	
31	13	PLYMOUTH ARGYLE	1-2	Goddard (p)	8758	5	8		7	1			9		3		11			4			2			10				6	
32	15	NEWPORT COUNTY	4-1	Goddard 3, Wheeler (og)	7926	5	8		7	1			9		3		11			4				2		10	6				
33	22	Torquay United	3-1	Armstrong, Burns, Rounce	4335	5	8		7	1			9		3		11			4				2		10	6				
34	27	BRIGHTON & HOVE ALB	3-1	Goddard 2, Marsden (og)	6578	5	8			1			9		3		11			7	4			2		10	6				
35	29	MERTHYR TOWN	2-0	Goddard, Rounce	10568	5	8		7	1			9		3		11			4				2		10	6				
36	Apr 5	Plymouth Argyle	0-4		18897	5	8		7	1		4	9		3		11							2		10	6				
37	12	SWINDON TOWN	8-3	Rounce 3, Coward, Goddard 4	7534	5	8		7	1			9				11						3	2		10	4	6			
38	18	BRENTFORD	2-1	Goddard (p), Rounce	22179	5	8		7	1			9		3		11			4			2			10		6			
39	19	Brighton & Hove Albion	3-2	Goddard 3	6411	5	8		7	1			9		3		11			4				2		10	6				
40	21	Brentford	0-3		18549	5	8		7	1			9		3		11			4				2		10	6				
41	26	BRISTOL ROVERS	2-1	H Wiles, Armstrong	7616	5	8			1			9		3		11			4			2			10	6		7		
42	May 3	Fulham	2-0	Rounce, Goddard	17030	5	8			1			9				11			4			2			10	6	3	7		
		Apps				20	31	22	25	36	1	2	41	4	17	1	28	22	15	36	13	1	25	27	1	40	15	5	10	10	14
		Goals				3	2		3				37				5		3							16			6		1

Four own goals

F.A. Cup

#	Date	Opponent	Score	Scorers	Att	Burns JC	Cockburn WO	Coward WC	Cunningham J	Goddard G	Howe HG	McNab JS	Neil A	Pickett TR	Pierce W	Pollard R	Rounce GA	Young H
R1	Nov 30	Luton Town	3-2	Goddard, Coward, Pierce (p)	9000	8	5	7		9	11	4	6	1	3	2	10	
R2	Dec 12	LINCOLN CITY	2-1	Burns 2	13097	8	5	7	1	9	11	4	6		2	3	10	
R3	Jan 11	Charlton Athletic	1-1	Goddard	22300	8	5	7	1	9	11	4	6		3	2	10	
rep	16	CHARLTON ATH.	0-3		22000	8	5	7	1	9		4	6		3	2	10	11

		P	W	D	L	F	A	W	D	L	F	A	Pts
1	Plymouth Argyle	42	18	3	0	63	12	12	5	4	35	26	68
2	Brentford	42	21	0	0	66	12	7	5	9	28	32	61
3	QUEEN'S PARK RGS.	42	13	5	3	46	26	8	4	9	34	42	51
4	Northampton Town	42	14	6	1	53	20	7	2	12	29	38	50
5	Brighton & Hove A.	42	16	2	3	54	20	5	6	10	33	43	50
6	Coventry City	42	14	3	4	54	25	5	6	10	34	48	47
7	Fulham	42	12	6	3	54	33	6	5	10	33	50	47
8	Norwich City	42	14	4	3	55	28	4	6	11	33	49	46
9	Crystal Palace	42	14	5	2	56	26	3	7	11	25	48	46
10	Bournemouth	42	11	6	4	47	24	4	7	10	25	37	43
11	Southend United	42	11	6	4	41	19	4	7	10	28	40	43
12	Clapton Orient	42	10	8	3	38	21	4	5	12	17	41	41
13	Luton Town	42	13	4	4	42	25	1	8	12	22	53	40
14	Swindon Town	42	10	7	4	42	25	3	5	13	31	58	38
15	Watford	42	10	4	7	37	30	5	4	12	23	43	38
16	Exeter City	42	10	6	5	45	29	2	5	14	22	44	35
17	Walsall	42	10	4	7	45	24	3	4	14	26	54	34
18	Newport County	42	9	9	3	48	29	3	1	17	26	56	34
19	Torquay United	42	9	6	6	50	38	1	5	15	14	56	31
20	Bristol Rovers	42	11	3	7	45	31	0	5	16	22	62	30
21	Gillingham	42	9	5	7	38	28	2	3	16	13	52	30
22	Merthyr Town	42	5	6	10	39	49	1	3	17	21	86	21

#	Date	Opponent	Score	Scorers	Att	Armstrong JH	Burns JC	Coward WC	Cunningham J	Daniels AWC	Embleton SW	Ferguson C	Goddard G	Harris B	Hoten RV	Howe HG	Legge AE	Lewis JW	Nixon T	Pickett TR	Pierce W	Pollard R	Rounce GA	Sales A	Shepherd W	Smith N(1)	Stephenson H	Tutt W	Vango AJ	Whatmore EL	Wiles GH	Wiles HS
1	Aug 30	THAMES	3-0	Hoten 2, Goddard	13103	5	8		1	11			9	3	10		7		2						4					6		
2	Sep 3	Bournemouth	0-2		6685	5			1	11			9	3	10		7					2	8		4					6		
3	Sep 6	Norwich City	1-1	Goddard	12472	5	8		1	11			9		10		7					2			4					6	3	
4	Sep 11	WATFORD	2-3	Daniels, Goddard	8114	5	8		1	11			9		10		7		2			3			4					6		
5	Sep 13	BRIGHTON & HOVE ALB	4-1	Coward, Burns, Rounce 2	6582	5	6	7	1	11		8		3								2	10		4							9
6	Sep 17	Watford	4-0	H Wiles, Daniels, Coward, Rounce	6606	5	6	7	1	11		8		3								3	10		4							9
7	Sep 20	WALSALL	3-0	Ferguson, H Wiles, Burns	9214	5	6	7	1	11		8		3								2	10		4							9
8	Sep 27	Coventry City	0-2		12529	5	6	7	1	11		8	9									2	10		4						3	9
9	Oct 4	FULHAM	0-2		14280	5	6	7	1	11		8										2	10		4						3	9
10	Oct 11	Swindon Town	1-4	Coward	6151	5		7	1	11					10				2		3		8	4						6		9
11	Oct 18	Torquay United	2-6	Burns, H Wiles	5123	5	8	7		11									2	1	3		10	4						6		9
12	Oct 25	NORTHAMPTON T	0-2		8362	5	8	7		11									2	1		3		4	10					6		9
13	Nov 1	Brentford	3-5	Coward, H Wiles, Nixon	10857	5	8	7								11			2	1		3	10	4						6		9
14	Nov 8	CRYSTAL PALACE	4-0	Rounce 3 (1p), Coward	12040	5	8	7	1					3		11						2	10	4	9					6		
15	Nov 15	Southend United	0-2		5060	5		7	1					3		11						2	10	4	9					6		
16	Nov 22	LUTON TOWN	3-1	Burns, Rounce, Sheppard	6388	5	8	7	1					3		11						2	10	4	9					6		
17	Dec 6	NEWPORT COUNTY	7-1	Rounce, Burns 2, Armstrong, Goddard 3	6566	5	8	7	1				9	3		11						2	10	4						6		
18	Dec 17	Gillingham	2-2	Goddard, Howe	2204	5		7	1			8	9	3		11						2		4	10					6		
19	Dec 20	EXETER CITY	7-2	Goddard 4, Rounce 2, Coward	7333		8	7	1				9	3		11						2	10	4		5				6		
20	Dec 25	NOTTS COUNTY	4-1	Burns 3, Goddard	14501		8	7	1				9	3		11						2	10	4		5				6		
21	Dec 26	Notts County	0-2		13696		8	7	1			11	9	3								2	10	4		5				6		
22	Dec 27	Thames	0-1		3899		8	7	1	11			9	3								2	10	4		5				6		
23	Jan 3	NORWICH CITY	3-1	Goddard 2, Rounce	6553		8		1				9	3		11						2	10	4		5				6		7
24	Jan 14	Bristol Rovers	0-3		3669				1				9	3	10		7					2	8	4				11	5	6		
25	Jan 17	Brighton & Hove Albion	1-1	Rounce	10532		8		1				9	3		11	7					2	10	4		5				6		
26	Jan 24	Walsall	2-0	John (og), Hoten	4573		8		1			6	9	3	11		7				2		10	4		5				6		
27	Jan 31	COVENTRY CITY	2-0	Howe, Rounce	7180			7	1			6	9	3		11							8	4		5				10	2	
28	Feb 7	Fulham	2-0	Goddard, Coward	18955		8	7	1			6	9	3		11							10	4		5					2	
29	Feb 14	SWINDON TOWN	1-2	Daniels	7914			7	1	11		6	9	3									8	4		5				10	2	
30	Feb 21	TORQUAY UNITED	1-2	Burns	9830	5	8	7	1				9	3		11							10	4						6	2	
31	Feb 28	Northampton Town	0-6		5198	5	8		1				9	3		11	7					2			10					6		
32	Mar 7	BRENTFORD	3-1	Howe, Goddard 2	10331	5	8		1		7	6	9			11						2	10	4							3	
33	Mar 14	Crystal Palace	0-4		14316	5	8		1		7	6	9			11						2	10	4							3	
34	Mar 21	SOUTHEND UNITED	0-2		7114	5		7	1			6	9	2		11								4	10	8					3	
35	Mar 28	Luton Town	1-5	Shepherd	6035	5	8	7				6	9									1	2	10	4	11					3	
36	Apr 3	CLAPTON ORIENT	4-2	Whatmore, Shepherd, Goddard 2 (1p)	7374	5	8	7					9	3								1	10	4	11					6		
37	Apr 4	BRISTOL ROVERS	2-0	Rounce, Goddard	8628	5	8	7					9	3							2	1	10	4	11					6		
38	Apr 6	Clapton Orient	3-2	H Wiles, Goddard, Rounce	5804	5	8						9	3								1	10	4	11					6		7
39	Apr 11	Newport County	3-2	Goddard 2, Shepherd	2899		8						9	3		11						1	2	10	4				5	6		7
40	Apr 18	GILLINGHAM	1-0	H Wiles	6890	5	8	7						3								1	2	10	4					6		9
41	Apr 25	Exeter City	0-2		3280	5	8	7						3				9				1	2	10	4					6		
42	May 2	BOURNEMOUTH	3-0	Hoten, Lewis, Rounce	6193	5		7						3	9	11		8				1	2	10	4					6		
		Apps				30	33	29	31	14	2	15	28	28	9	18	9	1	11	11	4	29	35	28	13	24	2	1	2	31	12	12
		Goals				1	10	7		3		1	23		4	3	1		1				16		4					1		6

One own goal

F.A. Cup

#	Date	Opponent	Score	Scorers	Att	Armstrong JH	Burns JC	Coward WC	Cunningham J	Goddard G	Harris B	Howe HG	Pickett TR	Pierce W	Pollard R	Rounce GA	Sales A	Shepherd W	Smith N(1)	Whatmore EL	Wiles HS
R1	Nov 29	THAMES	5-0	Goddard 2(1p), Burns 2, Rounce	9000	5	8	7		9	3	11	1		2	10	4			6	
R2	Dec 13	Crewe Alexandra	4-2	Goddard 2, Howe, Rounce	8200	5	8	7	1	9	3	11			2	10	4			6	
R3	Jan 10	Bristol Rovers	1-3	Coward	24000		8	7	1	9	3	11			2	10	4		5	6	

	Team	P	W	D	L	F	A	W	D	L	F	A	Pts
1	Notts County	42	16	4	1	58	13	8	7	6	39	33	59
2	Crystal Palace	42	17	2	2	71	20	5	5	11	36	51	51
3	Brentford	42	14	3	4	62	30	8	3	10	28	34	50
4	Brighton & Hove A.	42	13	5	3	45	20	4	10	7	23	33	49
5	Southend United	42	16	0	5	53	26	6	5	10	23	34	49
6	Northampton Town	42	10	6	5	37	20	8	6	7	40	39	48
7	Luton Town	42	15	3	3	61	17	4	5	12	15	34	46
8	QUEEN'S PARK RGS.	42	15	0	6	57	23	5	3	13	25	52	43
9	Fulham	42	15	3	3	49	21	3	4	14	28	54	43
10	Bournemouth	42	11	7	3	39	22	4	6	11	33	51	43
11	Torquay United	42	13	5	3	56	26	4	4	13	24	58	43
12	Swindon Town	42	15	5	1	68	29	3	1	17	21	65	42
13	Exeter City	42	12	6	3	55	35	4	2	14	29	55	42
14	Coventry City	42	11	4	6	55	28	5	5	11	20	37	41
15	Bristol Rovers	42	12	3	6	49	36	4	5	12	26	56	40
16	Gillingham	42	10	6	5	40	29	4	4	13	21	47	38
17	Walsall	42	9	5	7	44	38	5	4	12	34	57	37
18	Watford	42	9	4	8	41	29	5	3	13	31	46	35
19	Clapton Orient	42	12	3	6	47	33	2	4	15	16	58	35
20	Thames	42	12	5	4	34	20	1	3	17	20	73	34
21	Newport County	42	10	5	6	45	31	1	1	19	24	80	28
22	Norwich City	42	10	7	4	37	20	0	1	20	10	56	28

1931/32   13th in Division 3(S)

Match results

No	Date	Opponent	Score	Scorers	Att
1	Aug 29	Brentford	0-1		20739
2	31	Bristol Rovers	1-1	Haley	9213
3	Sep 5	BOURNEMOUTH	0-3		18938
4	10	SWINDON TOWN	1-2	Lewis	7646
5	12	Crystal Palace	1-1	Goddard	11000
6	16	Swindon Town	2-1	Goddard, Cribb	5065
7	19	WATFORD	4-4	Goddard 4	16497
8	26	Mansfield Town	2-2	England (og), Lewis	8461
9	Oct 3	BRIGHTON & HOVE ALB	1-1	Goddard	13813
10	10	Norwich City	1-2	Lewis	13165
11	17	Exeter City	2-6	Coward, Lewis	6152
12	24	COVENTRY CITY	1-1	Wilson	12634
13	31	Gillingham	0-1		5457
14	Nov 7	LUTON TOWN	3-1	Cribb 2, Goddard	10993
15	14	Cardiff City	4-0	Goddard, Roberts (og), Cribb 2	3491
16	21	NORTHAMPTON T	3-2	Cribb 2, Coward	12117
17	Dec 5	SOUTHEND UNITED	2-1	Robinson (og), Goddard	17898
18	19	THAMES	6-0	Goddard 3, Tutt 2, Wilson (p)	7397
19	25	Torquay United	3-2	Cribb, Collins 2	4999
20	26	TORQUAY UNITED	3-1	Wilson, Cribb, Goddard	24133
21	28	Fulham	3-1	Goddard 2, Cribb	22236
22	Jan 2	BRENTFORD	1-2	Cribb (p)	33553
23	13	Reading	2-3	Blackman 2	5038
24	16	Bournemouth	2-2	Armstrong, Coward	5641
25	28	CRYSTAL PALACE	2-2	Blackman, Rounce	8369
26	30	Watford	2-2	Howe, Blackman	12286
27	Feb 6	MANSFIELD TOWN	1-1	Blackman	12079
28	13	Brighton & Hove Albion	0-1		7033
29	20	NORWICH CITY	2-2	Blackman, Cribb	9632
30	27	EXETER CITY	1-0	Blackman	14418
31	Mar 5	Coventry City	0-1		12815
32	10	GILLINGHAM	7-0	H Wiles 4, Coward, Haley 2	3881
33	19	Luton Town	1-4	H Wiles	5768
34	25	Clapton Orient	0-3		9040
35	26	CARDIFF CITY	2-3	Rounce, Haley	8324
36	28	CLAPTON ORIENT	3-2	H Wiles, Coward, Tutt	11533
37	Apr 2	Northampton Town	1-6	H Wiles	6444
38	9	READING	2-0	H Wiles 2	6755
39	16	Southend United	0-0		5669
40	23	FULHAM	3-1	H Wiles 2, Haley	21572
41	30	Thames	2-3	Rounce 2	1143
42	May 7	BRISTOL ROVERS	2-1	Goddard, Whatmore	7186

Appearances / goals

	Apps	Goals
Adlam LW	28	
Armstrong JH	40	1
Blackman JJ	10	7
Collins JH	11	2
Coward WC	26	5
Cribb SR	28	12
Cunningham J	8	
Goddard G	25	17
Goodier E	28	
Haley WT	17	5
Hall EW	36	
Harris B	15	
Howe HG	3	1
Lewis JW	11	4
Nixon T	22	
Pickett TR	34	
Pollard R	10	
Rounce GA	31	4
Sales A	7	
Smith N(1)	2	
Tutt W	6	3
Vango AJ	10	
Whatmore EL	11	1
Wiles GH	1	
Wiles HS	11	11
Wilson AN	20	3
Wyper HTH	11	

Three own goals

F.A. Cup

Rnd	Date	Opponent	Score	Scorers	Att
R1	Nov 28	Barnet	7-3	Cribb 3, Goddard 2, Coward 2	6853
R2	Dec 12	Scunthorpe United	4-1	Rounce 3, Cribb	7943
R3	Jan 9	LEEDS UNITED	3-1	Cribb 2, Rounce	41097
R4	23	Huddersfield Town	0-5		31394

Division 3 (South) final table

		P	W	D	L	F	A	W	D	L	F	A	Pts
1	Fulham	42	15	3	3	72	27	9	6	6	39	35	57
2	Reading	42	19	1	1	65	21	4	8	9	32	46	55
3	Southend United	42	12	5	4	41	18	9	6	6	36	35	53
4	Crystal Palace	42	14	7	0	48	12	6	4	11	26	51	51
5	Brentford	42	11	6	4	40	22	8	4	9	28	30	48
6	Luton Town	42	16	1	4	62	25	4	6	11	33	45	47
7	Exeter City	42	16	3	2	53	16	4	4	13	24	46	47
8	Brighton & Hove A.	42	12	4	5	42	21	5	8	8	31	37	46
9	Cardiff City	42	14	2	5	62	29	5	6	10	25	44	46
10	Norwich City	42	12	7	2	51	22	5	5	11	25	45	46
11	Watford	42	14	4	3	49	27	5	4	12	32	52	46
12	Coventry City	42	17	2	2	74	28	1	6	14	34	69	44
13	QUEEN'S PARK RGS.	42	11	6	4	50	30	4	6	11	29	43	42
14	Northampton Town	42	12	3	6	48	26	4	4	13	21	43	39
15	Bournemouth	42	8	8	5	42	32	5	4	12	28	46	38
16	Clapton Orient	42	7	8	6	41	35	5	3	13	36	55	35
17	Swindon Town	42	12	2	7	47	31	2	4	15	23	53	34
18	Bristol Rovers	42	11	6	4	46	30	2	2	17	19	62	34
19	Torquay United	42	9	6	6	49	39	3	3	15	23	67	33
20	Mansfield Town	42	11	5	5	54	45	0	5	16	21	63	32
21	Gillingham	42	8	6	7	26	26	2	2	17	14	56	28
22	Thames	42	6	7	8	35	35	1	2	18	18	74	23

1932/33 16th in Division 3(S)

#	Date	Opponent	Score	Scorers	Att	Adlam LW	Armstrong JH	Ashman D	Barrie WB	Beecham EC	Blackman JJ	Brown AR	Collins JH	Goddard G	Gofton G	Goodier E	Hall EW	Hill J	Howe HG	Jobson JT	Jones CH	March R	Marcroft EH	Nixon T	Rounce GA	Russell SEJ	Wiles HS
1	Aug 27	BRENTFORD	2-3	Goddard, Brown	24381	4		2		1		11	10	9		6	3	5							8		
2	Sep 1	ALDERSHOT	2-2	Rounce, Goddard	5998	4	5	2		1		11		9		6	3	8					7		10		
3	Sep 3	Southend United	1-0	Rounce	7408	4	5	3		1				9		6		8	11				7	2	10		
4	Sep 7	Aldershot	0-2		4924	4	5	3		1		11		9		6		8					7	2	10		
5	Sep 10	CRYSTAL PALACE	2-1	Wiles, Blackman	15955	4	5	3		1	8	11		9		6							10	2			7
6	Sep 17	Gillingham	1-4	Brown	7375	4	5	3		1	8	11		9		6							10	2			7
7	Sep 24	WATFORD	2-1	Brown, Marcroft	10653	4	5	2		1		11		9		6	3	8					7		10		
8	Oct 1	Cardiff City	5-2	Marcroft 3, Goodier, Blackman	7842	4	5	2		1	9	11				6	3	8					7		10		
9	Oct 8	READING	0-3		11250	4	5	2		1	9	11				6	3	8					7		10		
10	Oct 15	Norwich City	2-3	Marcroft, Goddard	9457	4		2		1	9	10	8			6	3	11	5				7				
11	Oct 22	COVENTRY CITY	3-3	Gofton, Collins, Brown	7612	4	5	2		1		10	8		9	6	3	11					7				
12	Oct 29	Bristol City	3-2	Brown 2, Gofton	7128	4	5	2		1		10	8		9	6	3	11					7				
13	Nov 5	NORTHAMPTON T	1-1	Gofton	8895	4	5	2		1		10	8		9	6	3	11					7				
14	Nov 12	Clapton Orient	2-2	Howe, Gofton	6110	4	5	2		1		10	8		9	6	3	11					7				
15	Nov 19	SWINDON TOWN	4-2	Goddard 2, Gofton 2	5802	4	5	2		1		11		8	9	6	3						7		10		
16	Dec 3	NEWPORT COUNTY	8-1	Brown 2, Gofton 2, Rounce, Marcroft	6514	4	5	2		1		11		8	9	6	3						7		10		
17	Dec 17	EXETER CITY	1-3	Rounce	7485	4	5	2		1		11		8	9	6	3						7		10		
18	Dec 24	Torquay United	1-3	Goddard	2825			3	2	1	8	11		9		6			7	5		4			10		
19	Dec 26	BRIGHTON & HOVE ALB	0-1		9177		5	3	2	1	8	11		9		6			7			4			10		
20	Dec 27	Brighton & Hove Albion	1-4	Brown	14544	5			2	1	8	11		9		6						4	7	3	10		
21	Dec 31	Brentford	0-2		14981	8	5		2	1	7	11		9		6	3	4							10		
22	Jan 7	SOUTHEND UNITED	6-1	* See below	5588		5		2	1	7	11		9		6	3	4							10		8
23	Jan 18	Bournemouth	0-3		2645		6		2	1		11	8	9			3	4			5		7		10		
24	Jan 21	Crystal Palace	1-0	Rounce	8157		6	2		1			8	9		5	3	4	11				7		10		
25	Jan 28	GILLINGHAM	1-1	Wiles	4189		6	2		1			8			5	3	4	11				7		10		9
26	Feb 4	Watford	2-2	Howe, Rounce	6055		6	2		1	7		8	9		5		4	11						10	3	
27	Feb 11	CARDIFF CITY	5-1	Rounce 2, Goddard 2, Collins	5347		6	2		1	7		8	9		5		4	11						10	3	
28	Feb 18	Reading	1-3	Goddard	7606		3	2		1	7		8	9		5	6		11				4				
29	Feb 25	NORWICH CITY	2-2	Goodier, Howe	4586		6	2		1		11	8	9		5			7				4		10	3	
30	Mar 4	Coventry City	0-7		12312		6	2		1		11	8	9		5			7				4		10	3	
31	Mar 11	BRISTOL CITY	1-1	Blackman	6342		5		2	1	9	11	8			6	3		7				4		10		
32	Mar 18	Northampton Town	1-2	Brown	5293		5		2	1	9	10	8			6	3	11					4				7
33	Mar 25	CLAPTON ORIENT	2-1	Howe, Blackman	5320		5		2	1	9					6		8	11	10	4	7				3	
34	Apr 1	Swindon Town	0-0		3848	4	5		2	1	9	11				6			8		10		7			3	
35	Apr 8	BOURNEMOUTH	3-1	Hill, Jones, Blackman	4176	4	5		2	1	9	11				6			8		10		7			3	
36	Apr 14	BRISTOL ROVERS	1-1	Blackman	6683	4	5		2	1	9	11				6			8		10		7			3	
37	Apr 15	Newport County	1-5	Marcroft	4120	4	5		2	1	9	11	10	8		6							7			3	
38	Apr 17	Bristol Rovers	1-4	Brown	7550	4	5		2	1	8	10				6	3	11					7				9
39	Apr 18	Luton Town	1-3	Blackman	2402	4	5		2	1	8					6	3	11			10		7				9
40	Apr 22	LUTON TOWN	3-1	Blackman 2, Marcroft	2837	4	5		2	1	8	11				6	3				10		7				9
41	Apr 29	Exeter City	0-2		3358	4	5		2	1	8	11				6	3				10		7				9
42	May 6	TORQUAY UNITED	1-1	Blackman	3079	4	5		2	1	9	11	8			6	3				10		7				
		Apps				28	31	15	36	42	23	36	11	30	7	41	26	15	20	4	13	9	29	5	24	8	9
		Goals									11	13	2	11	8	2		1	4		1		8		8		2

Scorers in game 22: J Wilson (og), Goddard 2, Brown 2, Blackman.

One own goal

F.A. Cup

Rd	Date	Opponent	Score	Scorers	Att	Adlam LW	Armstrong JH	Ashman D	Barrie WB	Beecham EC	Blackman JJ	Brown AR	Collins JH	Goddard G	Gofton G	Goodier E	Hall EW	Hill J	Howe HG	Jobson JT	Jones CH	March R	Marcroft EH	Nixon T	Rounce GA	Russell SEJ	Wiles HS
R1	Nov 26	Merthyr Town	1-1	Rounce	6500	4	5	2		1		11			8	9	6	3					7		10		
rep	Nov 28	MERTHYR TOWN	5-1	Goddard 3, Marcroft, Rounce	6000	4	5	2		1		11			8	9	6	3					7		10		
R2	Dec 10	Torquay United	1-1	Rounce	5000	4	5	2		1		11			8	9	6	3					7		10		
rep	Dec 12	TORQUAY UNITED	3-1	Rounce 3	7000	4	5	2		1		11			8	9	6	3					7		10		
R3	Jan 14	Darlington	0-2		7839		5	2		1	7	11		9			3	4			6				10		8

Final Table

		P	W	D	L	F	A	W	D	L	F	A	Pts
1	Brentford	42	15	4	2	45	19	11	6	4	45	30	62
2	Exeter City	42	17	2	2	57	13	7	8	6	31	35	58
3	Norwich City	42	16	3	2	49	17	6	10	5	39	38	57
4	Reading	42	14	5	2	68	30	5	8	8	35	41	51
5	Crystal Palace	42	14	4	3	51	21	5	4	12	27	43	46
6	Coventry City	42	16	1	4	75	24	3	5	13	31	53	44
7	Gillingham	42	14	4	3	54	24	4	4	13	18	37	44
8	Northampton Town	42	16	5	0	54	11	2	3	16	22	55	44
9	Bristol Rovers	42	13	5	3	38	22	2	9	10	23	34	44
10	Torquay United	42	12	7	2	51	26	4	5	12	21	41	44
11	Watford	42	11	8	2	37	22	5	4	12	29	41	44
12	Brighton & Hove A.	42	13	3	5	42	20	4	5	12	24	45	42
13	Southend United	42	11	5	5	39	27	4	6	11	26	55	41
14	Luton Town	42	12	8	1	60	32	1	5	15	18	46	39
15	Bristol City	42	11	5	5	59	37	1	8	12	24	53	37
16	QUEEN'S PARK RGS.	42	9	8	4	48	32	4	3	14	24	55	37
17	Aldershot	42	11	6	4	37	21	2	4	15	24	51	36
18	Bournemouth	42	10	7	4	44	27	2	5	14	16	54	36
19	Cardiff City	42	12	4	5	48	30	0	3	18	21	69	31
20	Clapton Orient	42	7	8	6	39	35	1	5	15	20	58	29
21	Newport County	42	9	4	8	42	42	2	3	16	19	63	29
22	Swindon Town	42	7	9	5	36	29	2	2	17	24	76	29

23

1933/34 4th in Division 3(S)

#	Date	Opponent	Score	Scorers	Att	Allen, Joe	Ashman D	Barrie WB	Beecham EC	Blackman JJ	Blake AG	Brown AR	Clarke GB	Devine, Joe	Eaton F	Emmerson GAH	Farmer A	Goddard G	Goodier E	Hammond JH	Jones CH	Langford W	March R	Mason WS	Rivers W	Russell SEJ
1	Aug 26	BRIGHTON & HOVE ALB	2-0	Clarke 2	11986		3	2	1		6		11	10	8	7		9	5						4	
2	30	Swindon Town	1-3	Emmerson	9342		3	2	1		6		11	10	8	7		9	5						4	
3	Sep 2	Aldershot	1-3	Devine	6020		3	2	1		6		11	10	8	7		9	5				4			
4	7	SWINDON TOWN	1-0	Eaton	5956		3	2	1		6		11	10	8	7		9	5				4			
5	9	LUTON TOWN	2-1	Emmerson, Clarke	10110		3	2	1		6		11		8	7		9	5			10	4			
6	16	Northampton Town	1-2	Devine	7025		3	2	1		6		11	10	8	7		9	5				4			
7	23	TORQUAY UNITED	2-0	Blackman, Emmerson	6400		3	2	1	9	6		11	10	8	7			5				4			
8	30	Exeter City	1-1	Blackman	7126	8	3	2	1	9	6		11	10		7			5				4			
9	Oct 7	Newport County	2-1	Jones (og), Blackman	7483	8	3	2	1	9	6		11	10		7			5				4			
10	14	NORWICH CITY	5-2	Emmerson 2, Blackman 2, Clarke	8573	8	3	2	1	9	6		11	10		7			5				4			
11	21	CARDIFF CITY	4-0	Blake 2, Emmerson, Blackman	12169	8	3	2	1	9	6		11	10		7			5				4			
12	28	Bournemouth	2-3	Allen, Clarke	6324	8	3		1	9	6		11	10		7			5				4			2
13	Nov 4	CHARLTON ATHLETIC	2-1	Blackman, Clarke	15677	8	3	2	1	9	6		11	10		7			5				4			
14	11	Watford	0-0		14299	8	3	2	1	9	6		11	10		7			5				4			
15	18	Reading	0-0		11867	8	3	2	1	9	6		11	10		7			5				4			
16	Dec 2	SOUTHEND UNITED	4-0	Brown, Devine, Emmerson, Blake	8191	8	3	2	1	9	6	11		10		7			5				4			
17	16	CRYSTAL PALACE	2-1	Blackman, Blake	12849		3	2	1	9	6	11		10	8	7			5				4			
18	23	Gillingham	4-1	Blackman 3, Eaton	6979		3	2	1	9	6	11		10	8	7			5				4			
19	25	CLAPTON ORIENT	2-0	Blackman, Brown	19347		3	2	1	9	6	11		10	8	7			5				4			
20	26	Clapton Orient	2-2	Blackman 2	6274		3	2	1	9	6	11		10	8	7			5				4			
21	30	Brighton & Hove Albion	1-0	Blackman	6579		3	2	1	9	6	11		10	8	7			5				4			
22	Jan 6	ALDERSHOT	2-4	Devine, Blake	13100		3	2	1	9	6	11		10	8	7			5				4			
23	18	Coventry City	1-0	Emmerson	9701		3	2		9	6	11			8	7			5		1	10	4			
24	20	Luton Town	2-4	Kingham 2 (2og)	8098		3	2		9	6	11			8	7			5		1	10	4			
25	31	NORTHAMPTON T	2-1	Brown 2	5368	8	3	2		9	6	11		10		7			5		1		4			
26	Feb 3	Torquay United	1-1	Brown	3153	8	3	2		9	6	11		10		7	5						4	1		
27	10	EXETER CITY	2-0	Emmerson, Blackman	12380	8	3	2		9		11		10		7	5					6	4	1		
28	17	NEWPORT COUNTY	2-1	Devine, Allen	7278	8	3	2		9		11		10		7	5					6	4	1		
29	24	Norwich City	0-1		20390	8	3	2		9		11		10		7			5			6	4	1		
30	Mar 3	Cardiff City	1-3	Brown	6140	8	3	2		9	6	11		10		7			5				4	1		
31	10	BOURNEMOUTH	1-0	Brown	7149	8	3	2	1	9		11		10		7			5				4		6	
32	17	Charlton Athletic	2-1	Emmerson, Blackman	14491	8	3	2	1	9	6	11		10		7	5						4			
33	24	WATFORD	0-0		8205	8	3	2	1	9	6	11		10		7	5						4			
34	30	BRISTOL CITY	1-0	Blackman	12912	8	3	2	1	9	6	11		10		7			5				4			
35	31	Reading	0-5		10864	8	3	2	1	9	6	11		10		7			5				4			
36	Apr 2	Bristol City	2-0	Devine, Blackman	11441	8	3	2	1	9	6	11		10		7	5						4			
37	7	COVENTRY CITY	0-1		9562	8	3	2	1	9	6	11		10		7	5						4			
38	14	Southend United	2-0	Devine, Blackman	5249	8	3	2	1	9	6	11		10			5			7			4			
39	18	Bristol Rovers	1-4	Hammond	4875	8	3	2	1	9	6	11		10			5			7			4			
40	21	BRISTOL ROVERS	1-0	March	6248	8	3	2	1	9	6			10			5			7		11	4			
41	28	Crystal Palace	1-4	Blackman	7777	8	3	2	1	9	6			10			5			7		11	4			
42	May 5	GILLINGHAM	5-0	Blackman 3, Hammond, Devine	5129	8	3	2	1	9	6			10			5			7		11	4			
		Apps				26	42	41	34	36	38	24	15	37	15	37	12	6	30	5	3	9	40	8	3	1
		Goals				2				24	5	7	6	8	2	10			2	2			1			

Three own goals

F.A. Cup

#	Date	Opponent	Score	Scorers	Att	Allen, Joe	Ashman D	Barrie WB	Beecham EC	Blackman JJ	Blake AG	Brown AR	Clarke GB	Devine, Joe	Eaton F	Emmerson GAH	Farmer A	Goddard G	Goodier E	Hammond JH	Jones CH	Langford W	March R	Mason WS	Rivers W	Russell SEJ
R1	Nov 25	KETTERING TOWN	6-0	Blackman 2, Emmerson 2, Allen, Brown	14000	8	3	2	1	9	6	11		10		7			5				4			
R2	Dec 9	NEW BRIGHTON	1-1	Blackman	12000	8	3	2	1	9	6	11		10		7			5				4			
rep	11	New Brighton	4-0	Blackman 4	5062		3	2	1	9	6	11		10	8	7			5				4			
R3	Jan 13	Nottingham Forest	0-4		21170		3	2	1	9	6	11		10	8	7			5				4			

Division 3(S) Cup

#	Date	Opponent	Score	Scorers	Allen, Joe	Ashman D	Barrie WB	Beecham EC	Blackman JJ	Blake AG	Brown AR	Clarke GB	Devine, Joe	Eaton F	Emmerson GAH	Farmer A	Goddard G	Goodier E	Hammond JH	Jones CH	Langford W	March R	Mason WS	Rivers W	Russell SEJ
R2	Feb 28	READING	2-0	Brown 2	10	2					11			8	7	5		9		6			1	4	3
R3	Mar 8	BRIGHTON & HOVE ALB.	1-2	Hammond		3	2			6	11		10	8	7		5	9					4	1	

Final Table

		P	W	D	L	F	A	W	D	L	F	A	Pts
1	Norwich City	42	16	4	1	55	19	9	7	5	33	30	61
2	Coventry City	42	16	3	2	70	22	5	9	7	30	32	54
3	Reading	42	17	4	0	60	13	4	8	9	22	37	54
4	QUEEN'S PARK RGS.	42	17	2	2	42	12	7	4	10	28	39	54
5	Charlton Athletic	42	14	5	2	53	27	8	3	10	30	29	52
6	Luton Town	42	14	3	4	55	28	7	7	7	28	33	52
7	Bristol Rovers	42	14	4	3	49	21	6	7	8	28	26	51
8	Swindon Town	42	13	5	3	42	25	4	6	11	22	43	45
9	Exeter City	42	12	5	4	43	19	4	6	11	25	38	43
10	Brighton & Hove A.	42	12	7	2	47	18	3	6	12	21	42	43
11	Clapton Orient	42	14	4	3	60	25	2	6	13	15	44	42
12	Crystal Palace	42	11	6	4	40	25	5	3	13	31	42	41
13	Northampton Town	42	10	6	5	45	32	4	6	11	26	46	40
14	Aldershot	42	8	6	7	28	27	5	6	10	24	44	38
15	Watford	42	12	4	5	43	16	3	3	15	28	47	37
16	Southend United	42	9	6	6	32	27	3	4	14	19	47	34
17	Gillingham	42	8	8	5	49	41	3	3	15	26	55	33
18	Newport County	42	6	9	6	25	23	2	8	11	24	47	33
19	Bristol City	42	7	8	6	33	22	3	5	13	25	63	33
20	Torquay United	42	10	4	7	32	28	3	3	15	21	65	33
21	Bournemouth	42	7	7	7	41	37	2	2	17	19	65	27
22	Cardiff City	42	6	4	11	32	43	3	2	16	25	62	24

1934/35 13th in Division 3(S)

Results & Appearances

#	Date		Opponent	Score	Scorers	Att
1	Aug	25	Swindon Town	1-3	Reed	12176
2		29	CRYSTAL PALACE	3-3	Blake (p), Crawford, Blackman	9415
3	Sep	1	ALDERSHOT	2-0	Reed 2	12040
4		5	Crystal Palace	3-2	Hammond, Blackman, Reed	15853
5		8	Cardiff City	1-2	Farquarson (og)	12683
6		15	BRIGHTON & HOVE ALB	2-1	Blackman, Abel	9410
7		22	Luton Town	1-1	Crawford	7233
8		29	SOUTHEND UNITED	1-1	Abel	9989
9	Oct	6	Bristol Rovers	0-2		7835
10		13	CHARLTON ATHLETIC	0-3		12554
11		20	Gillingham	0-0		5898
12		27	READING	2-0	Dutton, Wilson	8433
13	Nov	3	Millwall	0-2		12001
14		10	COVENTRY CITY	1-1	Crawford	7442
15		17	Watford	0-2		8066
16	Dec	1	Exeter City	0-3		4359
17		15	Northampton Town	0-1		5008
18		22	BOURNEMOUTH	2-1	Crawford, Blackman	4300
19		25	CLAPTON ORIENT	6-3	*See below	9244
20		26	Clapton Orient	1-3	Crawford	11446
21		29	SWINDON TOWN	1-1	Blake	6150
22	Jan	1	BRISTOL CITY	4-1	Blackman, Crawford, Allen, Emmerson	7797
23		5	Aldershot	0-1		3625
24		12	NEWPORT COUNTY	4-1	Blackman 2, Dutton, Emmerson	4511
25		19	CARDIFF CITY	2-2	Blackman, Dutton	5548
26		26	Brighton & Hove Albion	1-5	Allen	5098
27	Feb	2	LUTON TOWN	3-0	Blackman 2, Crawford	6201
28		9	Southend United	0-2		5681
29		16	BRISTOL ROVERS	2-0	Abel, Dutton	2834
30		23	Charlton Athletic	1-3	Allen	17897
31	Mar	2	GILLINGHAM	2-0	Farmer, Blackman	8157
32		9	Reading	0-0		6631
33		16	MILLWALL	1-0	Farmer	8279
34		23	Coventry City	1-4	Blackman	8096
35		30	WATFORD	2-1	Blackman, Blake (p)	6732
36	Apr	6	Newport County	1-2	Blackman	2912
37		13	EXETER CITY	1-1	Farmer	5500
38		19	TORQUAY UNITED	5-1	Blackman 2, Blake, Farmer, Dutton	6082
39		20	Bristol City	1-5	Bridge (og)	5868
40		22	Torquay United	0-7		3445
41		27	NORTHAMPTON T	3-1	Farmer 2, Blackman	3603
42	May	4	Bournemouth	2-0	Farmer, Dutton	4970

Scorers in game 19: Blackman 2, Emmerson, Crawford, Devine, Allen.

Appearance grid

#	Abel SC	Allen, Joe	Ashman D	Barnie WB	Bartlett FL	Beecham EC	Blackman JJ	Blake AG	Connor R	Crawford JF	Devine, Joe	Dutton T	Emmerson GAH	Farmer A	Goodier E	Hammond JH	Langford W	March R	Mason WS	Reed G	Ridley JG	Russell SEJ	Trodd W	Watson G	Wright E
1	8		3	2		1				11	10	6		7	5			4		9					
2			3	2		1	8	6		11	10			7	5			4		9					
3			3	2		1	8	6		11	10			7	5			4		9					
4			3	2		1	8	6		11	10			7	5			4		9					
5			3	2		1	8	6		11	10			7	5			4		9					
6	8			2		1	9	6		7	10				5			4				3	11		
7	8			2		1	9	6		7	10				5			4				3	11		
8	8			2		1	9	6		7	10				5			4				3	11		
9	8			2		1	9	6		11	10				5			4				3		7	
10		8		2		1		6		11	10		7		5			4				3		9	
11			3	2			8			7	10	6		4	5					9	1		11		
12			3	2			8	4			10	6	7		5					9	1		11		
13			3	2	5		7	4			8	10			6					9	1		11		
14	9		3	2					4	11	8	10	7		5	6					1				
15	9		3	2					4	11	8	10	7	6	5						1				
16			3	2						9	11	8		7	5	6		4	10		1				
17		8			5					9	11	10				6	7	4			1				
18		8			5		9			11	10					6	7	4			1	2	3		
19		8		2			9	6		11	10		7		5			4			1	3			
20		8		2			9	6		11		10	7		5			4			1	3			
21		8	3	2			9	6		11	10		7		5			4			1				
22		8	3	2			9	6		11	10		7		5			4			1				
23		8	3	2			9	6		11			7		5			4	10		1				
24		8					9	6		11		10	7		5			4			1	2	3		
25		8		2			9	6		11		10	7		5			4			1	3			
26		8	3				9	6	11				7		5			4			1	2			10
27	7	8					9	6		11				10	5			4			1	2	3		
28	7	8	3				9	6		11				10	5			4			1	2			
29	7	8	3				9	6		11		10			5			4			1	2			
30	7	8	3				9	6		11				10	5			4			1	2			
31	9						8	6		11				10	5	7		4			1	2	3		
32	7						9	6		11	8			10	5			4			1	2	3		
33							9	6	11		8		7	10	5			4			1	2	3		
34	7	4					9	6	11		8			10	5						1	2	3		
35	7	4					9	6	11				8	10	5						1	2	3		
36	7	4					9	6	11				8	10	5						1	2	3		
37	7	8					9	6		11				10	5						1	2	3	4	
38	7	8					9	6		11				10	5						1	2	3	4	
39	7	8					9	6		11				10	5						1	2	3	4	
40	7	8	3	2			9	6		11				10	5						1			4	
41	7	8	3	2			9	6		11				10	5						1			4	
42		8	3	2			9	6		11			7	10	5						1			4	

	Abel SC	Allen, Joe	Ashman D	Barnie WB	Bartlett FL	Beecham EC	Blackman JJ	Blake AG	Connor R	Crawford JF	Devine, Joe	Dutton T	Emmerson GAH	Farmer A	Goodier E	Hammond JH	Langford W	March R	Mason WS	Reed G	Ridley JG	Russell SEJ	Trodd W	Watson G	Wright E
Apps	20	25	21	25	3	10	38	37	5	26	20	23	15	26	40	8	2	24	32	9	17	21	6	8	1
Goals	3	4					19	4		8	1	6	3	7		1				4					1

Two own goals

F.A. Cup

#	Date		Opponent	Score	Scorers	Att	Abel	Allen	Ashman	Barnie	Bartlett	Beecham	Blackman	Blake	Connor	Crawford	Devine	Dutton	Emmerson	Farmer	Goodier	Hammond	Langford	March	Mason	Reed	Ridley	Russell	Trodd	Watson	Wright
R1	Nov	24	WALTHAMSTOW AVE.	2-0	Emmerson, Devine	9000	9		3	2				4		11	8	10	7	5					6		1				
R2	Dec	8	BRIGHTON & HOVE ALB.	1-2	Crawford	14000		8		4	5		9			11	10			6	7				1			2	3		

Division 3(S) Cup

#	Date		Opponent	Score	Scorers	Abel	Allen	Ashman	Barnie	Bartlett	Beecham	Blackman	Blake	Connor	Crawford	Devine	Dutton	Emmerson	Farmer	Goodier	Hammond	Langford	March	Mason	Reed	Ridley	Russell	Trodd	Watson	Wright
R2	Oct	18	LUTON TOWN	2-1	Blackman, Crawford		8	3	2			9			11	10	6	7	5				4			1				
R3	Feb	13	Watford	1-1	Blackman	7	8	3				9	6		11				10	5			4	1			2			
rep		28	WATFORD	1-1	Blake	7	8	3				9	6		11				10	5			4	1			2			
rep2	Mar	14	WATFORD	0-2		7						9	11				8		10	5			4	1			2	3	6	

R3 replay 2 a.e.t.

League table

		P	W	D	L	F	A	W	D	L	F	A	Pts
1	Charlton Athletic	42	17	2	2	62	20	10	5	6	41	32	61
2	Reading	42	16	5	0	59	23	5	6	10	30	42	53
3	Coventry City	42	14	5	2	56	14	7	4	10	30	36	51
4	Luton Town	42	12	7	2	60	23	7	5	9	32	37	50
5	Crystal Palace	42	15	3	3	51	14	4	7	10	35	50	48
6	Watford	42	14	2	5	53	19	5	7	9	23	30	47
7	Northampton Town	42	14	4	3	40	21	5	4	12	25	46	46
8	Bristol Rovers	42	14	6	1	54	27	3	4	14	19	50	44
9	Brighton & Hove A.	42	15	4	2	51	16	2	5	14	18	46	43
10	Torquay United	42	15	2	4	60	22	3	4	14	21	53	42
11	Exeter City	42	11	5	5	48	29	5	4	12	22	46	41
12	Millwall	42	11	4	6	33	26	6	3	12	24	36	41
13	QUEEN'S PARK RGS.	42	14	6	1	49	22	2	3	16	14	50	41
14	Clapton Orient	42	13	3	5	47	21	2	7	12	18	44	40
15	Bristol City	42	14	3	4	37	18	1	6	14	15	50	39
16	Swindon Town	42	11	7	3	45	22	2	5	14	22	56	38
17	Bournemouth	42	10	5	6	36	26	5	2	14	18	45	37
18	Aldershot	42	12	6	3	35	20	1	4	16	15	55	36
19	Cardiff City	42	11	6	4	42	27	2	3	16	20	55	35
20	Gillingham	42	10	7	4	36	25	1	6	14	19	50	35
21	Southend United	42	10	4	7	40	29	1	5	15	25	49	31
22	Newport County	42	7	4	10	36	40	3	1	17	18	72	25

League Matches

#	Date	Opponent	Score	Scorers	Att
1	Aug 31	MILLWALL	2-3	Blackman, Lowe	13089
2	Sep 4	Brighton & Hove Albion	1-1	Hammond	8303
3	7	Torquay United	2-4	Hammond, Samuel	5432
4	12	BRIGHTON & HOVE ALB	3-2	Cheetham 2, Lowe	6236
5	14	ALDERSHOT	5-0	Cheetham 4, Hammond	9667
6	16	Luton Town	0-2		8220
7	21	Swindon Town	2-2	Crawford, Lowe	11628
8	28	COVENTRY CITY	0-0		11529
9	Oct 5	Newport County	4-3	Cheetham 3, Lowe	6033
10	12	EXETER CITY	3-1	Cheetham 2, Abel	11311
11	19	Notts County	0-3		7369
12	26	BRISTOL ROVERS	4-0	Cheetham (p), Lumsden 2, Farmer	9062
13	Nov 2	Clapton Orient	0-1		12815
14	9	BOURNEMOUTH	2-0	Cheetham, Overstone	10042
15	16	Northampton Town	4-1	Ballantyne, Cheetham 2, Ovenstone	6472
16	23	CRYSTAL PALACE	3-0	Cheetham 3	13414
17	Dec 7	CARDIFF CITY	5-1	Lumsden 3, Cheetham 2	5048
18	21	SOUTHEND UNITED	2-1	Ballantyne, Cheetham	8252
19	25	WATFORD	3-1	Cheetham 2, Ballantyne	14573
20	26	Watford	1-2	Lowe	14251
21	28	Millwall	0-2		14529
22	Jan 4	TORQUAY UNITED	2-1	Cheetham, Samuel	10244
23	15	Reading	2-1	Cheetham 2	5123
24	18	Aldershot	3-1	Lowe 2, Abel	3867
25	25	SWINDON TOWN	5-1	Cheetham 2, Lowe 2, Abel	10797
26	Feb 1	Coventry City	1-6	Samuel	20785
27	8	NEWPORT COUNTY	1-1	Crawford	10419
28	15	Exeter City	0-0		4801
29	22	NOTTS COUNTY	2-2	Cheetham, Overstone	6497
30	29	Bournemouth	1-0	Cheetham	6138
31	Mar 7	GILLINGHAM	5-2	Cheetham 3, Lowe, Crawford	11119
32	14	Bristol Rovers	1-0	Cheetham	7710
33	21	NORTHAMPTON T	0-1		13687
34	28	Crystal Palace	2-0	Cheetham, Crawford	22389
35	Apr 4	READING	0-1		14378
36	10	BRISTOL CITY	4-1	Lowe 3, Crawford	15256
37	11	Cardiff City	2-3	Crawford, Lowe	8571
38	13	Bristol City	0-0		10838
39	18	CLAPTON ORIENT	4-0	Lowe, Banks, Crawford, Farmer	10811
40	22	Gillingham	2-2	Banks, Cheetham	2405
41	25	Southend United	1-0	Farmer	4969
42	May 2	LUTON TOWN	0-0		17951

Player appearances (shirt numbers) and totals

#	Abel SC	Allen, Jimmy	Ballentyne J	Banks R	Bernie WB	Bartlett FL	Blackman JJ	Blake AG	Carr WP	Cheetham TM	Clarke C(t)	Coggins WH	Crawford JF	Farmer A	Fletcher J	Hammond JH	Lowe HP	Lumsden FL	March R	Mason WS	Molloy P	Ovenstone DG	Rowe J	Russell SEJ	Samuel DJ	Vincent E
1	7		11				9	6	2								8		4	1			3		10	5
2								6	2	9			11			7	8	10	4	1			3			5
3	9							6	2				11			7	8		4	1			3		10	5
4								6	2	9			11			7	8	10	4	1			3			5
5		4				5			2	9			11			7	8	10	6	1			3			
6		4				5			2	9			11			7	8	10	6	1			3			
7		4				5			2	9			11		8		10	7	6	1			3			
8		4				5			2	9			11		8		10	7	6	1				3		
9		4				5			2	9			11		8		10	7	6	1				3		
10		4				5			2	9			11		8		10	7	6	1				3		
11		4				5			2	9			11		8		10	7	6	1				3		
12		4			2	5				9			11	6	8		10	7		1			3			
13		4	11		2	5		6		9					8		10	7		1			3			
14		4			2	5				9					8		10	7	6	1		11	3			
15		4	10		2	5				9					8			7	6	1		11	3			
16		4	10		2	5				9					8			7	6	1		11	3			
17		4	10		2	5				9					8			7	6	1		11	3			
18		4	10		2	5		6		9					8			7		1		11	3			
19		4	10		2	5				9					8			7	6	1		11	3			
20		4			2	5				9					8		10	7	6	1		11	3			
21					2	5				9	1			10	8			7	6			11	3			4
22	7				2	5				9					8				6	1		11	3		10	4
23	7	4				5				9					8				6	1		11	3	2	10	
24	7	4				5				9							8		6	1		11	3	2	10	
25	7	4				5				9							8		6	1		11	3	2	10	
26	7	4		11	2	5				9							8		6	1			3		10	
27		4		11	2	5				9			7	10			8		6	1			3			
28		4			2	5				9					8			7	6	1		11	3		10	
29		4			2	5				9		10	8					7	6	1		11	3			
30		4	10		2	5				9			8					7	6	1		11	3			
31		4	10		2	5				9			11				8	7	6	1			3			
32		4	10		2	5				9			11				8	7	6	1			3			
33		4	10		2	5				9			11				8	7	6	1			3			
34		4	10		2	5				9			11				8	7	6	1			3			
35		4	10		2	5				9			11				8	7	6	1			3			
36		4	10		2	5							11	8			9	7	6	1			3			
37		4	10		2	5							11	8			9	7	6	1			3			
38		4	10		2	5							11	8			9	7	6	1			3			
39			10	7	2	5							11	8			9		6	1			3			4
40				11	2	5				9			7	10			8		6	1			3			4
41	9			11	2	5							7	10			8		6	1			3			4
42		4		11		5			2	9			7	10			8		6	1			3			
Apps	8	33	15	9	26	38	1	6	14	35	1	6	24	9	21	5	34	25	37	36	3	15	32	12	9	8
Goals	3		3	2			1			36			7	3		3	15	5				3			3	

F.A. Cup

#	Date	Opponent	Score	Scorers	Att
R1	Nov 30	Margate	1-3	Cheetham	7000

Team (shirt numbers): Allen 4, Ballentyne 10, Bernie 2, Bartlett 5, Cheetham 9, Fletcher 8, Lumsden 7, March 6, Mason 1, Ovenstone 11, Rowe 3.

Division 3(S) Cup

#	Date	Opponent	Score	Scorers
R2	Oct 23	Brighton & Hove Albion	1-2	Crawford

Team (shirt numbers): Allen 4, Ballentyne 10, Bernie 2, Bartlett 5, Cheetham 9, Crawford 11, Farmer 6, Fletcher 8, Lumsden 7, Mason 1, Rowe 3.

Division 3(S) Table

		P	W	D	L	F	A	W	D	L	F	A	Pts
1	Coventry City	42	19	1	1	75	12	5	8	8	27	33	57
2	Luton Town	42	13	6	2	56	20	9	6	6	25	25	56
3	Reading	42	18	0	3	52	20	8	2	11	35	42	54
4	QUEEN'S PARK RGS.	42	14	4	3	55	19	8	5	8	29	34	53
5	Watford	42	12	3	6	47	29	8	6	7	33	25	49
6	Crystal Palace	42	15	4	2	64	20	7	1	13	32	54	49
7	Brighton & Hove A.	42	13	4	4	48	25	5	4	12	22	38	44
8	Bournemouth	42	9	6	6	36	26	7	5	9	24	30	43
9	Notts County	42	10	5	6	40	25	5	7	9	20	32	42
10	Torquay United	42	14	4	3	41	27	2	5	14	21	35	41
11	Aldershot	42	9	6	6	29	21	5	6	10	24	40	40
12	Millwall	42	9	8	4	33	21	5	4	12	25	50	40
13	Bristol City	42	11	5	5	32	21	4	5	12	16	38	40
14	Clapton Orient	42	13	2	6	34	15	3	4	14	21	46	38
15	Northampton Town	42	12	5	4	38	24	3	3	15	24	66	38
16	Gillingham	42	9	5	7	34	25	5	4	12	32	52	37
17	Bristol Rovers	42	11	6	4	48	31	3	3	15	21	64	37
18	Southend United	42	8	7	6	38	21	5	3	13	23	41	36
19	Swindon Town	42	10	5	6	43	33	4	3	14	21	40	36
20	Cardiff City	42	11	5	5	37	23	2	5	14	23	50	36
21	Newport County	42	8	4	9	36	44	3	5	13	24	67	31
22	Exeter City	42	7	5	9	38	41	1	6	14	21	52	27

1936/37   9th in Division 3(S)

#	Date		Opponent	Score	Scorers	Att	Abel SC	Allen, Jimmy	Ballentyne J	Banks R	Barrie WB	Bartlett FL	Bott WE	Cameron K	Carr WP	Charlton W	Cheetham TM	Clarke C(1)	Crawford JF	Farmer A	Fitzgerald AM	James NL	Jefferson A	Lowe HP	Lumsden FL	McMahon HJ	March R	Mason WS	Moralee WE	Rowe J	Swinfen R	Vincent E
1	Aug 29		Bristol City	2-3	Cheetham, Lowe	13689		4				2	5	11	10	3	9		7				3	8			6	1				
2	31		Millwall	0-2		16227		4				2	5	11	10		9		7				3	8			6	1				
3	Sep 5		TORQUAY UNITED	3-0	Bott 2 (1p), Lowe	10385		4	10			2	5	11			9		7				3	8			6	1				
4	12		Notts County	2-1	Bott 2 (1p)	5013		4	10			2	5	11			9						3	8		7	6	1				
5	17		MILLWALL	0-1		10824		4	10			2	5	11			9						3	8		7	6	1				
6	19		CLAPTON ORIENT	2-1	Banks, Lowe	15448		4		11		2	5				9						3	10		7	6	1			8	
7	23		Crystal Palace	0-0		9467		4						11			9						2	8		7	6	1		3	10	5
8	26		Walsall	4-2	Cheetham 2, Allen, Lowe	8984		4			8			11			9						2	10		7	6	1		3		5
9	Oct 3		LUTON TOWN	2-1	Bott, Lowe (p)	20437	7	4			8			11			9						2	10			6	1		3		5
10	10		Cardiff City	0-2		21897	7	4			8			11			9						2	10			6	1		3		5
11	17		SWINDON TOWN	1-1	Lowe	12405	7				8		5	11			9						2	10			6	1		3		4
12	24		Aldershot	0-0		5050					8			11			9			5			2	10	7		6	1		3		4
13	31		GILLINGHAM	0-1		5687					8			11			9					5	2	10	7		6	1		3		4
14	Nov 7		Newport County	2-1	Lowe 2	10267								11			9				10	5	2	8	7		6	1		3		4
15	14		SOUTHEND UNITED	7-2	*see below	11446											9				10	5	2	8	7	11	6	1		3		4
16	21		Watford	0-2		12349											9				10	5	2	8	7	11	6	1		3		4
17	Dec 5		Bournemouth	1-3	Fitzgerald	7120							7				9				10	5	2	8			6	1		3		4
18	19		Bristol Rovers	1-1	Cheetham	8114							7			8	9			5	10		2			11	6	1		3		4
19	25		EXETER CITY	4-0	Bott, Fitzgerald, Cheetham, Charlton	12507							7			8	9			5	10		2	4		11	6	1		3		
20	26		BRISTOL CITY	5-0	Cheetham 2, Fitzgerald, Charlton, Bott	9576							7			8	9			5	10		2	4		11	6	1		3		
21	28		Exeter City	3-0	Bott, Cheetham, Charlton	4817							7			8	9			5	10		2	4		11	6	1		3		
22	Jan 2		Torquay United	1-1	Fitzgerald	3179			8				7				9			5	10		2	4		11	6	1		3		
23	9		NOTTS COUNTY	0-2		14938							7			8	9			5	10		2	4		11	6	1		3		
24	21		BRIGHTON & HOVE ALB	2-3	Bott, Lowe	4742							7			9	8			5	10		2	4		11	6	1		3		
25	23		Clapton Orient	0-0		7606		4				2	7				9			5	10		3	8		11		1	6		9	
26	Feb 4		WALSALL	2-0	Lowe 2	3850						2	7				9			5	10		3	8		11	4	1	6			
27	6		Luton Town	1-0	Charlton	13767						2					9			5	10			8	7	11	4	1	6	3		
28	13		CARDIFF CITY	6-0	Charlton 3, Fitzgerald 3	11408						2					9			5	10			8	7	11	4	1	6			
29	18		NORTHAMPTON T	3-2	Fitzgerald 2, Charlton	3751						2			3	8	9			5	10			4	7	11	6	1				
30	20		Swindon Town	1-1	Fitzgerald	6741						2				3	9			5	10			8	7	11	6	1				4
31	27		ALDERSHOT	3-0	Fitzgerald 2, Lumsden	8843						2				3	9			5	10			8	7	11	6	1				4
32	Mar 6		Gillingham	0-0		6965						2				3	9			5	10			8	7	11	6	1				4
33	13		NEWPORT COUNTY	6-2	Swinfen 3, Fitzgerald, Lowe, Lumsden	11738						2				3				5	10			8	7	11	4	1	6		9	
34	20		Southend United	2-3	Fitzgerald 2	8675						2				3	9			5	10			8	7	11	4	1	6			
35	26		READING	0-0		16297										3		7		5	10			8		11	4	1	6		9	2
36	27		WATFORD	1-2	McMahon	12945						2				3		7		5	10			8		11	6	1			9	4
37	29		Reading	0-2		13050						2			8	3	9			5	10				7	11	6	1				4
38	Apr 3		Brighton & Hove Albion	1-4	Barrie	9176						2			10	3	9	8		5				7		11	6	1				4
39	10		BOURNEMOUTH	1-2	Cameron	6002					7	2		8		3				5	10			9		11	4	1	6			
40	17		Northampton Town	1-0	Lowe	4056					7	2		8		3				5	10			9		11	4	1	6			
41	24		BRISTOL ROVERS	2-1	Lowe 2	6802						2			8		9			5	10			7		11	4	1	6			3
42	May 1		CRYSTAL PALACE	1-3	McMahon	6142						2			8	7					10	5		9		11	4	1	6	3		

Scorers in game 15: Fitzgerald 2, Lowe 2, Lumsden, March, Cheetham

	Abel SC	Allen, Jimmy	Ballentyne J	Banks R	Barrie WB	Bartlett FL	Bott WE	Cameron K	Carr WP	Charlton W	Cheetham TM	Clarke C(1)	Crawford JF	Farmer A	Fitzgerald AM	James NL	Jefferson A	Lowe HP	Lumsden FL	McMahon HJ	March R	Mason WS	Moralee WE	Rowe J	Swinfen R	Vincent E
Apps	3	11	10	3	23	7	23	8	14	16	28	2	3	25	28	6	25	41	13	33	41	42	11	20	6	20
Goals		1			1	1	9	1		8	9				17			17	3	2	1				3	

F.A. Cup

#	Date		Opponent	Score	Scorers	Att	Bott WE	Cheetham TM	Carr WP	Farmer A	Fitzgerald AM	Jefferson A	Lowe HP	McMahon HJ	March R	Mason WS	Rowe J	Vincent E
R1	Nov 28		BRIGHTON & HOVE ALB.	5-1	Fitzgerald 3, Cheetham, McMahon	16000	7	9		5	10	2	8	11	6	1	3	4
R2	Dec 12		South Liverpool	1-0	Fitzgerald	6000	7	9		5	10	2	8	11	6	1	3	4
R3	Jan 16		Bury	0-1		13638	7	9	8	5	10	2	4	11	6	1	3	

Division 3(S) Cup

#	Date		Opponent	Score	Scorers	Abel SC	Allen, Jimmy	Banks R	Cheetham TM	Jefferson A	Lowe HP	McMahon HJ	March R	Mason WS	Swinfen R	Vincent E
R1	Oct 7		Reading	1-2	McMahon	7	4	3	9	2	10	11	6	1	8	5

		P	W	D	L	F	A	W	D	L	F	A	Pts
1	Luton Town	42	19	1	1	69	16	8	3	10	34	37	58
2	Notts County	42	15	3	3	44	23	8	7	6	30	29	56
3	Brighton & Hove A.	42	15	5	1	49	16	9	0	12	25	27	53
4	Watford	42	14	4	3	53	21	5	7	9	32	39	49
5	Reading	42	14	5	2	53	23	5	6	10	23	37	49
6	Bournemouth	42	17	3	1	45	20	3	6	12	20	39	49
7	Northampton Town	42	15	4	2	56	22	5	2	14	29	46	46
8	Millwall	42	12	4	5	43	24	6	6	9	21	30	46
9	QUEEN'S PARK RGS.	42	12	2	7	51	24	6	7	8	22	28	45
10	Southend United	42	10	8	3	49	23	7	3	11	29	44	45
11	Gillingham	42	14	5	2	36	18	4	3	14	16	48	44
12	Clapton Orient	42	10	8	3	29	17	4	7	10	23	35	43
13	Swindon Town	42	12	4	5	52	24	2	7	12	23	49	39
14	Crystal Palace	42	11	7	3	45	20	2	5	14	17	41	38
15	Bristol Rovers	42	14	3	4	49	20	2	1	18	22	60	36
16	Bristol City	42	13	3	5	42	20	2	3	16	16	50	36
17	Walsall	42	11	3	7	38	34	2	7	12	25	51	36
18	Cardiff City	42	10	5	6	35	24	4	2	15	19	63	35
19	Newport County	42	7	7	7	37	28	5	3	13	30	70	34
20	Torquay United	42	9	5	7	42	32	2	5	14	15	48	32
21	Exeter City	42	9	5	7	36	37	1	7	13	23	51	32
22	Aldershot	42	5	6	10	29	29	2	3	16	21	60	23

1937/38   3rd in Division 3(S)

Player column key (left→right): Barrie WB · Bott WE · Cape JP · Charlton W · Cheetham TM · Clarke C(1) · Farmer A · Fitzgerald AM · Gilfillan JE · James NL · Jefferson A · Lowe HP · McCarthy LD · McMahon HJ · Mallett J · March R · Mason WS · Moralee WE · Pattison JM · Prior SJ · Reay EP · Ridyard A · Smith N(2) · Stock AWA · Swinfen R

#	Date	Match		Scorers	Att	Bar	Bot	Cap	Cha	Che	Cla	Far	Fit	Gil	Jam	Jef	Low	McC	McM	Mal	Mar	Mas	Mor	Pat	Pri	Rea	Rid	Smi	Sto	Swi
1	Aug 28	BRIGHTON & HOVE ALB	2-1	Cheetham, Fitzgerald	16090			7		9		5	10			3	8			11	4	1	6					2		
2	30	Millwall	4-1	Lowe, Cape, Cheetham, Fitzgerald	16725			7		9		5	10			3	8			11	4	1	6					2		
3	Sep 4	Bournemouth	1-1	Cape	8882			7		9		5	10			3	8			11	4	1	6					2		
4	9	MILLWALL	0-2		8334			7		9		5	10			3	8			11	4	1	6					2		
5	11	CARDIFF CITY	2-1	Cape, Lowe	15300			7		9			10		5	3	8			11	4	1	6					2		
6	15	Torquay United	2-0	Fitzgerald, Lowe	4782		11	7					10		5	3	8				4	1	6		9			2		
7	18	Walsall	3-0	Prior 2, Bott	8155		11	7					10		5	3	8				4	1	6		9			2		
8	25	NORTHAMPTON T	1-1	Cape	13982		11	7				5	10			3	8				4	1	6		9			2		
9	Oct 2	Bristol Rovers	1-1	Prior	12503		11	7			8				5	3	10				4	1	6		9			2		
10	9	MANSFIELD TOWN	1-1	Bott	14142		11	7			8				5	3	10				4	1	6		9			2		
11	16	Reading	0-1		10267		11	7			8		10	1	5	3					4		6		9			2		
12	23	CRYSTAL PALACE	1-0	McMahon	12982			7		9			10	1	5	3	4		11	8		6						2		
13	30	Notts County	2-2	Cape, Cheetham	11705			7		9				1	5	3	4	10	11	8		6						2		
14	Nov 6	NEWPORT COUNTY	0-0		11558			7		9				1	5	3	4	10	11	8		6						2		
15	13	Bristol City	0-2		17343		11	9					10	1	5	3	7			8	6							2		4
16	20	WATFORD	2-0	Bott (p), Cheetham	12533		11	7		9			10	1	5	3	4			8	6							2		
17	Dec 4	EXETER CITY	4-0	Bott 2, Fitzgerald, Cheetham	10681		11	7		9			10	1	5	3	4			8	6							2		
18	18	ALDERSHOT	3-0	Fitzgerald, Cheetham, Mallett	9300		11	7		9			10	1	5	3	4			8	6							2		
19	25	SOUTHEND UNITED	1-0	Fitzgerald	17934		11	7		9			10	1	5	3	4			8	6							2		
20	27	Southend United	1-2	Fitzgerald	16531		11	7		9			10	1	5	3	4			8	6							2		
21	28	Swindon Town	3-1	Cheetham 2, Bott	7255		11	7		9			10	1	5	3	4			8	6							2		
22	Jan 1	Brighton & Hove Albion	1-3	Bott	13244		11	7		9			10	1	5	3	4			8	6							2		
23	8	Gillingham	5-1	Fitzgerald, Mallett, Bott 2, Hartley (og)	7699		11	7		9			10	1	5	3	4			8	6							2		
24	15	BOURNEMOUTH	1-2	Bott	12846		11	7		9			10	1	5	3	4			8	6							2		
25	22	Cardiff City	2-2	Cape, Fitzgerald	26268		11	7		9			10	1	5	3	4			8	6							2		
26	29	WALSALL	3-1	Charlton, Fitzgerald, Shelton (og)	11934		11	7	9				10	1	5	3	4			8	6							2		
27	Feb 5	Northampton Town	2-0	Cape, Fitzgerald	9270		11	7	9				10	1	5	3	4			8	6							2		
28	12	BRISTOL ROVERS	4-0	Bott 2, Mallett, Fitzgerald	11407		11	7	9				10	1	5	3	4			8	6							2		
29	19	Mansfield Town	2-3	Cape, Charlton	9072		11	7	9				10	1	5	3	4			8	6							2		
30	26	READING	3-0	Fitzgerald 2, Stock	19725		11	7					10	1	5	3	4			8	6							2	9	
31	Mar 5	Crystal Palace	0-4		25522		11	7	9				10	1	5	3	4			8	6							2		
32	12	NOTTS COUNTY	2-1	Fitzgerald, Smith	19078		7					6	9		5	3	4	10		8		1		11				2		
33	19	Newport County	1-1	Cape	10225		11	7					10		5	3	4			8	6	1						2	9	
34	26	BRISTOL CITY	0-2		23113		11	7					10		5	3	4			8	6	1						2	9	
35	Apr 2	Watford	1-3	Bott	20456		11	7					10		5		4			8	6	1			3			2	9	
36	9	GILLINGHAM	2-0	Cheetham, Mallett	10356	2	7			9		6					4	10		8		1		11		3	5			
37	15	Clapton Orient	1-1	Pattison	12881	2	7			9							4	10		8	6	1		11		3	5			
38	16	Exeter City	4-0	Cheetham 2, Bott, McCarthy	7885	2	11			9			10				4	7		8	6	1				3	5			
39	18	CLAPTON ORIENT	3-2	Bott, Fitzgerald, McCarthy	15816	2	11			9			10				4	7		8	6	1				3	5			
40	23	SWINDON TOWN	3-0	Bott, Cheetham, McCarthy	15482	2	11	7		9			10				4			8	6	1				3	5			
41	30	Aldershot	0-1		4949	2	11	7		9			10				4			8	6	1				3	5			
42	May 7	TORQUAY UNITED	6-3	Cheetham 2, McCarthy 2, Fitzgerald, Bott	7177		11	7		9		6					4	10		8		1				3	5	2		
		Apps				6	31	40	4	26	3	7	36	21	30	34	41	10	8	29	39	21	11	3	6	5	7	39	4	1
		Goals					17	9	2	14			17				3	5	1	4				1	3			1	1	

Two own goals

F.A. Cup

Rd	Date	Match		Scorers	Att	Bot	Cap	Che	Fit	Gil	Jam	Jef	Low	Mal	Mar	Smi
R1	Nov 27	Bristol Rovers	8-1	Fitzgerald 3, Cheetham 3, Bott 2	7000	11	7	9	10	1	5	3	4	8	6	2
R2	Dec 11	Swindon Town	1-2	Cape	9000	11	7	9	10	1	5	3	4	8	6	2

Division 3(S) Cup

Rd	Date	Match		Scorers	Bot	Cap	Che	Cla	Fit	Gil	Jam	Jef	Low	McC	Mal	Mor	Swi
R2	Nov 11	CLAPTON ORIENT	2-0	Lowe, Fitzgerald	11	7			10		5	3	9		8	1 6	4
R3	Mar 1	WATFORD	2-3	Cheetham, McCarthy	11		9	2	10	1	5	3		8		6	4

Played in R2: SC Abel (at 2). In R3, Ives (7).

League table — Division 3(S)

		P	W	D	L	F	A	W	D	L	F	A	Pts
1	Millwall	42	15	3	3	53	15	8	7	6	30	22	56
2	Bristol City	42	14	6	1	37	13	7	7	7	31	27	55
3	QUEEN'S PARK RGS.	42	15	3	3	44	17	7	6	8	36	30	53
4	Watford	42	14	4	3	50	15	7	7	7	23	28	53
5	Brighton & Hove A.	42	15	3	3	40	16	6	6	9	24	28	51
6	Reading	42	17	2	2	44	21	3	9	9	27	42	51
7	Crystal Palace	42	14	4	3	45	17	4	8	9	22	30	48
8	Swindon Town	42	12	4	5	33	19	5	6	10	16	30	44
9	Northampton Town	42	12	4	5	30	19	5	5	11	21	38	43
10	Cardiff City	42	13	7	1	57	22	2	5	14	10	32	42
11	Notts County	42	10	6	5	29	17	6	3	12	21	33	41
12	Southend United	42	12	5	4	43	23	3	5	13	27	45	40
13	Bournemouth	42	8	10	3	36	20	6	2	13	20	37	40
14	Mansfield Town	42	12	5	4	46	26	3	4	14	16	41	39
15	Bristol Rovers	42	10	7	4	28	20	3	6	12	18	41	39
16	Newport County	42	9	10	2	31	15	2	6	13	13	37	38
17	Exeter City	42	10	4	7	37	32	3	8	10	20	38	38
18	Aldershot	42	11	4	6	23	14	4	1	16	16	45	35
19	Clapton Orient	42	10	7	4	27	19	3	0	18	15	42	33
20	Torquay United	42	7	5	9	22	28	2	7	12	16	45	30
21	Walsall	42	10	4	7	34	37	1	3	17	18	51	29
22	Gillingham	42	9	5	7	25	25	1	1	19	11	52	26

#		Date	Opponent	Score	Scorers	Att	Abel SC	Allen AR	Black S	Bott WE	Cape JP	Cheetham TM	Devine John	Fitzgerald AM	Gilmore HP	James NL	Jefferson A	Lowe HP	McCarthy LD	McEwan W	Mallett J	March R	Mason WS	Pattison JM	Pearson H	Powell IV	Reay EP	Ridyard A	Smith N(2)	Stock AWA	Swinfen R	Warburton A
1	Aug	27	Reading	4-2	Fitzgerald 2, Bott, Fulwood (og)	12966	3			11	7	9	8	10		5		4				6	1								2	
2	Sep	1	EXETER CITY	5-0	Cheetham 2, Bott 2, Fitzgerald	9259	3			11	7	9	8	10		5		4				6	1								2	
3		3	BRISTOL ROVERS	1-1	Devine	16266	3			11	7	9	8	10		5		4				6	1								2	
4		10	Southend United	1-2	McCarthy	6999	3			11	7	9		10		5		4	8			6	1								2	
5		10	Brighton & Hove Albion	1-3	Bott	11708	3			11	7	9				5		4	8			6	1								2	10
6		17	BOURNEMOUTH	2-0	Cheetham, James	12157					7	9		10		5		4				6	1	11		3					2	8
7		24	Walsall	1-0	Cheetham	8760					7	9		10		5		4				6	1	11		3					2	8
8	Oct	1	MANSFIELD TOWN	3-0	Bott, Cape, Cheetham	12519				11	7	9		10		5		4				6	1			3					2	8
9		8	Swindon Town	2-2	Bott, Lowe	12268				11		9		10		5		4				6	1		7	3					2	8
10		15	PORT VALE	2-2	Cheetham 2	13853				11		9		10		5		4				6	1		7	3					2	8
11		22	Torquay United	3-2	Cheetham 2, Fitzgerald	4496				11		9		10		5		4				6	1		7	3					2	8
12		29	CRYSTAL PALACE	1-2	Fitzgerald	17440				11		9		10		5		4				6	1		7	3					2	8
13	Nov	5	Bristol City	2-2	Cheetham 2	11386				11		9				5	3	4	10			6	1		7						2	8
14		12	ALDERSHOT	7-0	Cheetham 4, McCarthy, March, Swinfen	14811						9				5	3	4	10			6	1	11	7						2	8
15		19	Notts County	0-0		13363				11		9				5	3	4	10			6	1		7						2	8
16	Dec	3	Newport County	0-2		12338		1		11		9				5	3	4	10			6			7						2	8
17		17	Watford	1-4	Pearson	11254		1		11		9				5	3	4	10			6			7						2	8
18		24	READING	2-2	Bott, Devine	4329		1		11		9	8	10	6	5	3	4							7						2	
19		26	Cardiff City	0-1		26744		1		11	7	9	8	10	6	5	3	4													2	
20		27	CARDIFF CITY	5-0	Cheetham 2, Devine, McCarthy, Cape	14799		1		11	7	9	8				3	4	10			6						5	2			
21		31	Bristol Rovers	0-0		9046		1	11		7	9	8		6		3	4	10									5	2			
22	Jan	9	NORTHAMPTON T	3-0	Cheetham 3	3492		1	11		7	9					3	4	10			6						5	2			8
23		14	BRIGHTON & HOVE ALB	1-2	Cheetham	11387		1	11		7	9					3	4	10			6						5	2			8
24		21	Bournemouth	2-4	Cape, Lowe	5206		1	11		7	9		10	6		3	4										5	2			8
25		28	WALSALL	3-0	Cheetham, Lowe, Fitzgerald	10390		1	11		7	9		10			3	4	8			6						5	2			
26	Feb	4	Mansfield Town	2-2	Stimpson (Og), Lowe	5523		1			7	9		10		5	3	4	8			6		11					2			
27		11	SWINDON TOWN	2-1	Bott, Mallett	11635		1		11	7					5	3	4			8	6							2	9		10
28		18	Port Vale	2-1	Fitzgerald 2	7210		1		11	7			10		5	3	4			8	6							2	9		
29		25	TORQUAY UNITED	1-1	Lowe	7783		1		11	7			10		5	3	4			8	6							2	9		
30	Mar	4	Crystal Palace	1-0	McEwan	13328		1						10			3	4		7	8	6		11				5	2	9		
31		11	BRISTOL CITY	3-1	Fitzgerald, McEwan, Stock	9339		1						10		5	3	4		7	8	6		11					2	9		
32		18	Aldershot	0-2		4880		1						10		5	3	4		7	8	6		11					2	9		
33		25	NOTTS COUNTY	0-1		9164		1						10	6	5	3	4		7	8			11					2	9		
34	Apr	1	Northampton Town	0-1		7381		1						10		5	3	4		7	8	6		11					2	9		
35		7	IPSWICH TOWN	0-0		14663		1								6	3	4	10	7	8			11				5	2	9		
36		8	NEWPORT COUNTY	0-0		14864		1								6	3	4	10	9	8			11				5	2	7		
37		10	Ipswich Town	0-1		18963		1						10	6	5	3	4		7	8			11					2	9		
38		15	Clapton Orient	1-2	Smith (p)	8090		1						10	6	5	3	4		7	8			11					2	9		
39		22	WATFORD	1-0	Mallett	7364		1		11				10			3	4		7	8	6						5	2	9		
40		24	CLAPTON ORIENT	1-1	Swinfen	2834		1		11				10			3	4		7	8						6	5	2	9		
41		29	Exeter City	1-1	Stock	3348		1		10							3	4		7	8			11			6	5	2	9		
42	May	6	SOUTHEND UNITED	1-1	McCarthy	5702		1						8			3	4	10	7				11			6	5	2	9		
			Apps				5	27	5	21	21	26	7	30	6	32	30	42	12	13	15	30	15	14	11	8	6	10	29	12	18	17
			Goals							8	3	22	3	9				1	5	4	2	2			1				1	2	2	

Two own goals

F.A. Cup

	Date	Opponent	Score	Scorers	Att	Allen AR	Bott WE	Cape JP	Cheetham TM	Gilmore HP	James NL	Jefferson A	Lowe HP	McCarthy LD	March R	Pearson H	Ridyard A	Smith N(2)	Swinfen R	Warburton A
R1	Nov 26	Crystal Palace	1-1	Cheetham	33276	1	11		9		5	3	4	10	6	7			2	8
rep	28	CRYSTAL PALACE	3-0	Cheetham 2, Bott (p)	16000	1	11		9		5	3	4	10	6	7			2	8
R2	Dec 10	Hartlepools United	2-0	Cheetham, McCarthy	11094	1	11		9		5	3	4	10	6	7			2	8
R3	Jan 7	WEST HAM UNITED	1-2	Cheetham	22408	1	11	7	9	6		3	4	10			5	2		8

Division 3(S) Cup

	Date	Opponent	Score	Scorers	Allen AR	Bott	Cheetham	Devine	Fitzgerald	James	Jefferson	Lowe	McCarthy	McEwan	Mallett	March	Pattison	Pearson	Powell	Reay	Ridyard	Smith	Stock	Swinfen
R2	Jan 30	ALDERSHOT	1-0	Bott	1	10		9	8		6	5				7		11	4	3		2		
R3	Feb 20	BOURNEMOUTH	3-2	Stock 2, Fitzgerald					10	6	3			7	8		1	11		4	2		9	
SF	May 4	PORT VALE	0-0		1	10		9	6		3	4		8				7			2	5		

Replay held over until season 1939/40, but not played due to outbreak of World War II.

Played in R3: A Farmer (at 5). Played in SF: Stevens (at 11).

		P	W	D	L	F	A	W	D	L	F	A	Pts
1	Newport County	42	15	4	2	37	16	7	7	7	21	29	55
2	Crystal Palace	42	15	4	2	49	18	5	8	8	22	34	52
3	Brighton & Hove A.	42	14	5	2	43	14	5	6	10	25	35	49
4	Watford	42	14	6	1	44	15	3	6	12	18	36	46
5	Reading	42	12	6	3	46	23	4	8	9	23	36	46
6	QUEEN'S PARK RGS.	42	10	8	3	44	15	5	6	10	24	34	44
7	Ipswich Town	42	14	3	4	46	21	2	9	10	16	31	44
8	Bristol City	42	14	5	2	42	19	2	7	12	19	44	44
9	Swindon Town	42	15	4	2	53	25	3	4	14	19	52	44
10	Aldershot	42	13	6	2	31	15	3	6	12	22	51	44
11	Notts County	42	12	6	3	36	16	5	3	13	23	38	43
12	Southend United	42	14	5	2	38	13	2	4	15	23	51	41
13	Cardiff City	42	12	1	8	40	28	3	10	8	21	37	41
14	Exeter City	42	9	9	3	40	32	4	5	12	25	50	40
15	Bournemouth	42	10	8	3	38	22	3	5	13	14	36	39
16	Mansfield Town	42	10	8	3	33	19	2	7	12	11	43	39
17	Northampton Town	42	13	5	3	41	20	2	3	16	10	38	38
18	Port Vale	42	10	5	6	36	23	4	4	13	16	35	37
19	Torquay United	42	7	5	9	27	28	7	4	10	27	42	37
20	Clapton Orient	42	10	9	2	40	16	1	4	16	13	39	35
21	Walsall	42	9	6	6	47	23	2	5	14	21	46	33
22	Bristol Rovers	42	8	8	5	30	17	2	5	14	25	44	33

1946/47 2nd in Division 3(S)

League – Division 3 (South)

No	Date	Opponent	Score	Scorers	Att
1	Aug 31	WATFORD	2-1	Mallett 2	19446
2	Sep 4	Bournemouth	1-1	Neary	5738
3	7	Walsall	2-0	Neary 2	13894
4	11	LEYTON ORIENT	2-0	Pattison, Neary	15344
5	14	READING	2-0	Heath, McEwan	20021
6	21	Crystal Palace	0-0		27517
7	25	BOURNEMOUTH	3-0	Pattison 2, Mallett	17207
8	28	TORQUAY UNITED	0-0		23117
9	Oct 5	Mansfield Town	3-0	Neary, Durrant, Pattison	13459
10	12	Bristol Rovers	0-2		20668
11	19	Cardiff City	2-2	Durrant, Hatton	44010
12	26	NORWICH CITY	1-1	Hatton	15581
13	Nov 2	Notts County	2-1	Neary, Heathcote	26734
14	9	NORTHAMPTON T	1-0	McEwan	17798
15	16	Aldershot	2-1	Shepperd (og), Pattison	8163
16	23	BRIGHTON & HOVE ALB	2-0	Hatton 2	17739
17	Dec 7	PORT VALE	2-0	Harris, Mills	14251
18	21	SWINDON TOWN	7-0	*see below	9576
19	25	IPSWICH TOWN	1-3	Hatton	15503
20	26	Ipswich Town	1-1	Hatton	20267
21	28	Watford	2-0	Mallett 2	18610
22	Jan 4	WALSALL	1-0	Boxshall	16289
23	18	Reading	0-1		19300
24	25	CRYSTAL PALACE	1-2	Pattison	13022
25	Feb 8	MANSFIELD TOWN	3-1	Boxshall, Durrant, Pattison	7776
26	15	Bristol Rovers	1-3	Durrant	18258
27	Mar 1	Norwich City	1-0	Mills	15233
28	5	Exeter City	0-3		3679
29	8	NOTTS COUNTY	4-1	Pattison, Durrant 2, Chapman	9455
30	15	Northampton Town	4-4	Parkinson 2, Mills, Durrant	9907
31	22	ALDERSHOT	4-1	Hatton 3, Durrant	12600
32	29	Brighton & Hove Albion	2-0	McEwan 2	8432
33	Apr 4	SOUTHEND UNITED	1-0	Durrant	20307
34	5	EXETER CITY	2-0	Durrant, Pattison	18287
35	7	Southend United	3-1	Durrant, McEwan, Mills	17295
36	12	Port Vale	2-2	Durrant, Boxshall	12500
37	19	BRISTOL CITY	1-0	McEwan	19665
38	26	Swindon Town	2-3	Durrant, Hatton	20884
39	May 3	Leyton Orient	1-1	Hatton	13956
40	10	Bristol City	1-1	Durrant	20861
41	17	Torquay United	0-0		7162
42	24	CARDIFF CITY	2-3	Wardle (og), Pattison	23272

Scorers in game 18: Pattison 2, McEwan 2, Hatton, Mills, Powell

Appearances / Goals (totals)

	Add AW	Allen AR	Armitage S	Barr JM	Blizzard LWB	Boxshall D	Chapman RFJ	Daniels HAG	Dudley RA	Durrant FH	Harris N	Hatton C	Heath WJ	Heathcote W	Jefferson A	McEwan W	Mallett J	Mills DG	Neary HF	Parkinson AA	Pattison JM	Powell IV	Reay EP	Ridyard A	Rose J	Saphin RFE	Smith AW	Swinfen R
Apps	3	41	2	4	5	12	27	7	26	22	1	26	6	5	40	35	26	18	9	10	37	41	2	7	15	1	33	1
Goals						3	1			14	1	12	1	1		8	5	5	6	2	12	1						

Two own goals

F.A. Cup

Rd	Date	Opponent	Score	Scorers	Att
R1	Nov 30	POOLE TOWN	2-2	Pattison, Hatton	15000
rep	Dec 4	Poole Town	6-0	Mallett 2, Hatton, Harris, Pattison 2	9000
R2	12	Norwich City	4-4	Pattison, McEwan, Mills 2	26307
rep	18	NORWICH CITY	2-0	Hatton, Mills	13900
R3	Jan 11	MIDDLESBROUGH	1-1	Pattison	24549
rep	15	Middlesbrough	1-3	Boxshall	31270

Division 3 (South) — Final Table

		P	W	D	L	F	A	W	D	L	F	A	Pts
1	Cardiff City	42	18	3	0	60	11	12	3	6	33	19	66
2	QUEEN'S PARK RGS.	42	15	2	4	42	15	8	9	4	32	25	57
3	Bristol City	42	13	4	4	56	20	7	7	7	38	36	51
4	Swindon Town	42	15	4	2	56	25	4	7	10	28	48	49
5	Walsall	42	11	6	4	42	25	6	6	9	32	34	46
6	Ipswich Town	42	11	5	5	33	21	5	9	7	28	32	46
7	Bournemouth	42	12	4	5	43	20	6	4	11	29	34	44
8	Southend United	42	9	7	5	38	22	8	3	10	33	38	44
9	Reading	42	11	6	4	53	30	5	5	11	30	44	43
10	Port Vale	42	14	4	3	51	28	3	5	13	17	35	43
11	Torquay United	42	11	5	5	33	23	4	7	10	19	38	42
12	Notts County	42	11	4	6	35	19	4	6	11	28	44	40
13	Northampton Town	42	11	5	5	46	33	4	5	12	26	42	40
14	Bristol Rovers	42	9	6	6	34	26	7	2	12	25	43	40
15	Exeter City	42	11	6	4	37	27	4	3	14	23	42	39
16	Watford	42	11	4	6	39	27	6	1	14	22	49	39
17	Brighton & Hove A.	42	8	7	6	31	35	5	5	11	23	37	38
18	Crystal Palace	42	9	7	5	29	19	4	4	13	20	43	37
19	Leyton Orient	42	10	5	6	40	28	2	3	16	14	47	32
20	Aldershot	42	6	6	9	24	25	5	4	12	23	52	32
21	Norwich City	42	6	3	12	38	48	4	5	12	26	52	28
22	Mansfield Town	42	8	5	8	31	38	1	5	15	17	58	28

1947/48 — Champions of Division 3(S)

League matches

#	Date	Opponents	Score	Scorers	Att
1	Aug 23	NORWICH CITY	3-1	Hatton, McEwan, Pattison	18704
2	27	Brighton & Hove Albion	5-0	Hatton 3, Durrant 2	14288
3	30	Bristol Rovers	1-0	Durrant	19528
4	Sep 4	BRIGHTON & HOVE ALB	2-0	McEwan, Hatton	18116
5	6	NORTHAMPTON T	2-0	McEwan, Pattison	21419
6	11	Notts County	1-1	Durrant	19335
7	13	Aldershot	4-1	Durrant 2, Pattison, Hatton	8915
8	18	NOTTS COUNTY	4-1	Pattison 2, Hatton, McEwan	15708
9	20	CRYSTAL PALACE	1-0	Chapman	25199
10	25	EXETER CITY	3-1	Hatton 2, Durrant	18090
11	27	Torquay United	1-1	G Smith	10402
12	Oct 2	SOUTHEND UNITED	3-2	Hatton 2, Pattison	17585
13	4	SWINDON TOWN	0-2		25092
14	11	Swansea Town	1-3	Durrant	22171
15	18	BOURNEMOUTH	1-0	Durrant	21639
16	25	Ipswich Town	0-1		24361
17	Nov 1	BRISTOL CITY	2-0	Boxshall, Pattison	28358
18	8	Reading	2-3	Durrant, Boxshall	23258
19	15	WALSALL	2-1	Hatton, Hartburn	26119
20	22	Leyton Orient	3-1	Durrant, Hatton 2	16915
21	Dec 6	Newport County	0-0		13230
22	26	Watford	1-0	Jones (og)	22406
23	27	WATFORD	5-1	Pattison, Boxshall 2, Hatton, McEwan	19373
24	Jan 3	BRISTOL ROVERS	5-2	McEwan, Hatton, Boxshall 2, Hartburn	22518
25	31	ALDERSHOT	0-0		21691
26	Feb 14	TORQUAY UNITED	3-3	Ramscar, Boxshall, Hatton	21791
27	21	Swindon Town	0-0		14683
28	Mar 13	IPSWICH TOWN	2-0	Hatton, Boxshall	22135
29	15	Crystal Palace	1-0	Hartburn	22086
30	20	Bristol City	1-2	Hatton	21184
31	26	Port Vale	2-0	Boxshall 2	17889
32	27	READING	2-0	Boxshall, Hatton	23998
33	29	PORT VALE	2-1	Addinall, A Smith	24053
34	Apr 3	Walsall	1-0	Addinall	17872
35	8	Northampton Town	1-1	Hartburn	11260
36	10	LEYTON ORIENT	1-2	Stewart	27480
37	14	Bournemouth	1-0	Durrant	25495
38	17	Exeter City	2-1	Hartburn 2	11617
39	21	Norwich City	2-5	Hatton, A Smith	30052
40	24	NEWPORT COUNTY	1-0	I Powell	20905
41	26	SWANSEA TOWN	0-0		27757
42	May 1	Southend United	0-0		13827

Appearances / goals (shirt numbers)

#	Adams EW	Addinall AW	Allen AR	Boxshall D	Chapman RFJ	Daniels HAG	Dudley RA	Durrant FH	Hartburn J	Hatton C	Heath WJ	Jefferson A	McEwan W	Mills DG	Parkinson AA	Pattison JM	Powell GR	Powell IV	Ramscar FT	Reay EP	Ridyard A	Rose J	Saphin RFE	Smith AW	Smith GC	Stewart G
1			1					2	9	7	10	6	3	8		11		4							5	
2			1					2	9	7	10	6	8			11		4			3				5	
3			1					2	9	7	10	6	8			11		4			3				5	
4			1					2	9	7	10	6	8			11		4			3				5	
5			1					2	9	7	10	6	8			11		4			3				5	
6			1				6	2	9	7	10		8			11		4			3				5	
7			1				6	2	9	10			7	8		11		4			3				5	
8			1				6	2	9	10			7	8		11		4			3				5	
9			1		10		6	2	9	7			3	8		11		4							5	
10			1		10		6	2	9	7			3	8		11		4							5	
11			1		10		6	2	9	7			3	8		11		4							5	
12			1		10		6	2	9	7			3		8	11		4							5	
13			1		10		6	2	9	7			3	8		11		4							5	
14			1		10		6	2	9	7			3	8		11		4							5	
15			1		10		6	2	9	7			3	8		11		4							5	
16			1		10		6	2	9	7			3	8		11		4							5	
17			1	7	10		6	2	9				3	8		11		4							5	
18			1	8	6			2	9					7		11	2	4		10					5	
19			1	8			6		9	11		10	3	7			2	4	8						5	
20			1		6			2	9	11		10	3	7			2	4	8			5				
21			1		6			2	9	11		10	3	7			2	4	8							
22			1		6			2	9	11		10	3	7			2	4	8							
23			1	7	6			2	9	10			3	9		11	2	4	8						5	
24			1	7	6			2	11	10			3	9			2	4	8						5	
25			1	9	6				11	10			3	7			2	4	8						5	
26			1	9					11	10			3	7			2	4	8						5	
27			1	9					11	10			3	7			2	4	8					6	5	
28				7					11	9			3			2		4	10					1	6	5	8
29				7					11	9			3			2		4	10					1	6	5	8
30									9	11	10		3					2	4				1	6	5	7
31	9			7					11				3					2	4					1	6	5	8
32				7					11	9			3					2	4					1	6	5	8
33	9			7					11				3					2	4					1	6	5	8
34	9			7					11				3					2	4					1	6	5	8
35				7					11			9	3					2	4					1	6	5	8
36				7					11				3					2	4	8					6	5	9
37			1					9	7	8			3					2	4	11				6	5	
38			1					9	11	8			3					2	4					6	5	7
39			1					9	11	8			3					2	4					6	5	7
40	7		1						11	9			3						4			5	2	6		8
41	7		1						11	9			3						4			5	2	6		8
42			1	7					9				3					2	4					5		8
Apps	2	3	34	17	14	7	17	27	31	35	6	26	26	16	1	20	23	41	16	16	4	2	8	18	38	14
Goals		2		11	1			12	6	21			6			8		1	1					2	1	1

One own goal

F.A. Cup

Rnd	Date	Opponents	Score	Scorers	Att
R3	Jan 10	Gillingham	1-1	Boxshall	23002
rep	17	GILLINGHAM	3-1	Hatton, Hartburn, McEwan	28000
R4	24	STOKE CITY	3-0	Hatton 2, Ramscar	24100
R5	Feb 7	LUTON TOWN	3-1	Boxshall, Hatton, McEwan	30564
R6	28	DERBY COUNTY	1-1	Hartburn	28358
rep	Mar 6	Derby County	0-5		31588

F.A. Cup appearances (shirt numbers)

Rnd	Allen	Boxshall	Dudley	Hartburn	Hatton	McEwan	Mills	Pattison	Powell GR	Powell IV	Ramscar	Smith AW	Smith GC
R3	1	9	6		10	3	7	11	2	4	8		5
rep	1	9	6	11	10	3	7		2	4	8		5
R4	1	9	6	11	10	3	7		2	4	8		5
R5	1	9	6	11	10	3	9		2	4	8		5
R6	1	7		11	10	3	9		2	4	8	6	5
rep	1	9		11	10	3	7		2	4	8	6	5

Final table — Division 3 (South)

		P	W	D	L	F	A	W	D	L	F	A	Pts
1	QUEEN'S PARK RGS.	42	16	3	2	44	17	10	6	5	30	20	61
2	Bournemouth	42	13	5	3	42	13	11	4	6	34	22	57
3	Walsall	42	13	5	3	37	12	8	4	9	33	28	51
4	Ipswich Town	42	16	1	4	42	18	7	2	12	25	43	49
5	Swansea Town	42	14	6	1	48	14	4	6	11	22	38	48
6	Notts County	42	12	4	5	44	27	7	4	10	24	32	46
7	Bristol City	42	11	4	6	47	26	7	3	11	30	39	43
8	Port Vale	42	14	4	3	48	18	2	7	12	15	36	43
9	Southend United	42	11	8	2	32	16	4	5	12	19	42	43
10	Reading	42	10	5	6	37	28	5	6	10	19	30	41
11	Exeter City	42	11	6	4	34	22	4	5	12	21	41	41
12	Newport County	42	9	8	4	38	28	5	5	11	23	45	41
13	Crystal Palace	42	12	5	4	32	14	1	8	12	17	35	39
14	Northampton Town	42	10	5	6	35	28	4	6	11	23	44	39
15	Watford	42	6	6	9	31	37	8	4	9	26	42	38
16	Swindon Town	42	6	10	5	21	20	4	6	11	20	26	36
17	Leyton Orient	42	8	5	8	31	32	5	1	15	20	41	36
18	Torquay United	42	7	6	8	40	29	4	7	10	23	33	35
19	Aldershot	42	5	10	6	22	26	5	5	11	23	41	35
20	Bristol Rovers	42	7	3	11	39	34	6	5	10	32	41	34
21	Norwich City	42	8	3	10	33	34	5	5	11	28	42	34
22	Brighton & Hove A.	42	8	4	9	26	31	3	8	10	17	42	34

1948/49 13th in Division 2

#	Date	Opponent	Score	Scorers	Att	Adams EW	Addinall AW	Allen AR	Bennett EE	Dudley RA	Duggan EJ	Durrant FH	Farrow DA	Gibbons JR	Hartburn J	Hatton C	Heath WJ	Hill CJ	Hudson SR	Jefferson A	McEwan W	Mills DG	Parkinson AA	Pattison JM	Pointon WJ	Powell GR	Powell IV	Ramscar FT	Reay EP	Smith AW	Smith GC	Stewart G	Wardle G
1	Aug 21	Luton Town	0-0		23764		9	1							11	10				3	7	8				2	4			6	5		
2	26	LEICESTER CITY	4-1	Addinall 3, Hartburn	23827		9	1							11	10				3	7	8				2	4			6	5		
3	28	BRADFORD PARK AVE.	1-0	Addinall	27666		9	1							11	10				3	7	8				2	4			6	5		
4	30	Leicester City	3-2	Hatton 2, Mills	34063		9	1							11	10				3	7	8				2	4			6	5		
5	Sep 4	Southampton	0-3		27303		9	1							11	10				3	7	8				2	4			6	5		
6	9	CARDIFF CITY	0-0		25337		9	1							11	10				3	7	8				2	4			6	5		
7	11	BARNSLEY	2-2	Addinall 2	20791		9	1							11	10				3	7	8				2				6	5		
8	13	Cardiff City	0-3		36223			1								10					7	8		11		2	4			6	5		
9	18	Grimsby Town	1-4	Pattison	15140		9	1		2					7	10				3		8		11			4			6	5		
10	25	NOTTM. FOREST	2-1	Hartburn, Pattison	19381		9	1		3					7	10						8		11		2	4			6	5		
11	Oct 2	Fulham	0-5		38667		9	1							7	10				3		8		11		2	4			6	5		
12	9	BRENTFORD	2-0	Hartburn, Hudson	25814		9	1					6		7	10			11	3						2	4	8			5		
13	16	Tottenham Hotspur	0-1		69718		9	1					6		7	10		5	11	3						2	4	8					
14	23	WEST HAM UNITED	2-1	Hatton, Hudson	27950			1			9		6		7	10		5	11	3						2	4	8					
15	30	Bury	0-0		19238	11		1			9		6		7	10		5		3						2	4	8					
16	Nov 6	WEST BROMWICH ALB.	0-2		24459	7		1					6	9	11	10				3						2	4	8			5		
17	13	Chesterfield	1-2	Hartburn	10837			1					6	9	11	10				3	7					2	4	8			5		
18	20	LINCOLN CITY	2-0	Hatton, Gibbons	19465			1					6	9	11	10				3	7					2	4	8			5		
19	27	Sheffield Wednesday	0-2		34776			1					6	9	11	10				3	7					2	4	8			5		
20	Dec 4	COVENTRY CITY	0-3		16693			1					6	9	11	10				3	7					2	4				5		
21	11	Leeds United	2-1	Gibbons, Pattison	26420			1					6	9	7	10				3			4	11		2		8			5		
22	18	LUTON TOWN	0-3		16557			1					6	9	7	10				3			4	11		2		8			5		
23	25	Blackburn Rovers	0-2		31526			1							7	10	6		11	3			4			2		8			5	9	
24	27	BLACKBURN ROVERS	4-2	Parkinson 2, Hatton, Hartburn	17091			1				9	6		7	10			11	3			4			2		8			5		
25	Jan 1	Bradford Park Avenue	0-0		15178			1				9	6		7	10			11	3			4			2		8			5		
26	22	Barnsley	0-4		20596			1			7		6			10			11	3			4		9	2		8			5		
27	29	SOUTHAMPTON	1-3	Pointon	23317			1								10	6		11	3			4		9	2					5	8	7
28	Feb 5	GRIMSBY TOWN	1-2	Hudson	19813		10	1			8						6		11	3			4		9	2					5		7
29	19	Nottingham Forest	0-0		26164		10	1			8						6		11	3			4		9	2					5		7
30	26	FULHAM	1-0	Ramscar	27440			1			8						6		11	3			4		9	2		10			5		7
31	Mar 5	Brentford	3-0	Hudson, Pointon, Duggan	29420		10	1			7						6		11	3			4		9	2		8			5		
32	12	TOTTENHAM HOTSPUR	0-1		25416		10	1			7						6		11	3			4		9	2		8			5		
33	19	West Ham United	0-2		25039			1	10		8						6			3			4		9	2					5		7
34	26	BURY	3-1	Duggan, Jefferson, Ramscar	17547			1	11		10						6			3			4		9	2		8			5		7
35	Apr 2	West Bromwich Albion	1-1	Pointon	35293			1			7					10	6			3			4		9	2		8			5		11
36	9	CHESTERFIELD	1-1	Hill	17898			1			7					10	6	5		3			4		9	2		8					11
37	15	PLYMOUTH ARGYLE	2-1	Stewart, Pointon	22552			1			7					10	6	5	11	3			4		9	2						8	
38	16	Lincoln City	0-0		11306		10	1			7						6		11	3			4		9	2					5	8	
39	18	Plymouth Argyle	1-3	Addinall	19454		10	1			7						6		11	3			4		9	2					5	8	
40	23	SHEFFIELD WEDNESDAY	1-3	Heath	18456		10	1			7						6			3			4		9				2		5	8	11
41	30	Coventry City	1-1	Stewart	14518		10	1			7						6			3			4		9				2		5	8	11
42	May 7	LEEDS UNITED	2-0	Addinall 2	16730		10	1			7						6			3					9				2		5	8	11
		Apps				2	22	40	2	2	15	2	17	8	27	22	18	5	10	39	13	11	21	11	17	39	20	21	3	11	37	12	11
		Goals					9				2			2	5	5	1	1	4			1	2	3	4			2				2	

Played in one game: JH Millbank (game 7, at 4), WM Muir (game 8, at 3),
AV Lennon (game 20, at 8), CB Nicholas (game 42, at 4).

F.A. Cup

Rd	Date	Opponent	Score	Att	Allen AR	Duggan EJ	Farrow DA	Hartburn J	Hatton C	Hudson SR	Jefferson A	McEwan W	Parkinson AA	Powell GR	Ramscar FT	Smith GC
R3	Jan 8	HUDDERSFIELD T	0-0	26000	1	9	6	7	10	11	3		4	2	8	5
rep	15	Huddersfield Town	0-5	31075	1	9	6		10	11	3	10	4	2	8	5

Played in replay: D Campbell (at 7)

League table

		P	W	D	L	F	A	W	D	L	F	A	Pts
1	Fulham	42	16	4	1	52	14	8	5	8	25	23	57
2	West Bromwich Alb.	42	16	3	2	47	16	8	5	8	22	23	56
3	Southampton	42	16	4	1	48	10	7	5	9	21	26	55
4	Cardiff City	42	14	4	3	45	21	5	9	7	17	26	51
5	Tottenham Hotspur	42	14	4	3	50	18	3	12	6	22	26	50
6	Chesterfield	42	9	7	5	24	18	6	10	5	27	27	47
7	West Ham United	42	13	5	3	38	23	5	5	11	18	35	46
8	Sheffield Wed.	42	12	6	3	36	17	3	7	11	27	39	43
9	Barnsley	42	10	7	4	40	18	4	5	12	22	43	40
10	Luton Town	42	11	6	4	32	16	3	6	12	23	41	40
11	Grimsby Town	42	10	5	6	44	28	5	5	11	28	48	40
12	Bury	42	12	5	4	41	23	5	1	15	26	53	40
13	QUEEN'S PARK RGS.	42	11	4	6	31	26	3	7	11	13	36	39
14	Blackburn Rovers	42	12	5	4	41	23	3	3	15	12	40	38
15	Leeds United	42	11	6	4	36	21	1	7	13	19	42	37
16	Coventry City	42	12	3	6	35	20	3	4	14	20	44	37
17	Bradford Park Ave.	42	8	8	5	37	26	5	3	13	28	52	37
18	Brentford	42	7	10	4	28	21	4	4	13	14	32	36
19	Leicester City	42	6	10	5	41	38	4	6	11	21	41	36
20	Plymouth Argyle	42	11	4	6	33	25	1	8	12	16	39	36
21	Nottingham Forest	42	9	6	6	22	14	5	1	15	28	40	35
22	Lincoln City	42	6	7	8	31	35	2	5	14	22	56	28

1949/50   20th in Division 2

#	Date		Opponent	Score	Scorers	Att
1	Aug	20	Leeds United	1-1	Pointon	31589
2		24	BRENTFORD	3-3	Pattison 2(2p), Pointon	20931
3		27	SOUTHAMPTON	1-0	Hudson	23040
4		31	Brentford	2-0	Hatton, Wardle	25741
5	Sep	3	Coventry City	0-0		22606
6		7	PRESTON NORTH END	0-0		20113
7		10	LUTON TOWN	3-0	Addinall, Duggan, Hatton	20674
8		14	Preston North End	2-3	Addinall, Robertson (og)	26515
9		17	Barnsley	1-3	Addinall	19787
10		24	WEST HAM UNITED	0-1		24578
11	Oct	1	Sheffield United	1-1	Ramscar	28150
12		8	HULL CITY	1-4	Duggan	28725
13		15	Sheffield Wednesday	0-1		31728
14		22	PLYMOUTH ARGYLE	0-2		16381
15		29	Chesterfield	1-2	Neary	12202
16	Nov	5	BRADFORD PARK AVE.	0-1		8873
17		12	Leicester City	2-3	Addinall, Parkinson	27058
18		19	BURY	1-0	Neary	15257
19		26	Tottenham Hotspur	0-3		62783
20	Dec	3	CARDIFF CITY	0-1		15954
21		10	Blackburn Rovers	0-0		16808
22		17	LEEDS UNITED	1-1	Best	13256
23		24	Southampton	2-1	Neary 2	21382
24		26	Grimsby Town	1-1	Hudson	22053
25		27	GRIMSBY TOWN	1-2	Addinall	22994
26		31	COVENTRY CITY	2-0	McEwan, Best	16847
27	Jan	14	Luton Town	2-1	Neary, Mills	16291
28		21	BARNSLEY	0-5		16597
29	Feb	4	West Ham United	0-1		25440
30		18	SHEFFIELD UNITED	1-3	McKay	20264
31		25	Hull City	1-1	Mills	24586
32	Mar	4	SHEFFIELD WEDNESDAY	0-0		23273
33		11	Plymouth Argyle	2-0	Addinall, Best	22093
34		18	CHESTERFIELD	3-2	Addinall 2, Wardle	18502
35		25	Bradford Park Avenue	0-1		18063
36	Apr	1	TOTTENHAM HOTSPUR	0-2		29771
37		7	SWANSEA TOWN	0-0		23217
38		8	Cardiff City	0-4		21102
39		10	Swansea Town	1-0	Hudson	18405
40		15	LEICESTER CITY	2-0	Addinall 2	15311
41		22	Bury	0-0		11383
42		29	BLACKBURN ROVERS	2-3	Addinall, Hatton	10352

Player appearances (shirt numbers worn):

#	Adams EW	Addinall AW	Allen AR	Best TH	Chapman RFJ	Dudley RA	Duggan EJ	Farrow DA	Hatton C	Heath WJ	Hill CJ	Hudson SR	Jefferson A	McEwan W	McKay J	Mills DG	Neary HF	Nelson D	Parkinson AA	Pattison JM	Pointon WJ	Powell GR	Ramscar FT	Reay EP	Saphin RFE	Wardle G	Woodward HJ
1			1					7	10		6		3						4	11	9		8	2			5
2			1					7	10		6		3						4	11	9		8	2			5
3			1				2	7	10		6	11	3						4		9		8				5
4			1				2	7	10		6	11	3						4		9		8				5
5		9	1				2	7	10	3	6	11							4				8				5
6		9	1				2	7	10		6	11	3						4				8				5
7		9	1				2	7	10		6	11	3						4				8				5
8		9	1				2	7	10		6	11	3						4				8				5
9		9	1				2	7	10		6	11	3						4				8				5
10		9	1				2	7	10		6		3						4	11			8				5
11		9	1	5			2	7	10		6		3						4		11		8				
12		9	1				3		10		4	6								11	2		8			7	5
13		9	1				2	7	6	10	3								4				8			11	5
14			1				2	7	6	10			3						4		9		8			11	5
15		10	1					7	6	8			3				9		4	11		2					5
16	7	10	1						6	8			3				9		4	11		2					5
17		7	1						10	5	6		3				9		8	11		2					4
18		8	1	5					10			6	3		11		9					2				7	4
19			1	5					6	8		10	3		11		9					2				7	4
20			1	5					6	10			3			8	9	7				2				11	4
21		10	1	8	5				6		4		3				9	7				2				11	
22		10	1	8	5				6		4		3				9	7				2				11	
23		10	1	8	5				6		4		3				9	7				2				11	
24		10	1		5				6		4	11	3	8			9	7				2					
25		10	1		5				6		4	11	3	8			9	7				2					
26			1	10	5				6		4		3	8			9				11	2				7	
27			1	9	5				6		4		3	8		10	7				11	2					
28				9	5				6		4		3	8		10	7					2			1	11	
29			1	10	5				6		4		3	8	11		9					2				7	
30			1			8			6				3		11	10	9	4				2				7	5
31			1			8			6				3		11	10	9	4				2				7	5
32			1			8			6				3		11	10	9	4				2				7	5
33		8	1	9					6				3		11	10		4				2				7	5
34		8	1	9					6				3		11	10		4				2				7	5
35		8	1	9			10		6				3		11			4				2				7	5
36		8	1	9					6				3		11	10		4				2				7	5
37		8	1	9					6				3		11	10		4				2				7	5
38		8	1	9		2			6				3		11			4				2				7	5
39		8	1	9					6			10	3		11			4				2				7	5
40		9	1						6		8		3		11	10		4				2				7	5
41		9	1						6		8		3		11	10		4				2				7	5
42		9	1						6		8		3		11	10		4				2				7	5
Apps	1	28	41	13	13	13	20	22	37	25	16	12	17	9	13	13	18	13	17	7	9	28	14	2	1	28	32
Goals		11		3			2		3			3		1	1	2	5		1	2	2		1			2	

One own goal

F.A. Cup

	Date		Opponent	Score	Att	Allen AR	Best TH	Chapman RFJ	Hatton C	Hill CJ	Hudson SR	Jefferson A	McEwan W	Neary HF	Powell GR	Wardle G
R3	Jan	7	EVERTON	0-2	22433	1	10	5	6	4	11	3	8	9	2	7

		P	W	D	L	F	A	W	D	L	F	A	Pts
1	Tottenham Hotspur	42	15	3	3	51	15	12	4	5	30	20	61
2	Sheffield Wed.	42	12	7	2	46	23	6	9	6	21	25	52
3	Sheffield United	42	9	10	2	36	19	10	4	7	32	30	52
4	Southampton	42	13	4	4	44	25	6	10	5	20	23	52
5	Leeds United	42	11	8	2	33	16	6	5	10	21	29	47
6	Preston North End	42	12	5	4	37	21	6	4	11	23	28	45
7	Hull City	42	11	8	2	39	25	6	3	12	25	47	45
8	Swansea Town	42	11	3	7	34	18	6	6	9	19	31	43
9	Brentford	42	11	5	5	21	12	4	8	9	23	37	43
10	Cardiff City	42	13	3	5	28	14	3	7	11	13	30	42
11	Grimsby Town	42	13	5	3	53	25	3	3	15	21	48	40
12	Coventry City	42	8	6	7	32	24	5	7	9	23	31	39
13	Barnsley	42	11	6	4	45	28	2	7	12	19	39	39
14	Chesterfield	42	12	3	6	28	16	3	6	12	15	31	39
15	Leicester City	42	8	9	4	30	25	4	6	11	25	40	39
16	Blackburn Rovers	42	10	5	6	30	15	4	5	12	25	45	38
17	Luton Town	42	8	9	4	28	22	2	9	10	13	29	38
18	Bury	42	10	8	3	37	19	4	1	16	23	46	37
19	West Ham United	42	8	7	6	30	25	4	5	12	23	36	36
20	QUEEN'S PARK RGS.	42	6	5	10	21	30	5	7	9	19	27	34
21	Plymouth Argyle	42	6	6	9	19	24	2	10	9	25	41	32
22	Bradford Park Ave.	42	7	6	8	34	34	3	5	13	17	43	31

1950/51   16th in Division 2

No	Mon	Date	Opponent	Res	Scorers	Att	Addinall AW	Cameron R	Chapman RFJ	Clayton L	Davies E	Duggan EJ	Farrow DA	Gullan SK	Hatton C	Heath WJ	Ingham A	McKay J	Mills DG	Muir WM	Nelson D	Nicholas CB	Parkinson AA	Poppitt J	Powell GR	Saphin RFE	Shepherd E	Smith WC	Stewart G	Wardle G	Waugh WL	Woodward HJ
1	Aug	19	CHESTERFIELD	1-1	Hatton	18381	9								8	3			10		4			6	2	1	11				7	5
2		24	NOTTS COUNTY	1-0	Hatton	15962	9								10	3			8		4			6	2	1	11				7	5
3		26	Leicester City	2-6	Addinall, Shepherd	28911	9						6		10	3			8		4		5		2	1	11			7		
4		31	Notts County	3-3	Addinall 2, Wardle	33631	9		5				6		10	3			8		4				2	1	11			7		
5	Sep	2	MANCHESTER CITY	1-2	Hatton	21696	9		5				6		10	3			8		4				2	1	11			7		
6		6	Bury	1-0	Addinall	8888	9		5				6	1	10	3			8		4				2				11	7		
7		9	Coventry City	0-3		22298	9		5	4		10	6	1		3			8						2		11			7		
8		16	CARDIFF CITY	3-2	Hatton (p), Heath, Wardle	19236	9		5				6	1	10	3			8		4				2		11			7		
9		23	Birmingham City	1-1	Addinall	26583	9		5				6	1	10	3			8		4			2			11			7		
10		30	GRIMSBY TOWN	7-1	Shepherd 3, Addinall 2, Hatton 2	16331	9		5				6	1	10	3			8		4			2			11			7		
11	Oct	7	West Ham United	1-4	Addinall	26375	9		5				6	1	10	3			8		4			2			11			7		
12		14	SWANSEA TOWN	1-1	Addinall	19256	9		5	7			6	1	8	3			10		4			2			11					
13		21	Luton Town	0-2		15692	9		5	7			6	1		3		8	10		4			2			11					
14		28	LEEDS UNITED	3-0	Shepherd, Hatton (p), Mills	15935	9		5				6	1	10	3			8		4			2			11			7		
15	Nov	4	Barnsley	0-7		17927	9		5				6	1	10	3			8		4			2			11			7		
16		11	SHEFFIELD UNITED	2-1	Hatton, Addinall	16299	9		5				6	1	10	3			8		4			2			11			7		
17		18	Hull City	1-5		33866	9		5				6	1	10	3			8		4			2			11			7		
18		25	DONCASTER ROVERS	1-2	Hatton	16861	9		5				6	1	10	3			8		4		7	2			11					
19	Dec	2	Brentford	1-2	Addinall	23121	9		5				6	1	10	3					4		8	2			11			7		
20		9	BLACKBURN ROVERS	3-1	Addinall 2, Hatton (p)	13585	9						6	1	10		3					4	8	2			11				7	5
21		16	Chesterfield	1-3	Addinall	7421	9						6	1	10		3					4	8	2			11				7	5
22		23	LEICESTER CITY	3-0	Addinall, Hatton, Shepherd	11095	9						6	1	10		3					4	8	2			11				7	5
23		25	PRESTON NORTH END	1-4	Waugh	16881	9						6	1	10		3					4	8	2			11				7	5
24		26	Preston North End	0-1		38993	9					10	6				3					4	8	2		1	11				7	5
25	Jan	13	COVENTRY CITY	3-1	Addinall, Hatton (p), Shepherd	17380	9	8				10	6				3						4	2		1	11				7	5
26		20	Cardiff City	2-4	Shepherd 2	21017	9	8				10	6				3						4	2		1	11				7	5
27		27	BRENTFORD	1-1	Davies	26290	10			6	9	8					3						4	2		1	11				7	5
28	Feb	3	BIRMINGHAM CITY	2-0	Farrow (p), Shepherd	12295	9						6		10		3			8			4	2		1	11				7	5
29		17	Grimsby Town	2-2	Farrow, Shepherd	14005	9					8	6		10		3						4	2		1	11				7	5
30		24	WEST HAM UNITED	3-3	Clayton, Farrow, Duggan	21444	9			8		10	6				3						4	2		1	11				7	5
31	Mar	3	Swansea Town	0-1		18611	9					8	6		10		3						4	2		1	11				7	5
32		10	LUTON TOWN	1-1	Shepherd	13708	9					8	6		10		3						4	2		1	11				7	5
33		17	Leeds United	2-2	Shepherd, Smith	18094	9						6		10		3						4	2		1	11	8			7	5
34		23	SOUTHAMPTON	2-0		19814	9						6		10		3						4	2		1	11	8			7	5
35		24	BARNSLEY	2-1	Waugh, Smith	15868	9						6		10		3						4	2		1	11	8			7	5
36		26	Southampton	2-2	Addinall 2	20875	9					8	6		10		3						4	2		1	11				7	5
37		31	Sheffield United	0-2		16035	9						6		10		3						4	2		1	11	8			7	5
38	Apr	4	Manchester City	2-5		21573	9						6		10		3						4	2		1	11	8			7	5
39		7	HULL CITY	3-1	Farrow 2, Smith	14628						10	6	1	9		3						4	2			11	8			7	5
40		14	Doncaster Rovers	2-0	Clayton, Smith	16344				10			6	1	9		3						4	2			11	8			7	5
41		25	Blackburn Rovers	1-2	Hatton	9770						10	6	1	9		3						4	2			11	8			7	5
42	May	5	BURY	3-2	Hatton, Shepherd, Smith	11244						10	6	1	9		3						4	2			11	8			7	5
			Apps				38	2	16	16	1	12	39	22	26	21	23	1	18	1	18	5	27	33	8	20	41	9	1	14	25	25
			Goals				18			2	1	1	6		16	1			1								14	7		2	2	

F.A. Cup

No	Mon	Date	Opponent	Res	Scorers	Att	Addinall AW	Cameron R	Chapman RFJ	Clayton L	Davies E	Duggan EJ	Farrow DA	Gullan SK	Hatton C	Heath WJ	Ingham A	McKay J	Mills DG	Muir WM	Nelson D	Nicholas CB	Parkinson AA	Poppitt J	Powell GR	Saphin RFE	Shepherd E	Smith WC	Stewart G	Wardle G	Waugh WL	Woodward HJ
R3	Jan	6	MILLWALL	3-4	Parkinson 2, Addinall	25777	9			4		10	6				3						8	2		1	11				7	5

		P	W	D	L	F	A	W	D	L	F	A	Pts
1	Preston North End	42	16	3	2	53	18	10	2	9	38	31	57
2	Manchester City	42	12	6	3	53	25	7	8	6	36	36	52
3	Cardiff City	42	13	7	1	36	20	4	9	8	17	25	50
4	Birmingham City	42	12	6	3	37	20	8	3	10	27	33	49
5	Leeds United	42	14	4	3	36	17	6	4	11	27	38	48
6	Blackburn Rovers	42	13	3	5	39	27	6	5	10	26	39	46
7	Coventry City	42	15	3	3	51	25	4	4	13	24	34	45
8	Sheffield United	42	11	4	6	44	27	5	8	8	28	35	44
9	Brentford	42	13	3	5	44	25	5	5	11	31	49	44
10	Hull City	42	12	5	4	47	28	4	6	11	27	42	43
11	Doncaster Rovers	42	9	6	6	37	32	6	7	8	27	36	43
12	Southampton	42	10	9	2	38	27	5	4	12	28	46	43
13	West Ham United	42	10	5	6	44	33	6	5	10	24	36	42
14	Leicester City	42	10	4	7	42	28	5	7	9	26	30	41
15	Barnsley	42	9	5	7	42	22	6	5	10	32	46	40
16	QUEEN'S PARK RGS.	42	13	5	3	47	25	2	5	14	24	57	40
17	Notts County	42	7	7	7	37	34	6	6	9	24	26	39
18	Swansea Town	42	14	1	6	34	25	2	3	16	20	52	36
19	Luton Town	42	7	9	5	34	23	2	5	14	23	47	32
20	Bury	42	9	4	8	33	27	3	4	14	27	59	32
21	Chesterfield	42	7	7	7	30	28	2	5	14	14	41	30
22	Grimsby Town	42	6	8	7	37	38	2	4	15	24	57	28

#	Date		Opponent	Score	Scorers	Att	Addinall AW	Brown HT	Cameron R	Chapman RFJ	Clayton L	Farrow DA	Gilberg H	Gullan SK	Hatton C	Heath WJ	Hill WL	Hold O	Ingham A	McKay J	Muir WM	Nicholas CB	Poppitt J	Powell GR	Richardson AJ	Shepherd E	Smith WC	Spence WJ	Stewart G	Tomkys MG	Underwood ED	Waugh WL
1	Aug	18	WEST HAM UNITED	2-0	Addinall, Shepherd	19541	9	1		5	4		6		10	3							2			11	8					7
2		20	HULL CITY	1-1	Smith	15809	9	1		5	4		6			3							2			11	8	10				
3		25	Coventry City	0-0		22646	9	1		5	4		6			3				11	7		2				8	10				
4		30	Hull City	1-4	Smith	19661	9	1		5	4		6			3				11	7		2				8	10				
5	Sep	1	SWANSEA TOWN	1-1	Smith	18369	9	1		5	4		6			3					7		2			11	8	10				
6		3	BLACKBURN ROVERS	2-1	Addinall 2	13392	9	1		10	4		6	5									2	3		11	8					7
7		8	Bury	1-3	Clayton	13115	9	1		10	4		6	5									2	3		11	8					7
8		15	LUTON TOWN	0-0		17391	9	1		10	5		6	4									2			11	8					7
9		22	Notts County	0-0		27734	9			5	4		6		10	1							2	3		11	8					7
10		29	BRENTFORD	3-1	Gilberg, Shepherd, Smith	25339		1	8	5	4		6		10								2	3		11	9					7
11	Oct	1	Everton	0-3		38172		1	8	5	4		6		10								2	3		11	9					7
12		6	Doncaster Rovers	0-4		17673	9	1		5	4		6		10								2	3		11	8					7
13		13	EVERTON	4-4	Shepherd 2, Waugh, Gilberg	17256	9	1		5	4		6		10								2	3		11	8					7
14		20	Southampton	1-1		19150	9	1		5	4		6		10								2	3		11	8					7
15		27	SHEFFIELD WEDNESDAY	2-2	Addinall, Smith	18541	9	1		5	4		6		10								2	3		11	8					7
16	Nov	3	Leeds United	0-3		22875	9	1			4		6		10				5				2	3		11	8					7
17		10	ROTHERHAM UNITED	2-3	Gilberg, Smith	19072	9	1					6		4				5				2	3		11	8	10				7
18		17	Cardiff City	1-3	Gilberg	21211	9	1					6		4				5		3		2			11	8	10		7		
19		24	BIRMINGHAM CITY	0-2		14945	9	1					6		4				5	8	3		2			11		10				7
20	Dec	1	Leicester City	0-4		23123	9	1					6		10	4			5				2	3		11	8					7
21		8	NOTTM. FOREST	4-3	Smith, Hatton(p), Shepherd, Gilberg	12113	9	1					6		10	4			5				2	3		11	8					7
22		15	West Ham United	2-4	Gilberg, Hatton(p)	17549		1		5			6		8	10					4		2	3		11	9					7
23		22	COVENTRY CITY	1-4	Smith	12888		1					6		8	10				7			4	2	3		9	5				11
24		25	Barnsley	1-3	Hatton	15067		1					6		8	10				7			4	2	3		9	5				11
25		26	BARNSLEY	1-1	Smith	13862	9	1							8		6			7		3		4			10	5				11
26		29	Swansea Town	3-2	Gilberg, Hill, Addinall	16146	9	1							8		6			7		3		4			10	5				11
27	Jan	1	Blackburn Rovers	2-4	Nicholas, Addinall	28671	9	1							8		6			7		3		4			10	5				11
28		5	BURY	3-2	Addinall, Gilberg, Smith	13539	9						6		4	1			10				3	2		11	8	5				7
29		19	Luton Town	1-0	Addinall	15242	9						6		4				10				3	2		11	8	5			1	7
30		26	NOTTS COUNTY	1-4	Gilberg	18891	9						6		4				10	3				2		11	8	5			1	7
31	Feb	9	Brentford	0-0		25645							6		8	1			4	7		3		2			10	5	10			11
32		16	DONCASTER ROVERS	0-2		14783	9						6		8	1			4		3	11		2			10	5				7
33	Mar	8	SOUTHAMPTON	2-1	Addinall, Hold	19040	9	1					6		4			8	3		7			2			10	5				11
34		15	Sheffield Wednesday	1-2	Muir	41712	9	1					6		4			8	3		7			2			10	5				11
35		22	LEEDS UNITED	0-0		15195	9	1					6		4			8	3		7			2			10	5				11
36		29	Rotherham United	0-1		9311	9	1				4	6		10				3					2		11	8	5				7
37	Apr	5	CARDIFF CITY	1-1	Smith	17938	9	1				4	6		10				3					2		11	8	5				7
38		12	Birmingham City	0-1		28286	9	1				4	6		10				3					2		11	8	5				7
39		14	SHEFFIELD UNITED	4-2	Addinall 2, Farrow, Muir	12714	9	1				4	6		10				3		7		3	2			8	5				11
40		19	LEICESTER CITY	1-0	Addinall	16827	9	1				4	6						3	8			2			11	10	5				7
41		26	Nottingham Forest	1-3	Muir	18975	9	1				4	6	8					3		7		2			11	10	5				
42	May	3	Sheffield United	2-1	Stewart, Smith	11310	9	1				4	6						3				2			11	8	5	10			7
	Apps						36	36	5	15	22	32	40	4	6	19	10	3	17	3	10	6	25	33	2	29	41	20	9	1	2	36
	Goals						12				1	1	9		3		1	1		1	3	1	3	1		5	13		1			1

F.A. Cup

	Date		Opponent	Score	Scorers	Att	Addinall AW	Brown HT	Chapman RFJ	Clayton L	Gilberg H	Hatton C	Ingham A	Poppitt J	Shepherd E	Smith WC	Spence WJ	Waugh WL
R3	Jan	12	Brentford	1-3	Shepherd	35000	9	1		4	6	10	3	2	11	8	5	7

		P	W	D	L	F	A	W	D	L	F	A	Pts
1	Sheffield Wed.	42	14	4	3	54	23	7	7	7	46	43	53
2	Cardiff City	42	18	2	1	52	15	2	9	10	20	39	51
3	Birmingham City	42	11	6	4	36	21	10	3	8	31	35	51
4	Nottingham Forest	42	12	6	3	41	22	6	7	8	36	40	49
5	Leicester City	42	12	6	3	48	24	7	3	11	30	40	47
6	Leeds United	42	13	7	1	35	15	5	4	12	24	42	47
7	Everton	42	12	5	4	42	25	5	5	11	22	33	44
8	Luton Town	42	9	7	5	46	35	7	5	9	31	43	44
9	Rotherham United	42	11	4	6	40	25	6	4	11	33	46	42
10	Brentford	42	11	7	3	34	20	4	5	12	20	35	42
11	Sheffield United	42	13	2	6	57	28	5	3	13	33	48	41
12	West Ham United	42	13	5	3	48	29	2	6	13	19	48	41
13	Southampton	42	11	6	4	40	25	4	5	12	21	48	41
14	Blackburn Rovers	42	11	3	7	35	30	6	3	12	19	33	40
15	Notts County	42	11	5	5	45	27	5	2	14	26	41	39
16	Doncaster Rovers	42	9	4	8	29	28	4	8	9	26	32	38
17	Bury	42	13	2	6	43	22	2	5	14	24	47	37
18	Hull City	42	11	5	5	44	23	2	6	13	16	47	37
19	Swansea Town	42	10	4	7	45	26	2	8	11	27	50	36
20	Barnsley	42	8	7	6	39	33	3	7	11	20	39	36
21	Coventry City	42	9	5	7	36	33	5	1	15	23	49	34
22	QUEEN'S PARK RGS.	42	8	8	5	35	35	3	4	14	17	46	34

#	Date	Opponent	Score	Scorers	Att	Addinall AW	Brown HT	Cameron R	Chapman RFJ	Clayton L	Crickson GE	Farrow DA	Gilberg H	Gullan SK	Harrison JH	Hatton C	Higgins RV	Hold O	Ingham A	Muir WM	Mountford GF	Nicholas CB	Parsons DJ	Poppitt J	Powell GR	Powell MP	Quinn GP	Shepherd E	Smith WC	Spence WJ	Stewart G	Tomkys MG	Waugh WL
1	Aug 23	Exeter City	2-2	Smith 2	14897	9	1		4				6						3					2				11	8	5	10		7
2	25	WATFORD	2-2	Stewart, Smith	23125	9	1		4				6						3					2				11	8	5	10		7
3	30	COVENTRY CITY	0-4		14335	9	1		4				6					10	3					2				11	8	5			7
4	Sep 4	Watford	1-1	Shepherd	22875	9	1		4				6					10	3					2				11	8	5			7
5	6	Norwich City	0-2		26449		1	10					8								4			2	3	5		11	7	6		9	
6	8	WALSALL	4-2	Tomkys 2, Gilberg, Smith	9362		1	10					8								4			2	3	5		11	7	6		9	
7	13	COLCHESTER UNITED	1-0	Muir	13925		1	10					8						3	7	4			2		5		11		6		9	
8	18	Walsall	1-1	Cameron	7028		1	10				6	8						3	7	4			2		5		11				9	
9	20	Aldershot	1-4	Shepherd	8316		1	10				6	8						3	7	4			2		5		11				9	
10	25	Leyton Orient	0-5		8754	9	1	10				6	8						3	11	4			2								7	
11	27	SWINDON TOWN	1-1	Addinall	10762	9	1	10				6	11						3	7	4			2		5				8			
12	Oct 2	Shrewsbury Town	3-0	Shepherd 2, Smith	5988	9	1	10	4				6	7					3					2				11	8	5			
13	4	SOUTHEND UNITED	3-2	Smith 2, Addinall	14777	9	1	10	4				6	7					3					2				11	8	5			
14	11	Brighton & Hove Albion	0-2		18987	9	1	10	4				6	7					3					2				11	8	5			
15	18	NEWPORT COUNTY	4-2	Quinn, Shepherd 2, Addinall	14902	9	1		4				6						3			7		2			10	11	8	5			
16	25	Crystal Palace	2-4	Addinall, Ingham	19181	9	1		4				6						3			7		2			10	11	8	5			
17	Nov 1	BRISTOL CITY	2-1	Mountford, Addinall	14718	9	1						6						3		4	7		2			10	11	8	5			
18	8	Torquay United	1-1	Parsons	6638	9	1	10					8						3		4	7	6	2				11		5			
19	15	NORTHAMPTON T	2-2	Shepherd, Gilberg	14661	9	1	10					8						3		4	7	6	2				11		5			
20	29	IPSWICH TOWN	2-2	Addinall 2	9983	9	1	10					6						3		4	7		2				11	8	5			
21	Dec 13	BOURNEMOUTH	2-1	Nicholas, Cameron	8015	9	1	10				6	8						3		4	7		2				11		5			
22	20	EXETER CITY	1-1	Clayton	6310	9	1	10		8		6							3		4	7		2				11		5			
23	26	BRISTOL ROVERS	0-1		13592	9	1	10				6	8						3		4	7		2				11		5			
24	27	Bristol Rovers	1-2	Gilberg	30995		1	10				6	8						3		4	7		2				11		5		9	
25	Jan 3	Coventry City	0-2		15097	9	1	10		8			6						3		4	7						11		5			
26	10	Gillingham	0-3		11907	9	1	10		8			6						3		4	7		2		5		11					
27	17	NORWICH CITY	3-1	Tomkys, Waugh 2	13084		1	10		5			8						3		4			2				11		6		9	7
28	24	Colchester United	1-1	Harrison (og)	7959		1	10		5			8						3		4			2				11		6		9	7
29	31	GILLINGHAM	1-1	Tomkys	10585		1	10		5			8						3		4			2				11		6		9	7
30	Feb 7	ALDERSHOT	2-2	Smith, Waugh	10713		1			5						10			3		4			2				11	8	6		9	7
31	14	Swindon Town	3-1	Hatton 2, Smith	7387		1			5						10			3		4			2				11	8	6		9	7
32	21	Southend United	0-2		9252		1			5						10			3		4			2				11	8	6		9	7
33	28	BRIGHTON & HOVE ALB	3-3	Higgins, Hatton, Jennings (og)	15238		1			5						10	9		3		4			2				11	8	6			7
34	Mar 7	Newport County	0-2		7971		1			5			8			10	9		3		4			2				11		6			7
35	14	CRYSTAL PALACE	1-1	Cameron	12972		1	10		5			8						3		4	7		2				11		6		9	
36	21	Bristol City	4-4	Mountford, Cameron, Smith 2	20052		1	10		5									3		4	7		2				11	8	6		9	
37	28	TORQUAY UNITED	0-1		8059		1	10		5									3		4	7		2				11	8	6		9	
38	Apr 3	Millwall	1-2	Smith	23962		1	10		5							9		3		4	7		2				11	8	6			
39	4	Northampton Town	2-4	Tomkys, Cameron	12546		1	10											3		4	7		2		5		11	8	6		9	
40	6	MILLWALL	1-3	Smith	12607		1			6	4								3					2		5		11	8			9	7
41	11	LEYTON ORIENT	0-1		11018		1	10		6	4								3			7		2		5			8			9	11
42	18	Ipswich Town	1-0	Hatton	8682		1		4				8		9	10			3			7		2		5		11		6			
43	20	SHREWSBURY TOWN	1-0	Shepherd	7206		1		4				8		9	10			3			7		2		5		11		6			
44	25	READING	1-0	Harrison	10433		1		4				8		9	10			3			7		2		5		11		6			
45	29	Reading	0-2		6367		1		4				8		9	10			3			7		2		5		11		6			
46	May 2	Bournemouth	0-1		8276		1	10							9				3		4	7		2				11	8	6			
	Apps					20	43	34	12	25	2	8	26	3	6	10	3	2	43	5	25	31	2	34	14	17	3	43	25	31	2	19	16
	Goals					7		5		1			3		1	4	1		1	1	2	1	1		1		1	8	13		1	5	3

Played in one game: WJ Heath (game 10, at 5), PJ Woods (game 25, at 2).

Two own goals

F.A. Cup

	Date	Opponent	Score	Scorers	Att	Addinall AW	Brown HT	Cameron R	Chapman RFJ	Clayton L	Crickson GE	Farrow DA	Gilberg H	Gullan SK	Harrison JH	Hatton C	Higgins RV	Hold O	Ingham A	Muir WM	Mountford GF	Nicholas CB	Parsons DJ	Poppitt J	Powell GR	Powell MP	Quinn GP	Shepherd E	Smith WC	Spence WJ	Stewart G	Tomkys MG	Waugh WL
R1	Nov 22	SHREWSBURY T	2-2	Cameron 2	11475	9	1	10					8						3		4	7	6	2				11		5			
rep	27	Shrewsbury Town	2-2	Addinall, Smith	5000	9	1	10					8						3		4	7		2				11	6	5			
rep2	Dec 2	Shrewsbury Town	1-4	Smith	3799	9	1	10	4				8						3			7		2				11	6	5			

Replay 2 at Villa Park.

		P	W	D	L	F	A	W	D	L	F	A	Pts
1	Bristol Rovers	46	17	4	2	55	19	9	8	6	37	27	64
2	Millwall	46	14	7	2	46	16	10	7	6	36	28	62
3	Northampton Town	46	18	4	1	75	30	8	6	9	34	40	62
4	Norwich City	46	16	6	1	56	17	9	4	10	43	38	60
5	Bristol City	46	13	8	2	62	28	9	7	7	33	33	59
6	Coventry City	46	15	5	3	52	22	4	7	12	25	40	50
7	Brighton & Hove A.	46	12	6	5	48	30	7	6	10	33	45	50
8	Southend United	46	15	5	3	41	21	3	8	12	28	53	49
9	Bournemouth	46	15	3	5	49	23	4	6	13	25	46	47
10	Watford	46	12	8	3	39	21	3	9	11	23	42	47
11	Reading	46	17	3	3	53	18	2	5	16	16	46	46
12	Torquay United	46	15	4	4	61	28	3	5	15	26	60	45
13	Crystal Palace	46	12	7	4	40	26	3	6	14	26	56	43
14	Leyton Orient	46	12	7	4	52	28	4	3	16	16	45	42
15	Newport County	46	12	4	7	43	34	4	6	13	27	48	42
16	Ipswich Town	46	10	7	6	34	28	3	8	12	26	41	41
17	Exeter City	46	11	8	4	40	24	2	6	15	21	47	40
18	Swindon Town	46	9	5	9	38	33	5	7	11	26	46	40
19	Aldershot	46	8	8	7	36	29	4	7	12	25	48	39
20	QUEEN'S PARK RGS.	46	9	9	5	37	34	3	6	14	24	48	39
21	Gillingham	46	10	7	6	30	26	2	8	13	25	48	39
22	Colchester United	46	9	9	5	35	21	3	5	15	19	47	38
23	Shrewsbury Town	46	11	5	7	38	35	1	7	15	30	56	36
24	Walsall	46	5	9	9	35	46	2	1	20	21	72	24

1953/54   18th in Division 3(S)

League Matches

No	Date	Opponent	Score	Scorers	Att
1	Aug 19	BRIGHTON & HOVE ALB	1-2	Shepherd	16649
2	22	Bristol City	2-1	Petchey, Cameron	20819
3	26	Norwich City	2-2	Clayton, Hawkins	23432
4	29	ALDERSHOT	0-2		12146
5	31	NORWICH CITY	0-2		11742
6	Sep 5	Swindon Town	1-0	Cameron	15157
7	7	SOUTHAMPTON	0-1		11308
8	12	WALSALL	2-0	Petchey, Hawkins	12273
9	16	Southampton	1-3	Hawkins	16246
10	19	Shrewsbury Town	1-1	Smith	10153
11	21	CRYSTAL PALACE	1-1	Shepherd	7485
12	26	EXETER CITY	0-0		13041
13	30	Crystal Palace	3-0	Smith 2, Shepherd	9409
14	Oct 3	Newport County	1-2	Hurrell	6817
15	10	NORTHAMPTON T	1-1	Shepherd	13300
16	17	Torquay United	2-2	Smith 2	8328
17	24	WATFORD	0-4		15560
18	Nov 7	SOUTHEND UNITED	1-0	Tomkys	9975
19	14	Reading	1-3	Shepherd	14866
20	28	Millwall	0-4		17497
21	Dec 5	IPSWICH TOWN	3-1	Petchey, Woods, Shepherd	13815
22	19	BRISTOL CITY	0-1		8126
23	25	Colchester United	0-5		6155
24	26	COLCHESTER UNITED	0-0		10715
25	Jan 2	Aldershot	4-1	Petchey 3, Cameron	5497
26	16	SWINDON TOWN	0-2		9122
27	23	Walsall	0-2		8734
28	30	COVENTRY CITY	0-3		5300
29	Feb 6	SHREWSBURY TOWN	0-0		7851
30	13	Exeter City	0-0		8133
31	20	NEWPORT COUNTY	5-1	Cameron 3, Kerrins, Smith	10533
32	27	Northampton Town	1-2	Clark	8259
33	Mar 6	TORQUAY UNITED	5-1	Clark, Smith 2, Kerrins, Cameron	11233
34	18	Leyton Orient	2-2	Clark, Angell	5114
35	20	MILLWALL	4-0	Kerrins, Clark, Pounder, Smith	13503
36	27	Southend United	1-4	Angell	7110
37	Apr 3	READING	2-0	Smith, Tomkys	9942
38	7	Bournemouth	1-0	Clark	5721
39	10	Ipswich Town	1-2	Cameron	15380
40	12	Coventry City	1-3	Clark	4785
41	16	Gillingham	0-1		10769
42	17	BOURNEMOUTH	2-1	Shepherd, Smith	10007
43	19	GILLINGHAM	3-1	Smith, Kerrins, Lewin (og)	9576
44	24	Watford	2-0	Angell, Cameron	12431
45	26	LEYTON ORIENT	2-1	Cameron, Aldous (og)	9412
46	30	Brighton & Hove Albion	1-3	Pounder	10493

Appearances grid

No	Allen JC	Angell PF	Barley DC	Brown HT	Cameron R	Clark W	Clayton L	Fallon PD	Gullan SK	Hawkins BW	Hurrel WP	Ingham A	Kerrins PM	Mountford GF	Nicholas CB	Petchey GW	Poppitt J	Pounder AW	Powell MP	Quinn GP	Shepherd E	Smith WC	Spence WJ	Taylor GA	Taylor JG	Tomkys MG	Woods PJ
1				1	8		6			9		3		7		10	2				11			4	5		
2				1	8		6			9		3		7		10	2				11			4	5		
3				1	8		6			9		3		7		10	2				11			4	5		
4			9	1	8		6					3		7		10	2				11			4	5		
5			9	1	8		6					3		7	4						11	10			5		
6			9	1	8		6					3		7	4	10	2				11				5		
7			9	1	8		6					3		7	4	10	2				11				5		
8	11			1	8		6			9		3		7	4	10									5		2
9				1						9	8	3		7							11	10	6		5		2
10				1	8	4	6			9		3		7							11	10			5		2
11				1	8		6			9		3			4						11	10			5	7	2
12				1			6			9		3			4						11	10			5	7	2
13		6		1	8					9		3			4						11	10			5	7	2
14		6		1	9						10	3			4						11	8			5	7	2
15		6		1	9							3			4				5	8	11	10				7	2
16		6		1	9							3			4				5	8	11	10				7	2
17		6		1	9							3			4						11	10			5	7	2
18				1	8		6					3			4	9					11	10			5	7	2
19		6		1	8						10	3			4	9					11				5	7	2
20		6		1	8						10	3			4	9					11				5	7	2
21		6		1	8						10	3			4	9					11				5	7	2
22		6		1	8						10	3			4	9					11				5	7	2
23		6		1	8							3			4	9					11	10		7	5		
24		6		1	10							3			4	9				8	11			7	5		
25		6		1	10							3			4	9				8			11		5		
26		6		1	10							3			4	9				8	11				5	7	2
27		6		1	10							3			4	8		9			11				5	7	2
28		6		1	10		4					3				8		9			11				5	7	2
29		6		1	10		9					3			4						11	8		2	7		
30		6		1	8	9						3	11		4			7	5			10					2
31		6		1	8	9						3	11		4			7	5			10					2
32		6		1	8	9						3	11		4			7	5			10					2
33		6		1	8	9						3	11		4			7	5			10					2
34		6			8	9		1				3	11		4			7	5			10					2
35		6		1	8	9						3	11		4			7	5			10					2
36		6		1	8	9						3	11		4			7	5			10					2
37		6			8	9	4		1			3							5			10				7	2
38	7	6			8	9	4		1			3							5		11	10					2
39		6			8	9	4		1			3						7	5		11	10					2
40		6			8	9	4		1			3						7	5		11	10					2
41		6			8	9	4		1			3							5		11	10				7	2
42						9	4		1					7		6			5	8	11	10					3
43						9	4		1									6	5	8	11	10					3
44		6			8	9	4					3		7					5		11	10					2
45		6			8	9	4					3	11					7	5			10					2
46		6			8	9	4					3	11					7	5			10					2
Apps	1	31	4	33	38	18	28	1	13	8	6	41	13	10	30	21	14	11	21	10	34	29	5	2	41	20	23
Goals		3			10	6	1			3	1		4			6		2			7	12			2	1	

Two own goals

F.A. Cup

Rd	Date	Opponent	Score	Scorers	Att	Angell PF	Brown HT	Cameron R	Clark W	Hurrel WP	Ingham A	Nicholas CB	Petchey GW	Shepherd E	Taylor JG	Tomkys MG	Woods PJ
R1	Nov 21	SHREWSBURY T	2-0	Hurrell 2	13076	6	1	8		10	3	4	9	11	5	7	2
R2	Dec 12	NUNEATON BOROUGH	1-1	Tomkys	18316	6	1	8	5	10	3	4	9	11		7	2
rep	17	Nuneaton Borough	2-1	Petchey, Shepherd	13083	6	1	8		10	3	4	9	11	5	7	2
R3	Jan 9	PORT VALE	0-1		17474	6	1	10			3	4	9	11	5	7	

Division 3 (South) — Final Table

		P	W	D	L	F	A	W	D	L	F	A	Pts
1	Ipswich Town	46	15	5	3	47	19	12	5	6	35	32	64
2	Brighton & Hove A.	46	17	3	3	57	31	9	6	8	29	30	61
3	Bristol City	46	18	3	2	59	18	7	3	13	29	48	56
4	Watford	46	16	3	4	52	23	5	7	11	33	46	52
5	Northampton Town	46	18	4	1	63	18	2	7	14	19	37	51
6	Southampton	46	17	5	1	51	22	5	2	16	25	41	51
7	Norwich City	46	13	5	5	43	28	7	6	10	30	38	51
8	Reading	46	14	3	6	57	33	6	6	11	29	40	49
9	Exeter City	46	12	2	9	39	22	8	6	9	29	36	48
10	Gillingham	46	14	3	6	37	22	5	7	11	24	44	48
11	Leyton Orient	46	14	5	4	48	26	4	6	13	31	47	47
12	Millwall	46	15	3	5	44	24	4	6	13	30	53	47
13	Torquay United	46	10	10	3	48	33	7	2	14	33	55	46
14	Coventry City	46	14	5	4	36	15	4	4	15	25	41	45
15	Newport County	46	14	4	5	42	28	5	2	16	19	53	44
16	Southend United	46	15	2	6	46	22	3	5	15	23	49	43
17	Aldershot	46	11	5	7	45	31	6	4	13	29	55	43
18	QUEEN'S PARK RGS.	46	10	5	8	32	25	6	4	13	28	43	42
19	Bournemouth	46	12	5	6	47	27	4	3	16	20	43	40
19	Swindon Town	46	13	5	5	48	21	2	5	16	19	49	40
21	Shrewsbury Town	46	8	3	12	34	34	4	1	17	17	42	40
22	Crystal Palace	46	11	7	5	41	30	3	5	15	19	56	40
23	Colchester United	46	7	9	7	35	29	3	3	17	15	49	30
24	Walsall	46	8	5	10	22	27	1	3	19	18	60	26

1954/55   15th in Division 3(S)

	Date		Opponent	Score	Scorers	Att	Angell PF	Brown HT	Cameron R	Clark W	Fidler TG	Gullan SK	Ingham A	Kerrins PM	Longbottom A	Nicholas CB	Petchey GW	Pounder AW	Powell MP	Rutter KG	Shepherd E	Silver A	Smith WC	Tomkys MG	Woods PJ
1	Aug 21		WATFORD	2-1	Cameron, Clark	19686	6	1	8	9			3			4			7	5			11		10	2
2	24		Southend United	2-2	Cameron, Smith	8505	6	1	8		9					4			7	5	3		11		10	2
3	28		Bournemouth	2-2	Smith 2	13865	6	1	8		9					4			7	5	3		11		10	2
4	30		SOUTHEND UNITED	1-1	Shepherd	11894	6		8		9	1				4			7	5	3		11		10	2
5	Sep 4		Brentford	1-1	Clark	18756			8		9	1				4	6		7	5	3		11		10	2
6	7		ALDERSHOT	5-0	Smith 2 (2p), Fidler 2, Petchey	11045			8		9	1				4	6		7	5	3		11		10	2
7	11		NEWPORT COUNTY	2-0	Shepherd, Rutter	13188			8	9		1				4	6		7	5	3		11		10	2
8	15		Aldershot	0-2		5169			8	9		1				4	6		7	5	3		11		10	2
9	18		Exeter City	1-2	Cameron	8911			8	9		1	3			4	6		7	5	2		11		10	
10	22		Swindon Town	0-2		6423	6	1	8	9			3	7		4	10			5	2		11			
11	25		COLCHESTER UNITED	4-1	Pounder, Clark, Cameron, Elder(og)	11926	6	1	8	9			3			4	10	7		5	2		11			
12	27		SWINDON TOWN	3-1	Smith 2(1p), Pounder	8241	6	1	8	9			3			4		7		5	2		11		10	
13	Oct 2		Norwich City	1-1	Smith	20353	6	1	8	9			3				4	7		5	2		11		10	
14	9		SOUTHAMPTON	2-2	Smith, Wilkins (og)	16899	6	1		9			3			4	8	7		5	2		11		10	
15	16		Millwall	1-0	Clark	21062	6	1	8	9			3				4	7		5	2		11		10	
16	23		LEYTON ORIENT	2-0	Smith, Clark	22114	6	1	8	9			3				4	7		5	2		11		10	
17	30		Brighton & Hove Albion	1-4	Shepherd	14825	6	1	8	9			3				4	7		5	2		11		10	
18	Nov 6		READING	2-3	Shepherd, Smith	13399	6	1	8	9			3				4	7		5	2		11		10	
19	13		Shrewsbury Town	0-1		7372	11	1	8		9		3				4	6		5				10	7	2
20	27		Bristol City	1-1	Tomkys	17657	6	1	8		9		3	11		4				5				10	7	2
21	Dec 4		TORQUAY UNITED	4-2	Smith 2(1p), Cameron 2	8339	6		8	9	7		3	11		1	4			5				10		2
22	18		Watford	1-1	Cameron	11427	6	1	8	9	7		3			4				5	11			10		2
23	25		NORTHAMPTON T	1-0	Clark	8718	6	1	8	9	7		3			4				5	11			10		2
24	27		Northampton Town	3-1	Clark 2, Angell	12623	6	1	8	9	7		3			4				5	2		11	10		
25	Jan 1		BOURNEMOUTH	1-1	Angell	9031	6	1	8	9			3			4				5	2		11	10	7	
26	15		BRENTFORD	1-1	Clark	9835	6	1	8	9				11		4				5	3			10	7	2
27	22		Newport County	0-4		5457	6	1		9			3	11		4	8			5	2			10	7	
28	29		COVENTRY CITY	3-2	Smith, Cameron, Kerrins	12523	6	1	8	9			3	7		4				5			11	10		2
29	Feb 5		EXETER CITY	1-2	Smith	9626	6	1	8	9			3	7		4				5			11	10		2
30	12		Colchester United	0-1		4903	6	1	10	9	7		3			4				5			11	8		2
31	19		NORWICH CITY	2-1	Angell, Cameron	6530	6	1	10	9			3	7		4				5			11	8		2
32	26		Southampton	2-2	Clark, Shepherd	12396	6	1	10	9			3	7		4				5			11	8		2
33	Mar 5		MILLWALL	1-2	Shepherd	12036	6	1	10	9			3	7		4				5			11	8		2
34	12		Leyton Orient	0-3		17513	6	1	10	9			3		8	4				5			11		7	2
35	19		BRIGHTON & HOVE ALB	3-2	Clark 2, Shepherd	9191	6	1	10	9			3	7	8	4				5			11			2
36	26		Reading	1-3	Kerrins	6066	6	1	10	9			3	7	8	4				5	2		11			
37	Apr 2		SHREWSBURY TOWN	2-0	Clark, Cameron	8461	6	1	10	9			3	7	8	4				5			11			2
38	8		Crystal Palace	1-2	Clark	17238	6	1	10	9			3			4		7		5			11	8		2
39	9		Walsall	1-4	Smith	13018	6	1	10	9			3	11		4		7		5				8		2
40	11		CRYSTAL PALACE	1-0	Clark	8974	6	1	10	9			3	7	8	4				5	11					2
41	16		BRISTOL CITY	1-1	Shepherd	12498	6	1	10	9			3		8	4		7		5	11					2
42	20		Gillingham	1-3	Pounder	9528	6	1	10	9			3		8	4		7		5	11					2
43	23		Torquay United	2-3	Longbottom, Cameron	6146	6	1	10	9			3		8		4	7		5	11					2
44	25		WALSALL	1-1	Cameron	6253	6	1	10	9			3		8	4		7		5	11					2
45	30		GILLINGHAM	1-1	Cameron	9104	6	1	10	9			3		8	4				5	11				7	2
46	May 2		Coventry City	1-5	Smith	7381	6	1	10	9			3		8	4				5	11				7	2

	Angell PF	Brown HT	Cameron R	Clark W	Fidler TG	Gullan SK	Ingham A	Kerrins PM	Longbottom A	Nicholas CB	Petchey GW	Pounder AW	Powell MP	Rutter KG	Shepherd E	Silver A	Smith WC	Tomkys MG	Woods PJ
Apps	41	39	44	39	12	6	38	15	11	40	17	23	36	32	40	0	33	8	32
Goals	3		13	15	2			2	1			1	3		1	8		17	1	

Two own goals

F.A. Cup

	Date		Opponent	Score	Scorers	Att	Angell	Brown	Cameron	Clark	Fidler		Ingham	Kerrins		Nicholas	Petchey	Pounder		Rutter	Shepherd	Silver	Smith	Tomkys	Woods
R1	Nov 20		WALTHAMSTOW AVE.	2-2	Fidler, Smith	16299	6	1	8		9		3			4		7	5			11		10		2
rep	23		Walthamstowe Avenue	2-2	Fidler, Tomkys	10500	6	1	8		9		3			4			5			11		10	7	2
rep2	29		Walthamstowe Avenue	0-4		11939	6		8	9			3	11		4			5			1		10	7	2

Replay 2 at Highbury.

		P	W	D	L	F	A	W	D	L	F	A	Pts
1	Bristol City	46	17	4	2	62	22	13	6	4	39	25	70
2	Leyton Orient	46	16	2	5	48	20	10	7	6	41	27	61
3	Southampton	46	16	6	1	49	19	8	5	10	26	32	59
4	Gillingham	46	12	8	3	41	28	8	7	8	36	38	55
5	Millwall	46	14	6	3	44	25	6	5	12	28	43	51
6	Brighton & Hove A.	46	14	4	5	47	27	6	6	11	29	36	50
7	Watford	46	11	9	3	45	26	7	5	11	26	36	50
8	Torquay United	46	12	6	5	51	39	6	6	11	31	43	48
9	Coventry City	46	15	5	3	50	26	3	6	14	17	33	47
10	Southend United	46	13	5	5	48	28	4	7	12	35	52	46
11	Brentford	46	11	6	6	44	36	5	8	10	38	46	46
11	Norwich City	46	13	5	5	40	23	5	5	13	20	37	46
13	Northampton Town	46	13	5	5	47	27	6	3	14	26	54	46
14	Aldershot	46	12	6	5	44	23	4	7	12	31	48	45
15	QUEEN'S PARK RGS.	46	13	7	3	46	25	2	7	14	23	50	44
16	Shrewsbury Town	46	14	5	4	49	24	2	5	16	21	54	42
17	Bournemouth	46	7	8	8	32	29	5	10	8	25	36	42
18	Reading	46	7	10	6	32	26	6	5	12	33	47	41
19	Newport County	46	8	8	7	32	29	3	8	12	28	44	38
20	Crystal Palace	46	9	11	3	32	24	2	5	16	20	56	38
21	Swindon Town	46	10	8	5	30	19	1	7	15	16	45	37
22	Exeter City	46	9	7	7	30	31	2	8	13	17	42	37
23	Walsall	46	9	6	8	49	36	1	8	14	26	50	34
24	Colchester United	46	7	6	10	33	40	2	7	14	20	51	31

38

1955/56 18th in Division 3(S)

#	Date		Opponent	Score	Scorers	Att	Angell PF	Brown HT	Cameron R	Clark W	Crickson GE	Dawson G	Dean J	Hellawell MS	Ingham A	Kerrins PM	Longbottom A	McKay W	Nelson WE	Petchey GW	Pounder AW	Powell MP	Quinn GP	Rhodes A	Rutter KG	Shepherd E	Smith WC	Springett RDG	Temby W	Tomkys MG	Woods PJ
1	Aug	20	Brighton & Hove Albion	1-1	Clark	14510	6	1	10	9					3	7	8			4		5				11					2
2		22	BRENTFORD	1-1	Cameron	11688	6	1	10	9	4				3	7	8			4		5				11					2
3		27	SOUTHAMPTON	4-0	Shepherd 2, Smith, Angell	10672	6	1	10	9					3	7				4		5				11	8				2
4		30	Brentford	0-2		12947	6	1	10			9			3	7				4		5				11	8				2
5	Sep	3	Shrewsbury Town	1-1	Shepherd	11223	6	1	10	9					3	7				4		5	8			11					2
6		5	CRYSTAL PALACE	0-3		9083	6	1	10	9					3	7				4		5	8			11					2
7		10	IPSWICH TOWN	1-1	Clark	11763	6	1	8	9					3	7				4		5	10			11					2
8		14	Crystal Palace	1-1	Shepherd	10543	6	1	10	9					3	7				4		5				11	8				2
9		17	Walsall	2-2	Smith, Clark	12427	6	1	10	9					3	7				4		5				11	8				2
10		19	Northampton Town	2-5	Smith 2	9735	6	1	10	9					3					4	7	5				11	8				2
11		24	TORQUAY UNITED	3-1	Cameron 2, Smith	10536	6	1	10	9					3					4	7	5				11	8				2
12		26	SWINDON TOWN	1-0	Cameron	5181	6	1	10	9					3					4	7	5				11	8				2
13	Oct	1	Newport County	1-2	Smith	7375	4	1	10	9					3	7				6		5				11	8				2
14		8	SOUTHEND UNITED	1-2	Shepherd	11885	6	1	10	9					3	7				4		5				11	8				2
15		15	Exeter City	0-2		8741	6	1	10	9					3					4	7				5	11	8				2
16		22	LEYTON ORIENT	0-1		11856	6	1	10	9					3	11	8			4	7				5						2
17		29	Colchester United	1-4	Clark	7339	6	1	10	9					3					4					5	11	8			7	2
18	Nov	5	NORWICH CITY	2-3	Petchey, Smith	10162	6		10						3					9					5	11	8	1	4	7	2
19		12	Bournemouth	0-1		6834	6		10						3	7				9					5	11	8	1	4		2
20		26	Millwall	0-2		7602	6	1	10		4		8		3					9	7				5	11					2
21	Dec	3	READING	3-3	Smith 2, Angell	7088	6	1	4						3					2	9	7	5	10		11	8				
22		17	BRIGHTON & HOVE ALB	2-1	Cameron, Clark	7648	6	1	10	9					3					4	7				5	11	8				2
23		24	Southampton	0-4		9502	6	1	10	9					3					4	7				5	11	8				2
24		26	Aldershot	2-1	Smith 2	6366	6	1	10						3					4	7				5	11	8			9	2
25		27	ALDERSHOT	2-2	Cameron 2	8378	6	1	10	9					3		11			4	7				5		8				2
26		31	SHREWSBURY TOWN	1-1	Smith	7779	6		10	9					3					4	7				5	11	8	1			2
27	Jan	7	GILLINGHAM	2-2	Smith 2	7345	11	1	10	9			6		3					4	7				5		8				2
28		14	Ipswich Town	1-4	Clark	12168	11	1	10	9			6		3					4	7				5		8				2
29		21	Walsall	3-2	Petchey 2, Pounder	6591	6	1	8	9					3					4	7				5	11	10				2
30		28	Watford	1-0	Angell	5784	6	1		9					3				8	4	7				5		10			11	2
31	Feb	4	Torquay United	0-2		5176	6	1		9					3				8	4	7				5		10			11	2
32		11	NEWPORT COUNTY	0-0		3910	6	1		9					3				8	4	7				5		10			11	2
33		18	Southend United	1-5	Smith	6951	6	1	8	9					3					4	7				5		10			11	2
34		25	EXETER CITY	1-0	Cameron	6898	6	1	9					11	3				8	4	7				5		10				2
35	Mar	3	Leyton Orient	1-7	Shepherd	12614	6	1	9						3				8	4	7				5	11	10				2
36		10	COLCHESTER UNITED	6-2	Shepherd 2, Kerrins, Cameron, Smith, Petchey	7954		1	10	9			6		3	7				4		5				11	8				2
37		17	Norwich City	0-1		13355	6	1	10	9					3	7				4		5				11	8				2
38		24	BOURNEMOUTH	0-1		5832	6	1	10	9	4				3	7						5				11	8				2
39		30	COVENTRY CITY	1-2	Cameron	10956	6	1	10	9	4				3	11	8	7				5									2
40		31	Gillingham	2-0	Clark, Cameron	5462	6	1	10	9	4				3	11	8				7	5									2
41	Apr	3	Coventry City	1-4	Clark	16714	6		10	9	4				3							5				11	8	1		7	2
42		7	MILLWALL	4-0	Clark, Shepherd, Ingham, Smith(p)	6497			10	9			6		3	7				4		5				11	8	1			2
43		14	Reading	1-3	Cameron	4697			10	9			6		3	7				4		5		2		11	8	1			
44		21	WATFORD	3-2	Kerrins, Cameron, Angell	7603	11		10	9			6		3	7				4		5		2			8	1			
45		25	Swindon Town	1-0	Smith	4617	11		10	9			6		3	7				4				2	5		8	1			
46		28	NORTHAMPTON T	3-2	Clark 2, Smith	7157	11		10	9			6		3	7				4				2	5		8	1			
			Apps				43	38	43	38	3	1	12	1	41	20	12	6	9	41	19	25	4	4	21	32	37	8	2	8	38
			Goals				4		13	11						1	2			4			1			9	19				

F.A. Cup

R1	Nov 19	Southend United	0-2		15000	6	1	10		4		8		3					9	7	5				11					2

Southern Professional Floodlight Cup

R1	Oct 31	LEYTON ORIENT	0-1		2790	6	1	10	9					3					4					5	11	8			7	2

		P	W	D	L	F	A	W	D	L	F	A	Pts
1	Leyton Orient	46	18	3	2	76	20	11	5	7	30	29	66
2	Brighton & Hove A.	46	20	2	1	73	16	9	5	9	39	34	65
3	Ipswich Town	46	16	6	1	59	28	9	8	6	47	32	64
4	Southend United	46	16	4	3	58	25	5	7	11	30	55	53
5	Torquay United	46	11	10	2	48	21	9	2	12	38	42	52
6	Brentford	46	11	8	4	40	30	8	6	9	29	36	52
7	Norwich City	46	15	4	4	56	31	4	9	10	30	51	51
8	Coventry City	46	16	4	3	54	20	4	5	14	19	40	49
9	Bournemouth	46	13	6	4	39	14	6	4	13	24	37	48
10	Gillingham	46	12	3	8	38	28	7	7	9	31	43	48
11	Northampton Town	46	14	3	6	44	27	6	4	13	23	44	47
12	Colchester United	46	14	4	5	56	37	4	7	12	20	44	47
13	Shrewsbury Town	46	12	9	2	47	21	5	3	15	22	45	46
14	Southampton	46	13	6	4	60	30	5	2	16	31	51	44
15	Aldershot	46	9	9	5	36	33	3	7	13	34	57	40
16	Exeter City	46	10	6	7	39	30	5	4	14	19	47	40
17	Reading	46	10	2	11	40	37	5	7	11	30	42	39
18	QUEEN'S PARK RGS.	46	10	7	6	44	32	4	4	15	20	54	39
19	Newport County	46	12	2	9	32	26	3	7	13	26	53	39
20	Walsall	46	13	5	5	43	28	2	3	18	25	56	38
21	Watford	46	8	5	10	31	39	5	6	12	21	46	37
22	Millwall	46	13	4	6	56	31	2	2	19	27	69	36
23	Crystal Palace	46	7	3	13	27	32	5	7	11	27	51	34
24	Swindon Town	46	4	10	9	18	22	4	4	15	16	56	30

1956/57 10th in Division 3(S)

#	Date	Opponent	Score	Scorers	Att	Andrews CJ	Angell PF	Balogun T	Cameron R	Dawson A	Dean J	Hellawell MS	Ingham A	Kerrins PM	Lay PJ	Locke LC	Longbottom A	Peacock T	Petchey GW	Powell MP	Quigley T	Quinn GP	Rhodes A	Rutter KG	Springett RDG	Temby W	Woods PJ
1	Aug 18	Reading	0-1		11417	6	11		10			7	3						4	5	9	8			1		2
2	20	Plymouth Argyle	2-1	Angell, Longbottom	15718	6	11					7	3				8		4		9	10		5	1		2
3	25	NEWPORT COUNTY	1-1	Hellawell	7863	6	11					7	3				8		4		9	10		5	1		2
4	27	PLYMOUTH ARGYLE	3-0	Quigley 2, Hellawell	8450	6	11					7	3			10	8		4		9			5	1		2
5	Sep 1	Colchester United	1-1	Quigley	8179	6	11					7	3			10	8		4		9			5	1		2
6	6	Northampton Town	0-3		7591	6	11					7	3			10	8		4		9			5	1		2
7	8	NORWICH CITY	3-1	Angell, Locke, Quigley	12631	6	11					7	3			10	8		4		9			5	1		2
8	10	NORTHAMPTON T	1-0	Longbottom	10785	6	11					7	3			10	8		4		9			5	1		2
9	15	Coventry City	1-5	Quigley	18160	6	11					7	3			10	8		4		9			5	1		2
10	19	Swindon Town	0-1		8705	6						7	3	11					4		9	10		5	1	8	2
11	22	SOUTHAMPTON	1-2	Hellawell	12792	6						7	3	11		10	8		4		9			5	1		2
12	24	SWINDON TOWN	3-0	Quigley 2, Temby	9526	6						7	3	11					4		9	10		5	1	8	2
13	29	Exeter City	0-0		7312	6	11					7	3			10			4		9			5	1	8	2
14	Oct 6	Aldershot	2-4	Cameron, Hellawell	5609	6	11		8			7	3			10			4		9			5	1		2
15	13	WATFORD	3-1	Hellawell, Balogun, Brown(og)	14211	6		9	8			7	3	11		10			4					5	1		2
16	20	Shrewsbury Town	0-0		8463	6		9	8			7	3	11		10			4					5	1		2
17	27	WALSALL	1-0	Kerrins	9461	6		9	8			7	3	11		10			4					5	1		2
18	Nov 3	Ipswich Town	0-4		12778	6		9	8			7	3	11		10			4					5	1		2
19	10	BOURNEMOUTH	2-1	Petchey, Locke	8554	6		9	8			7	3	11		10			4					5	1		2
20	24	MILLWALL	0-0		10427	6	11	9				7	3			10	8		4					5	1		2
21	Dec 1	Brighton & Hove Albion	0-1		9770	6	11					7	3			10	8		4		9			5	1		2
22	15	READING	1-1	Peacock	5472	6			10			7	3	11			8	9	4					5	1		2
23	22	Newport County	1-1	Peacock	7638	6			10			7	3	11			8	9	4					5	1		2
24	25	Crystal Palace	1-2	Peacock	9988	6			10			7	3	11			8	9	4					5	1		2
25	26	CRYSTAL PALACE	4-2	Cameron 2, Kerrins 2	5307	6			9			7	3	11	5	10	8		4						1		2
26	29	COLCHESTER UNITED	1-1	Kerrins	8801	6			9			7	3	11		10	8		4					5	1		2
27	Jan 12	Norwich City	2-1	Longbottom, Pointer(og)	11722	6			10			7	3	11			8	9	4					5	1		2
28	19	COVENTRY CITY	1-1	Petchey	7863	6			10			7	3	11			8	9	4					5	1		2
29	Feb 2	Southampton	2-1	Hellawell, Longbottom	17074	6			10			7	3	11			8	9	4					5	1		2
30	9	EXETER CITY	5-3	Longbottom 3, Kerrins, Andrews	8639	6			10			7	3	11			8	9	4					5	1		2
31	16	ALDERSHOT	0-1		10525	6			10			7	3	11			8	9	4					5	1		2
32	23	Watford	4-2	Temby, Cameron, Balogun, Shipwright(og)	4428	6		9	10			7	3	11					4					5	1	8	2
33	Mar 2	SHREWSBURY TOWN	2-1	Balogun, Temby	9984	6		9	10			7	3	11					4					5	1	8	2
34	9	Gillingham	1-0	Kerrins	7581	6		9	10			7	3	11			8		4					5	1		2
35	16	IPSWICH TOWN	0-2		12339	6		9	10			7	3	11			8		4					5	1		2
36	23	Bournemouth	0-1		12552	6		9	10			7	3	11			8		4					5	1		2
37	25	SOUTHEND UNITED	3-0	Peacock, Longbottom, Hellawell	6412	6			10		4	7	3	11			8	9						5	1		2
38	30	TORQUAY UNITED	0-1		9605	6			10		4	7	3	11			8	9						5	1		2
39	Apr 6	Millwall	0-2		10834	6			10		4	7	3	11			8					9		5	1		2
40	13	BRIGHTON & HOVE ALB	0-0		6957	6		9	10	7			3	11			8		4					5	1		2
41	15	Southend United	0-3		6052	6		9	10			7	3	11			8		4				2	5	1		
42	19	Brentford	0-2		13841	6			9		10	7	3	11			8		4					5	1		2
43	20	Walsall	2-0	Longbottom 2	10924	6	11		10				3	7			8	9	4					5	1		2
44	22	BRENTFORD	2-2	Longbottom, Dargie (og)	9661	6	11					7	3			10	8	9	4					5	1		2
45	27	Torquay United	0-3		8630	6	11		10			7	3				8	9	4					5	1		2
46	29	GILLINGHAM	5-0	Longbottom 3, Kerrins, Cameron	6237	6			10			7	3	11			8	9	4					5	1		2
		Apps				46	16	13	31	1	4	44	46	31	1	19	34	14	43	1	16	5	1	44	46	5	45
		Goals				1	2	3	5			7		7		2	14	4	2		7					3	

Four own goals

F.A. Cup

#	Date	Opponent	Score	Scorers	Att	Andrews CJ	Angell PF	Balogun T	Cameron R	Dawson A	Dean J	Hellawell MS	Ingham A	Kerrins PM	Lay PJ	Locke LC	Longbottom A	Peacock T	Petchey GW	Powell MP	Quigley T	Quinn GP	Rhodes A	Rutter KG	Springett RDG	Temby W	Woods PJ
R1	Nov 17	DORCHESTER	4-0	Hellawell, Balogun, Locke, Cameron	9764	6		9	8			7	3	11		10			4					5	1		2
R2	Dec 8	Tooting & Mitcham	2-0	Balogun, Longbottom	11450	6		9	10			7	3	11			8		4					5	1		2
R3	Jan 5	Sunderland	0-4		30577	6			10			7	3	11			8	9	4					5	1		2

Southern Professional Floodlight Cup

#	Date	Opponent	Score	Scorers	Att	Andrews CJ	Angell PF	Balogun T	Cameron R	Dawson A	Dean J	Hellawell MS	Ingham A	Kerrins PM	Lay PJ	Locke LC	Longbottom A	Peacock T	Petchey GW	Powell MP	Quigley T	Quinn GP	Rhodes A	Rutter KG	Springett RDG	Temby W	Woods PJ
R1	Oct 8	MILLWALL	5-2	Balogun 2, Locke 2, Woods (p)		6	11	9	8			7	3			10			4					5	1		2
R2	Nov 26	READING	1-2	McLaren (og)	3012	6	11					7	3			10	8		4		9			5	1		2

		P	W	D	L	F	A	W	D	L	F	A	Pts
1	Ipswich Town	46	18	3	2	72	20	7	6	10	29	34	59
2	Torquay United	46	19	4	0	71	18	5	7	11	18	46	59
3	Colchester United	46	15	8	0	49	19	7	6	10	35	37	58
4	Southampton	46	15	4	4	48	20	7	6	10	28	32	54
5	Bournemouth	46	15	7	1	57	20	4	7	12	31	42	52
6	Brighton & Hove A.	46	15	6	2	59	26	4	8	11	27	39	52
7	Southend United	46	14	3	6	42	20	4	9	10	31	45	48
8	Brentford	46	12	9	2	55	29	4	7	12	23	47	48
9	Shrewsbury Town	46	11	9	3	45	24	4	9	10	27	55	48
10	QUEEN'S PARK RGS.	46	12	7	4	42	21	6	4	13	19	39	47
11	Watford	46	11	6	6	44	32	7	4	12	28	43	46
12	Newport County	46	15	6	2	51	18	1	7	15	14	44	45
13	Reading	46	13	4	6	44	30	5	5	13	38	51	45
14	Northampton Town	46	15	5	3	49	22	3	4	16	17	51	45
15	Walsall	46	11	7	5	49	25	5	5	13	31	49	44
16	Coventry City	46	12	5	6	52	36	4	7	12	22	48	44
17	Millwall	46	13	7	3	46	29	3	5	15	18	55	44
18	Plymouth Argyle	46	10	8	5	38	31	6	3	14	30	42	43
19	Aldershot	46	11	5	7	43	35	4	7	12	36	57	42
20	Crystal Palace	46	7	10	6	31	28	4	8	11	31	47	40
21	Exeter City	46	8	8	7	37	26	4	5	14	24	50	37
22	Gillingham	46	7	8	8	29	29	5	5	13	25	56	37
23	Swindon Town	46	12	3	8	43	33	3	3	17	23	63	36
24	Norwich City	46	7	5	11	33	37	1	10	12	28	57	31

League

#		Date	Opponent	Score	Scorers	Att	Allum A	Andrews CJ	Angell PF	Cameron R	Colgan W	Dawson A	Drinkwater R	Finney CW	Fry RP	Ingham A	Kerrins PM	Locke LC	Longbottom A	Orr DM	Peacock T	Petchey GW	Powell MP	Rutter KG	Smith EWA	Springett RDG	Standley TL	Tomkys MG	Woods PJ
1	Aug	24	BRENTFORD	1-0	Petchey	15734		6	11	8				9		3						7		4	5	1	10		2
2		26	COLCHESTER UNITED	1-0	Cameron	12328		6	11	8				9		3						7		4	5	1	10		2
3		31	Southend United	0-6		15883		6	11	8				9		3						7		4	5	1	10		2
4	Sep	2	Colchester United	1-2	Finney	8992	7	6	11					9		3						8		4	5	1	10		2
5		7	BRIGHTON & HOVE ALB	0-1		11139		6	11					9		3	7					8		4	5	1	10		2
6		11	Swindon Town	1-1	Angell	10730		6	11					10		3	7					8	9	4	5	1			2
7		14	Southampton	0-5		15965		6	11					10		3	7					8	9	4	5	1			2
8		16	SWINDON TOWN	2-1	Locke 2	8413			6	9				8		3	7	10		11				4	5	1			2
9		21	NEWPORT COUNTY	1-1	Woods	9187			6	8				9		3	7	10		11				4	5	1			2
10		23	MILLWALL	3-0	Locke 3	11325		6	11	8						3		10			7			4	5	1	9		2
11		28	Port Vale	1-2	Locke	12816		6	11	8						3		10			7			4	5	1	9		2
12		30	Millwall	0-5		12784		6	11	8						3		10			7			4	5	1	9		2
13	Oct	5	PLYMOUTH ARGYLE	1-0	Locke	11354			6	8		9				3	11	10				7		4	5	1			2
14		12	Norwich City	0-2		19460			6	8		9				3	11	10				7		4	5	1			2
15		19	BOURNEMOUTH	3-0	Angell, Woods, Woollard(og)	9007			6	8		9				3	11	10				7		4	5	1			2
16		26	Walsall	2-1	Longbottom	7560			6			9				3	11	10	8			7		4	5	1			2
17	Nov	2	COVENTRY CITY	3-0	Kerrins 2, Locke	9246			6			9				3	11	10	8			7		4	5	1			2
18		9	Shrewsbury Town	1-2	Longbottom	6514			6			9				3	11	10	8			7		4	5	1			2
19		23	Northampton Town	5-1	Longbottom 4, E Smith	7525			6	9		10				3	11		8			7		4	5	1			2
20		30	WATFORD	3-0	Ingham, Longbottom, Petchey	10236			6	9		10				3	11		8			7		4	5	1			2
21	Dec	14	TORQUAY UNITED	1-1	Woods	6093			6	9		10			1	3	11		8			7		4	5				2
22		21	Brentford	1-1	Cameron	12804			6	10						3	11		8			7		4	5	1	9		2
23		25	Gillingham	1-1	Standley	7233			6	10						3	11		8			7		4	5	1	9		2
24		26	GILLINGHAM	1-1	Woods	8658		6		10						3	11		8			7		4	5	1	9		2
25		28	SOUTHEND UNITED	1-1	Standley	10072			6	10	2					3	11		8			7		4	5	1	9		
26	Jan	11	Brighton & Hove Albion	1-1	Longbottom	13322			6	10						3	11		8			7		4	5	1	9		2
27		18	SOUTHAMPTON	3-2	Longbottom 2, Woods(p)	8611			6	10						3	11		8			7		4	5	1	9		2
28		25	Reading	0-3		11455			6	10						3	11		8			7		4	5	1	9		2
29	Feb	1	Newport County	2-4	Dawson, Longbottom	7543			6	10		9				3	11		8			7		4	5	1			2
30		8	PORT VALE	2-1	Cameron, Longbottom	7594			6	10		9				3	11		8			7		4	5	1			2
31		15	Plymouth Argyle	1-3	Cameron	17068			6	10		9				3	11		8			7		4	5	1			2
32		22	NORWICH CITY	1-1	Cameron	7935			6	10		9		8		3	11					7		4	5	1			2
33	Mar	1	Bournemouth	1-4	Dawson	12711			6	10	2	9				3	11		8			7		4	5	1			
34		3	ALDERSHOT	0-1		7744			6	10		9				3	11		8			7		4	5	1			2
35		8	WALSALL	1-0	Cameron	6548			6	9						3		10	8			7		4	5	1		11	2
36		15	Coventry City	1-1	Locke	7673	11	6					1			3		10	8			7		4	5			9	2
37		17	READING	3-0	Woods, Longbottom, Petchey	8838		6					1			3		10	8			7		4	5		9	11	2
38		22	NORTHAMPTON T	1-0	Longbottom	7531		6					1			3		10	8			7		4	5		9	11	2
39		29	Torquay United	1-3	Locke	5172		6					1			3		10	8			7		4	5		9	11	2
40	Apr	4	EXETER CITY	1-1	Cameron	10223		6		9			1			3		10	8	11		7		4	5				2
41		7	Exeter City	0-0		7078		6					1			3		10	8	11		7		4	5		9		2
42		12	Watford	0-0		8022		6					1			3	11	10	8			7		4	5		9		2
43		16	Crystal Palace	3-2	Longbottom, Kerrins, Locke	18712		6					1			3	11	10	8	9		7		4	5				2
44		19	CRYSTAL PALACE	4-2	Kerrins, Longbottom, Cameron, Locke	11868		6					1			3	11	10	8	9		7		4	5				2
45		23	Aldershot	1-1	Kerrins	4050		6					1			3	9	10	8	11		7		4	5				2
46		28	SHREWSBURY TOWN	3-0	Kerrins 2, Locke	6193		6					1			3	9	10	8	11		7		4	5				2
			Apps				1	12	45	37	2	33	11	10	1	46	31	22	40	5	2	46	1	46	17	34	15	5	44
			Goals					2	8	2		1		1		1	7	13	17			3			1		2		6

One own goal

F.A. Cup

		Date	Opponent	Score	Scorers	Att	Allum A	Andrews CJ	Angell PF	Cameron R	Colgan W	Dawson A	Drinkwater R	Finney CW	Fry RP	Ingham A	Kerrins PM	Locke LC	Longbottom A	Orr DM	Peacock T	Petchey GW	Powell MP	Rutter KG	Smith EWA	Springett RDG	Standley TL	Tomkys MG	Woods PJ
R1	Nov	16	Clapton	1-1	Dawson	8000			6			9				3	11	10	8			7		4	5	1			2
rep		18	CLAPTON	3-1	Longbottom, Locke, Walsh(og)	12786			6			9				3	11	10	8			7		4	5	1			2
R2	Dec	7	Hereford United	1-6	E Smith	14000		6				9				3	11		8			7		4	5	1	10		2

Southern Professional Floodlight Cup

		Date	Opponent	Score	Scorers	Att	Allum A	Andrews CJ	Angell PF	Cameron R	Colgan W	Dawson A	Drinkwater R	Finney CW	Fry RP	Ingham A	Kerrins PM	Locke LC	Longbottom A	Orr DM	Peacock T	Petchey GW	Powell MP	Rutter KG	Smith EWA	Springett RDG	Standley TL	Tomkys MG	Woods PJ
R1	Oct	4	READING	0-0				9	6	8						3	11					7		4	5	1	10		2
rep	Nov	6	Reading	2-5	Kerrins, Locke				6				1			3	11	10	8			7		4	5		9		2

Division 3 (South) Final Table

		P	W	D	L	F	A	W	D	L	F	A	Pts
1	Brighton & Hove A.	46	13	6	4	52	30	11	6	6	36	34	60
2	Brentford	46	15	5	3	52	24	9	5	9	30	32	58
3	Plymouth Argyle	46	17	4	2	43	17	8	4	11	24	31	58
4	Swindon Town	46	14	7	2	47	16	7	8	8	32	34	57
5	Reading	46	14	5	4	52	23	7	8	8	27	28	55
6	Southampton	46	16	3	4	78	31	6	7	10	34	41	54
7	Southend United	46	14	5	4	56	26	7	7	9	34	32	54
8	Norwich City	46	11	9	3	41	28	8	6	9	34	42	53
9	Bournemouth	46	16	5	2	54	24	5	4	14	27	50	51
10	QUEEN'S PARK RGS.	46	15	6	2	40	14	3	8	12	24	51	51
11	Newport County	46	12	6	5	40	24	5	8	10	33	43	48
12	Colchester United	46	13	5	5	45	27	4	8	11	32	52	47
13	Northampton Town	46	13	1	9	60	33	6	5	12	27	46	44
14	Crystal Palace	46	12	5	6	46	30	3	8	12	24	42	43
15	Port Vale	46	12	6	5	49	24	4	4	15	18	34	42
16	Watford	46	9	8	6	34	27	4	8	11	25	50	42
17	Shrewsbury Town	46	10	6	7	29	25	5	4	14	20	46	40
18	Aldershot	46	7	9	7	31	34	5	7	11	28	55	40
19	Coventry City	46	10	9	4	41	24	3	4	16	20	57	39
20	Walsall	46	10	7	6	37	24	4	2	17	24	51	37
21	Torquay United	46	9	7	7	33	34	2	6	15	16	40	35
22	Gillingham	46	12	5	6	33	24	1	4	18	19	57	35
23	Millwall	46	6	6	11	37	36	5	3	15	26	55	31
24	Exeter City	46	10	4	9	37	35	1	5	17	20	64	31

1958/59   13th in Division 3

Player columns (in order): Anderson TC · Angell PF · Cameron R · Clark C · Colgan W · Dawson A · Drinkwater R · Ingham A · Kelly WB · Kerrins PM · Locke LC · Longbottom A · Pearson JA · Petchey GW · Powell MP · Richardson S · Rutter KG · Tomkys MG · Welton RP · Whitelaw G · Woods PJ

#	Date	Opponent	Score	Scorers	Att	And	Ang	Cam	Clk	Col	Daw	Dri	Ing	Kel	Ker	Loc	Lon	Pea	Pet	Pow	Ric	Rut	Tom	Wel	Whi	Woo
1	Aug 23	Reading	2-2	Longbottom 2	16961		6	10			7	1	3		9	11	8		4			5				2
2	25	TRANMERE ROVERS	1-1	Cameron	12393		6	10			7	1	3		9	11	8		4			5				2
3	30	COLCHESTER UNITED	4-2	Kerrins 2, Longbottom, Locke	9852		6	10			7	1	3		9	11	8		4			5				2
4	Sep 1	Tranmere Rovers	0-2		13959		6	10			7	1	3		9		8	11	4			5				2
5	6	Bournemouth	0-2		11890		6	10		11	7	1	3		9		8		4			5				2
6	9	Doncaster Rovers	0-2		10725		6	10			7	1	3		9	11	8		4			5				2
7	13	NORWICH CITY	2-1	Longbottom, Kerrins	10498		6	10				1	3		9	11	8		4			5	7			2
8	15	DONCASTER ROVERS	3-1	Longbottom, Cameron, Kerrins	10118		6	10			7	1	3		9	11	8		4			5				2
9	20	Southend United	0-4		13534		6	10			7	1	3		9	11	8		4			5				2
10	22	Stockport County	3-2	Longbottom 3	12182		6	10			7	1	3		9		8		4			5	11			2
11	27	BURY	2-1	Tomkys 2	9796		6				7	1	3		9	10	8		4			5	11			2
12	29	STOCKPORT COUNTY	0-0		7458		6	10			7	1	3		9	11	8		4			5				2
13	Oct 4	Mansfield Town	4-3	Longbottom, Dawson, Cameron, Angell	10033		6	10			7	1	3		9	11	8		4			5				2
14	7	Rochdale	2-2	Cameron, Tomkys	4276		6	10			7	1	3		9		8		4			5	11			2
15	11	CHESTERFIELD	2-2	Kerrins, Tomkys	9452		6	10			7	1	3		9		8		4			5	11			2
16	20	Newport County	1-3	Cameron	8400		6	10			7	1	3		9		8		4			5	11			2
17	25	HALIFAX TOWN	3-1	Longbottom 3	9607		6	10			7	1	3		9		8		4			5	11			2
18	Nov 1	Accrington Stanley	4-2	Dawson 2, Tomkys, Longbottom	6498		6	10			7	1	3		9		8		4			5	11			2
19	8	SOUTHAMPTON	2-2	Longbottom, Petchey	11287		6	10			7	1	3		9		8		4			5	11			2
20	22	BRENTFORD	1-2	Kerrins	13784		6	10			7	1	3		9		8		4			5	11			2
21	29	Hull City	0-1		11705	7	6	10				1	3		9		8		4			5	11			2
22	Dec 13	Swindon Town	0-2		8037		6	10				1	3	9	11		8		4			5	7			2
23	20	READING	2-0	Kerrins, Pearson	6909		6					1	3	9	11		8	10	4			5	7			2
24	26	Plymouth Argyle	2-3	Angell, Tomkys	30665		6					1	3	9	11		8	10	4			5	7			2
25	27	PLYMOUTH ARGYLE	2-1	Pearson, Longbottom	15768		6					1	3	9	11		8	10	4			5	7			2
26	Jan 3	Colchester United	0-3		8719							1	3	9	11		8	10	4		6	5	7			2
27	17	BOURNEMOUTH	0-4		6041		6					1	3	9	11		8	10	4			5	7			2
28	31	Norwich City	1-5	Longbottom	16781		6	9	11			1	3		7	10	8		4			5				2
29	Feb 7	SOUTHEND UNITED	1-3	Petchey	6361		6		11		7		3		9		8	10	4			5		1		2
30	14	Bury	1-3	Clarke	5072		6		11		7		3			10	8		4	9		5		1		2
31	21	MANSFIELD TOWN	1-1	Locke	5007		6		11		7		3			10	8		4	9		5		1		2
32	28	Chesterfield	3-2	Locke 2, Tomkys	8711		6		11		7	1	3			10	8		4			5	9			2
33	Mar 7	NEWPORT COUNTY	4-2	Longbottom 2, Locke, Angell	5707		6		11		7	1	3			10	8		4			5	9			2
34	14	Halifax Town	1-2	Locke	5586		6		11		7	1	3			10	8		4			5	9			2
35	16	BRADFORD CITY	3-0	Pearson 2, Whitelaw	7578	7	6		11			1	3				8	10	4			5			9	2
36	21	ACCRINGTON STANLEY	3-1	Anderson, Pearson, Tigue (og)	8005	7	6		11			1	3				8	10	4			5			9	2
37	27	NOTTS COUNTY	2-1	Whitelaw, Pearson	12044	7	6		11			1	3				8	10	4			5			9	2
38	28	Southampton	0-1		9808		6		11			1	3			10	8		4			5	7		9	2
39	30	Notts County	1-0	Angell	6956	7	6				2	1	3			11	8	10	4			5			9	
40	Apr 4	WREXHAM	5-0	Anderson 2, Whitelaw, Angell, Longbottom	8670	7	6		11			1	3			10	8		4			5			9	2
41	8	Wrexham	0-1		5738	7	6		11			1	3			10	8		4			5			9	2
42	11	Brentford	0-1		15905	7	6		11			1	3			10	8		4			5			9	2
43	18	HULL CITY	1-1	Whitelaw	9325	7	6		11			1	3			10	8		4			5			9	2
44	20	ROCHDALE	3-0	Angell, Longbottom, Whitelaw	7280	7	6		11			1	3			10	8		4			5			9	2
45	25	Bradford City	0-1		6895		6		11			1	3			10	8		4	9		5	7			2
46	27	SWINDON TOWN	2-1	Angell, Tomkys	7628		6		11			1	3			10	8		4	9		5	7			2
		Apps				10	45	22	19	1	25	43	46	6	29	25	41	16	46	4	1	44	25	3	11	44
		Goals				3	7	5	1		3				7	6	20	6	2				8		5	

One own goal

F.A. Cup

	Date	Opponent	Score	Scorers	Att	And	Ang	Cam	Daw	Dri	Ing	Ker	Lon	Pet	Rut	Tom	Woo
R1	Nov 15	Walsall	1-0	Dawson	15123		6	10	7	1	3	9	8	4	5	11	2
R2	Dec 6	SOUTHAMPTON	0-1		13166		6	10	7	1	3	11	8	4	5	9	2

Southern Professional Floodlight Cup

	Date	Opponent	Score	Att	Ang	Cam	Daw	Dri	Ing	Ker	Lon	Pet	Rut	Tom	Woo
R1	Oct 13	FULHAM	0-4	8497	6	10	7	1	3	9	8	4	5	11	2

		P	W	D	L	F	A	W	D	L	F	A	Pts
1	Plymouth Argyle	46	14	7	2	55	27	9	9	5	34	32	62
2	Hull City	46	19	3	1	65	21	7	6	10	25	34	61
3	Brentford	46	15	5	3	49	22	6	10	7	27	27	57
4	Norwich City	46	13	6	4	51	29	9	7	7	38	33	57
5	Colchester United	46	15	2	6	46	31	6	8	9	25	36	52
6	Reading	46	16	4	3	51	21	5	4	14	27	42	50
7	Tranmere Rovers	46	15	3	5	53	22	6	5	12	29	45	50
8	Southend United	46	14	6	3	52	26	7	2	14	33	54	50
9	Halifax Town	46	14	5	4	48	25	7	3	13	32	52	50
10	Bury	46	12	9	2	51	24	5	5	13	18	34	48
11	Bradford City	46	13	4	6	47	25	5	7	11	37	51	47
12	Bournemouth	46	12	9	2	40	18	5	3	15	29	51	46
13	QUEEN'S PARK RGS.	46	14	6	3	49	28	5	2	16	25	49	46
14	Southampton	46	12	7	4	57	33	5	4	14	31	47	45
15	Swindon Town	46	13	4	6	39	25	3	9	11	20	32	45
16	Chesterfield	46	12	5	6	40	26	5	5	13	27	38	44
17	Newport County	46	15	2	6	43	24	2	7	14	26	44	43
18	Wrexham	46	12	6	5	40	30	2	8	13	23	47	42
19	Accrington Stanley	46	10	8	5	42	31	5	4	14	29	56	42
20	Mansfield Town	46	11	5	7	38	42	3	8	12	35	56	41
21	Stockport County	46	9	7	7	33	23	4	3	16	32	55	36
22	Doncaster Rovers	46	13	2	8	40	32	1	3	19	10	58	33
23	Notts County	46	5	9	9	33	39	3	4	16	22	57	29
24	Rochdale	46	8	7	8	21	26	0	5	18	16	53	28

#			Opponent	Score	Scorers	Att	Andrews JP	Angell PF	Bedford NB	Cini J	Clark C	Collins JW	Drinkwater R	Golding NJ	Hasty PJ	Ingham A	Keen MT	Kerrins PM	Locke LC	Longbottom A	Pearson JA	Petchey GW	Pinner MJ	Rutter KG	Whitelaw G	Whitfield K	Woods PJ
1	Aug	22	SWINDON TOWN	2-0	Longbottom, Whitelaw	12206	11	6	10	7						3				8		4	1	5	9		2
2		24	Southend United	2-3	Whitelaw 2	12197	11	6	10	7						3				8		4	1	5	9		2
3		29	Chesterfield	4-0	Pearson 2, Bedford, Whitelaw	8890	11	6	8							3				7	10	4	1	5	9		2
4		31	SOUTHEND UNITED	0-0		13488	10	6	8		11					3				7		4	1	5	9		2
5	Sep	5	NEWPORT COUNTY	3-0	Bedford 2, Longbottom	10774	11	6	8							3				7	10	4	1	5	9		2
6		7	York City	1-2	Pearson	10593	11		8							3	6			7	10	4	1	5	9		2
7		12	Accrington Stanley	2-1	Andrews, Longbottom	5336	11	6	8							3				7	10	4	1	5	9		2
8		14	YORK CITY	0-0		11857	11	6	8					7		3					10	4	1	5	9		2
9		19	BOURNEMOUTH	3-0	Bedford, Golding, Nelson(og)	11410	11	6	10					7		3				8		4	1	5	9		2
10		21	Coventry City	0-0		16759	11	6	10					7		3				8		4	1	5	9		2
11		26	Tranmere Rovers	3-0	Golding 2, Bedford	11252	11	6	9				1	7		3				8		4		5		10	2
12		28	COVENTRY CITY	2-1	Golding 2	16154	11	6	9				1	7		3				8		4		5		10	2
13	Oct	3	WREXHAM	2-1	Angell 2	12732	11	6	9				1	7		3				8		4		5		10	2
14		5	GRIMSBY TOWN	0-0		15257	11	6					1	7		3	10			8		4		5	9		2
15		10	Mansfield Town	3-4	Locke 2, Petchey	7526	11	6					1	7		3	10		9	8		4		5			2
16		13	Grimsby Town	1-3	Angell	6024	11	6								3	10	7	8			4	1	5	9		2
17		17	HALIFAX TOWN	3-0	Longbottom, Whitelaw, Petchey	13787	11	6	10					7		3				8		4	1	5	9		2
18		24	Bury	0-2		10079	11	6	10					7		3				8		4	1	5	9		2
19		31	BRENTFORD	2-4	Bedford 2	19532	11	6	10					7		3				8		4	1	5	9		2
20	Nov	7	Southampton	1-2		18619	11	6	10				1	7		3	9			8		4		5			2
21		21	Shrewsbury Town	1-1	Bedford	10084	11	6	10				1	7		3	4			8		9		5			2
22		28	PORT VALE	2-2	Bedford 2	8775	11	6	10		7					3	4			8		9	1	5			2
23	Dec	12	Barnsley	1-2	Bedford	4450	11	6	10		7					3	4			8		9	1	5			2
24		19	Swindon Town	1-2	Andrews	5798	11		9		7		1			3	6			8		4		5		10	2
25		26	COLCHESTER UNITED	3-1	Bedford 2, Angell	6480	10	6	9		7					3			11	8		4	1	5			2
26		28	Colchester United	0-2		9095	10	6	9		7					3			11	8		4	1	5			2
27	Jan	16	Newport County	3-2	Bedford 3	4194	10		9				1			3	4	7	11	8		6		5			2
28		23	ACCRINGTON STANLEY	5-1	Andrews 2, Kerrins, Locke, Bedford	4721	10		9				1			3	4	7	11	8		6		5			2
29		30	Norwich City	0-1		17053	10		9				1			3	4	7	11	8		6		5			2
30	Feb	6	Bournemouth	1-1	Bedford	9855	10		9				1			3	4	7	11	8		6		5			2
31		13	TRANMERE ROVERS	2-1	Andrews, Keen	5019	10		9		11		1			3	4	7		8		6		5			2
32		27	MANSFIELD TOWN	2-0	Woods (p), Longbottom	7834	10	6	9		11		1			3	4	7		8				5			2
33	Mar	5	Halifax Town	1-3	Woods (p)	6731	11	10	9				1	7		3	4			8		6		5			2
34		7	READING	2-0	Andrews, Bedford	6715	10	6	9	8	11		1			3	4		7					5			2
35		12	BURY	2-0	Cini, Andrews	9088	10	6	9	8	11		1			3	4		7					5			2
36		19	Port Vale	0-0		7049	10	6	8	7	11		1			3	4		9					5			2
37		26	SOUTHAMPTON	0-1		11734	10	6	9		11		1			3	4		7	8				5			2
38		28	CHESTERFIELD	3-3	Bedford 2, Petchey	4346	10	6	8		11		1			3	4		7			9		5			2
39	Apr	2	Reading	0-2		8975	10	6	9		11		1	7		3	4			8				5			2
40		9	SHREWSBURY TOWN	1-1	Bedford	6831	10	6	9		11		1	7		3				8		4		5			2
41		15	BRADFORD CITY	5-0	Bedford 2, Longbottom, Petchey, Andrews	6798	10		9		11		1	7		3	4			8		6		5			2
42		16	Brentford	1-1	Golding	16025	10		9		11		1	7		3	4			8		6		5			2
43		18	Bradford City	1-3	Andrews	6265	10		9		11		1	7		3	4			8		6		5			2
44		23	NORWICH CITY	0-0		15319	10		9		11		1	7		3	4			8		6		5			2
45		30	BARNSLEY	1-0	Andrews	5700	10		9		11	8	1	7		3	4					6		5			2
46	May	4	Wrexham	1-1	Woods	2819	10		9			8	1	7	11	3	4					6		5			2
			Apps				46	33	44	7	18	2	27	22	1	46	27	7	10	37	5	41	19	46	15	7	46
			Goals				10	4	25	1				6			1	1	3	6	3	4			5		3

One own goal

F.A. Cup

R			Opponent	Score	Scorers	Att	Andrews JP	Angell PF	Bedford NB	Cini J	Clark C	Collins JW	Drinkwater R	Golding NJ	Hasty PJ	Ingham A	Keen MT	Kerrins PM	Locke LC	Longbottom A	Pearson JA	Petchey GW	Pinner MJ	Rutter KG	Whitelaw G	Whitfield K	Woods PJ
R1	Nov	14	Colchester United	3-2	Petchey, Bedford, Angell	8866	11	6	10					7		3	4			8		9	1	5			2
R2	Dec	5	PORT VALE	3-3	Longbottom 2, Bedford	11143	11	6	9		7					3	4			8			1	5		10	2
rep		7	Port Vale	1-2	Andrews	9513	11	6	9		7		1			3	4			8				5		10	2

Southern Professional Floodlight Cup

R			Opponent	Score	Scorers	Att	Andrews JP	Angell PF	Bedford NB	Cini J	Clark C	Collins JW	Drinkwater R	Golding NJ	Hasty PJ	Ingham A	Keen MT	Kerrins PM	Locke LC	Longbottom A	Pearson JA	Petchey GW	Pinner MJ	Rutter KG	Whitelaw G	Whitfield K	Woods PJ
R1	Oct	26	LEYTON ORIENT	1-2	Longbottom	5758	11	6	10					7		3				8		4	1	5	9		2

		P	W	D	L	F	A	W	D	L	F	A	Pts
1	Southampton	46	19	3	1	68	30	7	6	10	38	45	61
2	Norwich City	46	16	4	3	53	24	8	7	8	29	30	59
3	Shrewsbury Town	46	12	7	4	58	34	6	9	8	39	41	52
4	Grimsby Town	46	12	7	4	48	27	6	9	8	39	43	52
5	Coventry City	46	14	6	3	44	22	7	4	12	34	41	52
6	Brentford	46	13	6	4	46	24	8	3	12	32	37	51
7	Bury	46	13	4	6	36	23	8	5	10	28	28	51
8	QUEEN'S PARK RGS.	46	14	7	2	45	16	4	6	13	28	38	49
9	Colchester United	46	15	6	2	51	22	3	5	15	32	52	47
10	Bournemouth	46	12	8	3	47	27	5	5	13	25	45	47
11	Reading	46	13	3	7	49	34	5	7	11	35	43	46
12	Southend United	46	15	3	5	49	28	4	5	14	27	46	46
13	Newport County	46	15	2	6	59	36	4	4	14	21	43	46
14	Port Vale	46	16	4	3	51	19	3	4	16	29	60	46
15	Halifax Town	46	13	3	7	42	27	5	7	11	28	45	46
16	Swindon Town	46	12	6	5	39	30	7	2	14	30	48	46
17	Barnsley	46	13	6	4	45	25	2	8	13	20	41	44
18	Chesterfield	46	13	3	7	41	31	5	4	14	30	53	43
19	Bradford City	46	10	7	6	39	28	5	5	13	27	46	42
20	Tranmere Rovers	46	11	8	4	50	29	3	5	15	22	46	41
21	York City	46	11	5	7	38	26	2	7	14	19	47	38
22	Mansfield Town	46	11	4	8	55	48	4	2	17	26	64	36
23	Wrexham	46	12	5	6	39	30	2	3	18	29	71	36
24	Accrington Stanley	46	4	5	14	31	53	7	0	16	26	70	27

1960/61   3rd in Division 3

#	Date	Opponent	Score	Scorers	Att	Andrews JP	Angell PF	Baker PR	Barber MJ	Bedford NB	Bottoms MC	Carey PR	Clark C	Cockell DJ	Drinkwater R	Evans B	Golding NJ	Ingham A	Keen MT	Lazarus M	Longbottom A	Rutter KG	Whitaker C	Whitfield K	Woods PJ
1	Aug 20	Bournemouth	0-1		12222	10	6			9		2	11		1		7	3	4		8	5			
2	25	Notts County	1-2	Andrews	15174	10	6			9		2	11		1		7	3	4		8	5			
3	27	BRADFORD CITY	1-0	Bedford	7075		6			10		4	11		1		7	3			8	5		9	2
4	29	NOTTS COUNTY	2-0	Clark 2	8385	10	6			9		4	11		1		7	3			8	5			2
5	Sep 3	Barnsley	3-3	Whitfield 2, Bedford	6162	10	6			8		4	11		1		7	3				5		9	2
6	5	Coventry City	4-4	Bedford 2, Andrews, Clark	15804	10	6		7	8		4	11		1			3				5		9	2
7	10	NEWPORT COUNTY	2-0	Whitfield, Barber	7353	10	6		7	8		4	11		1			3				5		9	2
8	12	COVENTRY CITY	2-1	Bedford, Woods	9199	10	6		7	8		4	11		1			3				5		9	2
9	17	Colchester United	1-0	Lazarus	5750	10	6			8		4	11		1			3		7		5		9	2
10	19	BRENTFORD	0-0		12823	11	6			8		4			1			3		7	10	5		9	2
11	24	GRIMSBY TOWN	2-0	Andrews, Longbottom	11042	10	6					4	11		1			3		7	8	5		9	2
12	27	Brentford	0-2		15282	10	6					4	11		1			3		7	8	5		9	2
13	Oct 1	Hull City	1-3	Bedford	9333	10	6			8		4	11		1		7	3				5		9	2
14	3	READING	5-2	Bedford 2, Lazarus 2, Barber	8426	10	6		7	9			11		1			3	4	8		5			2
15	8	TORQUAY UNITED	3-3	Lazarus 2, Bedford	7901	10	6		7	9			11		1			3	4	8		5			2
16	15	Port Vale	1-0	Bedford	8802		6		7	9	10		11		1			3	4	8		5			2
17	22	SOUTHEND UNITED	2-1	Woods, Bedford	6122		6		7	9			11		1			3	4	8	10	5			2
18	29	Chesterfield	1-0	Carey	4474		6		11	10		8			1			3	4	7		5		9	2
19	Nov 12	Walsall	3-4	Bedford 2, Lazarus	10044		6			10		8			1			3	4	7	11	5		9	2
20	19	SHREWSBURY TOWN	1-1	Bedford	7680		6			10					1			3	4	7	11	5			2
21	Dec 3	TRANMERE ROVERS	9-2	*see below	4921	10	6			8			11		1	9		3	4	7		5			2
22	10	Watford	3-0	Lazarus, Woods, Clark	15546	10	6			8			11		1	9		3	4	7		5			2
23	17	BOURNEMOUTH	3-1	Bedford 2, Evans	6952	10	6			8			11		1	9		3	4	7		5			2
24	26	Bristol City	1-1	Bedford	10794	10	6			8					1	9		3	4	7	11	5			2
25	27	BRISTOL CITY	1-1	Woods	15391	10	6			8			11		1	9		3	4	7		5			2
26	31	Bradford City	1-1	Evans	8405	10	6			8			11	4	1	9		3		7		5			2
27	Jan 14	BARNSLEY	4-2	Bedford, Andrews, Evans, Keen	8859	11	6			8				4	1	9		3	10	7		5			2
28	23	Newport County	3-1	Evans 2, Bedford	6610	11	6			8				4	1	9		3	10	7		5			2
29	28	BURY	3-1	Bedford 3	14672	11	6			8				4	1	9		3	10		7	5			2
30	Feb 4	COLCHESTER UNITED	3-2	Evans, Bedford, Lazarus	10348	11	6			8				4	1	9		3	10	7		5			2
31	11	Grimsby Town	1-3	Bedford	10599		6		7	8	10				1	9		3	4		11	5			2
32	18	HULL CITY	2-1	Keen, Bedford	12210		6			8					1	9		3	4	7	10	5	11		2
33	25	Tranmere Rovers	2-1	Evans, Woods	9226		6			8					1	9	7	3	4		10	5	11		2
34	Mar 4	PORT VALE	1-0	Evans	12711		6	2		8					1	9	7	3	4		10	5	11		
35	11	Southend United	0-0		10987		6	2		8					1	9		3	4	7	10	5	11		
36	18	CHESTERFIELD	1-2	Bedford	8858	10	6	2		8					1	9		3	4	7		5	11		
37	25	Bury	0-1		14701		6	2		8				4	1	9		3	10		7	5			
38	31	SWINDON TOWN	3-1	Angell, Barber, Evans	14436	10	11	2	7	8				6	1	9		3	4			5			
39	Apr 1	WALSALL	1-0	Longbottom	14288	10	6	2		8					1	9		3	4		7	5	11		
40	3	Swindon Town	0-1		11568	10	6	2		8					1	9		3	4		7	5	11		
41	8	Shrewsbury Town	1-4	Evans	8386		6	2		8					1	9		3	4	7	11	5		10	
42	15	HALIFAX TOWN	5-1	Bedford 4, Lazarus	9069	11	6	2		10					1	9		3	4	7	8	5			
43	17	Halifax Town	1-1	Andrews	4194	11	6	2		10					1	9		3	4	7	8	5			
44	22	Torquay United	6-1	Evans 3, Lazarus, Bedford, Bettany(og)	5436	11	6	2		10					1	9		3	4	7	8	5			
45	26	Reading	1-3	Longbottom	15058		6	2	11	10					1	9		3	4	7	8	5			
46	29	WATFORD	2-1	Evans, Longbottom	10328		6	2	11	10					1	9		3	4	7	8	5			

Scorers in game 21: Bedford 2, Clark 2, Lazarus 2, Evans 2, Andrews

						Andrews JP	Angell PF	Baker PR	Barber MJ	Bedford NB	Bottoms MC	Carey PR	Clark C	Cockell DJ	Drinkwater R	Evans B	Golding NJ	Ingham A	Keen MT	Lazarus M	Longbottom A	Rutter KG	Whitaker C	Whitfield K	Woods PJ
Apps						32	46	13	12	44	2	15	21	8	46	27	8	46	34	29	26	46	8	12	31
Goals						6	1		3	33		1	6			16			2	12	4			3	5

One own goal

F.A. Cup

	Date	Opponent	Score	Scorers	Att	Andrews JP	Angell PF	Baker PR	Barber MJ	Bedford NB	Bottoms MC	Carey PR	Clark C	Cockell DJ	Drinkwater R	Evans B	Golding NJ	Ingham A	Keen MT	Lazarus M	Longbottom A	Rutter KG	Whitaker C	Whitfield K	Woods PJ
R1	Nov 5	WALTHAMSTOW AVE.	3-2	Bedford 3	5373	11	6			10		8			1			3	4	7		5		9	2
R2	26	COVENTRY CITY	1-2	Longbottom	8927					10			11	6	1			3	4	7	8	5		9	2

F.L. Cup

	Date	Opponent	Score	Scorers	Att	Andrews JP	Angell PF	Baker PR	Barber MJ	Bedford NB	Bottoms MC	Carey PR	Clark C	Cockell DJ	Drinkwater R	Evans B	Golding NJ	Ingham A	Keen MT	Lazarus M	Longbottom A	Rutter KG	Whitaker C	Whitfield K	Woods PJ
R1	Oct 17	PORT VALE	2-2	Lazarus, Rutter	6600				7	9	10	4	11	6				3		8		5			2
rep	19	port Vale	1-3	Bedford		10	6		7	9			11		1			3	4	8		5			2

Played in first game: MJ Pinner (at 1).

		P	W	D	L	F	A	W	D	L	F	A	Pts
1	Bury	46	18	3	2	62	17	12	5	6	46	28	68
2	Walsall	46	19	4	0	62	20	9	2	12	36	40	62
3	QUEEN'S PARK RGS.	46	18	4	1	58	23	7	6	10	35	37	60
4	Watford	46	12	7	4	52	27	8	5	10	33	45	52
5	Notts County	46	16	3	4	52	24	5	6	12	30	53	51
6	Grimsby Town	46	14	4	5	48	32	6	6	11	29	37	50
7	Port Vale	46	13	5	5	63	30	2	12	9	33	49	49
8	Barnsley	46	15	5	3	56	30	6	2	15	27	50	49
9	Halifax Town	46	14	7	2	42	22	2	10	11	29	56	49
10	Shrewsbury Town	46	13	7	3	54	26	2	9	12	29	49	46
11	Hull City	46	13	6	4	51	28	4	6	13	22	45	46
12	Torquay United	46	8	12	3	37	26	6	5	12	38	57	45
13	Newport County	46	12	7	4	51	30	5	4	14	30	60	45
14	Bristol City	46	15	4	4	50	19	2	6	15	20	49	44
15	Coventry City	46	14	6	3	54	25	2	6	15	26	58	44
16	Swindon Town	46	13	6	4	41	16	1	9	13	21	39	43
17	Brentford	46	10	9	4	41	28	3	8	12	15	42	43
18	Reading	46	13	5	5	48	29	1	7	15	24	54	40
19	Bournemouth	46	8	7	8	34	39	7	3	13	24	37	40
20	Southend United	46	10	8	5	38	26	4	3	16	22	50	39
21	Tranmere Rovers	46	11	5	7	53	50	4	3	16	26	65	38
22	Bradford City	46	8	8	7	37	36	3	6	14	28	51	36
23	Colchester United	46	8	5	10	40	44	3	6	14	28	57	33
24	Chesterfield	46	9	6	6	42	29	1	6	16	25	58	32

1961/62 4th in Division 3

No	Date		Opponent	Result	Scorers	Att	Anderton SJ	Andrews JP	Angell PF	Baker PR	Barber MJ	Bedford NB	Bentley RTF	Cockell DJ	Collins JW	Drinkwater R	Evans B	Francis GE	Ingham A	Keen MT	Lazarus M	McCelland JB	Rutter KG	Slack RG	Towers EJ	Williams WT
1	Aug	19	BRENTFORD	3-0	Towers, Bedford, Evans	16796			6	2	11	8	5			1	9		3	4	7				10	
2		21	READING	3-6	Lazarus 2, Angell	12847		11	6	2		8	5			1	9		3	4	7				10	
3		26	Barnsley	4-2	Bedford, Angell(p), Towers, Evans	7668		11	6			8	2			1	9		3	4	7		5		10	
4		30	Reading	2-0	Towers 2	20003		11	6			8	2			1	9		3	4	7		5		10	
5	Sep	2	PORTSMOUTH	0-1		13010		11	6			8	2			1	9		3	4	7		5		10	
6		4	SWINDON TOWN	6-1	Lazarus 2, Towers 2, Barber, Evans	10255			6		11	8	2			1	9		3	4	7		5		10	
7		9	Crystal Palace	2-2	Lazarus 2	27179			6		11	8	2			1	9		3	4	7		5		10	
8		16	BOURNEMOUTH	1-1	Lazarus	13088			6	2	11	8				1		9		4	7		5		10	3
9		23	Watford	2-3	Towers, McCelland	15555			6	2	11	8				1	9		3	4		7	5		10	
10		25	HALIFAX TOWN	6-2	Bedford 3, Evans 2, McCelland	11907			6	2	11	8				1	9		3	4		7	5		10	
11		30	HULL CITY	1-1	Francis	10076			6	2	11	8				1		9	3	4		7	5		10	
12	Oct	7	Newport County	4-2	McCelland, Bedford, Barber, Evans	5440			6	2	11	8				1	9		3	4		7	5		10	
13		9	LINCOLN CITY	1-3	Evans	10151			6	2	11	8				1	9		3	4		7	5		10	
14		14	SOUTHEND UNITED	5-3	Bedford 4, Angell	10665			6		11	8	2		10	1	9		3	4		7	5			
15		17	Swindon Town	0-0		11320			6		11	8	2		10	1	9			4		7	5			3
16		21	Grimsby Town	1-1	Collins	6630			6		11	8	2		10	1	9			4		7	5			3
17		28	COVENTRY CITY	4-1	Barber 2, Bedford, Evans	10008			6		11	8	2		10	1	9			4		7	5			3
18	Nov	11	PORT VALE	2-1	Bedford, Angell (p)	7087			6			8	2		10	1	9			4		7	5		11	3
19		18	Bristol City	0-2		10892			6		11	8	2		10	1	9			4		7	5			3
20	Dec	2	Notts County	0-0		7980			6			8	2		10	1	9		3	4		7	5		11	
21		9	SHREWSBURY TOWN	3-1	Bedford 3	7433			6		11	8	2			1	9		3	4		7	5		10	
22		16	Brentford	4-1	Bedford 2, McCelland, Reeves(og)	11771			6		11	8	2			1	9		3	4		7	5		10	
23		26	Torquay United	2-2	McCelland, Keen	4574			6		11	8	2			1	9		3	4		7	5		10	
24		30	TORQUAY UNITED	6-0	Evans 3, Towers 2, Collins	9193			6		11		2		8	1	9		3	4		7	5		10	
25	Jan	13	Portsmouth	1-4	Towers	17727			6		11	8	2			1	9		3	4		7	5		10	
26		20	CRYSTAL PALACE	1-0	Evans	18003	6					8	2		11	1	9		3	4		7	5		10	
27	Feb	3	Bournemouth	1-3	Towers	11645	6				11		2		10	1	9		3	4		7	5		8	
28		10	WATFORD	1-2	McCelland	11288	6				11		2		10	1	9		3	4		7	5		8	
29		16	Hull City	1-3	Bedford	3237	6				11	8			10	1	9		3	4		7	5			2
30		19	Peterborough United	1-5	Collins	11922					11	8		6	10	1	9		3	4		7	5			2
31		24	NEWPORT COUNTY	4-0	Bedford, McCelland, Lazarus 2	7813			6			8			10	1	9		3	4	11	7	5			2
32	Mar	3	Southend United	3-2	Bedford, Collins, Shields(og)	8298			6			8			10	1	9		3	4	11	7	5			2
33		10	GRIMSBY TOWN	3-2	Bedford 2, Angell	8490			6			8			10	1	9		3	4	11	7	5			2
34		16	Coventry City	3-2	Bedford	8629			6			8			10	1	9		3	4	11	7	5			2
35		19	BARNSLEY	3-0	Keen, Bedford, Evans	10310			6			8			10	1	9		3	4	11	7	5			2
36		24	PETERBOROUGH UTD.	3-3	Evans, McCelland, Bedford	13430			6			8			10	1	9		3	4	11	7	5			2
37		31	Port Vale	3-2	Collins, Bedford, Angell	4936			6			8			10	1	9		3	4	11	7	5			2
38	Apr	7	BRISTOL CITY	4-1	Evans 2, Bedford 2	11482			6			8			10	1	9		3	4	11	7	5			2
39		11	BRADFORD PARK AVE.	1-2	Lazarus	11462			6			8			10	1	9		3	4	11	7	5			2
40		14	Bradford Park Avenue	3-3	Bedford 3	8744			6			8	2			1	9		3	4	11	7	5		10	
41		21	NOTTS COUNTY	2-0	Bedford, McCelland	10043			6			8	2			1	9		3	4	11	7	5		10	
42		23	NORTHAMPTON T	2-0	Evans, Towers	10953			6			8	2			1	9		3	4	11	7	5		10	
43		24	Northampton Town	1-1	McCelland	12533						8	2		10	1	9		3	4	11	7	5			6
44		28	Shrewsbury Town	2-1	Towers, McCelland	5823						8	2			1	9		3	4	11	7	5		10	6
45		30	Lincoln City	5-0	Lazarus 2, Towers 2, Collins	6815			6			8	2		10	1			3	4	11	7	5		9	
46	May	3	Halifax Town	1-1	Evans	2316			6			8	2		10		9		3	4	11	7	5	1		
			Apps				4	4	39	8	23	43	29	1	25	45	43	2	40	46	24	38	43	1	28	20
			Goals						6		4	34			6		18	1		2	12	11			15	

Two own goals

F.A. Cup

	Date		Opponent	Result	Scorers	Att	Angell PF	Barber MJ	Bedford NB	Bentley RTF	Collins JW	Drinkwater R	Evans B	Ingham A	Keen MT	McCelland JB	Rutter KG	Towers EJ	Williams WT
R1	Nov	4	Barry Town	1-1	McLellan(og)	5500	6		8	2	10	1	9		4	7	5	11	3
rep		6	BARRY TOWN	7-0	Bedford 3, Collins 2, Evans 2	11328	6	11	8	2	10	1	9		4	7	5		3
R2		25	Ashford Town	3-0	Collins, McCelland, Evans	5000	6		8	2	10	1	9	3	4	7	5	11	
R3	Jan	6	Burnley	1-6	Evans	28352	6		8	2	11	1	9	3	4	7	5	10	

F.L. Cup

	Date		Opponent	Result	Scorers	Att	Angell PF	Baker PR	Barber MJ	Bedford NB	Bentley RTF	Cockell DJ	Drinkwater R	Evans B	Francis GE	Ingham A	Keen MT	Lazarus M	Rutter KG	Towers EJ
R1	Sep	13	CRYSTAL PALACE	5-2	Bedford 2, Francis 2, Angell	10565	6	2	11	8			1		9	3	4	7	5	10
R2	Oct	11	NOTTM FOREST	1-2	Towers	11198	6		11	8	2	7	1	9		3	4		5	10

		P	W	D	L	F	A	W	D	L	F	A	Pts
1	Portsmouth	46	15	6	2	48	23	12	5	6	39	24	65
2	Grimsby Town	46	18	3	2	49	18	10	3	10	31	38	62
3	Bournemouth	46	14	8	1	42	18	7	9	7	27	27	59
4	QUEEN'S PARK RGS.	46	15	3	5	65	31	9	8	6	46	42	59
5	Peterborough Utd.	46	16	0	7	60	38	10	6	7	47	44	58
6	Bristol City	46	15	3	5	56	27	8	5	10	38	45	54
7	Reading	46	14	5	4	46	24	8	4	11	31	42	53
8	Northampton Town	46	12	6	5	52	24	8	5	10	33	33	51
9	Swindon Town	46	14	4	4	48	26	6	7	10	30	45	49
10	Hull City	46	15	2	6	43	20	5	6	12	24	34	48
11	Bradford Park Ave.	46	13	5	5	47	27	7	2	14	33	51	47
12	Port Vale	46	12	4	7	41	23	5	7	11	24	35	45
13	Notts County	46	14	5	4	44	23	3	4	16	23	51	43
14	Coventry City	46	11	6	6	38	26	5	5	13	26	45	43
15	Crystal Palace	46	8	8	7	50	41	6	6	11	33	39	42
16	Southend United	46	10	7	6	31	26	3	9	11	26	43	42
17	Watford	46	10	9	4	37	26	4	4	15	26	48	41
18	Halifax Town	46	9	9	5	34	35	6	5	12	28	49	40
19	Shrewsbury Town	46	8	7	8	46	37	5	5	13	27	47	38
20	Barnsley	46	9	6	8	45	41	4	6	13	26	54	38
21	Torquay United	46	9	4	10	48	44	6	2	15	28	56	36
22	Lincoln City	46	4	10	9	31	43	5	7	11	26	44	35
23	Brentford	46	11	3	9	34	29	2	5	16	19	64	34
24	Newport County	46	6	5	12	29	38	1	3	19	17	64	22

No	Date		Opponent	Score	Scorers	Att	Angell PF	Baker PR	Barber MJ	Bedford NB	Bentley RTF	Collins JW	Drinkwater R	Dugdale JR	Evans B	Ingham A	Keen MT	Large F	Lazarus M	Leary SE	Malcolm A	McCelland JB	Rutter KG	Smith FA	Springett PJ	Taylor B	Williams WT
1	Aug	18	BRIGHTON & HOVE ALB	2-2	Lazarus, Bedford	12022	6			8	2				1	9	3	4	10			11	7	5			
2		20	HALIFAX TOWN	5-0	Bedford 2, McCelland, Keen, Lazarus	11143				8	2	10			1	9	3	4	6			11	7	5			
3		24	Carlisle United	5-2	Lazarus 2(1p), Bedford 2, Evans	8116				8	2	10			1	9	3	4	6			11	7	5			
4		27	Halifax Town	4-1	McCelland, Angell(p), Bedford, Lazarus	7353	6			8	2	10			1		3	4	9			11	7	5			
5	Sep	1	SWINDON TOWN	2-2	McCelland, Large	12573	6			8	2	10			1		3	4	9			11	7	5			
6		3	CRYSTAL PALACE	4-1	Bedford 2, Angell (p), Large	16853	6			8	2	10			1		3	4	9			11	7	5			
7		8	Peterborough United	2-1	McCelland, Bedford	14481	6			8	2	10			1		3	4	9			11	7	5			
8		12	Crystal Palace	0-1		21958	6			8	2	10			1		3	4	9			11	7	5			
9		15	BARNSLEY	2-1	Large 2	11246	6			8	2	10	1					4	9			11	7	5			3
10		17	WREXHAM	1-2	Lazarus	13175	6			8	2	10	1					4	9			11	7	5			3
11		22	Northampton Town	0-1		15469	3		11	8			1			9		4	6			10	7	5			2
12		29	Southend United	3-1	Barber, lazarus, McCelland	12597	6		11		2	10	1					4	9			8	7	5			3
13	Oct	6	NOTTS COUNTY	0-1		15594	6		11		2	10	1					4	9			8	7	5			3
14		10	Wrexham	1-3	Lazarus	15592	6		11	10			1			9	3	4	8				7	5			2
15		13	Bournemouth	1-2	Bedford	11410	6		11	10		8	1			9	3	4					7	5			2
16		22	HULL CITY	4-1	Bedford 3, Lazarus	18281	6			8	2	10	1	5		9	3		11		4	7					
17		27	Bradford Park Avenue	3-0	McCelland 3	8552	6			8	2	10	1	5		9	3		11		4	7					
18	Nov	10	Bristol City	4-2	Bedford 2, Barber, McCelland	13262	6		11	8	2	10	1	5			3		7		4	9					
19		17	READING	3-2	Large, Collins, Malcolm	10313	6			8	2	10	1	5			3	9	11		4	7					
20	Dec	1	SHREWSBURY TOWN	0-0		10347	6	2		8			1	5			3	10	9		4	11	7				
21		8	Millwall	0-0		13763	6	2		8		10	1	5			3		9		4	11	7				
22		15	Brighton & Hove Albion	2-2	Bedford, Lazarus	11529	6	2		8			1	5			3	10	11		9	4	7				
23		22	CARLISLE UNITED	2-2	Lazarus 2	9723	6	2		8			1	5			3	10	11		9	4	7				
24	Jan	12	Swindon Town	0-5		7625	2		10	8			1				3	5	6	11	9	4	7				
25	Feb	9	NORTHAMPTON T	1-3	Bedford	14238	2			8		10	1				3	6	11		9	4	7	5			
26		23	Notts County	2-3	Lazarus, Bedford	8268	2		11	10			1				3	6	8		9	4	7	5			
27	Mar	2	BOURNEMOUTH	1-0	Bedford	8393	6		11	10			1	5			3	6	8		9	4	7				
28		9	Coventry City	1-4	Leary	15029	6		11	10			1	5			3		8	9	4	7				1	2
29		16	BRADFORD PARK AVE.	1-2	Malcolm	7355	2		11	8			1				3	6	10	9	4	7			1		5
30		23	Watford	5-2	Bedford 2, Lazarus 2, Malcolm	10597			11	8			1				3	4	10	9	6	7			1	2	5
31		30	BRISTOL CITY	3-1	Collins, Leary, Barber	5716			11	8		7	1				3	4	10	9	6				1	2	5
32	Apr	1	COLCHESTER UNITED	1-2	Malcolm	7688			11	8		7	1				3	4	10	9	6				1	2	5
33		5	Reading	1-1	Bedford	7946			11	8		7	1				3	4	10	9	6				1	2	5
34		8	SOUTHEND UNITED	1-2	Lazarus	7552			11	8		7	1				3	4	10	9	6				1	2	5
35		12	BRISTOL ROVERS	3-5	Bedford, Leary, lazarus	10169			11	8		6	1				3	5	8	9	4	7			1	2	
36		13	PORT VALE	3-1	Leary 2, Collins	5690			11	8		10	1				3	6	7	9	4				1	2	5
37		15	Bristol Rovers	0-0		10954			11	8		10	1				3	6	7	9	4				1	2	5
38		20	Shrewsbury Town	3-0	Lazarus, Malcolm, leary	3890			11	8		10	1				3	6	7	9	4				1	2	5
39		22	Colchester United	1-2	McCelland	6556			11	8		10	1				3	6		9	4	7			1	2	5
40		25	Hull City	1-4	Leary	5894			11	8		10	1				3	6		9	4	7			1	2	5
41		27	MILLWALL	2-3	Leary, McCelland	8583			11	8		10	1				3	6		9	4	7			1	2	5
42		29	Port Vale	2-3	Leary, Sproson(og)	5974	2		11	8		10	1				3	6	7	9	4				1	2	5
43	May	10	Barnsley	0-0		4934		2	11	8		10	1				3	6	7	9	4				1		5
44		13	WATFORD	2-2	Barber, Collins	5052		2	11	8		10	1				3	6	7	9	4				1		5
45		18	PETERBOROUGH UTD.	0-0		5977	2		11			10					3	4	7	9	8				1	6	5
46		22	COVENTRY CITY	1-3	Collins	3261	2		11	9		10					3	8	7		4				1	6	5

	Angell	Baker	Barber	Bedford	Bentley	Collins	Drinkwater	Dugdale	Evans	Ingham	Keen	Large	Lazarus	Leary	Malcolm	McCelland	Rutter	Smith	Springett	Taylor	Williams
Apps	30	6	28	43	16	33	27	10	8	41	41	18	42	24	31	33	17	17	2	14	25
Goals	2		4	23		5					1	5	18	9	5	11					

One own goal

F.A. Cup

	Date		Opponent	Score	Scorers	Att	Angell PF	Barber MJ	Bedford NB	Bentley RTF	Collins JW	Drinkwater R	Dugdale JR	Ingham A	Keen MT	Lazarus M	Leary SE	Malcolm A	McCelland JB	Rutter KG
R1	Nov	3	NEWPORT COUNTY	3-2	Barber 2, Large	12252	6	11		2	10	1	5		3			9	7	4 8
R2		24	HINCKLEY ATHLETIC	7-2	*See below	13008	6		8	2	10	1	5		3	9		11	4	7
R3	Jan	26	Swansea Town	0-2		12500	2		10			1	5		3	8	6	11	9	4 7

Scorers in R2: Bedford 3, McClelland, Collins, Lazarus, Large.

F.L. Cup

	Date		Opponent	Score	Scorers	Att	Angell PF	Bedford NB	Collins JW	Evans B	Keen MT	Large F	Lazarus M	Rutter KG	Smith FA	Springett PJ	Williams WT
R1	Sep	24	PRESTON NORTH END	1-2	Collins	11005	3	8	10	9	4	6	11	7	5	1	2

		P	W	D	L	F	A	W	D	L	F	A	Pts
1	Northampton Town	46	16	6	1	64	19	10	4	9	45	41	62
2	Swindon Town	46	18	2	3	60	22	4	12	7	27	34	58
3	Port Vale	46	16	4	3	47	25	7	4	12	25	33	54
4	Coventry City	46	14	6	3	54	28	4	11	8	29	41	53
5	Bournemouth	46	11	12	0	39	16	7	4	12	24	30	52
6	Peterborough Utd.	46	11	5	7	48	33	9	6	8	45	42	51
7	Notts County	46	15	3	5	46	29	4	10	9	27	45	51
8	Southend United	46	11	7	5	38	24	8	5	10	37	53	50
9	Wrexham	46	14	6	3	54	27	6	3	14	30	56	49
10	Hull City	46	12	6	5	40	22	7	4	12	34	47	48
11	Crystal Palace	46	10	7	6	38	22	7	6	10	30	36	47
12	Colchester United	46	11	6	6	41	35	7	5	11	32	58	47
13	QUEEN'S PARK RGS.	46	9	6	8	44	36	8	5	10	41	40	45
14	Bristol City	46	10	9	4	54	38	6	4	13	46	54	45
15	Shrewsbury Town	46	13	4	6	57	41	3	8	12	26	40	44
16	Millwall	46	11	6	6	50	32	4	7	12	32	55	43
17	Watford	46	12	3	8	55	40	5	5	13	27	45	42
18	Barnsley	46	12	6	5	39	28	3	5	15	24	46	41
19	Bristol Rovers	46	11	8	4	45	29	4	3	16	25	59	41
20	Reading	46	13	4	6	51	30	3	4	16	23	48	40
21	Bradford Park Ave.	46	9	4	4	43	36	4	3	16	36	61	40
22	Brighton & Hove A.	46	7	6	10	28	38	5	6	12	30	46	36
23	Carlisle United	46	12	4	7	41	37	1	5	17	20	52	35
24	Halifax Town	46	8	3	12	41	51	1	9	13	23	55	30

1963/64   15th in Division 3

No	Date	Opponent	Score	Scorers	Att	Angell PF	Bedford NB	Brady PJ	Brady TR	Collins JW	Gibbs DW	Graham M	Keen MT	Lazarus M	Leary SE	McLeod GJ	McQuade TJ	Malcolm A	Sibley FP	Smith FA	Springett PJ	Taylor B	Vafiadis O	Whittaker R
1	Aug 24	Oldham Athletic	1-2	Graham	13029	3	8		5	11	6	10	4	7	9						1			2
2	26	Shrewsbury Town	2-1	Bedford 2	8051	3	8		5	11	6	10	4	7	9						1			2
3	31	PETERBOROUGH UTD.	3-0	Leary 2, Angell	10762	3	8		5	10	4	11	6	7	9						1			2
4	Sep 7	Southend United	3-1	Lazarus 2, Leary	14069	3	8		5	10	4	11	6	7	9						1			2
5	9	SHREWSBURY TOWN	3-4	Graham 2, Bedford	11090	3	8		5	10	4	11	6	7	9						1			2
6	14	WATFORD	1-0	Bedford	10829	3	8		5	10	4	11	6	7	9						1			2
7	17	Bristol Rovers	0-0		12328	3	8		5	10			6	7	9	11	4				1			2
8	21	Colchester United	0-2		5418	3	8		5	10			6	7	9	11	4				1			2
9	28	MILLWALL	2-0	Bedford, McQuade	9858	3	8		5	10	6		4		9		11				1		7	2
10	30	BRISTOL ROVERS	1-0	Lazarus	8793	3	8		5	10	6		4	7	9						1		11	2
11	Oct 4	Barnsley	1-3	Bedford	5791	3	8		5	10	6		4	7	9	11					1			2
12	7	BOURNEMOUTH	1-0	Angell	10045	3	8		5	10	6		4	7	9						1		11	2
13	12	Mansfield Town	0-1		10869	3	8			10	4	11	6		9						1	5	7	2
14	16	Bournemouth	2-4	Collins, Vafiadis	8915	3	8		5	10	6		4	7	9						1		11	2
15	19	NOTTS COUNTY	3-2	Collins, Lazarus, Birkinshaw(og)	7175	3	8		5	10	6		4	7	9						1		11	2
16	21	HULL CITY	0-2		9836	3			5	10	8		6	7	9	11	4				1			2
17	26	Crewe Alexandra	0-2		5114	3	8		5	11		10	4	7	9		6				1			2
18	30	Hull City	0-3		7932	3		2	5	10	9		4	7			6				1		11	
19	Nov 2	CRYSTAL PALACE	3-4	Collins 2, Bedford	9826	3	10	2	5	11	6		8	7	9		4				1			
20	9	Walsall	2-0	Lazarus, Graham	7961	3	8	2	5			10	6	7	9	11		4			1			
21	23	Luton Town	4-4	Leary 2, Graham, McQuade	6598	3	9	2	5		4	10	6	7	8	11					1			
22	30	COVENTRY CITY	3-6	Bedford 2, Keen	10997	3	8	2	5	10			6	7	8	11		4			1			
23	Dec 14	OLDHAM ATHLETIC	3-2	Bedford 2, Leary	5265	2	10	3	5		9		6	7	8	11		4			1			
24	21	Peterborough United	1-2	Angell	6418	2	8	3	5		9		6	7	10	11		4			1			
25	28	BRISTOL CITY	0-2		8916	2	8	3	5		9		6	7	10	11		4			1			
26	Jan 11	SOUTHEND UNITED	4-5	Leary 2, Vafiadis, Bedford	4380		8	3	5				10	6	9		11	4			1	2	7	
27	18	Watford	1-3	Graham	11550		8	3	5				10	6	9		11	4		1		2	7	
28	Feb 1	COLCHESTER UNITED	0-0		5225			3	5	8	9	10	6			11	7	4		1		2		
29	8	Millwall	2-2	McLeod, Leary	11154	3	8	2	5	7			10	6	9		11	4		1				
30	22	MANSFIELD TOWN	2-0	Humble (og), Bedford	4780	3	8	2	5				10	6	9		11	4		1				
31	29	Brentford	2-2	Bedford 2	12226	3	8	2	5				10	6	9	11	7	4		1				
32	Mar 7	CREWE ALEXANDRA	2-0	Graham, Riggs (og)	3676	3	8	2	5		6	10	4		9	11	7			1				
33	10	Bristol City	1-2	McLeod	8869	3	8	2			6	10	5		9	11		4	7	1				
34	14	Crystal Palace	0-1		15370	3	8	2	5	7		10	6		9	11		4		1				
35	20	BRENTFORD	2-2	Bedford 2	9351	3	8	2	5	11		10	6		9			4		1				
36	27	WREXHAM	1-0	Collins	7867	3	8	2	5	10			6		9	11	7	4		1				
37	28	Reading	2-1	McLeod 2	7947		8	3	5	10			6		9	11	7	4		1		2		
38	30	Wrexham	1-0	Collins	7885		8	3	5	10			6		9	11	7	4		1		2		
39	Apr 6	Port Vale	0-2		7167		8	3	5	10			6		9	11	7	4		1		2		
40	11	Coventry City	2-4	Collins 2	27384	2	8	3	5	7	6		10		9	11		4		1				
41	14	READING	4-2	Bedford, Keen, Vafiadis, Leary	5542	3	8	2	5	10			6		9	11		4		1			7	
42	18	PORT VALE	3-0	Bedford 2, Leary	4955	3	8	2	5	10			6		9	11		4		1			7	
43	25	Notts County	2-2	Vafiadis, Leary	2862	3	8	2	5	10			6		9	11		4		1			7	
44	27	BARNSLEY	2-2	Bedford 2	8434	3	8	2	5	11			10	6	9			4		1			7	
45	29	LUTON TOWN	1-1	Bedford	5005	3	8	2		10			6		9			4		1		5	7	
46	May 1	WALSALL	3-0	Keen 2, Collins	5625		8	3	5	10			6		9	11		4		1		2	7	
		Apps				39	44	29	43	35	25	21	46	23	43	17	20	31	3	20	26	9	15	17
		Goals				3	23			9		7	4	5	12	4	2						4	

Three own goals

F.A. Cup

No	Date	Opponent	Score	Scorers	Att	Angell PF	Bedford NB	Brady PJ	Brady TR	Collins JW	Gibbs DW	Graham M	Keen MT	Lazarus M	Leary SE	McLeod GJ	McQuade TJ	Malcolm A	Sibley FP	Smith FA	Springett PJ	Taylor B	Vafiadis O	Whittaker R
R1	Nov 16	GILLINGHAM	4-1	Bedford, Leary, Malcolm, Graham	12141	3	9	2	5			10	6	7	8		11	4			1			
R2	Dec 7	Colchester United	1-0	Leary	6841	2	8	3	5		9		6	7	10	11	4				1			
R3	Jan 4	Carlisle United	0-2		15359	2		3	5	10	9		6	7	8	11	4				1			

F.L. Cup

No	Date	Opponent	Score	Scorers	Att	Angell PF	Bedford NB	Brady PJ	Brady TR	Collins JW	Gibbs DW	Graham M	Keen MT	Lazarus M	Leary SE	McLeod GJ	McQuade TJ	Malcolm A	Sibley FP	Smith FA	Springett PJ	Taylor B	Vafiadis O	Whittaker R
R1	Sep 4	Aldershot	1-3	Bedford	6800		8	3	5				10	6	9	11	7	4			1			2

		P	W	D	L	F	A	W	D	L	F	A	Pts
1	Coventry City	46	14	7	2	62	32	8	9	6	36	29	60
2	Crystal Palace	46	14	4	2	38	14	6	10	7	35	37	60
3	Watford	46	16	6	1	57	28	7	6	10	22	31	58
4	Bournemouth	46	17	4	2	47	15	7	4	12	32	43	56
5	Bristol City	46	13	7	3	52	24	7	8	8	32	40	55
6	Reading	46	15	5	3	49	26	6	5	12	30	36	52
7	Mansfield Town	46	15	8	0	51	20	5	3	15	25	42	51
8	Hull City	46	16	3	4	45	27	5	8	10	28	41	49
9	Oldham Athletic	46	13	3	7	44	35	7	5	11	29	35	48
10	Peterborough Utd.	46	13	6	4	52	27	5	5	13	23	43	47
11	Shrewsbury Town	46	15	6	2	43	19	5	5	13	30	61	47
12	Bristol Rovers	46	9	6	8	52	34	10	2	11	39	45	46
13	Port Vale	46	13	6	4	35	13	3	8	12	18	36	46
14	Southend United	46	9	10	4	42	26	6	5	12	35	52	45
15	QUEEN'S PARK RGS.	46	13	4	6	47	34	5	5	13	29	44	45
16	Brentford	46	11	4	8	54	36	4	10	9	33	44	44
17	Colchester United	46	10	8	5	45	26	2	11	10	25	42	43
18	Luton Town	46	12	2	9	42	41	4	8	11	22	39	42
19	Walsall	46	7	9	7	34	35	6	5	12	25	41	40
20	Barnsley	46	9	9	5	34	29	3	6	14	34	65	39
21	Millwall	46	9	4	10	33	29	5	6	12	20	38	38
22	Crewe Alexandra	46	10	5	8	29	26	1	7	15	21	51	34
23	Wrexham	46	9	4	10	50	42	4	2	17	25	65	32
24	Notts County	46	7	8	8	29	26	2	1	20	16	66	27

1964/65 14th in Division 3

No	Date	Opponent	Score	Scorers	Att	Angell PF	Bedford NB	Brady PJ	Brady TR	Collins JW	Gibbs DW	Hazell AP	Hunt RG	Jacks GC	Keen MT	Leach MJC	Leary SE	McAdams WJ	McLeod GJ	Malcolm A	Morgan IA	Morgan RE	Nash RG	Sibley FP	Smith FA	Springett PJ	Taylor B
1	Aug 22	Barnsley	0-0		5688	6	8	2	5	7					10		9		11	4					1		3
2	24	SOUTHEND UNITED	2-0	Bedford, Leary	6709	6	8	2	5	7					10		9		11	4					1		3
3	28	SCUNTHORPE UNITED	2-1	Keen 2	6764	6	8	2	5	7					10		9		11	4					1		3
4	31	Southend United	0-0		10862	6	8	2	5	7					10		9		11	4					1		3
5	Sep 5	Walsall	1-4	Collins	4190	6	8	2	5	7					10		9		11	4					1		3
6	7	READING	0-1		7233	6	8	2	5	7	4				10		9		11						1		3
7	11	WATFORD	2-2	Bedford, Leary	8833	6	8	2	5	7					10		9		11	4					1		3
8	16	Reading	3-5	Keen 2, Bedford	10422	6	8	2	5	7	4				10		9		11						1		3
9	18	Workington	0-0		7394	6	8	2	5	10					4		9							7	1		3
10	25	HULL CITY	2-1	Keen, McAdams	6639		10	2	5	8					6			9	11	4	7		3		1		
11	Oct 3	Gillingham	2-2	Keen, Bedford	12581		10	2	5	8		4			6			9			7	11	3		1		
12	5	SHREWSBURY TOWN	2-1	Bedford, R Morgan	5772		10	2	5	8		4			6			9			7	11	3		1		
13	9	BRENTFORD	1-3	Keen	11063		10	2	5	8					6			9		4	7	11	3		1		
14	13	Bristol City	0-2		11133		10	2	5	8					6			9		4	7	11	3		1		
15	17	Colchester United	2-1	Collins, Jones(og)	3529		10	2	5	8					6			9		4	7	11	3		1		
16	19	BRISTOL CITY	1-0	Bedford	5560		10	2	5	8					6			9		4	7	11	3		1		
17	23	PORT VALE	3-1	Bedford, I Morgan, R Morgan	4489		10	2	5	8					6			9		4	7	11	3		1		
18	30	Carlisle United	0-2		9483		10	2	5	8					6			9		4	7	11	3		1		
19	Nov 6	LUTON TOWN	7-1	Bedford 3, Keen 3(2p), R Morgan	5175		10	2	5	8					6			9		4	7	11	3		1		
20	21	GRIMSBY TOWN	1-1	R Morgan	6213		10		5	8		4			6			9			7	11	3		1		2
21	28	Peterborough United	1-6	Collins	8337		10		5	8		4			6			9			7	11	3		1		2
22	Dec 11	BARNSLEY	3-2	Bedford 3	3350		10	2	5						6			9	11	4	7		3		1		
23	18	Scunthorpe United	1-2	McAdams	5344		10	2	5	8					6			9	11	4	7				1		
24	26	Bristol Rovers	1-3	R Morgan	17698		10	2	5	8					6			9		4	7	11			1		
25	28	BRISTOL ROVERS	3-1	Bedford 2, Keen	5220		10		3	8		2	5		6			9		4	7	11			1		
26	Jan 1	WALSALL	1-0	Bedford	4844		10		3	8		2	5		6			9		4	7	11			1		
27	16	Watford	2-0	Leary, I Morgan	7526				3	10		2	5		6	8	9			4	7	11				1	
28	29	BOURNEMOUTH	1-1	Bedford	3520		8		3	10		2	5		6			9		4	7	11				1	
29	Feb 6	Hull City	1-3	McAdams	23574		10		3			2	5		6	8		9	11	4	7					1	
30	13	GILLINGHAM	3-1	Bedford, Collins, McAdams	6633		10		3	8		2	5		6			9		4	7	11				1	
31	20	Brentford	2-5	I Morgan, Keen	12398		10		3	8		2	5		6			9		4	7	11				1	
32	26	COLCHESTER UNITED	5-0	McAdams 3, Bedford, Leach	4220		10			6		2	5		4	8		9			7	11	3			1	
33	Mar 6	Bournemouth	0-2		5937					8		2	5		6	10		9	11	4	7		3			1	
34	12	CARLISLE UNITED	1-2	Bedford	5834		8			10		2	5		6			9		4	7	11				1	
35	15	Mansfield Town	1-8	Bedford	9168		8		5	10		2			6			9		4	7	11				1	3
36	20	Luton Town	0-2		3998		8	2	5	10		4			6			9			7	11				1	3
37	26	MANSFIELD TOWN	2-0	Bedford, Collins	5400		8	2	5	10		4			6			9			7	11				1	3
38	31	Exeter City	2-2	Leary 2	5615			2	5						6	10		9	8		7	11				1	3
39	Apr 3	Grimsby Town	0-0		4207			2	5			4			6	10		9	8		7	11				1	3
40	5	WORKINGTON	2-1	Hazell, Leary	4642		10	2	5			4			6	8		9			7	11				1	3
41	10	PETERBOROUGH UTD.	3-2	Bedford, Leary, Collins	4972		8	2	5	10		4			6			9			7	11				1	3
42	12	Shrewsbury Town	2-3	McAdams, I Morgan	3415			2	5	8					6			9	10	4	7	11				1	3
43	16	Oldham Athletic	3-5	Collins 2, Keen	7951			2	5	8					6			9	10	4	7	11				1	3
44	17	Port Vale	0-0		4816		8	2	5	7					6			9	10	4		11				1	3
45	19	OLDHAM ATHLETIC	1-1	Leary	3260		10	2	5	8					6			9		4	7	11		3		1	
46	23	EXETER CITY	0-0		4060		8	2	5	7				10	6			9		4		11				1	3
		Apps				9	40	33	44	40	2	29	10	1	46	5	26	27	24	22	30	27	17	6	26	20	22
		Goals					23			8	1				13	1	8	8			4	5					

One own goal

F.A. Cup

Rd	Date	Opponent	Score	Scorers	Att	Angell PF	Bedford NB	Brady PJ	Brady TR	Collins JW	Gibbs DW	Hazell AP	Hunt RG	Jacks GC	Keen MT	Leach MJC	Leary SE	McAdams WJ	McLeod GJ	Malcolm A	Morgan IA	Morgan RE	Nash RG	Sibley FP	Smith FA	Springett PJ	Taylor B
R1	Nov 14	BATH CITY	2-0	Collins, Leary	7398		10	2	5	8		4			6			9			7	11	3		1		
R2	Dec 5	PETERBOROUGH UTD.	3-3	R Brady, Keen(p), Bedford	6502	3	9		5	8		2			6		10			4	7	11			1		
rep	9	Peterborough United	1-2	McAdams	15000		10	2	5	7		3			6			9	8		4	11			1		

F.L. Cup

Rd	Date	Opponent	Score	Scorers	Att	Angell PF	Bedford NB	Brady PJ	Brady TR	Collins JW	Gibbs DW	Hazell AP	Hunt RG	Jacks GC	Keen MT	Leach MJC	Leary SE	McAdams WJ	McLeod GJ	Malcolm A	Morgan IA	Morgan RE	Nash RG	Sibley FP	Smith FA	Springett PJ	Taylor B
R1	Sep 2	ALDERSHOT	5-2	Bedford 2, Collins 2, Angell	3528	6	8	2	5	7					10		9			4					1		3
R2	23	Reading	0-4		7271	6	10	2	5	7					4		8		11					9		1	3

Played in R1: McQuade (at 11)

	P	W	D	L	F	A	W	D	L	F	A	Pts
1 Carlisle United	46	14	5	4	46	24	11	5	7	30	29	60
2 Bristol City	46	14	6	3	53	18	10	5	8	39	37	59
3 Mansfield Town	46	17	4	2	61	23	7	7	9	34	38	59
4 Hull City	46	14	6	3	51	25	9	6	8	40	32	58
5 Brentford	46	18	4	1	55	18	6	5	12	28	37	57
6 Bristol Rovers	46	14	7	2	52	21	6	8	9	30	37	55
7 Gillingham	46	16	5	2	45	13	7	4	12	25	37	55
8 Peterborough Utd.	46	16	3	4	61	33	6	4	13	24	41	51
9 Watford	46	13	8	2	45	21	4	8	11	26	43	50
10 Grimsby Town	46	11	10	2	37	21	5	7	11	31	46	49
11 Bournemouth	46	12	4	7	40	24	6	7	10	32	39	47
12 Southend United	46	14	4	5	48	24	5	4	14	30	47	46
13 Reading	46	12	8	3	45	26	4	6	13	25	44	46
14 QUEEN'S PARK RGS.	46	15	5	3	48	23	2	7	14	24	57	46
15 Workington	46	11	7	5	30	22	6	5	12	28	47	46
16 Shrewsbury Town	46	10	6	7	42	38	5	6	12	34	46	42
17 Exeter City	46	8	7	8	33	27	4	10	9	18	25	41
18 Scunthorpe United	46	9	8	6	42	27	5	4	14	23	45	40
19 Walsall	46	9	4	10	34	36	6	3	14	21	44	37
20 Oldham Athletic	46	10	8	5	30	39	3	7	13	21	44	36
21 Luton Town	46	8	8	5	32	36	5	3	15	19	58	33
22 Port Vale	46	7	6	10	27	33	2	8	13	14	43	32
23 Colchester United	46	8	4	11	30	30	3	4	16	20	55	30
24 Barnsley	46	8	5	10	33	31	1	6	16	21	59	29

1965/66   3rd in Division 3

League matches

#	Date	Opponent	Score	Scorers	Att
1	Aug 21	Brentford	1-6	R Morgan	15209
2	23	BRIGHTON & HOVE ALB	4-1	Keen(p), Collins, Allen, McAdams	10480
3	28	MANSFIELD TOWN	1-2	McAdams	6405
4	Sep 4	Hull City	3-1	Allen 2, R Morgan	20478
5	11	READING	0-2		6800
6	14	Scunthorpe United	2-1	Allen, Collins	5362
7	18	Exeter City	0-0		6174
8	25	PETERBOROUGH UTD.	2-1	Collins, Langley(p)	5094
9	Oct 2	Millwall	1-2	Leach	14465
10	4	SCUNTHORPE UNITED	1-0	Keen	6726
11	9	York City	2-2	Allen, I Morgan	6553
12	16	OXFORD UNITED	2-3	Sanderson, Allen	8448
13	23	Swansea Town	2-4	Collins, Allen	8430
14	30	WALSALL	2-1	Sibley, Langley(p)	5228
15	Nov 5	Workington	1-1	McAdams	4464
16	20	Southend United	3-1	Allen 2, Lazarus	6690
17	23	Brighton & Hove Albion	2-0	Allen 2	10689
18	27	SWINDON TOWN	3-2	Allen 3	6872
19	Dec 11	GRIMSBY TOWN	3-0	Collins, R Morgan, Thompson(og)	6671
20	18	Oxford United	3-1	Allen 2, R Morgan	8786
21	Jan 1	YORK CITY	7-2	Allen 3, Collins 2, Lazarus, R Morgan	7811
22	8	Bournemouth	1-1	R Morgan	7616
23	15	SWANSEA TOWN	6-2	R Morgan 3, Collins 2, Lazarus	7042
24	29	BRENTFORD	1-0	R Morgan	14506
25	Feb 5	Mansfield Town	1-2	Collins	4166
26	15	WATFORD	1-1	Langley(p)	8191
27	19	HULL CITY	3-3	Collins 3	12327
28	Mar 5	Watford	2-1	Keen, R Morgan	11600
29	12	EXETER CITY	1-0	Allen	7542
30	19	Peterborough United	1-1	Collins	7487
31	26	MILLWALL	6-1	Marsh 2, Collins, Allen, Lazarus, R Morgan	16610
32	Apr 2	WORKINGTON	4-1	Allen 2, Marsh, Lazarus	8016
33	8	BRISTOL ROVERS	4-1	Allen, Collins, Marsh, Lazarus	13372
34	9	Shrewsbury Town	0-0		4791
35	12	Bristol Rovers	0-1		9203
36	16	SOUTHEND UNITED	2-1	Lazarus 2	7028
37	23	Swindon Town	1-2	Keen	13802
38	25	Gillingham	1-3	Marsh	7582
39	30	SHREWSBURY TOWN	2-1	Allen, Marsh	5713
40	May 2	OLDHAM ATHLETIC	1-1	Allen	6850
41	7	Grimsby Town	2-4	R Morgan, Marsh	5586
42	13	Reading	1-2	Collins	6554
43	18	Gillingham	1-3	Collins	7147
44	21	BOURNEMOUTH	5-0	Lazarus 3, Allen 2	4732
45	25	Oldham Athletic	2-0	Allen, Marsh	7969
46	28	Walsall	1-0	Allen	8103

Appearances and goals

	Allen LW	Brady TR	Collins JW	Hazell AP	Hunt RG	Keen MT	Langley EJ	Lazarus M	Leach MJC	Leary SE	McAdams WJ	Marsh RW	Morgan IA	Morgan RE	Mortimore JH	Moughton CE	Sanderson K	Sibley FP	Smith FA	Springett PJ	Taylor B	Watson IL
Apps	44	1	36	19	32	46	46	29	10	1	6	16	10	44	10	3	42	29	3	43	5	40
Goals	30		18			4	3	11	1		3	8	1	13				1	1			

One own goal

F.A. Cup

R	Date	Opponent	Score	Scorers	Att
R1	Nov 13	Colchester United	3-3	Collins, Allen, Sanderson	6693
rep	17	COLCHESTER UNITED	4-0	Allen 2, R Morgan, Sanderson	6166
R2	Dec 4	GUILDFORD CITY	3-0	Hunt(og), Sibley, Lazarus	8343
R3	Jan 22	SHREWSBURY TOWN	0-0		15738
rep	26	Shresbury Town	0-1		14779

F.L. Cup

R	Date	Opponent	Score	Scorers	Att
R1	Sep 1	WALSALL	1-1	Sissons(og)	3529
rep	7	Walsall	2-3	R Morgan, Collins	12236

Played in R1: NB Bedford (at 10)

Division 3 final table

		P	W	D	L	F	A	W	D	L	F	A	Pts
1	Hull City	46	19	2	2	64	24	12	5	6	45	38	69
2	Millwall	46	19	4	0	47	13	8	7	8	29	30	65
3	QUEEN'S PARK RGS.	46	16	3	4	62	29	8	6	9	33	36	57
4	Scunthorpe United	46	9	8	6	44	34	12	3	8	36	33	53
5	Workington	46	13	6	4	38	18	6	8	9	29	39	52
6	Gillingham	46	14	4	5	33	19	8	4	11	29	35	52
7	Swindon Town	46	11	8	4	43	18	8	5	10	31	30	51
8	Reading	46	13	5	5	36	19	6	8	9	34	44	51
9	Walsall	46	13	7	3	48	21	7	3	13	29	43	50
10	Shrewsbury Town	46	13	7	3	48	22	6	4	13	25	42	49
11	Grimsby Town	46	15	6	2	47	25	2	7	14	21	37	47
12	Watford	46	12	4	7	33	19	5	9	9	22	32	47
13	Peterborough Utd.	46	13	6	4	50	26	4	6	13	30	40	46
14	Oxford United	46	11	3	9	38	33	8	5	10	32	41	46
15	Brighton & Hove A.	46	13	4	6	48	28	3	7	13	19	37	43
16	Bristol Rovers	46	11	10	2	38	15	4	4	16	26	49	42
17	Swansea Town	46	14	4	5	61	37	1	7	15	20	59	41
18	Bournemouth	46	9	8	6	24	19	4	4	15	14	37	38
19	Mansfield Town	46	10	5	8	31	36	5	3	15	28	53	38
20	Oldham Athletic	46	8	7	8	34	33	4	6	13	21	48	37
21	Southend United	46	15	1	7	43	28	1	3	19	11	55	36
22	Exeter City	46	9	6	8	36	28	3	5	15	17	51	35
23	Brentford	46	9	4	10	34	30	1	8	14	14	39	32
24	York City	46	5	7	11	30	44	4	2	17	23	62	27

1966/67 Champions of Division 3: Promoted

#	Date	Opponent	Score	Scorers	Att	Allen LW	Clement DT	Collins JW	Hazell AP	Hunt RG	Keen MT	Keetch RD	Langley EJ	Lazarus M	Leach MJC	Marsh RW	Morgan IA	Morgan RE	Moughton CE	Sanderson K	Sibley FP	Springett PJ	Watson IL	Wilks A
1	Aug 20	SHREWSBURY TOWN	2-2	Allen, Marsh	6343	9		8	3	5	4		7			10		11			6	1	2	
2	27	Watford	0-1		9860	9			2	5	4		3	7		10		11		8	6	1		
3	Sep 3	SWINDON TOWN	3-1	Lazarus 2, R Morgan	7900	9			3	5	4			7		10		11		8	6	1		
4	6	MIDDLESBROUGH	4-0	Marsh 3, Allen	8807	9			3	5	4			7		10		11		8	6	1	2	
5	10	Reading	2-2	Langley(p), I Morgan	8148	9			3		5		12	7		10	8	11		4	6	1	2	
6	17	DONCASTER ROVERS	6-0	R Morgan 2, Keen 2, Sanderson, Marsh	8090	9			2	5	4		3	7		10		11		8	6	1		
7	24	Mansfield Town	7-1	Marsh 3, Allen 2, Langley(p), Sanderson	6260	9			2	5	4		3			10	7	11		8	6	1		
8	28	Middlesbrough	2-2	Marsh, Lazarus	13091	9			2	5	4		3	7		10		11		8	6	1		
9	Oct 1	GRIMSBY TOWN	5-1	Allen 2, Marsh, Lazarus, R Morgan	9097	9			2	5	4		3	7		10	8	11			6	1		
10	8	SWANSEA TOWN	4-2	Allen, Sanderson, Marsh	11047	9			2	5	4		3	7		10		11		8	6	1		
11	15	Bournemouth	3-1	R Morgan 2, Marsh	12164	9			2	5	4		3	7		10		11		8	6	1		
12	19	Torquay United	1-1	Langley(p)	7887					5	4		3	7	9	10		11		8	6	1	2	
13	22	ORIENT	4-1	Allen 2, Lazarus, Marsh	16719	9			2	5	4		3	7		10		11		8	6	1		
14	29	Gillingham	2-2	Keen, Marsh	11951	9			2	5	4		3	7		10		11		8	6	1		
15	Nov 5	WORKINGTON	4-1	Marsh 2, Langley(p), Allen	9094	9			2	5	4		3	7		10		11		8	6	1		
16	12	Scunthorpe United	2-0	Marsh 2	5052	9			2	5	4		3	7		10		11		8	6	1		
17	15	TORQUAY UNITED	2-1	R Morgan, Allen	10385	9			2	5	4		3	7		10		11		8	6	1		
18	19	OLDHAM ATHLETIC	0-1		14413	9			2	5	4		3	7		10		11		8	6	1		
19	Dec 3	BRISTOL ROVERS	3-0	Allen, Sanderson, Lazarus	13312	9				5	4		3	7		10		11		8	6	1	2	
20	10	Colchester United	3-1	R Morgan 2, Marsh	8195	9				5	4		3	7		10		11		8	6	1	2	
21	17	Shrewsbury Town	0-0		6520	9				5	4		3	7		10	12	11		8	6	1	2	
22	26	BRIGHTON & HOVE ALB	3-0	Sanderson, Lazarus, Marsh	17875	9				5	4		3	7		10		11		8	6	1	2	
23	27	Brighton & Hove Albion	2-2	R Morgan, Wilks	22947					5	4		3	7		10		11		8	6	1	2	9
24	31	WATFORD	4-1	Marsh 2, Sibley, Lazarus	17703	9				5	4		3	7		10		11		8	6	1	2	
25	Jan 14	READING	2-1	Marsh, R Morgan	14341	9				5	4		3	7		10		11		8	6	1	2	
26	21	Doncaster Rovers	1-1	Keen	12062	9				5	4		3	7		10		11		8	6	1	2	
27	Feb 4	MANSFIELD TOWN	0-0		14728	9			2	5	4		3	7		10		11		8	6	1		
28	11	Grimsby Town	1-1	I Morgan	7157	9			2	5	4		3	7		10	8	11			6	1		
29	20	Peterborough United	2-0	Crawford(og), Lazarus	6411	9			2	5	4		3	7		10		11		8	6	1		
30	25	Swansea Town	3-1	Lazarus 3	10141	9			2	5	4		3	7		10	12	11		8	6	1		
31	Mar 7	BOURNEMOUTH	4-0	Marsh 2, Allen, Keen	21558				2	5	4		3	7		10	12	11		8	6	1		9
32	11	PETERBOROUGH UTD.	0-0		16716	9			2	5	4	3		7		10	8	11			6	1		
33	18	Orient	0-0		14607	9			2	5	4		3	7		10		11		8	6	1		
34	24	DARLINGTON	4-0	Marsh, Langley(p), Lazarus, Allen	18601	9			2	5	4		3	7		10	11			8	6	1		
35	25	GILLINGHAM	2-0	I Morgan, Marsh	14612	9			2	5	4		3	7		10	11			8	6	1		
36	27	Darlington	0-0		9914	9			2	5	4		3	7		10		11		8	6	1		
37	Apr 1	Workington	2-0	I Morgan, Langley(p)	4010	9			2	5	4		3	7		10	12	11	6	8		1		
38	8	SCUNTHORPE UNITED	5-1	Marsh 2, Lazarus 2, Keen	13113	9	5		2		4		3	7		10		11	6	8		1		
39	11	Walsall	0-2		11881	9			2	5	4	12	3	7		10				8	6	1		
40	15	Oldham Athletic	1-0	Wilks	14279	9			2	5	4		3				7	11		8	6	1	12	10
41	22	OXFORD UNITED	3-1	Wilks 2, Lazarus	15365	9			2	5	4		3	7				11		8	6	1		10
42	25	WALSALL	0-0		11880	9			2	5	4		3	7				11		8	6	1		10
43	29	Bristol Rovers	1-2	Leach	17721				3	5	4			7	9		8	11	6			1	2	10
44	May 2	Swindon Town	1-1	Wilks	21367	9			6	5	4		3	7			8	11				1	2	10
45	6	COLCHESTER UNITED	2-1	Sanderson, Allen	10935	9			2	5	4		3	7		10		11		8	6	1		
46	13	Oxford United	1-2	Marsh	10189	9			2	5	4		3	7		10		11		8	6	1		
				Apps		42	1	1	37	44	46	2	41	44	2	41	14	44	3	40	42	46	16	7
				Goals		16					6		6	16	1	30	4	11			6			5

One own goal

F.A. Cup

	Date	Opponent	Score	Scorers	Att	Allen LW	Clement DT	Collins JW	Hazell AP	Hunt RG	Keen MT	Keetch RD	Langley EJ	Lazarus M	Leach MJC	Marsh RW	Morgan IA	Morgan RE	Moughton CE	Sanderson K	Sibley FP	Springett PJ	Watson IL	Wilks A
R1	Nov 26	POOLE TOWN	3-2	Marsh 3	9534	9			2	5	4		3	7		10	12	11		8	6			
R2	Jan 7	BOURNEMOUTH	2-0	Langley(p), Lazarus	12102	9				5	4		3	7		10		11		8	6	1	2	
R3	28	Sheffield Wednesday	0-3		40038	9				5	4		3	7		10	12	11		8	6	1	2	

Played in R1: Kelly (at 1)

F.L. Cup

	Date	Opponent	Score	Scorers	Att	Allen LW	Clement DT	Collins JW	Hazell AP	Hunt RG	Keen MT	Keetch RD	Langley EJ	Lazarus M	Leach MJC	Marsh RW	Morgan IA	Morgan RE	Moughton CE	Sanderson K	Sibley FP	Springett PJ	Watson IL	Wilks A
R1	Aug 23	COLCHESTER UNITED	5-0	Marsh 4, Lazarus	5497	9				5	4		3	7		10		11		8	6	1	2	
R2	Sep 14	Aldershot	1-1	Allen	5349	9			2	5	4		3	7		10	8	11			6	1		
rep	20	ALDERSHOT	2-0	Langley(p), Marsh	7848	9			2	5	4		3	7		10		11		8	6	1		
R3	Oct 12	SWANSEA TOWN	2-1	Hazell, Keen	12998	9			3	5	4			7		10		11		8	6	1	2	
R4	25	LEICESTER CITY	4-2	Allen 2, R Morgan, Lazarus	20735	9			2	5	4		3	7		10		11		8	6	1		
R5	De 7	CARLISLE UNITED	2-1	Marsh 2	19146	9				5	4		3	7		10		11		8	6	1	2	
SF1	Jan 17	Birmingham City	4-1	Marsh, R Morgan, Lazarus, Allen	34295	9				5	4		3	7		10		11		8	6	1	2	
SF2	Feb 7	BIRMINGHAM CITY	3-1	Marsh 2, Keen	24604	9			2	5	4		3	7		10		11		8	6	1		
F	Mar 4	West Bromwich Albion	3-2	R Morgan, Marsh, Lazarus	97952	9			2	5	4		3	7		10		11		8	6	1		

Final at Wembley Stadium.

		P	W	D	L	F	A	W	D	L	F	A	Pts
1	QUEEN'S PARK RGS.	46	18	4	1	66	15	8	11	4	37	23	67
2	Middlesbrough	46	16	3	4	51	20	7	6	10	36	44	55
3	Watford	46	15	5	3	39	17	5	9	9	22	29	54
4	Reading	46	13	7	3	45	20	9	2	12	31	37	53
5	Bristol Rovers	46	13	8	2	47	28	7	5	11	29	39	53
6	Shrewsbury Town	46	15	5	3	48	24	5	7	11	29	38	52
7	Torquay United	46	17	3	3	57	20	4	6	13	16	34	51
8	Swindon Town	46	14	5	4	53	21	6	5	12	28	38	50
9	Mansfield Town	46	12	4	7	48	37	8	5	10	36	42	49
10	Oldham Athletic	46	15	4	4	51	16	4	6	13	29	47	48
11	Gillingham	46	11	9	3	36	18	4	7	12	22	44	46
12	Walsall	46	12	8	3	37	16	6	2	15	28	56	46
13	Colchester United	46	14	3	6	52	30	3	7	13	24	43	44
14	Orient	46	10	9	4	36	27	3	9	11	22	41	44
15	Peterborough Utd.	46	12	4	7	40	31	2	11	10	28	40	43
16	Oxford United	46	10	8	5	41	29	5	5	13	20	37	43
17	Grimsby Town	46	13	5	5	46	23	4	4	15	15	45	43
18	Scunthorpe United	46	13	4	6	39	26	4	4	15	19	47	42
19	Brighton & Hove A.	46	10	8	5	37	27	3	7	13	24	44	41
20	Bournemouth	46	8	10	5	24	24	4	7	12	15	33	41
21	Swansea Town	46	9	9	5	50	30	3	6	14	35	59	39
22	Darlington	46	8	7	8	26	28	5	4	14	21	53	37
23	Doncaster Rovers	46	11	6	6	40	40	1	2	20	18	77	32
24	Workington	46	9	3	11	35	35	3	4	16	20	54	31

1967/68   2nd in Division 2: Promoted

#		Date	Opponent	Score	Scorers	Att	Allen LW	Clarke FJ	Clement DT	Finch RJ	Harris AJ	Hazell AP	Hunt RG	Keen MT	Keetch RD	Kelly MJ	Lazarus M	Leach MJC	McGovern MJ	Marsh RW	Morgan IA	Morgan RE	Sanderson K	Sibley FP	Springett RDG	Watson IL	Wilks A
1	Aug	19	Portsmouth	1-1	R Morgan	23267	9		2		3	6		4	5		7	10			8	11			1		
2		22	Bristol City	2-0	Leach 2	20228	9		2		3	6		4	5		7	10			8	11			1		
3		26	NORWICH CITY	2-0	Keen, I Morgan	14526	9		2		3	6	5	4			7	10			8	11			1	12	
4		29	BRISTOL CITY	3-1	I Morgan, Allen, R Morgan	15448	9		2		3	6	5	4		1	7	10			8	11				12	
5	Sep	2	Rotherham United	3-1	Leach, Allen, Lazarus	8111	9				3	6	5	4			7	10			8	11	12		1	2	
6		5	ASTON VILLA	3-0	Sanderson 2, Lazarus	21438			2		3	6	5	4			7	10			8	11	9		1		
7		9	DERBY COUNTY	0-1		18431	12		2		3	6	5	4			7	9			8	11	10		1		
8		16	Preston North End	2-0	R Morgan, Leach	15792	9		2		3	6	5	4			12	10			7	11	8		1		
9		23	CHARLTON ATHLETIC	2-0	I Morgan, Allen	18933	9		2		3	6	5	4			7	10			8	11			1		
10		30	Crystal Palace	0-1		38006	9		2		3	6	5	4	12		7	10			8	11			1		
11	Oct	7	BOLTON WANDERERS	1-0	Wilks	16848			2		3	6	12	4	5			9			7	11	8		1		10
12		14	Hull City	0-2		14240	8		2		3	6		4	5			9			7	11			1		10
13		21	MILLWALL	3-1	R Morgan, Keen, Allen	23887	9				3	2		4	5		7				8	11		6	1		10
14		28	Blackpool	1-0	Allen	21635	9		2		3	6		4	5		7	12			8	11		10	1		
15	Nov	11	Carlisle United	1-3	Sibley	12544	9		2		3	6		4	5		7				8	11		10	1		
16		18	MIDDLESBROUGH	1-1	Marsh	17557	9				3	2		4	5		7			10	8	11		6	1		
17		25	Huddersfield Town	0-1		14615	9				3	2		4	5		7			10	8	11	12	6	1		
18	Dec	2	IPSWICH TOWN	1-0	Marsh	16266			2		3	6		4	5					10	8	11			1		7
19		9	Birmingham City	0-2		25281	9		2		3	6		4	5					10	7	11	8		1		12
20		12	BLACKBURN ROVERS	3-1	Marsh, Wilks, Sanderson	12917			2		3	6		4	5					10	7	11	8		1		9
21		16	PORTSMOUTH	2-0	I Morgan, Keen	20195			2		3	6		4	5					10	7	11	8		1		9
22		23	Norwich City	0-0		23593			2		3	6		4	5					10	7	11	8		1	12	9
23		26	Plymouth Argyle	1-0	Keen (p)	21003			2		3	6		4	5				9	10	7	11	8		1		
24		30	PLYMOUTH ARGYLE	4-1	Marsh 2, Keen 2	15889			2		3	6		4	5					10	7	11	8		1		9
25	Jan	6	ROTHERHAM UNITED	6-0	I Morgan 2, Leach 2, R Morgan, Marsh	16782			2		3	6		4	5			9		10	7	11	8		1		
26		20	PRESTON NORTH END	2-0	Marsh 2	16633			2		3	6		4	5			9		10	7	11	8		1		
27	Feb	3	Charlton Athletic	3-3	R Morgan 2, Marsh	21507			2		3	6		4	5			9		10	7	11	8		1		
28		10	CRYSTAL PALACE	2-1	Wilks, I Morgan	18954			2		3	6		4	5					10	7	11	8		1		9
29		17	Derby County	0-4		22854			2		3	6		4	5			9		10	7	11	8		1		
30		24	Bolton Wanderers	1-1	R Morgan	14956		9	2		3	6		4	5					10	7	11	8		1		
31	Mar	9	HULL CITY	1-1	Marsh (p)	17705		9			3	6		4	5					10	8	11			1	2	7
32		16	Millwall	1-1	Marsh	21436	8	9	2		3	6		4	5					10	7	11			1		
33		23	BLACKPOOL	2-0	I Morgan, Clarke	18498	8	9	2		3	6		4	5					10	7	11			1		
34		30	Blackburn Rovers	1-0	Clarke	16141	8	9	2		3	6		4	5					10	7	11			1		
35	Apr	6	CARLISLE UNITED	1-0	Clarke	18103	8	9	2		3	6		4	5					10	7	11			1	12	
36		12	CARDIFF CITY	1-0	I Morgan	23043	8	9			3	6		4	5						7	11			1	2	10
37		13	Middlesbrough	1-3	Allen	20849	8	9			3	6	5	4					12		7	11			1	2	10
38		16	Cardiff City	0-1		20021		9		2	3	6	5	4		1		8		10	7	11					
39		20	HUDDERSFIELD T	3-0	Marsh 2, Legg(og)	19646		9		2	3	6	5	4	5	1		8		10	7	11					
40		27	Ipswich Town	2-2	Marsh (p), Leach	28152	12	9		2	3	6		4	5	1		8		10	7	11					
41	May	4	BIRMINGHAM CITY	2-0	Leach, I Morgan	25895	11	9			3	6		4	5	1		8		10	7					2	12
42		11	Aston Villa	2-1	Leach, Bradley(og)	33835	11	9			3	6		4	5	1		8		10	7					2	
			Apps				26	13	30	3	42	42	11	42	33	6	15	23	1	25	42	40	18	5	36	10	14
			Goals				6	3						6			2	9	1	14	10	8	3	1			3

Two own goals

F.A. Cup

R3	Jan 27	PRESTON NORTH END	1-3	Keen	18425			2		3	6		4	5				9	10	7	11	8		1		12

F.L. Cup

R2	Sep 12	HULL CITY	2-1	Leach, Keen	16609	9		2		3	6	5	4			7	10			8	11			1		
R3	Oct 10	OXFORD UNITED	5-1	Wilks 5	16989	8		2		3		5	4	6			9			7	11			1		10
R4	31	BURNLEY	1-2	Sibley	24213	9		2		3	6		4	5		7				8	11		10	1		

		P	W	D	L	F	A	W	D	L	F	A	Pts
1	Ipswich Town	42	12	7	2	45	20	10	8	3	34	24	59
2	QUEEN'S PARK RGS.	42	18	2	1	45	9	7	6	8	22	27	58
3	Blackpool	42	12	6	3	33	16	12	4	5	38	27	58
4	Birmingham City	42	12	6	3	54	21	7	8	6	29	30	52
5	Portsmouth	42	13	6	2	43	18	5	7	9	25	37	49
6	Middlesbrough	42	10	7	4	39	19	7	5	9	21	35	46
7	Millwall	42	9	10	2	35	16	5	7	9	27	34	45
8	Blackburn Rovers	42	13	5	3	34	16	3	6	12	22	33	43
9	Norwich City	42	12	4	5	40	30	4	7	10	20	35	43
10	Carlisle United	42	9	9	3	38	22	5	4	12	20	30	41
11	Crystal Palace	42	11	4	6	34	19	3	7	11	22	37	39
12	Bolton Wanderers	42	8	6	7	37	28	5	7	9	23	35	39
13	Cardiff City	42	9	6	6	35	29	4	6	11	25	37	38
14	Huddersfield Town	42	10	6	5	29	23	3	6	12	17	38	38
15	Charlton Athletic	42	10	6	5	43	25	2	7	12	20	43	37
16	Aston Villa	42	10	3	8	35	30	5	4	12	19	34	37
17	Hull City	42	6	8	7	25	23	6	5	10	33	50	37
18	Derby County	42	8	5	8	40	35	5	5	11	31	43	36
19	Bristol City	42	7	7	7	26	25	6	3	12	22	37	36
20	Preston North End	42	8	7	6	29	24	4	4	13	14	41	35
21	Rotherham United	42	7	4	10	22	32	3	7	11	20	44	31
22	Plymouth Argyle	42	5	4	12	26	36	4	5	12	12	36	27

1968/69   Bottom of Division 1: Relegated

#	Date	Opponent	Score	Scorers	Att	Allen LW	Bridges BJ	Clarke FJ	Clement DT	Finch RJ	Francis GCJ	Gillard IT	Glover AR	Harris AJ	Hazell AP	Hunt RG	Keen MT	Keetch RD	Kelly MJ	Leach MJC	McGovern MJ	Marsh RW	Metchick DJ	Morgan IA	Morgan RE	Sanderson K	Sibley FP	Spratley AS	Springett RDG	Watson IL	Wilks A
1	Aug 10	LEICESTER CITY	1-1	Allen	21494	12		9	2					3	6	4								7	11		8		1	5	10
2	14	Leeds United	1-4	Wilks	31612	9			2					3	6	4								7	11		8		1	5	10
3	17	Wolverhampton Wan.	1-3	I Morgan	30858									3	6	4		5	1	9				7	11		8			2	10
4	20	SUNDERLAND	2-2	Allen, Clarke	20669	8		9						3	2	4			1	10				7	11	12	6			5	
5	24	MANCHESTER CITY	1-1	Bridges	19716	8	9							3	2	4			1					7	11	10	6			5	
6	27	Ipswich Town	0-3		24049		9	10						3	2	4			1	8				7			6			5	11
7	31	Arsenal	1-2	Wilks	44407	11	9		2					3	8	4			1	10				7			6			5	12
8	Sep 7	Liverpool	0-2		46025		11	9						3	8	12	4	5						7		10	6		1	2	
9	14	CHELSEA	0-4		26358			9						3	8	12	4	5		11				7		10	6		1	2	
10	21	Stoke City	1-1	R Morgan	15585	10	9							3	4			5	1	8				7	11		6			2	12
11	28	SOUTHAMPTON	1-1	Allen	20760	10	9							3	4	5			1	8				7	11		6			2	
12	Oct 5	West Bromwich Albion	1-3	Clarke	22944		10	9						3	4	5			1	8			12	7	11		6			2	
13	8	IPSWICH TOWN	2-1	Bridges, R Morgan	17992		9	7						3	6		4	5	1	8					11					2	10
14	12	SHEFFIELD WEDNESDAY	3-2	Wilks, Bridges, Leach	19044		9	7						3	6	5	4		1	8			12		11					2	10
15	19	Newcastle United	2-3	Wilks, Moncur(og)	35503		9	7						3	6	5	4		1	8					11					2	10
16	26	MANCHESTER UNITED	2-3	Leach, Wilks	31138		9	7						3	6	5	4		1	8					11					2	10
17	Nov 2	West Ham United	3-4	Leach 2, Bridges	36008		9	7						3	6	5	4			8					11				1	2	10
18	9	BURNLEY	0-2		22572		9	7						3	6	5	4			8				12	11				1	2	10
19	16	Everton	0-4		43552		9	7	3						6	8	5		1			10			11		4			2	
20	23	NOTTM. FOREST	2-1	Marsh, Hazell	18857		9		2		3				6				1		8	10		7	11		4			5	
21	Dec 7	COVENTRY CITY	0-1		17921				2					3	6					9		10		7	11		4		1	5	8
22	14	Sheffield Wednesday	0-4		21280		7							3	6	5	4			9		10		8	11				1	2	
23	21	NEWCASTLE UNITED	1-1	Bridges	18444		7	9						3	6	5	8	4				10			11				1	2	
24	26	WEST BROMWICH ALB.	0-4		18649	12	7	9						3	6	5	8	4				10			11				1	2	
25	Jan 11	WEST HAM UNITED	1-1	Clarke	28645		9	3				12			5		6			8		10		7	11		4		1	2	
26	18	Burnley	2-2	Marsh, Leach	12674		9	3				12			5		6			8		10		7	11		4		1	2	
27	24	LEEDS UNITED	0-1		26163		9	3				12			5		6		1	8		10		7	11		4			2	
28	29	Tottenham Hotspur	2-3	Clement, Clarke(p)	38766		9	3				12			5		6		1			10		7	11		4			2	8
29	Feb 1	EVERTON	0-1		26476		9	3									4	5	1			10		7	11		6			2	8
30	15	TOTTENHAM HOTSPUR	1-1	Clarke	30013	8	11	9	3								4	5	1			10		7			6			2	8
31	25	Coventry City	0-5		26449		11	9	3						6		4	5	1	8		10		7						2	
32	Mar 4	Nottingham Forest	0-1		21035		9	12	3						6		4	5		8		10		7					1	2	11
33	8	WOLVERHAMPTON W.	0-1		17901		9	12				3	8		6		4	5						7					1	2	11
34	12	Leicester City	0-2		25587		9					11	3		6		4	5		8		10		7					1	2	
35	15	Manchester City	1-3	Leach	28859		9					3	11		6		4	5		8		10		7					1	2	
36	19	Manchester United	1-8	Marsh	36638		9	3					11				4	5		8		10		7			6		1	2	
37	22	ARSENAL	0-1		23076	8		3					11				4	5		9		10		7			6	1		2	
38	29	LIVERPOOL	1-2	Bridges	16792	11	9						12	3	6		4	5		8		10							1	2	7
39	Apr 5	Southampton	2-3	Marsh, Bridges	22103	11	9		2					3	6			5		8		10		7					1	4	
40	7	Sunderland	0-0		18928	11			2					3	6			5		9		10		7				8	1	4	10
41	12	STOKE CITY	2-1	Leach 2	12489	11	9		2					3	6			5				10		7				8	1	4	12
42	19	Chelsea	1-2	Bridges	41263	11	9		2					3	6			5		8		10		7					1	4	
		Apps				16	27	23	19	2	1	6	6	29	39	31	19	17	20	30	1	22	2	33	25	4	25	13	9	42	20
		Goals				3	8	5	1						1					8		4		1	2						5

One own goal

F.A. Cup

Rd	Date	Opponent	Score	Scorers	Att	Players
R3	Jan 4	Aston Villa	1-2	I Morgan	39854	Bridges 9, Clarke 3, Hunt 10, Keen 5, Keetch 4, Leach 8, Morgan IA 7, Morgan RE 11, Sibley 6, Springett 1, Watson 2

F.L. Cup

Rd	Date	Opponent	Score	Scorers	Att	Players
R2	Sep 3	Peterborough United	2-4	Keen, Clarke	11408	Allen 11, Bridges 9, Clarke 12, Clement 2, Finch 3, Hazell 8, Hunt 4, Kelly 1, Morgan IA 7, Sibley 6, Watson 5, Wilks 10

Final Division 1 Table

		P	W	D	L	F	A	W	D	L	F	A	Pts
1	Leeds United	42	18	3	0	41	9	9	10	2	25	17	67
2	Liverpool	42	16	4	1	36	10	9	7	5	27	14	61
3	Everton	42	14	5	2	43	10	7	10	4	34	26	57
4	Arsenal	42	12	6	3	31	12	10	6	5	25	15	56
5	Chelsea	42	11	7	3	40	24	9	3	9	33	29	50
6	Tottenham Hotspur	42	10	8	3	39	22	4	9	8	22	29	45
7	Southampton	42	13	5	3	41	21	3	8	10	16	27	45
8	West Ham United	42	10	8	3	47	22	3	10	8	19	28	44
9	Newcastle United	42	12	7	2	40	20	3	7	11	21	35	44
10	West Bromwich Alb.	42	11	7	3	43	26	5	4	12	21	41	43
11	Manchester United	42	13	5	3	38	18	2	7	12	19	35	42
12	Ipswich Town	42	10	4	7	32	26	5	7	9	27	34	41
13	Manchester City	42	13	6	2	49	20	2	4	15	15	35	40
14	Burnley	42	11	6	4	36	25	4	3	14	19	57	39
15	Sheffield Wed.	42	7	9	5	27	26	3	7	11	14	28	36
16	Wolverhampton Wan.	42	7	10	4	26	22	3	5	13	15	36	35
17	Sunderland	42	10	6	5	28	18	1	6	14	15	49	34
18	Nottingham Forest	42	6	6	9	17	22	4	7	10	28	35	33
19	Stoke City	42	9	7	5	24	24	0	8	13	16	39	33
20	Coventry City	42	8	6	7	32	22	2	5	14	14	42	31
21	Leicester City	42	8	8	5	27	24	1	4	16	12	44	30
22	QUEEN'S PARK RGS.	42	4	7	10	20	33	0	3	18	19	62	18

1969/70   9th in Division 2

#	Date	Opponent	Score	Scorers	Att	Bridges BJ	Busby MG	Clark C	Clarke FJ	Clement DT	Ferguson MK	Francis GCJ	Gillard IT	Harris AJ	Hazell AP	Hunt RG	Kelly MJ	Leach MJC	McGovern MJ	Marsh RW	Metchick DJ	Mobley VJ	Morgan IA	Sibley FP	Spratley AS	Turpie RP	Venables TF	Watson IL	Wilks A
1	Aug 9	HULL CITY	3-0	Clark, Clarke, Leach	15781	7		11	9	3					6	5	1	12		10			8				4	2	
2	16	Preston North End	0-0		11181	7		11	9	3					6	5	1			10			8				4	2	
3	20	Watford	1-0	Bridges	27968	7			9	3			12		6	5	1	11		10				8			4	2	
4	23	MILLWALL	3-2	Bridges 2, Clement	19735	7			9	3			12		6	5	1	11		10				8			4	2	
5	26	BLACKPOOL	6-1	Marsh 3, Bridges 2, Venables(p)	19231	7		11		3					6	5	1	9		10				8			4	2	
6	30	Birmingham City	0-3		32660	7		11		3					6	5	1	9		10				8			4	2	
7	Sep 6	HUDDERSFIELD T	4-2	Marsh, I Morgan, Bridges, Venables(p)	18746	7				3					6	5	1	9		10			11	8			4	2	
8	13	Portsmouth	3-1	Clement, Francis, Bridges	22169	7			9	3		11			6	5	1			10				4		12		2	8
9	17	Blackburn Rovers	1-0	Leach	15945	7			9	2					6	5	1	7		10				4		3		2	8
10	20	SWINDON TOWN	2-0	Wilks, Clarke	22799				9	3					6	5		7		10			11	4	1			2	8
11	27	Cardiff City	2-4	Venables(p), Bridges	30048	7			9	3					6	5		8		10			11		1		4	2	
12	Oct 4	MIDDLESBROUGH	4-0	Bridges 2, Clarke, Clement	21421	7			9	3					6			8		10		5	11		1		4	2	
13	7	PRESTON NORTH END	0-0		21127	7			9	2			3		6		1			8		5	11	12			4		
14	11	Norwich City	0-1		20040	7			9	3					6	12	1	11		10		5		8			4	2	
15	18	Carlisle United	2-3	Clement, Clarke	11900	7			9	3					6	8	1	11		10		5					4	2	
16	25	CHARLTON ATHLETIC	1-1	Metchick	20577	7		11	9	3					6		1	8		10	12	5					4	2	
17	Nov 1	Aston Villa	1-1	Marsh	31525	7			9				12	3	6	8	1	11		10		5					4	2	
18	8	SHEFFIELD UNITED	2-1	Bridges, Clarke	19852	7		12	9					3	6	8	1	11		10		5					4	2	
19	11	WATFORD	2-1	Clarke, Hazell	19719	7		11	9					3	6	4	1	8		10		5						2	
20	15	Bristol City	0-2		18893	7		11	9	12				3	6	4	1	8		10		5						2	
21	22	LEICESTER CITY	1-1	Bridges	21027	11			9	2	8	7		3	6	5		4		10					1				
22	29	Bolton Wanderers	4-6	Leach, Bridges, Clement, Marsh	7253	11			9	2	8			3	6	5		7		10					1		4		
23	Dec 6	OXFORD UNITED	1-2	Bridges	12018	7			9	2	10	11		3	6	5		8							1		4		
24	13	PORTSMOUTH	2-0	Clarke, Bridges	11831	7			9	2	11			3	6		1			10				4			8	5	
25	26	Millwall	0-2		13952	7			9	2	10			3	6		1	11				5					8	4	
26	27	BIRMINGHAM CITY	2-1	Bridges 2	15688	7			9	2	10	11		3	6	4	1										8	5	
27	Jan 10	Swindon Town	0-0		18448	7			9	2	11			3	6		1			10				4			8	5	
28	17	CARDIFF CITY	2-1	Gillard, Marsh	22033	7			9	2	11		3		6					10				4	1		8	5	
29	20	Huddersfield Town	0-2		21699	7			9	2	11			3	6		1	12		10		5		4			8		
30	31	Middlesbrough	0-1		25821				9	2	11			3	6		1	12		10		5					8	4	7
31	Feb 14	Hull City	2-1	Marsh, Clarke	12698	7			9	2	11			3	6		1			10		5						4	
32	17	NORWICH CITY	4-0	Venables(p), Clarke, Bridges, Marsh	17270	7			9	2	11			3	6		1	12		10		5					8	4	
33	24	Sheffield United	0-2		25724	7				2	11			3	6		1	9		10		5	12					4	
34	28	ASTON VILLA	4-2	Bridges 2, Marsh 2	17057	7			9	2	11			3	6		1			10				8			4	5	
35	Mar 14	BOLTON WANDERERS	0-4		13596	7			9	2	11		3	12	6	5	1			10			8				4		
36	21	Oxford United	0-0		13828	7								3	6			9	4	10		5			1		8	2	11
37	27	CARLISLE UNITED	0-0		16343	7					12			3	6			9	4	10		5			1		8	2	11
38	28	BRISTOL CITY	2-2	Bridges, Francis	11017	7						11	8	3	6			9	4	10		5			1			2	
39	31	Charlton Athletic	1-1	Watson	13790	7						11	8	3	6			9	4	10		5			1		4	2	
40	Apr 4	Blackpool	1-1	Leach	19516	7						11	8	3	6			9		10		5			1		4	2	
41	14	BLACKBURN ROVERS	2-3	Venables(p), Hazell	11161	7						11	8	3	6			9		10		5	12		1		4	2	
42	18	Leicester City	1-2	Marsh (p)	20391		4		2		11		8	3	6			9		10		5	7		1				
		Apps				38	1	8	31	33	20	10	15	16	42	22	28	33	3	38	1	22	13	14	14	2	34	35	6
		Goals				21			9	5		2	1		1			2		12	1		1	1			5	1	1

F.A. Cup

Rd	Date	Opponent	Score	Scorers	Att	Bridges	Clarke	Clement	Ferguson	Francis	Harris	Hazell	Kelly	Leach	Marsh	Mobley	Venables	Watson
R3	Jan 3	SOUTH SHIELDS	4-1	Marsh 2, Clarke, Ferguson	16811	7	9	2	8	11	3	6	1		10		4	5
R4	24	Charlton Athletic	3-2	Marsh 2, Clarke	30262	7	9	2	11		3	6	1		10	5	8	4
R5	Feb 7	DERBY COUNTY	1-0	Mackay(og)	27685	7	9	2	11		3	6	1		10	5	8	4
R6	21	CHELSEA	2-4	Venables(p), Bridges	33572	7		2	11		3	6	1	9	10	5	8	4

F.L. Cup

Rd	Date	Opponent	Score	Scorers	Att	Bridges	Clarke	Clark	Clement	Gillard	Hazell	Hunt	Kelly	Leach	Marsh	Metchick	Mobley	Morgan	Sibley	Spratley	Venables	Watson	Wilks
R2	Sep 3	Mansfield Town	2-2	Bridges, Watson	9759	7		11	3		6	5	1	9	10				8		4	2	
rep	9	MANSFIELD TOWN	4-0	Venables(p), Clement, Marsh, Clarke	17315	7	12		3		6	5	1	9	10		11		8		4	2	
R3	23	TRANMERE ROVERS	6-0	Marsh 4, Leach, Clarke	17477		9		4	3	6	5		7	10			11		1		2	8
R4	Oct 15	WOLVERHAMPTON WAN.	3-1	Clarke 2, Bridges	29971	7	9	11	3		6		1	8	10	5					4	2	
R5	29	Manchester City	0-3		42058	7	9		3		6		1	8	10	5	11				4	2	

Division 2 final table:

		P	W	D	L	F	A	W	D	L	F	A	Pts
1	Huddersfield Town	42	14	6	1	36	10	10	6	5	32	27	60
2	Blackpool	42	10	9	2	25	16	10	4	7	31	29	53
3	Leicester City	42	12	6	3	37	22	7	7	7	27	28	51
4	Middlesbrough	42	15	4	2	36	14	5	6	10	19	31	50
5	Swindon Town	42	13	7	1	35	17	4	9	8	22	30	50
6	Sheffield United	42	16	2	3	50	18	6	3	12	23	28	49
7	Cardiff City	42	12	7	2	38	14	6	6	9	23	27	49
8	Blackburn Rovers	42	15	2	4	42	19	5	5	11	12	31	47
9	QUEEN'S PARK RGS.	42	13	5	3	47	24	4	6	11	19	33	45
10	Millwall	42	14	4	3	38	18	1	10	10	18	38	44
11	Norwich City	42	13	5	3	37	14	3	6	12	12	32	43
12	Carlisle United	42	10	6	5	39	28	4	7	10	19	28	41
13	Hull City	42	11	6	4	43	28	4	5	12	29	42	41
14	Bristol City	42	11	7	3	37	13	2	6	13	17	37	39
15	Oxford United	42	9	9	3	23	13	3	6	12	12	29	39
16	Bolton Wanderers	42	9	6	6	31	23	3	6	12	23	38	36
17	Portsmouth	42	8	4	9	39	35	5	5	11	27	45	35
18	Birmingham City	42	9	7	5	33	22	2	4	15	18	56	33
19	Watford	42	6	8	7	26	21	3	5	13	18	36	31
20	Charlton Athletic	42	7	8	6	23	28	0	9	12	12	48	31
21	Aston Villa	42	7	8	6	23	21	1	5	15	13	41	29
22	Preston North End	42	7	6	8	31	28	1	6	14	12	35	28

1970/71   11th in Division 2

#	Date	Opponent	Score	Scorers	Att	Bridges BJ	Busby MG	Clement DT	Evans IP	Ferguson MK	Francis GCJ	Gillard IT	Harris AJ	Hazell AP	Hunt RG	Leach MJC	McCulloch A	McGovern MJ	Marsh RW	Mobley VJ	Morgan IA	Parkes PBF	Salvage BJ	Saul FL	Sibley FP	Spratley AS	Venables TF	Watson IL	Wilks A
1	Aug 15	Birmingham City	1-2	Bridges	30785	7		2		11	3			6	5	10			10					9	8	1	4		
2	22	LEICESTER CITY	1-3	Venables(p)	17090	7		2		12	3			6	5	11			10			1		9	8		4		
3	29	Bolton Wanderers	2-2	Venables 2(1p)	11242	7		3	8					2	5	11			10			1		9	6		4		
4	Sep 2	Blackburn Rovers	2-0	Leach, Saul	7783	7		3		11	12			2	5	8			10			1		9	6		4		
5	5	WATFORD	1-1	Venables(p)	18856	7		3		11	8			2	5				10			1		9	6		4		
6	12	Sheffield Wednesday	0-1		14490	7	12	3		11	8			2	5				10			1		9	6		4		
7	19	BRISTOL CITY	2-1	Marsh, Bridges	13387	7		3		11	8			2	5				10			1		9	6		4		
8	26	Middlesbrough	2-6	Clement, Marsh	16788			3		11	8			2	5				10		7	1		9	6		4	12	
9	29	LUTON TOWN	0-1		19268		4	3		7									10	5	11	1		9	6		8	2	
10	Oct 3	ORIENT	5-1	Marsh 2, I Morgan 2, Venables(p)	14500		9	3		7				6	4				10	5	11	1			8			2	
11	10	Swindon Town	0-1		17682			2		7		3		6	4				10		11	1			9		8	5	
12	17	BIRMINGHAM CITY	5-2	Marsh 3, Venables, McCulloch	13074			2		11		3		6	4		9		10		7	1					8	5	
13	21	Oxford United	3-1	Venables, Ferguson, Francis	15194		9	2		11	12	3		6	5				10		7	1					8	4	
14	24	PORTSMOUTH	2-0	Clement, I Morgan	16049			2		11	9	3		6	4				10	5	7	1					8		
15	31	Millwall	0-3		16012			4			8	3	12	6	5		9		10		7	1				11		2	
16	Nov 7	CARDIFF CITY	0-1		14268	6		4		11		3		2	5	7			10			1			9		8		
17	14	Sheffield United	1-1	Hunt	19672	6		4		11	7	3		2	5	9			10			1					8		
18	21	Hull City	1-1	Leach	15606	6		4		11	7	3		2	5	9	12		10			1					8		
19	28	CHARLTON ATHLETIC	1-4	Leach	14027	4		2		11	7	3		6	5	9	8					1				10			
20	Dec 5	Sunderland	1-3	Leach	14891	6		2		11	7	3		4	5	10						1			9		8		
21	12	CARLISLE UNITED	1-1	Marsh	8884	6		2		11	7	3		4	5	9			10		12	1					8		
22	19	Leicester City	0-0		23880		4	3		11					5	9		7	10			1			8	6		2	
23	Jan 9	Luton Town	0-0		22024			3		11	8				5	9	12		10		7	1			6		4	2	
24	16	OXFORD UNITED	2-0	Francis, Marsh	10909			3		11	8			6	5	9			10		7	1					4	2	
25	Feb 6	SUNDERLAND	2-0	Venables, Leach	11707			3		11	8				5	9			10		7	1			6		4	2	12
26	13	Carlisle United	0-3		9074			3		11	8			12	5	9			10		7	1			6		4	2	
27	20	HULL CITY	1-1	Marsh	13418			3		11	8				5	9	12		10		7	1			6		4	2	
28	27	MILLWALL	2-0	Francis, Marsh	15698			3		11	8				5	9		12	10			1			6		4	2	7
29	Mar 6	Portsmouth	0-2		10402			3		11	8				5	9		4	10			1			6			2	7
30	13	SHEFFIELD UNITED	2-2	Marsh 2	12317			3		11	8			2	5	9		7	10			1			6		4		
31	20	Cardiff City	0-1		23309		12	3		8				2	5	9		11	10		7	1			6		4		
32	23	NORWICH CITY	0-1		9927			3		11	8			2	5	9			10		7	1			6		4		
33	27	Watford	2-1	Marsh 2	16625			2			8	3		6	5	7	4		10		12	1	11	9					
34	Apr 3	BOLTON WANDERERS	4-0	Marsh 3, Leach	8613			2			8	3		6	5	9			10			1	11				4		
35	6	SHEFFIELD WEDNESDAY	1-0	Marsh	11378			2	5	7	8	3		6		9	12		10			1	11				4		
36	10	Norwich City	0-3		14973			2	5	11	8	3		6			7		10			1		9			4		
37	12	Orient	1-0	McCulloch	11949	4		2	5	7	8	3		6			9		10			1				11	12		
38	17	SWINDON TOWN	4-2	Clement, Venables 2, McCulloch	11571	4		2	5		8	3		6			9		10		12	1				11	7		
39	20	Charlton Athletic	3-0	McCulloch 2, Marsh	16138			2	5		7	3		6	4		9		10		12	1				11	8		
40	24	Bristol City	0-0		12522		9		5		7	3		6	4				10			1				11	8	2	
41	27	BLACKBURN ROVERS	2-0	Marsh, Francis	9343			2	5	7	8	3		12	6		9		10			1				11	4		
42	May 1	MIDDLESBROUGH	1-1	Francis	10390			2	5		7	3		6	4		9		10			1				11	8		
		Apps				7	14	42	8	30	38	17	7	35	37	25	13	6	39	3	19	41	3	22	19	1	38	16	3
		Goals				2		3		1	5				1	6	5		21		3			1			10		

F.A. Cup

Rd	Date	Opponent	Score	Scorers	Att	Bridges BJ	Busby MG	Clement DT	Evans IP	Ferguson MK	Francis GCJ	Gillard IT	Harris AJ	Hazell AP	Hunt RG	Leach MJC	McCulloch A	McGovern MJ	Marsh RW	Mobley VJ	Morgan IA	Parkes PBF	Salvage BJ	Saul FL	Sibley FP	Spratley AS	Venables TF	Watson IL	Wilks A
R3	Jan 2	SWINDON TOWN	1-2	Marsh (p)	14840		4	3		11					5	9		7	10			1			6		8		2

F.L. Cup

Rd	Date	Opponent	Score	Scorers	Att	Bridges BJ	Busby MG	Clement DT	Evans IP	Ferguson MK	Francis GCJ	Gillard IT	Harris AJ	Hazell AP	Hunt RG	Leach MJC	McCulloch A	McGovern MJ	Marsh RW	Mobley VJ	Morgan IA	Parkes PBF	Salvage BJ	Saul FL	Sibley FP	Spratley AS	Venables TF	Watson IL	Wilks A
R2	Sep 8	CARDIFF CITY	4-0	Bridges, Saul, Marsh, Venables(p)	15025	7	12	3		11	8			2	5				10			1		9	6		4		
R3	Oct 6	Fulham	0-2		31729		9	3		7				6	4				10	5	11	1			8			2	

		P	W	D	L	F	A	W	D	L	F	A	Pts
1	Leicester City	42	12	7	2	30	14	11	6	4	27	16	59
2	Sheffield United	42	14	6	1	49	18	7	8	6	24	21	56
3	Cardiff City	42	12	7	2	39	16	8	6	7	25	25	53
4	Carlisle United	42	16	3	2	39	13	4	10	7	26	30	53
5	Hull City	42	11	5	5	31	16	8	8	5	23	25	51
6	Luton Town	42	12	7	2	40	18	6	9	9	22	25	49
7	Middlesbrough	42	13	6	2	37	16	4	8	9	23	27	48
8	Millwall	42	13	5	3	36	12	6	4	11	23	30	47
9	Birmingham City	42	12	7	2	30	12	5	5	11	28	36	46
10	Norwich City	42	11	8	2	34	20	4	6	11	20	32	44
11	QUEEN'S PARK RGS.	42	11	5	5	39	22	5	6	10	19	31	43
12	Swindon Town	42	12	7	2	38	14	3	5	13	23	37	42
13	Sunderland	42	11	6	4	34	21	4	6	11	18	33	42
14	Oxford United	42	8	8	5	23	23	6	6	9	18	25	42
15	Sheffield Wed.	42	10	7	4	32	27	2	5	14	19	42	36
16	Portsmouth	42	9	4	8	32	28	1	10	10	14	33	34
17	Orient	42	5	11	5	16	15	4	5	12	13	36	34
18	Watford	42	6	7	8	18	22	4	6	11	20	38	33
19	Bristol City	42	9	6	6	30	28	1	5	15	16	36	31
20	Charlton Athletic	42	7	6	8	28	30	1	8	12	13	35	30
21	Blackburn Rovers	42	5	8	8	20	28	1	7	13	17	41	27
22	Bolton Wanderers	42	6	5	10	22	31	1	5	15	13	43	24

1971/72 4th in Division 2

#	Date	Opponent	Score	Scorers	Att	Busby MG	Clement DT	Evans IP	Ferguson MK	Francis GCJ	Gillard IT	Hazell AP	Hunt RG	Leach MJC	McCulloch A	McGovern MJ	Mancini TJ	Marsh RW	Morgan IA	O'Rourke J	Parkes PBF	Salvage BJ	Saul FL	Seary RM	Venables TF	Watson IL
1	Aug 14	SHEFFIELD WEDNESDAY	3-0	Marsh 2 (1p), Francis	13270	7	2			8	3	6	5	11	9			10			1				4	
2	21	Middlesbrough	2-3	McCulloch, Marsh	20547	7	2			8	3	6	5	11	9			10			1		12		4	
3	28	MILLWALL	1-1	Marsh	16730	7	2			8	3	6	5	11	9			10			1				4	
4	31	Fulham	3-0	Saul, Matthewson(og), McCulloch	21187	7	2			8	3	6			9			10			1		11		4	
5	Sep 4	Swindon Town	0-0		16158	7	2				3	6	5		9			10			1		8	11	4	
6	11	PRESTON NORTH END	2-1	McCulloch, Saul	13578	7	2			8	3	6	5		9	12		10			1		11		4	
7	18	Burnley	0-1		13795	7	2			8	3	6	5		9			10			1		11		4	
8	25	WATFORD	3-0	Marsh 2, McCulloch	15698	7	2			8	3	6	5		9			10			1		11		4	
9	29	Oxford United	1-3	Busby	11902	7	2			8	3	6	5		9			10			1		11		4	
10	Oct 2	Norwich City	0-0		22695		2			8	3	6	5		9			10	7		1		11		4	
11	9	BIRMINGHAM CITY	1-0	Marsh	16039	7	2			8	3	6	5		9			10			1		11		4	
12	16	Sheffield Wednesday	0-0		16965	7	2				3	4	5	12	9		6	10			1		11		8	
13	19	LUTON TOWN	1-0	Leach	15858	7	2				3	6	12	8			5	10		9	1		11		4	
14	23	Blackpool	1-1	Marsh	16417	7	3					2	5	8	9		6	10			1		11		4	
15	30	PORTSMOUTH	1-1	Morgan	15934	7	3					2	5				6	10	12	9	1		11		4	
16	Nov 6	Cardiff City	0-0		16892		2			8	3	6			11		5	10	7	9	1		12		4	
17	13	BRISTOL CITY	3-0	O'Rourke, Merrick(og), Marsh	14898		2			8	3	6		9			5	10	7	11	1				4	
18	20	HULL CITY	2-1	O'Rourke, Morgan	12627		2			8	3	6		9			5	10	7	11	1		12		4	
19	27	Charlton Athletic	1-2	Clement	16268		2			8	3	5		9			6	10	7	11	1				4	
20	Dec 4	SUNDERLAND	2-1	Marsh, O'Rourke	13576		2			8	3	5		9			6	10	7	11	1				4	
21	11	Carlisle United	4-1	Leach, O'Rourke, Marsh(2)	9243		2			8	3	5		9	12		6	10	7	11	1				4	
22	18	SWINDON TOWN	3-0	Marsh 2, Venables	13517		2			8	3	5		9			6	10	7	11	1				4	
23	27	Orient	0-2		19081		2			8	3	5		9	12		6	10	7	11	1					
24	Jan 1	BURNLEY	3-1	Leach 2, Marsh	14614		2			8	3		5	9			6	10		11	1		7		4	
25	8	Millwall	0-0		24376		2			8	3		5	9			6	10		11	1		7		4	
26	22	OXFORD UNITED	4-2	Marsh 2, Saul, Leach	13283		2		11	8	3		5	9			6	10			1		7		4	
27	29	Luton Town	1-1	Francis	17280		2		11	8	3		5	9			6	10			1		7		4	
28	Feb 12	BLACKPOOL	0-1		13690	12	2		11	8	3		5	9			6	10			1		7		4	
29	19	Portsmouth	0-1		15563		2		11	8	3		5	9			6	10		7	1				4	
30	Mar 4	Bristol City	0-2		11105	8	2			7	3	5	4	12	9		6	10		11	1					
31	11	Birmingham City	0-0		35557	4	2	5	10	7	3	6	12	8						9	1	11				
32	18	MIDDLESBROUGH	1-0	Clement	11467	4	2	5	10	8	3	6		9						7	1	11				
33	25	Preston North End	1-1	O'Rourke	12304	4	2	5	10	8	3	6		9	12					7	1	11				
34	31	Watford	2-0	Evans, Salvage	14719	4	2	5	10	8	3	6		9						7	1	11				
35	Apr 1	ORIENT	1-0	O'Rourke	12042	4	2	5	10	8	3	6		9						7	1	11				
36	3	NORWICH CITY	0-0		25257	4	2	5	10	8	3	6		9						7	1	11				
37	8	Hull City	1-1	O'Rourke	12830	4	2	5	10	8	3	6		9	12					7	1	11				
38	15	CHARLTON ATHLETIC	2-0	Francis, Leach	12976	4	2	5	10	8	3	6		9	12					7	1	11				
39	22	Sunderland	1-0	Busby	13751	4	2		10	8	3	6		9			5			7	1	11				
40	25	FULHAM	0-0		20605	4	2		10	8	3	6		9	12		5			7	1	11				
41	29	CARLISLE UNITED	3-0	Clement, Leach, O'Rourke	7616	4	2		10	8		6		9			5			7	1	11				3
42	May 2	CARDIFF CITY	3-0	Ferguson, O'Rourke, Leach	8430	4	2		10	8		6		9			5			7	1	11				3
		Apps				29	42	8	16	38	24	42	30	31	23	1	23	30	10	26	42	15	21	1	27	2
		Goals				2	3	1	1	3				8	4			17	2	9		1	3		1	

Two own goals

F.A. Cup

	Date	Opponent	Score	Scorers	Att	Busby MG	Clement DT	Evans IP	Ferguson MK	Francis GCJ	Gillard IT	Hazell AP	Hunt RG	Leach MJC	McCulloch A	McGovern MJ	Mancini TJ	Marsh RW	Morgan IA	O'Rourke J	Parkes PBF	Salvage BJ	Saul FL	Seary RM	Venables TF	Watson IL
R3	Jan 15	FULHAM	1-1	Mancini	23707		2			8	3		5	9	12		6	10		11	1		7		4	
rep	18	Fulham	1-2	Clement	24181		2			8	3		5	9			6	10		11	1		7		4	

F.L. Cup

	Date	Opponent	Score	Scorers	Att	Busby MG	Clement DT	Evans IP	Ferguson MK	Francis GCJ	Gillard IT	Hazell AP	Hunt RG	Leach MJC	McCulloch A	McGovern MJ	Mancini TJ	Marsh RW	Morgan IA	O'Rourke J	Parkes PBF	Salvage BJ	Saul FL	Seary RM	Venables TF	Watson IL
R2	Sep 7	BIRMINGHAM CITY	2-0	Francis, Marsh	15032	7	2			8	3	6	5		9			10			1		11		4	
R3	Oct 5	LINCOLN CITY	4-2	Morgan, McCulloch, Marsh, Saul	12723		2			8	3	6	5		9			10	7		1		11		4	
R4	26	BRISTOL ROVERS	1-1	Marsh	17045	7	3	6		8		2	5	9				10	12		1		11		4	
rep	Nov 2	Bristol Rovers	0-1		24373		2	5	11	8	3	6						10	7	9	1		12		4	

	P	W	D	L	F	A	W	D	L	F	A	Pts
1 Norwich City	42	13	8	0	40	16	8	7	6	20	20	57
2 Birmingham City	42	15	6	0	46	14	4	12	5	14	17	56
3 Millwall	42	14	7	0	38	17	5	10	6	26	29	55
4 QUEEN'S PARK RGS.	42	16	4	1	39	9	4	10	7	18	19	54
5 Sunderland	42	11	7	3	42	24	6	9	6	25	33	50
6 Blackpool	42	12	6	3	43	16	8	1	12	27	34	47
7 Burnley	42	13	4	4	43	22	7	2	12	27	33	46
8 Bristol City	42	14	3	4	43	22	4	7	10	18	27	46
9 Middlesbrough	42	16	4	1	31	11	3	4	14	19	37	46
10 Carlisle United	42	12	6	3	38	22	5	3	13	23	35	43
11 Swindon Town	42	10	6	5	29	16	5	6	10	18	31	42
12 Hull City	42	10	6	5	33	21	4	4	13	16	32	38
13 Luton Town	42	7	8	6	25	24	3	10	8	18	24	38
14 Sheffield Wed.	42	11	7	3	33	22	2	5	14	18	36	38
15 Oxford United	42	10	8	3	28	17	2	6	13	15	38	38
16 Portsmouth	42	9	7	5	31	26	3	6	12	28	42	37
17 Orient	42	12	4	5	32	19	2	5	14	18	42	37
18 Preston North End	42	11	4	6	32	21	1	8	12	20	37	36
19 Cardiff City	42	9	7	5	37	25	1	7	13	19	44	34
20 Fulham	42	10	7	4	29	20	2	3	16	16	48	34
21 Charlton Athletic	42	9	7	5	33	25	3	2	16	22	52	33
22 Watford	42	5	5	11	15	25	0	4	17	9	50	19

1972/73 2nd in Division 2: Promoted

#		Date	Opponent	Score	Scorers	Att	Beck JA	Bowles S	Busby MG	Clement DT	Delve JF	Evans IP	Ferguson MK	Francis GCJ	Gillard IT	Givens DJ	Hazell AP	Hunt RG	Leach MJC	McCulloch A	Mancini TJ	Morgan IA	O'Rourke J	Parkes PBF	Salvage BJ	Spratley AS	Thomas D	Venables TF	Watson IL
1	Aug	12	Swindon Town	2-2	Busby, Leach	14383			7	2	5			8		11	6		10				9	1				4	3
2		19	SHEFFIELD WEDNESDAY	4-2	Francis, O'Rourke, Givens, Leach	12977			7	2	5			8		11	6		10				9	1				4	3
3		26	Preston North End	1-1	O'Rourke	9292			7	2	5			8		11	6		10				9	1				4	3
4	Sep	2	MIDDLESBROUGH	2-2	Givens, O'Rourke	10601			7	2	5			8		11	6		10				9	1				4	3
5		9	Burnley	1-1	Busby	10898			7	2	5			8		11	6					9	10	1	12		4	3
6		16	NOTTM. FOREST	3-0	Givens, Bowles, McCulloch	12528		10	7	2	5			8		11	6					9		1	12		4	3
7		19	BRISTOL CITY	1-1	Francis	11588		10	7	2	5			8		11	6			9				1				4	3
8		23	Orient	2-2	Leach, Bowles	9492		10	7	2	5			8			6		11	9				1				4	3
9		26	Hull City	1-4	Givens	8289		10	7	2	5			8		11	6			9				1				4	3
10		30	CARDIFF CITY	3-0	Givens 2, Bowles	11182		10	7	2	5		12	8	3	11	6			9				1				4	
11	Oct	7	CARLISLE UNITED	4-0	Leach, Busby, Evans, Francis	11755		10	7	2	5			8		11	6			9				1				4	3
12		14	Aston Villa	1-0	Francis	34045		10	7	2	5			8		11	6			9				1				4	3
13		17	Fulham	2-0	Bowles, Givens	20895		10	7	2	5			8		11	6			9	12			1				4	3
14		21	SUNDERLAND	3-2	Bowles 2, Givens	17356		10		2	5			8		11	6		9					1			7	4	3
15		28	Blackpool	0-2		14160		10		2	5			8		11	6		9					1			7	4	3
16	Nov	4	HULL CITY	1-1	Bowles	13619		10		2	5			8		11	6		9					1			7	4	3
17		11	Bristol City	2-1	Givens 2	12570		10		2	5			8		11	6		9					1			7	4	3
18		18	MILLWALL	1-3	Bowles	15857		10		2	5			8	3	11	6		9		12			1			7	4	
19		25	Portsmouth	1-0	Givens	8460		10		2				8	3	11	6		9		5			1			7	4	
20	Dec	2	OXFORD UNITED	0-0		9790		10		2				8	3	11	6		9		5			1			7	4	
21		9	Luton Town	2-2	Givens, Clement	13670		10		2				8	3	11	6		9		5			1			7	4	
22		23	Brighton & Hove Albion	2-1	Givens 2	13735		10		2				8	3	11	6		9		5			1			7	4	
23		26	ORIENT	3-1	Leach, Givens, Thomas	15062	12	10		2				8	3	11	6		9		5			1			7	4	
24		30	Sheffield Wednesday	1-3	Leach	19785		10			12			8	3	11	6		9		5			1			7	4	2
25	Jan	6	PRESTON NORTH END	3-0	Givens 2, Francis	10519		10				7		8		11	2	6	4		5			1		12	9		3
26		20	Middlesbrough	0-0		8398		10		3	12			8		11	6		4		5			1			9	7	2
27		27	BURNLEY	2-0	Leach, Givens	22518		10		2	4			8		11	6		9		5			1		1	7		3
28	Feb	6	HUDDERSFIELD T	3-1	Givens 2, Thomas	13539		10		2	4			8		11		6	9		5			1			7		3
29		10	Nottingham Forest	0-0		11617		10		2	4			8		11	6		9		5			1			7		3
30		17	SWINDON TOWN	5-0	Bowles 3, Francis, Givens	13472		10		2				8		11	6		9		5			1			7	4	3
31	Mar	3	Carlisle United	3-1	Thomas, Bowles, Clement	8733		10		2				8		11	6		9		5			1			7	4	3
32		6	Huddersfield Town	2-2	Francis, Leach	8627				2	10			8		11	6		9		5			1			7	4	3
33		10	ASTON VILLA	1-0	Leach	21578				2	10			8		11	6		9		5			1			7	4	3
34		24	BLACKPOOL	4-0	Bowles, Francis, Thomas, Hatton(og)	15714		10		2				8		11	6		9		5			1			7	4	3
35		31	PORTSMOUTH	5-0	Thomas, Lewis(og), Venables, Leach, Mancini	14086		10		2				8		11	6		9		5			1			7	4	3
36	Apr	7	Oxford United	0-2		12390		10		2				8		11	6		9		5			1			7	4	3
37		14	LUTON TOWN	2-0	Mancini, Givens	16471		10		2	12			8		11	6		9		5			1			7	4	3
38		18	Cardiff City	0-0		12033		10		2				8		11	6		9		5			1			7	4	3
39		21	Millwall	1-0	Givens	16138		10		2				8		11	6		9		5			1			7	4	3
40		24	BRIGHTON & HOVE ALB	2-0	Francis, Bowles	16625		10		2				8		11	6		9		5			1			7	4	3
41		28	FULHAM	2-0	Clement, Bowles	22187		10		2				8		11	6		9		5			1			7	4	3
42	May	9	Sunderland	3-0	Bowles 2, Thomas	43285		10		2				8		11	6		9		5			1			7	4	3
Apps							1	35	13	40	9	18	2	42	8	41	41	2	36	6	24	2	8	41	3	1	28	37	35
Goals								17	3	3		1		9		23			10	1	2		3				6	1	

Two own goals

F.A. Cup

		Date	Opponent	Score	Scorers	Att	Beck JA	Bowles S	Busby MG	Clement DT	Delve JF	Evans IP	Ferguson MK	Francis GCJ	Gillard IT	Givens DJ	Hazell AP	Hunt RG	Leach MJC	McCulloch A	Mancini TJ	Morgan IA	O'Rourke J	Parkes PBF	Salvage BJ	Spratley AS	Thomas D	Venables TF	Watson IL
R1	Jan	13	BARNET	0-0		13626		10		3		7				11	2	6	4		5			1		8	9		
rep		16	Barnet	3-0	Leach, Bowles, Mancini	10919		10		3		7		8		11	4		6		5			1			9		2
R2	Feb	3	Oxford United	2-0	Clement, Givens	16057		10		2	4			8		11	6		12	9	5			1			7		3
R3		24	Derby County	2-4	Leach, Givens	38100		10		2				8		11	6		9		5			1			7	4	3

F.L. Cup

		Date	Opponent	Score	Scorers	Att	Beck JA	Bowles S	Busby MG	Clement DT	Delve JF	Evans IP	Ferguson MK	Francis GCJ	Gillard IT	Givens DJ	Hazell AP	Hunt RG	Leach MJC	McCulloch A	Mancini TJ	Morgan IA	O'Rourke J	Parkes PBF	Salvage BJ	Spratley AS	Thomas D	Venables TF	Watson IL
R2	Sep	6	West Bromwich Albion	1-2	Givens	8282			7	2	5			8		11	6		10	12			9	1				4	3

		P	W	D	L	F	A	W	D	L	F	A	Pts
1	Burnley	42	13	6	2	44	18	11	8	2	28	17	62
2	QUEEN'S PARK RGS.	42	16	4	1	54	13	8	9	4	27	24	61
3	Aston Villa	42	12	5	4	27	17	6	9	6	24	30	50
4	Middlesbrough	42	12	6	3	29	15	5	7	9	17	28	47
5	Bristol City	42	10	7	4	34	18	7	5	9	29	33	46
6	Sunderland	42	12	6	3	35	17	5	6	10	24	32	46
7	Blackpool	42	12	6	3	37	17	6	4	11	19	34	46
8	Oxford United	42	14	2	5	36	18	5	5	11	16	25	45
9	Fulham	42	11	6	4	32	16	5	6	10	26	33	44
10	Sheffield Wed.	42	14	4	3	40	20	3	6	12	19	35	44
11	Millwall	42	12	5	4	33	18	4	5	12	22	29	42
12	Luton Town	42	6	9	6	24	23	9	2	10	20	30	41
13	Hull City	42	9	7	5	39	22	5	5	11	25	37	40
14	Nottingham Forest	42	12	5	4	32	18	2	7	12	15	34	40
15	Orient	42	11	6	4	33	18	1	6	14	16	35	36
16	Swindon Town	42	8	9	4	28	23	2	7	12	18	38	36
17	Portsmouth	42	7	6	8	21	22	5	5	11	21	37	35
18	Carlisle United	42	10	5	6	40	24	1	7	13	10	28	34
19	Preston North End	42	6	8	7	19	25	5	4	12	18	39	34
20	Cardiff City	42	11	4	6	32	21	0	7	14	11	37	33
21	Huddersfield Town	42	7	9	5	21	20	1	8	12	15	36	33
22	Brighton & Hove A.	42	7	8	6	32	31	1	5	15	14	52	29

1973/74 8th in Division 1

No	Date	Opponent	Res	Scorers	Att	Abbott RF	Beck JA	Bowles S	Busby MG	Clement DT	Delve JF	Evans IP	Francis GCJ	Gillard IT	Givens DJ	Hazell AP	Leach MJC	McLintock F	Mancini TJ	Parkes PBF	Thomas D	Venables TF	Watson IL
1	Aug 25	SOUTHAMPTON	1-1	Givens	18602			10		2	8				11	6	9		5	1	7	4	3
2	29	Norwich City	0-0		24285			10		2	8				11	6	9		5	1	7	4	3
3	Sep 1	Manchester United	1-2	Francis	44156			10		2			8		11	6	9		5	1	7	4	3
4	4	WEST HAM UNITED	0-0		28360			10		2			8		11	6	9		5	1	7	4	3
5	8	STOKE CITY	3-3	Leach, Venables(p), Mancini	18118			10		2			8		11	6	9		5	1	7	4	3
6	10	West Ham United	3-2	Givens 2, Abbott	26042	7		10		2			8		11	6	9		5	1		4	3
7	15	Everton	0-1		30795			10				6	8	3	11	2	9		5	1	7	4	
8	22	BIRMINGHAM CITY	2-2	Hynd(og), Bowles	18701			10	12	2			8		11	3	9	6	5	1	7	4	
9	29	Newcastle United	3-2	Thomas, Francis, Leach	31402			10		2			8		11	3	9	6	5	1	7	4	
10	Oct 6	CHELSEA	1-1	Bowles	30109			10		2			8		11	3	9	6	5	1	7	4	
11	13	Burnley	1-2	Thomas	18349			10		2		5	8		11	3	9	6		1	7	4	
12	20	Wolverhampton Wan.	4-2	Bowles 2, Leach, Francis(p)	19350			10		2	12		8		11	3	9	6	5	1	7	4	
13	27	ARSENAL	2-0	Givens, Bowles	29115			10		2			8		11	3	9	6	5	1	7	4	
14	Nov 3	Derby County	2-1	Francis, Bowles	28092			10		2			8		11	3	9	6	5	1	7	4	
15	10	COVENTRY CITY	3-0	Bowles, Francis, Venables	20416			10		2	12		8		11	3	9	6	5	1	7	4	
16	17	Manchester City	0-1		30486			10	9	2	12		8		11	3		6	5	1	7	4	
17	24	LIVERPOOL	2-2	Bowles, McLintock	26254			10		2			8		11	3	9	6	5	1	7	4	
18	Dec 1	Leeds United	2-2	Thomas, Bowles	32194			10		2			8		11	3	9	6	5	1	7	4	
19	8	SHEFFIELD UNITED	0-0		15843		12	10		2	4		8		11	3	9	6	5	1	7		
20	15	Leicester City	0-2		17614			10		2			8		11	3	9	6	5	1	7	4	
21	22	NEWCASTLE UNITED	3-2	Clement, Givens, Bowles	15757			10		2			8	3	11		9	6	5	1	7	4	
22	26	Tottenham Hotspur	0-0		30762			10		2			8	3	11		9	6	5	1	7	4	
23	29	Stoke City	1-4	Leach	18908		12	10		2		5	8	3	11		9	6		1	7	4	
24	Jan 1	MANCHESTER UNITED	3-0	Bowles 2, Givens	32339			10		2			8	3	11		9	6	5	1	7	4	
25	12	EVERTON	1-0	Givens	20051			10		2			8	3	11		9	6	5	1	7	4	
26	19	Southampton	2-2	Thomas, Francis(p)	22689			10		2			8	3	11	6	9		5	1	7	4	
27	Feb 2	LEICESTER CITY	0-0		22646			10		2			8	3	11		9	6	5	1	7	4	
28	5	NORWICH CITY	1-2	Bowles	12422			10		2			8	3	11		9	6	5	1	7	4	
29	23	Chelsea	3-3	Bowles 2, Givens	34264	12		10		2			8	3	11		9	6	5	1	7	4	
30	27	BURNLEY	2-1	Thomas, Bowles(p)	21306	4		10		2			8	3	11		9	6	5	1	7		
31	Mar 2	TOTTENHAM HOTSPUR	3-1	Givens, Bowles, Francis	25775	4		10		2			8	3	11	12	9	6	5	1	7		
32	16	WOLVERHAMPTON W.	0-0		21209			10		2			8	3	11	12	9	6	5	1	7	4	
33	23	Coventry City	1-0	Francis	18825	12		10		2			8	3	11		9	6	5	1	7		
34	30	DERBY COUNTY	0-0		19795			10	12	2			8	3	11		9	6	5	1	7	4	
35	Apr 6	Liverpool	1-2	Thomas	52027			10		2			8	3	11	6	9		5	1	7	4	
36	9	MANCHESTER CITY	3-0	Leach 2, Bowles	20461		4	10		2			8	3	11	6	9		5	1	7		
37	12	IPSWICH TOWN	0-1		27567		4	10		2			8	3	11	6	9		5	1	7		
38	15	Ipswich Town	0-1		26093	12		10		2			8	3	11	6	9		5	1	7	4	
39	20	Sheffield United	1-1	Givens	17833			10	9			6	8	3	11	2	12		5	1	7	4	
40	23	Birmingham City	0-4		39160			10	9			6	8	3	11	2			5	1	7	4	
41	27	LEEDS UNITED	0-1		35353			10		2			8	3	11	6	9		5	1	7	4	
42	30	Arsenal	1-1	Bowles	40396	12		10		2			8	3	11	6	9		5	1	7	4	
	Apps					7	5	42	6	38	6	5	40	23	42	31	40	26	40	42	41	36	6
	Goals					1		19		1			8		10		6	1	1		6	2	

One own goal

F.A. Cup

Rd	Date	Opponent	Res	Scorers	Att	Abbott RF	Beck JA	Bowles S	Busby MG	Clement DT	Delve JF	Evans IP	Francis GCJ	Gillard IT	Givens DJ	Hazell AP	Leach MJC	McLintock F	Mancini TJ	Parkes PBF	Thomas D	Venables TF	Watson IL
R3	Jan 5	Chelsea	0-0		31540			10		2			8	3	11		9	6	5	1	7	4	
rep	15	CHELSEA	1-0	Bowles	28573			10		2			8	3	11	12	9	6	5	1	7	4	
R4	26	BIRMINGHAM CITY	2-0	Leach, Givens	23387			10		2			8	3	11		9	6	5	1	7	4	
R5	Feb 16	Coventry City	0-0		30081			10					8	3	11	2	9	6	5	1	7	4	
rep	19	COVENTRY CITY	3-2	Givens, Thomas, Bowles	28010			10					8	3	11	2	9	6	5	1	7	4	
R6	Mar 9	LEICESTER CITY	0-2		34078			10		2			8	3	11		9	6	5	1	7	4	

F.L. Cup

Rd	Date	Opponent	Res	Scorers	Att	Abbott RF	Beck JA	Bowles S	Busby MG	Clement DT	Delve JF	Evans IP	Francis GCJ	Gillard IT	Givens DJ	Hazell AP	Leach MJC	McLintock F	Mancini TJ	Parkes PBF	Thomas D	Venables TF	Watson IL
R2	Oct 8	TOTTENHAM HOTSPUR	1-0	Givens	23353			10	12	2			8		11	3	9	6	5	1	7	4	
R3	Nov 6	SHEFFIELD WEDNESDAY	8-2	*see below	16043			10	12	2			8		11	3	9	6	5	1	7	4	
R4	20	PLYMOUTH ARGYLE	0-3		19072			10	9	2	12		8		11	3		6	5	1	7	4	

Scorers in R3: Cameron (og), Mullen (og), Francis, Bowles, Givens 2, Leach 2

		P	W	D	L	F	A	W	D	L	F	A	Pts
1	Leeds United	42	12	8	1	38	18	12	6	3	28	13	62
2	Liverpool	42	18	2	1	34	11	4	11	6	18	20	57
3	Derby County	42	13	7	1	40	16	4	7	10	12	26	48
4	Ipswich Town	42	10	7	4	38	21	8	4	9	29	37	47
5	Stoke City	42	13	6	2	39	15	2	10	9	15	27	46
6	Burnley	42	10	9	2	29	16	6	5	10	27	37	46
7	Everton	42	12	7	2	29	14	4	5	12	21	34	44
8	QUEEN'S PARK RGS.	42	8	10	3	30	17	5	7	9	26	35	43
9	Leicester City	42	10	7	4	35	17	3	9	9	16	24	42
10	Arsenal	42	9	7	5	23	16	5	7	9	26	35	42
11	Tottenham Hotspur	42	9	4	8	26	27	5	10	6	19	23	42
12	Wolverhampton Wan.	42	11	6	4	30	18	2	9	10	19	31	41
13	Sheffield United	42	7	7	7	25	22	7	5	9	19	27	40
14	Manchester City	42	10	7	4	25	17	4	5	12	14	29	40
15	Newcastle United	42	9	6	6	28	21	4	6	11	21	27	38
16	Coventry City	42	10	5	6	25	18	4	5	12	18	36	38
17	Chelsea	42	9	4	8	36	29	3	9	9	20	31	37
18	West Ham United	42	7	7	7	36	32	4	8	9	19	28	37
19	Birmingham City	42	10	7	4	30	21	2	6	13	22	43	37
20	Southampton	42	8	10	3	30	20	3	4	14	17	48	36
21	Manchester United	42	7	7	7	23	20	3	5	13	15	28	32
22	Norwich City	42	6	9	6	25	27	1	6	14	12	35	29

1974/75   11th in Division 1

#		Date	Opponent	Score	Scorers	Att	Abbott RF	Beck JA	Bowles S	Busby MG	Clement DT	Francis GCJ	Gillard IT	Givens DJ	Hazell AP	Leach MJC	McLintock F	Mancini TJ	Masson DS	Parkes PBF	Pritchett KB	Rogers DE	Shanks D	Teale RG	Thomas D	Venables TF	Webb DJ	Westwood D
1	Aug	17	Sheffield United	1-1	Francis	16032	9	10			2	8	3	11			5			1					7	4	6	
2		21	Leeds United	1-0	Francis	31497	9	10		12	2	8	3	11			5			1					7	4	6	
3		24	STOKE CITY	0-1		21117		9	10	4	2	8	3	11		12	5			1					7		6	
4		27	LEEDS UNITED	1-1	Givens	24965		9	10	12	2	8	3	11			5			1					7	4	6	
5		31	Luton Town	1-1	Bowles (p)	18535		9	10		2	8	3	11			5			1					7	4	6	
6	Sep	7	BIRMINGHAM CITY	0-1		16058		9	10	2		8	3	11	12		5			1					7	4	6	
7		14	Leicester City	1-3	Francis	19763			10	9	2	8	3	11	6	4				1					7		5	
8		21	NEWCASTLE UNITED	1-2	Keeley(og)	18594			10	9	2	8	3	11	6	4				1					7		5	
9		24	EVERTON	2-2	Givens, Busby	16638	10			9	2	8	3	11	6	4			12	1					7		5	
10		28	Manchester City	0-1		30647	10		4	9	2	8	3	11	6				12	1					7		5	
11	Oct	5	IPSWICH TOWN	1-0	Francis	19494		4	10		2	8	3	11	6	9	5		12	1					7			
12		12	Arsenal	2-2	Bowles 2(2p)	26690			10		2	8	3	11		4	5			1		9			7		6	
13		19	LIVERPOOL	0-1		27392		4	10		2	8	3	11			5			1		9			7		6	
14		26	Wolverhampton Wan.	2-1	Givens 2	20320			10		2	8	3	11	4		5			1		9			7		6	
15	Nov	2	COVENTRY CITY	2-0	Bowles, Givens	17256			10		2		3	11	4	9	5			1		8			7		6	
16		9	Derby County	2-5	Leach, Bowles	23339			10	12	2	8	3	11	4	9	5			1					7		6	
17		16	CARLISLE UNITED	2-1	Thomas, Bowles	15700			10		6	8	3	11	2	4	5			1		9			7			
18		23	Middlesbrough	3-1	Bowles, Givens, Rogers	27530			10		2	8	3	11	6	4	5			1		9			7			
19		27	Stoke City	0-1		22425			10		2	8	3	11	6	4	5			1		9			7			
20		30	WEST HAM UNITED	0-2		28357			10		2	8	3	11		4	5			1		9			7		6	
21	Dec	7	Burnley	0-3		16522			10		2	8	3	11		9	5			1					7		6	
22		14	SHEFFIELD UNITED	1-0	Rogers	13244	10				2	8	3	11		9	5		4	1		7					6	
23		21	Tottenham Hotspur	2-1	Bowles 2(1p)	21150		8	10		2		3	11		9	5		4	1					7		6	
24		26	LEICESTER CITY	4-2	Beck, Thomas, Givens, Westwood	17311		8			6		3	11		9	5		4	1				2	7		10	12
25		28	Chelsea	3-0	Givens 2, Francis	38917		9	10		2	8	3	11			5		4	1					7		6	
26	Jan	11	BURNLEY	0-1		19539		9	10		2	8	3	11			5		4	1					7		6	
27		18	West Ham United	2-2	Masson, Bowles (p)	28762		9	10		2	8	3	11			5		4	1					7		6	
28	Feb	1	DERBY COUNTY	4-1	Givens 3, Thomas	20686		9	10		2	8	3	11			5		4	1					7		6	
29		8	Coventry City	1-1	Leach	18830		9	10		2	8	3	11		12	5		4	1					7			
30		22	Carlisle United	2-1	Givens 2	13176		9	10	12	6		3	11			5		4	1		8	2		7			
31		25	MIDDLESBROUGH	0-0		18487		9	10		2	8	3	11			5		4	1					7		6	
32	Mar	1	LUTON TOWN	2-1	Givens, Rogers	19583		9	10	8	2		3	11			5		4	1		12			7			
33		8	Everton	1-2	Givens	39567		9	10	8	2		3	11			5		4	1					7			
34		15	MANCHESTER CITY	2-0	Rogers 2	22102			10	9		8	3				5		4	1		11	2		7		6	
35		18	CHELSEA	1-0	Thomas	25324			10	12		8	3				5		4	1		11	2		7		6	
36		22	Birmingham City	1-4	Thomas	32832			10	9		8	3	11			5		4	1		12	2		7		6	
37		29	TOTTENHAM HOTSPUR	0-1		25461		9				8	3	11			5		4	1		10	2		7		6	
38		31	Newcastle United	2-2	Francis (p), Gillard	29819		12	9			8	6	11		10	5		4	1	3		2		7			
39	Apr	5	WOLVERHAMPTON W.	2-0	Givens, Thomas	16596		12	9			8	6	11			5		4	1	3		2		7			
40		12	Ipswich Town	1-2	Gillard	28684		12	9	10		8	6	11			5		4	1	3		2		7			
41		19	ARSENAL	0-0		24362	5	9	10				6	11			8		4	1	3		2		7			
42		26	Liverpool	1-3	Francis (p)	42546	10	9				8	3	11			12		5	1			2		7		6	
			Apps				9	29	33	15	31	35	42	40	12	20	30	7	21	41	4	18	12	1	41	5	33	1
			Goals					1	10	1		7	2	17		2			1			5			6			1

One own goal

F.A. Cup

Rd		Date	Opponent	Score	Scorers	Att	Abbott RF	Beck JA	Bowles S	Busby MG	Clement DT	Francis GCJ	Gillard IT	Givens DJ	Hazell AP	Leach MJC	McLintock F	Mancini TJ	Masson DS	Parkes PBF	Pritchett KB	Rogers DE	Shanks D	Teale RG	Thomas D	Venables TF	Webb DJ	Westwood D
R3	Jan	4	Southend United	2-2	Gillard, Francis	18,100		7	10		2	8	3	11		9	5		4	1							6	
rep		7	SOUTHEND UNITED	2-0	Givens 2	21,484		9	10		2	8	3	11			5		4	1					7		6	
R4		24	NOTTS COUNTY	3-0	Thomas, Bowles (p), Givens	23,428		9	10		2	8	3	11			5		4	1					7		6	
R5	Feb	15	West Ham United	1-2	Clement	39,193		9	10		2		3	11		8	5		4	1					12		6	

F.L. Cup

Rd		Date	Opponent	Score	Scorers	Att	Abbott RF	Beck JA	Bowles S	Busby MG	Clement DT	Francis GCJ	Gillard IT	Givens DJ	Hazell AP	Leach MJC	McLintock F	Mancini TJ	Masson DS	Parkes PBF	Pritchett KB	Rogers DE	Shanks D	Teale RG	Thomas D	Venables TF	Webb DJ	Westwood D
R2	Sep	10	ORIENT	1-1	Francis	14,304			10	9	2	8	3	11			5							1	7	4	6	
rep		17	Orient	3-0	Francis, Givens, Bowles	11,750	2		10	6		8	3	11	4	9				1					7		5	
R3	Oct	8	NEWCASTLE UNITED	0-4		15,815		4	10		2	8	3	11	6		5			1					7		12	9

		P	W	D	L	F	A	W	D	L	F	A	Pts
1	Derby County	42	14	4	3	41	18	7	7	7	26	31	53
2	Liverpool	42	14	5	2	44	17	6	6	9	16	22	51
3	Ipswich Town	42	17	2	2	47	14	6	3	12	19	30	51
4	Everton	42	10	9	2	33	19	6	9	6	23	23	50
5	Stoke City	42	12	7	2	40	18	5	8	8	24	30	49
6	Sheffield United	42	12	7	2	35	20	6	6	9	23	31	49
7	Middlesbrough	42	11	7	3	33	14	7	5	9	21	26	48
8	Manchester City	42	16	3	2	40	15	2	7	12	14	39	46
9	Leeds United	42	10	8	3	34	20	6	5	10	23	29	45
10	Burnley	42	11	6	4	40	29	6	5	10	28	38	45
11	QUEEN'S PARK RGS.	42	10	4	7	25	17	6	6	9	29	37	42
12	Wolverhampton Wan.	42	12	5	4	43	21	2	6	13	14	33	39
13	West Ham United	42	10	6	5	38	22	3	7	11	20	37	39
14	Coventry City	42	8	9	4	31	27	4	6	11	20	35	39
15	Newcastle United	42	12	4	5	39	23	3	5	13	20	49	39
16	Arsenal	42	10	6	5	31	16	3	5	13	16	33	37
17	Birmingham City	42	10	4	7	34	28	4	5	12	19	33	37
18	Leicester City	42	8	7	6	25	17	4	5	12	21	43	36
19	Tottenham Hotspur	42	8	4	9	29	27	5	4	12	23	36	34
20	Luton Town	42	8	6	7	27	26	3	5	13	20	39	33
21	Chelsea	42	4	9	8	22	31	5	6	10	20	41	33
22	Carlisle United	42	8	2	11	22	21	4	3	14	21	38	29

1975/76   2nd in Division 1

No	Date	Opponent	Score	Scorers	Att	Abbott RF	Beck JA	Bowles S	Clement DT	Francis GCJ	Gillard IT	Givens DJ	Hollins JW	Leach MJC	McLintock F	Masson DS	Nutt PJ	Parkes PBF	Shanks D	Tagg AP	Thomas D	Webb DJ
1	Aug 16	LIVERPOOL	2-0	Francis, Leach	27113			10	2	8	3	11	4	12	5	9		1			7	6
2	19	ASTON VILLA	1-1	Francis	21966	6	12	10	2	8	3	11	4		5	9		1			7	
3	23	Derby County	5-1	Bowles 3 (1p), Thomas, Clement	27950	5	12	10	2	8	3	11	4			9		1		6	7	
4	26	Wolverhampton Wan.	2-2	Givens 2	19380	5		10	2	8	3	11	4			9		1		6	7	
5	30	WEST HAM UNITED	1-1	Givens	28408	5		10	2	8	3	11	4	12		9		1		6	7	
6	Sep 6	Birmingham City	1-1	Thomas	27305	5		10	2			11	8		4	9		1		6	7	3
7	13	MANCHESTER UNITED	1-0	Webb	29237			10	2	8	3	11	4		5	9		1			7	6
8	20	Middlesbrough	0-0		24887			10	2	8	3	11	4	12	5	9		1			7	6
9	23	LEICESTER CITY	1-0	Leach	19292			10	2	8	3	11	4		5	9		1			7	6
10	27	NEWCASTLE UNITED	1-0	Leach	22981			10	2	8	3	11	4		5	9		1			7	6
11	Oct 4	Leeds United	1-2	Bowles (p)	30943			10	2	8	3	11	4		5	9		1			7	6
12	11	EVERTON	5-0	Francis 2, Givens, Masson, Thomas	23435			10	2	8	3	11	4		5	9		1			7	6
13	18	Burnley	0-1		20378			10	2	8	3	11	5		4	9		1			7	6
14	25	SHEFFIELD UNITED	1-0	Givens	21161			10	2	8	3	11	4		5	9		1			7	6
15	Nov 1	Coventry City	1-1	Givens	18047			10	2	8	3	11	4		5	9		1			7	6
16	8	TOTTENHAM HOTSPUR	0-0		28434			10	2	8	3	11	4		5	9		1			7	6
17	15	Ipswich Town	1-1	Givens	25529				2	8	3	11	10	4	5	9		1			7	6
18	22	BURNLEY	1-0	Bowles	17390			10	2	8	3	11	4		5	9		1			7	6
19	29	STOKE CITY	3-2	Masson, Clement, Webb	22328		8	10	2		3		4	11	5	9	12	1			7	6
20	Dec 6	Manchester City	0-0		36066				2	8	3	11	4	10	5	9		1			7	6
21	13	DERBY COUNTY	1-1	Nutt	25465				2	8	3	11	4	10	5	9	12	1			7	6
22	20	Liverpool	0-2		39182			10	2	8	3	11	4		5	9		1			7	6
23	26	NORWICH CITY	2-0	Masson, Bowles	21774			10	2	8	3	11	4		5	9		1			7	6
24	27	Arsenal	0-2		39021			10	2	8	3	11	4		5	9		1			7	6
25	Jan 10	Manchester United	1-2	Givens	58312	12		10	2	8	3	11	4	7	5	9		1				6
26	17	BIRMINGHAM CITY	2-1	Masson 2	16759		8	10	2		3	11	4		5	9		1			7	6
27	24	West Ham United	0-1		26437		8		2		3	11	4	10	5	9	12	1			7	6
28	31	Aston Villa	2-0	Hollins, Francis	32223				2	8	3	11	4	10	5	9		1			7	6
29	Feb 7	WOLVERHAMPTON W.	4-2	Givens 2, Thomas, Francis (p)	17173			10	2	8	3	11	4		5	9		1			7	6
30	14	Tottenham Hotspur	3-0	Francis 2, Givens	28190			10	2	8	3	11	5		4	9		1			7	6
31	21	IPSWICH TOWN	3-1	Wark(og), Webb, Thomas	22593			10	2	8	3	11	5	4	12	9		1			7	6
32	25	Leicester City	1-0	Thomas	24340			10	2	8	3	11	4		5	9		1			7	6
33	28	Sheffield United	0-0		21949			10	2		3	11	4	8	5	9		1			7	6
34	Mar 6	COVENTRY CITY	4-1	Thomas, Francis, Givens, Masson	19731			10	2	8	3	11	4		5	9		1			7	6
35	13	Everton	2-0	Bowles, Leach	25006			10	2	8	3	11	4	12	5	9		1			7	6
36	20	Stoke City	1-0	Webb	22847			10	2		3	11	4	8	5	9		1			7	6
37	27	MANCHESTER CITY	1-0	Webb	29883			10			3	11	4	8	5	9		1	2		7	6
38	Apr 3	Newcastle United	2-1	McLintock, Bowles	30145			10			3	11	4	8	5	9		1	2		7	6
39	10	MIDDLESBROUGH	4-2	Francis 2(1p), Givens, Bowles	24342			10	2	8	3	11	4		5	9		1			7	6
40	17	Norwich City	2-3	Thomas, Powell(og)	30895			10	2	8	3	11	4		5	9		1			7	6
41	19	ARSENAL	2-1	McLintock, Francis(p)	30362			10	2	8	3	11	4		5	9		1			7	6
42	24	LEEDS UNITED	2-0	Thomas, Bowles	31002			10	2	8	3	11	4		5	9		1			7	6
Apps						6	5	37	40	36	41	41	30	31	35	42	3	42	2	4	41	38
Goals								10	2	12		13	1	4	2	6	1				9	5

Two own goals

F.A. Cup

Rnd	Date	Opponent	Score	Scorers	Att	Abbott RF	Beck JA	Bowles S	Clement DT	Francis GCJ	Gillard IT	Givens DJ	Hollins JW	Leach MJC	McLintock F	Masson DS	Nutt PJ	Parkes PBF	Shanks D	Tagg AP	Thomas D	Webb DJ
R3	Jan 3	NEWCASTLE UNITED	0-0		20102			10	2	8	3	11	4	12	5	9		1			7	6
rep	7	Newcastle United	1-2	Masson	37225			10	2	8	3	11	4		5	9		1				6

Played in replay: MG Busby (at 12).

F.L. Cup

Rnd	Date	Opponent	Score	Scorers	Att	Abbott RF	Beck JA	Bowles S	Clement DT	Francis GCJ	Gillard IT	Givens DJ	Hollins JW	Leach MJC	McLintock F	Masson DS	Nutt PJ	Parkes PBF	Shanks D	Tagg AP	Thomas D	Webb DJ
R2	Sep 9	Shrewsbury Town	4-1	Webb, Masson, Thomas, Leach	11250	6		10	2	8		11		4	5	9		1			7	3
R3	Oct 7	CHARLTON ATHLETIC	1-1	Bowles	20434			10	2	8	3	11	4		5	9		1			7	6
rep	14	Charlton Athletic	3-0	Thomas, Masson, Bowles	31583			10	2	8	3	11	4	12	5	9		1			7	6
R4	Nov 11	NEWCASTLE UNITED	1-3	Leach	21162			10	2	8	3	11	12	4	5	9		1			7	6

		P	W	D	L	F	A	W	D	L	F	A	Pts
1	Liverpool	42	14	5	2	41	21	9	9	3	25	10	60
2	QUEEN'S PARK RGS.	42	17	4	0	42	13	7	7	7	25	20	59
3	Manchester United	42	16	4	1	40	13	7	6	8	28	29	56
4	Derby County	42	15	3	3	45	30	6	8	7	30	28	53
5	Leeds United	42	13	3	5	37	19	8	6	7	28	27	51
6	Ipswich Town	42	11	6	4	36	23	5	8	8	18	25	46
7	Leicester City	42	9	9	3	29	24	4	10	7	19	27	45
8	Manchester City	42	14	5	2	46	18	2	6	13	18	28	43
9	Tottenham Hotspur	42	6	10	5	33	32	8	5	8	30	31	43
10	Norwich City	42	10	5	6	33	26	6	5	10	25	32	42
11	Everton	42	10	7	4	37	24	5	5	11	23	42	42
12	Stoke City	42	8	5	8	25	24	7	6	8	23	26	41
13	Middlesbrough	42	9	7	5	23	11	6	3	12	23	34	40
14	Coventry City	42	6	9	6	22	22	7	5	9	25	35	40
15	Newcastle United	42	11	4	6	51	26	4	5	12	20	36	39
16	Aston Villa	42	11	8	2	32	17	0	9	12	19	42	39
17	Arsenal	42	11	4	6	33	19	2	6	13	14	34	36
18	West Ham United	42	10	5	6	28	23	3	5	13	22	48	36
19	Birmingham City	42	11	5	5	36	28	2	2	17	21	49	33
20	Wolverhampton Wan.	42	7	8	6	27	25	3	4	14	24	43	30
21	Burnley	42	6	6	9	23	26	3	4	14	20	40	28
22	Sheffield United	42	4	7	10	19	32	2	3	16	14	50	22

1976/77   14th in Division 1

No	Date	Opponent	Score	Scorers	Att	Abbott RF	Bowles S	Busby MG	Clement DT	Cunningham TE	Eastoe PR	Francis GCJ	Gillard IT	Givens DJ	Hollins JW	Kelly EP	Leach MJC	McLintock F	Masson DS	Nutt PJ	Parkes PBF	Richardson DW	Shanks D	Thomas D	Webb DJ
1	Aug 21	EVERTON	0-4		24449		10	8	2				3	11	4		6	5	9		1		12	7	
2	23	West Ham United	0-1		31885	6	10		2				3	11	4			5	9		1			7	
3	28	Ipswich Town	2-2	Givens, Masson	24440	6	10		2				3	11	4			5	9		1			7	
4	Sep 4	WEST BROMWICH ALB.	1-0	Gillard	18876		10		2				3	11	4			5	9		1			7	6
5	11	ASTON VILLA	2-1	Masson, Clement	23602		10		2				3	11	4	8	12	5	9		1			7	6
6	18	Leicester City	2-2	Givens, Hollins	18439		10		2				3	11	4	8	12	5	9		1			7	6
7	25	STOKE CITY	2-0	Bowles, Givens	21621		10		2				3	11	4	8		5	9		1			7	6
8	Oct 2	Arsenal	2-3	Thomas, McLintock	39442		10		2	8			3	11	4			5	9	12	1			7	6
9	5	NORWICH CITY	2-3	Masson(Pen), Webb	16086		10		2				3	11	4	8		5	9		1			7	6
10	16	Manchester City	0-0		40751		10		2	12			3	11	4	8		5	9		1			7	6
11	23	SUNDERLAND	2-0	McLintock, Bowles	22408		10		2				3	11	4	8		5	9		1			7	6
12	30	Birmingham City	1-2	Eastoe	31471		10		2		7		3	11	4			5	9		1				6
13	Nov 6	DERBY COUNTY	1-1	Givens	22527		10		2				3	11	4	8		5	9		1			7	6
14	9	Coventry City	0-2		16184		10		2				3	11	4			5	9		1			7	6
15	20	MIDDLESBROUGH	3-0	Givens(Pen), Masson, Bowles	16037		10							11	3	8	4	5	9		1		2	7	6
16	27	Newcastle United	0-2		39045				2	10			3	11	4	8		5	9		1			7	6
17	Dec 11	Liverpool	1-3	Eastoe	37154		10		2		7		3	11	5	4	8		9		1				6
18	27	Norwich City	0-2		26652		10		2	12			3	11	5	4	8		9		1			7	6
19	Jan 11	TOTTENHAM HOTSPUR	2-1	Bowles, Clement	24266		10		2		7		3	11	4			5	9		1				6
20	22	Everton	3-1	Leach, Masson, Bowles	26875		10		2	12	7		3	11	4	8		5	9		1				6
21	Feb 12	West Bromwich Albion	1-1	Francis	18342		10		2			8	3	11	4			5	9		1			7	6
22	26	LEICESTER CITY	3-2	Givens, Hollins, Francis(p)	20356				2		9	8	3	11	4	10	12	5			1			7	6
23	Mar 5	Stoke City	0-1		15454		10		12				3	11	4			5	9		1			7	6
24	8	LEEDS UNITED	0-0		20386				2			8	3	11	4	10		5	9			1		7	6
25	12	ARSENAL	2-1	Francis, Hollins	26191				2	12		8	3	11	4	10		5	9			1		7	6
26	19	Bristol City	0-1		21956		10		2	8	7		3	11	4			5	9		1		12		6
27	22	MANCHESTER CITY	0-0		17619	5			2	8			3	11	4	10			9		1		12	7	6
28	Apr 2	Sunderland	0-1		27550	5				10	7		3	11	4		8		9		1		2		
29	4	WEST HAM UNITED	1-1	Eastoe	24930	6					7		3	11	4		8	5	9		1		2		10
30	9	Tottenham Hotspur	0-3		32680	5				10			3	11		4	8		9		1		2	7	6
31	11	COVENTRY CITY	1-1	Eastoe	15445	5				12	10		3	11		4	8		9		1		2	7	6
32	16	Middlesbrough	2-0	Abbott, Masson	14500	10			2		7		3	11	4		8	5	9		1				6
33	19	MANCHESTER UNITED	4-0	Eastoe 2, Givens, Kelly	28848	12			2		7		3	11	4	10		5	9		1				6
34	23	NEWCASTLE UNITED	1-2	Givens	20544	10					7		3	11	4	8		5	9		1		2		6
35	26	BRISTOL CITY	0-1		14576				2		7	8	3	11	4	10		5	9		1		12		6
36	30	Manchester United	0-1		50788				2		7	8	3	11	4	10		5	9		1				6
37	May 7	LIVERPOOL	1-1	Givens	29382				2		10	8	3	11	4			5	9		1			7	6
38	11	Derby County	0-2		21312				2		10		3	11	4	8		5	9		1		12	7	6
39	14	Leeds United	1-0	Eastoe	22226						10	8	3	11	2	4		5	9		1			7	6
40	16	IPSWICH TOWN	1-0	Givens	19171						10	8	3	11	2	4	12	5	9		1			7	6
41	20	Aston Villa	1-1	Abbott	28056	6			2		10		3	11	4	8		5	9		1			7	
42	23	BIRMINGHAM CITY	2-2	Masson, Webb	14976	12			2		10		3	11	2	4	8	5	9		1			7	6
		Apps				12	22	1	33	5	27	11	41	41	40	28	20	36	41	1	40	2	10	31	38
		Goals				2	5		2		6	3	1	10	3	1	1	2	8					1	2

F.A. Cup

No	Date	Opponent	Score	Scorers	Att	Abbott RF	Bowles S	Busby MG	Clement DT	Cunningham TE	Eastoe PR	Francis GCJ	Gillard IT	Givens DJ	Hollins JW	Kelly EP	Leach MJC	McLintock F	Masson DS	Nutt PJ	Parkes PBF	Richardson DW	Shanks D	Thomas D	Webb DJ
R1	Jan 8	SHREWSBURY TOWN	2-1	Bowles, Givens	18285		10		2		7		3	11	4		8	5	9		1				6
R2	29	Manchester United	0-1		57422		10		2		7		3	11	4		8	5	9		1	2			6

F.L. Cup

No	Date	Opponent	Score	Scorers	Att	Abbott RF	Bowles S	Busby MG	Clement DT	Cunningham TE	Eastoe PR	Francis GCJ	Gillard IT	Givens DJ	Hollins JW	Kelly EP	Leach MJC	McLintock F	Masson DS	Nutt PJ	Parkes PBF	Richardson DW	Shanks D	Thomas D	Webb DJ
R2	Sep 1	Cardiff City	3-1	Bowles, Thomas, Clement	23618		10		2				3	11	4	8		5	9		1		12	7	6
R3	21	BURY	2-1	McLintock, Givens	13069		10		2				3	11	4	8		5	9		1			7	6
R4	Oct 27	West Ham United	2-0	Bowles, Clement	24585		10		2				3	11	4	8	12	5	9		1			7	6
R5	Dec 1	ARSENAL	2-1	Masson, Webb	27621		10		2				3	11	4	8	12	5	9		1			7	6
SF1	Feb 1	ASTON VILLA	0-0		28739		10					11	3	12	4		8	5	9		1		2	7	6
SF2	16	Aston Villa	2-2	Francis, Eastoe	48439		10		2	12		8	3	11	4			5	9		1			7	6
rep	22	Aston Villa	0-3		40438		10		2		9	8	3	11				5	4		1			7	6

SF2 a.e.t. SF replay at Highbury

UEFA Cup

No	Date	Opponent	Score	Scorers	Att	Abbott RF	Bowles S	Busby MG	Clement DT	Cunningham TE	Eastoe PR	Francis GCJ	Gillard IT	Givens DJ	Hollins JW	Kelly EP	Leach MJC	McLintock F	Masson DS	Nutt PJ	Parkes PBF	Richardson DW	Shanks D	Thomas D	Webb DJ
R1/1	Sep 15	BRANN BERGAN	4-0	Bowles 3, Masson	14698		10		2				3	11	4	8		5	9		1			7	6
R1/2	29	Brann Bergan	7-0	Bowles 3, Givens 2, Thomas, Webb	11000		10	12	2				3	11	4	8		5	9		1			7	6
R2/1	Oct 20	Slovan Bratislava	3-3	Bowles 2, Givens	40000		10		2				3	11	4	8		5	9		1			7	6
R2/2	Nov 3	SLAVAN BRATISLAVA	5-2	Givens 3(1p), Bowles, Clement	22001		10		2				3	11	4	8		5	9		1			7	6
R3/1	24	FC COLOGNE	3-0	Givens, Webb, Bowles	21143		10		2				3	11	4	8		5	9		1			7	6
R3/2	Dec 7	FC Cologne	1-4	Masson	50000		10		2	12			3	11	4	8		5	9		1			7	6
QF1	Mar 2	AEK Athens	3-0	Francis 2(2p), Bowles	23009		10					8	3	11	2	4		5	9		1			7	6
QF2	16	AEK Athens	0-3		35000		10				7		3	11	4	8		5	9		1		2		6

R3 won on away goals rule. QF lost on penalties.

1977/78   19th in Division 1

#		Date	Opponent	Score	Scorers	Att	Abbott RF	Bowles S	Busby MG	Clement DT	Cunningham TE	Eastoe PR	Francis GCJ	Gillard IT	Givens DJ	Goddard P	Hollins JW	Howe EJ	James L	Leach MJC	McGee PG	Masson DS	Needham DW	Parkes PBF	Perkins SA	Richardson DW	Shanks D	Wallace BD	Webb DJ	Williams B
1	Aug	20	ASTON VILLA	1-2	Eastoe	25431		10		2		7	8	3	11		4					9	5	1					6	12
2		23	Wolverhampton Wan.	0-1		22278	8	10		2		7		3	11		4			12		9	5	1					6	
3		27	Norwich City	1-1	Needham	17249		10		2		7		3	11		4				8	9	5	1					6	12
4	Sep	3	LEICESTER CITY	3-0	Givens, Francis, Needham	14516		10		2		7	8		11		4					9	5	1			3		6	
5		10	West Ham United	2-2	Eastoe, Lock (og)	26922		10		2		7	8		11		4					9	5	1			3		6	12
6		17	MANCHESTER CITY	1-1	Francis	24668	12	10		2		7	8	3	11							9	5	1					6	4
7		24	CHELSEA	1-1	Masson	26267		10		2		7	8	3	11		4					9	5	1					6	12
8	Oct	1	Bristol City	2-2	Masson, Eastoe	20641	6	10	8	2		7		3	11		4					9	5	1						12
9		4	Birmingham City	1-2	Masson	21304	6	10	8	2		7			11					4		9	5	1			3			12
10		8	EVERTON	1-5	Eastoe	20495	6	10	8	2		7			11			12		4		9	5	1			3			
11		15	Arsenal	0-1		36172		10	8	2		7		3	11		4					9	5	1			6			
12		22	NOTTM. FOREST	0-2		24449		10	8	2		7		3	11		4					9	5	1			6			12
13		29	WEST BROMWICH ALB.	2-1	Eastoe, Bowles	18800	5	10		2		7		3	9		4		8					1			6	12		11
14	Nov	5	Middlesbrough	1-1	Busby	18215	6	10	7					3	9		4		8				5	1		2		12		11
15		12	LIVERPOOL	2-0	James, Bowles	25625		10			12	7		3	9		4		8				5	1		2				11
16		19	Coventry City	1-4	Givens	20390	12	10	6					3	9		4		8		7		5	1		2				11
17		26	MANCHESTER UNITED	2-2	Needham, Givens	25367		10						6	9		4		8		7		5	1		2				11
18	Dec	3	Leeds United	0-3		26507		10						6	9		4		8		7		5	1		2				11
19		10	NEWCASTLE UNITED	0-1		15251		10					8	6	9		4				7		5	1		2				11
20		17	Liverpool	0-1		38249		12					8	6	9		4	5		10				1		2			7	11
21		26	DERBY COUNTY	0-0		18917		10			11		8	6	9		4	5	7					1		2				
22		27	Ipswich Town	2-3	Bowles (p), McGee	22400		10			11		8	6	9		4	5	7		12			1		2				
23		31	WOLVERHAMPTON W.	1-3	Shanks	16067		10			9	8		6	11		4	5	7		12			1		2				
24	Jan	2	Aston Villa	1-1	Smith (og)	34750		10	12		9	8		6	11		4	5	7					1		2				
25		14	NORWICH CITY	2-1	Eastoe, Cunningham	14247		10			7	8		6	11		4	5			9			1		2				12
26		21	Leicester City	0-0		16288		10				8		6	11		4	5			9			1		2	7			12
27	Feb	11	Manchester City	1-2	Abbott	39860	6	10	8	2				3	11		4	5			9			1			7			
28		25	BRISTOL CITY	2-2	Bowles (p), Busby	17051	6	10	8	2				3	11		4	5			9			1			7			
29	Mar	4	Everton	3-3	Shanks, Hollins, Howe	33861		10	8	2	6			3	11		4	5			9			1			7	12		
30		14	WEST HAM UNITED	1-0	Cunningham	20394		10	8	2	6			3	11		4	5		12	9			1			7			
31		22	West Bromwich Albion	0-2		19536			8	2	6			3	11		4	5		10	9			1			7			
32		25	IPSWICH TOWN	3-3	McGee 2, James	15563		10	8	2	6			3	11		4	5		12	9			1			7			
33		27	Derby County	0-2		20155		10	8	2	6			3			4	5	11		9			1			7	12		
34	Apr	1	MIDDLESBROUGH	1-0	Busby	12925		10	8	2				3			4	5	11					1		6	7	9		
35		8	Manchester United	1-3	Bowles (p)	42677		10	8	2				3			4	5	11	12				1		6	7	9		
36		11	ARSENAL	2-1	Shanks, Bowles	25621		10	8	2				3	11	12	4	5	7		9			1		6				
37		15	COVENTRY CITY	2-1	Goddard, James	17062		10	8	2				3	11	7	4	5			9			1		6				12
38		18	Nottingham Forest	0-1		30339		10		2				3	11	7	4	5			9			1		6				8
39		22	Newcastle United	3-0	Givens, McGee, Hollins	13463		10		2				3	11	7	4	5			9			1		6				8
40		25	BIRMINGHAM CITY	0-0		16049		10		2				3	11	12	4	5			9			1	8	6	7			
41		29	LEEDS UNITED	0-0		23993		10		2				3	11	12	4	5			9			1	8	6	7			
42	May	2	Chelsea	1-3	James	22937		10		2				3	11	7	4	5	8		9			1		6				12
			Apps				10	40	21	29	16	19	13	38	37	7	40	23	27	7	17	12	18	31	2	11	36	13	7	19
			Goals				1	6	3		2	6	2		4	1	2	1	4		4	3	3				3			

Two own goals

F.A. Cup

	Date		Opponent	Score	Scorers	Att	Bowles S	Clement DT	Cunningham TE	Gillard IT	Givens DJ	Hollins JW	Howe EJ	James L	McGee PG	Parkes PBF	Richardson DW	Shanks D	Wallace BD	Williams B
R3	Jan	7	WEALDSTONE	4-0	Givens, James, Bowles (p), Howe	16158	10		6	3	11	4	5	9	7	1	2		8	12
R4		28	West Ham United	1-1	Howe	35556	10	6 (Abbott)		3	11	4	5	9	7	1		8		12
rep		31	WEST HAM UNITED	6-1	Givens, Hollins, Busby 2, Bowles (p), James	24057	10	8		3	11	4	5	9		1		7		
R5	Feb	18	NOTTM. FOREST	1-1	Busby	26803	10	8		3	11	4	5	9		1		7		
rep		27	Nottingham Forest	1-1	Shanks	40097	10	8		3	11	4	5	9	12	1		7		
rep2	Mar	2	Nottingham Forest	1-3	Bowles	32000	10	9	8	3	11	4	5	7		1		2		12

R5 replay a.e.t.

F.L. Cup

	Date		Opponent	Score	Scorers	Att	Abbott RF	Bowles S	Clement DT	Eastoe PR	Gillard IT	Givens DJ	Hollins JW	Masson DS	Needham DW	Parkes PBF	Richardson DW	Shanks D	Wallace BD	Webb DJ	Williams B
R2	Aug	31	Bournemouth	2-0	Givens, Eastoe	10006		10	2	7	3	11	4	9	5	1				6	12
R3	Oct	26	Aston Villa	0-1		34481	12	10	2	7	3	9	4		5	1	6	11			8

		P	W	D	L	F	A	W	D	L	F	A	Pts
1	Nottingham Forest	42	15	6	0	37	8	10	8	3	32	16	64
2	Liverpool	42	15	4	2	37	11	9	5	7	28	23	57
3	Everton	42	14	4	3	47	22	8	7	6	29	23	55
4	Manchester City	42	14	4	3	46	21	6	8	7	28	30	52
5	Arsenal	42	14	5	2	38	12	7	5	9	22	25	52
6	West Bromwich Alb.	42	13	5	3	35	18	5	9	7	27	35	50
7	Coventry City	42	13	5	3	48	23	5	7	9	27	39	48
8	Aston Villa	42	11	4	6	33	18	7	6	8	24	24	46
9	Leeds United	42	12	4	5	39	21	6	6	9	24	32	46
10	Manchester United	42	9	6	6	32	23	7	4	10	35	40	42
11	Birmingham City	42	8	5	8	32	30	8	4	9	23	30	41
12	Derby County	42	10	7	4	37	24	4	6	11	17	35	41
13	Norwich City	42	10	8	3	28	20	1	10	10	24	46	40
14	Middlesbrough	42	8	8	5	25	19	4	7	10	17	35	39
15	Wolverhampton Wan.	42	7	8	6	30	27	5	4	12	21	37	36
16	Chelsea	42	7	11	3	28	20	4	3	14	18	49	36
17	Bristol City	42	9	6	6	37	26	2	7	12	12	27	35
18	Ipswich Town	42	10	5	6	32	24	1	8	12	15	37	35
19	QUEEN'S PARK RGS.	42	8	8	5	27	26	1	7	13	20	38	33
20	West Ham United	42	8	6	7	31	28	4	2	15	21	41	32
21	Newcastle United	42	4	6	11	26	37	2	4	15	16	41	22
22	Leicester City	42	4	7	10	16	32	1	5	15	10	38	22

#	Date		Opponent	Score	Scorers	Att	Abbott RF	Allen CD	Bowles S	Busby MG	Clement DT	Cunningham TE	Eastoe PR	Elsey KW	Francis GCJ	Gillard IT	Goddard P	Hamilton WR	Harkouk RP	Hollins JW	Howe EJ	James L	McGee PG	Parkes PBF	Richardson DW	Roeder GV	Shanks D	Wallace BD	Walsh MA
1	Aug	19	Liverpool	1-2	McGee	50783			10	7	2		9		8	3				4	5		11	1			6		
2		22	WEST BROMWICH ALB.	0-1		15481			10	9	2		7		8	3				4	5	11	12	1			6		
3		26	NOTTM. FOREST	0-0		17971			10	9			7		8	3			12	4	5		11	1		2	6		
4	Sep	2	Arsenal	1-5	McGee	33883			10	9			7		8	3				4	5		11	1		6	2		
5		9	MANCHESTER UNITED	1-1	Gillard	23477			10	6			7		8	3	12		9	4	5		11	1			2		
6		16	Middlesbrough	2-0	Harkouk, Eastoe	12822	12		10	9		6	7			3			8	4	5		11	1			2		
7		23	ASTON VILLA	1-0	Harkouk	18410			10	9		6	7			3			8	4	5		11	1			2		
8		30	Wolverhampton Wan.	0-1		14250	12		10			6	7		8	3			9	4	5		11		1		2		
9	Oct	7	Bristol City	1-0	Busby	15707			10	12		6	7		8	3			9	4	5		11	1			2		
10		14	Southampton	1-1	Goddard	22897			10	6		7			9	3	12		11	4	5		8	1			2		
11		21	EVERTON	1-1	Gillard	21171			10	6			7		8	3			9	4	5		11	1			2		
12		28	Ipswich Town	1-2	Francis	20717			10	6	11		7		8	3			9	4	5		12	1			2		
13	Nov	4	CHELSEA	0-0		22876	12		10	6	11		7			3			9	4	5		8	1			2		
14		11	LIVERPOOL	1-3	Eastoe	26626			10	8	2		7			3			9	4	5		11	1			6		
15		18	Nottingham Forest	0-0		28032			10	9	2	11	7		8	3				4	5			1			6		
16		25	Derby County	1-2	Howe	19702			9		2	11	7		8	3				4	5		12	1			6		10
17	Dec	2	BOLTON WANDERERS	1-3	Harkouk	11635			9		2		7		8	3		12	11	4	5		10	1			6		
18		9	Coventry City	0-1		18693			10		2		7			3		12	9	4	5		11	1		8	6		
19		16	MANCHESTER CITY	2-1	Hamilton 2	12902			10		2				8	3		12	9	4	5		11	1		6	7		
20		26	TOTTENHAM HOTSPUR	2-2	Bowles (p), Shanks	24845			10		2				8	3		12	9	4	5		11	1		6	7		
21		30	LEEDS UNITED	1-4	Eastoe	17435	12		10		2		8			3	11		9	6	5			1		4	7		
22	Jan	20	MIDDLESBROUGH	1-1	Goddard	9899			10		2				8	3	11		9	6	5			1		4	7		
23		31	Norwich City	1-1	Francis	12401			10	12	2				8	3	11		9	4	5			1		6	7		
24	Feb	1	WOLVERHAMPTON W.	3-3	Roeder, Busby, Gillard	11814			10	12	2				8	3	11		9	4	5			1		6	7		
25		13	ARSENAL	2-2	Shanks	21125			10	6	2				8	3	11		9	4				1			7		
26		24	SOUTHAMPTON	0-1		13635	12		10	6	2				8	3	11		9	4					1		5		7
27		28	Manchester United	0-2		36085			10	6	2		9		8	3	11			4					1		5		7
28	Mar	3	Everton	1-2	Goddard	24809			10		2		9		8	3	11	12		4	5				1	6	7		
29		6	Birmingham City	1-3	Busby	12605			10	12	2		9		8	3	11			4	5				1	6	7		
30		17	Chelsea	3-1	Goddard, Roeder, Busby	26712			10	12	2		9		8	3	11			4	5				1	6	7		
31		20	Aston Villa	1-3	Allen	24310	12	11	10		2		9		8	3				4	5				1	6	7		
32		24	West Bromwich Albion	1-2	McGee	21063			9		2	11			8	3				4	5		10		1	6	7		
33		31	DERBY COUNTY	2-2	Goddard, Walsh	13988			10	12	2				8	3	11			4	5				1	6	7		9
34	Apr	3	Bristol City	0-2		16671	12		8	2							11			4	5		10		1	6	3	7	9
35		7	Bolton Wanderers	1-2	Goddard	21119			10		2				8		11			4	5		7		1	6	3		9
36		13	NORWICH CITY	0-0		14654	12		10		2						11			4	5		7		1	6	3		9
37		14	Tottenham Hotspur	1-1	Clement	28854			10	7	2				8		11			4	5				1	6	3		9
38		21	Manchester City	1-3	Busby	30694				4	2				8	3	11				5		10		1	6	7		9
39		28	COVENTRY CITY	5-1	Allen 3, Shanks, Walsh (p)	10951	11			7	2					3	10			4	5				1	6	8		9
40	May	4	Leeds United	3-4	Walsh, Roeder, Busby	20121	11			7			12		8	3	10			4	5				1	6	2		9
41		7	BIRMINGHAM CITY	1-3	Roeder	9600	11			7			7	8		3	10			4	5				1	6	2	12	9
42		11	IPSWICH TOWN	0-4		9819	11			7	2			8		3	10			4					1	5	6		9

	Abbott	Allen	Bowles	Busby	Clement	Cunningham	Eastoe	Elsey	Francis	Gillard	Goddard	Hamilton	Harkouk	Hollins	Howe	James	McGee	Parkes	Richardson	Roeder	Shanks	Wallace	Walsh
Apps	2	10	30	35	29	9	26	3	31	38	23	11	15	41	38	1	22	24	18	27	41	5	10
Goals		4	1	6	1		3		2	3	6	2	3		1		3			4	3		3

F.A. Cup

Rd	Date		Opponent	Score	Att	Players
R3	Jan	9	Fulham	0-2	21119	Bowles 10, Busby 11, Clement 2, Eastoe 4, Francis 8, Gillard 3, Harkouk 9, Hollins 12, Howe 6, Parkes 1, Shanks 5, Roeder 7

F.L. Cup

Rd	Date		Opponent	Score	Scorers	Att	Players
R2	Aug	29	Preston North End	3-1	Baxter (og), Eastoe 2	14913	Bowles 10, Busby 9, Eastoe 7, Francis 8, Gillard 3, Hollins 4, Howe 5, McGee 11, Parkes 1, Roeder 6, Shanks 2
R3	Oct	3	SWANSEA CITY	2-0	McGee, Eastoe	18513	Abbott 12, Bowles 10, Busby 6, Eastoe 7, Francis 8, Gillard 3, Harkouk 9, Hollins 4, Howe 5, McGee 11, Richardson 1, Shanks 2
R4	Nov	11	LEEDS UNITED	0-2		22769	Bowles 10, Busby 8, Clement 2, Cunningham 12, Eastoe 7, Gillard 3, Harkouk 9, Hollins 4, Howe 5, McGee 11, Parkes 1, Shanks 6

		P	W	D	L	F	A	W	D	L	F	A	Pts
1	Liverpool	42	19	2	0	51	4	11	6	4	34	12	68
2	Nottingham Forest	42	11	10	0	34	10	10	8	3	27	16	60
3	West Bromwich Alb.	42	13	5	3	38	15	11	6	4	34	20	59
4	Everton	42	12	7	2	32	17	5	10	6	20	23	51
5	Leeds United	42	11	4	6	41	25	7	10	4	29	27	50
6	Ipswich Town	42	11	4	6	34	21	9	5	7	29	28	49
7	Arsenal	42	11	8	2	37	18	6	6	9	24	30	48
8	Aston Villa	42	8	9	4	37	26	7	7	7	22	23	46
9	Manchester United	42	9	7	5	29	25	6	8	7	31	38	45
10	Coventry City	42	11	7	3	41	29	3	9	9	17	39	44
11	Tottenham Hotspur	42	7	8	6	19	25	6	7	8	29	36	41
12	Middlesbrough	42	10	5	6	33	21	5	5	11	24	29	40
13	Bristol City	42	11	6	4	34	19	4	4	13	13	32	40
14	Southampton	42	9	10	2	35	20	3	6	12	12	33	40
15	Manchester City	42	9	5	7	34	28	4	8	9	24	28	39
16	Norwich City	42	7	10	4	29	19	0	13	8	22	38	37
17	Bolton Wanderers	42	10	5	6	36	28	2	6	13	18	47	35
18	Wolverhampton Wan.	42	10	4	7	26	26	3	4	14	18	42	34
19	Derby County	42	8	5	8	25	25	2	6	13	19	46	31
20	QUEEN'S PARK RGS.	42	4	9	8	24	33	2	4	15	21	40	25
21	Birmingham City	42	5	9	7	24	25	1	1	19	13	39	22
22	Chelsea	42	3	5	13	23	42	2	5	14	21	50	20

1979/80   5th in Division 2

#		Date	Opponent	Score	Scorers	Att.	Allen CD	Bowles S	Burke SJ	Busby MG	Currie AW	Davidson PE	Elsey KW	Gillard IT	Goddard P	Hamilton WR	Harkouk RP	Hazell R	Hill GA	Howe EJ	McCreery D	Neal DJ	Pape AM	Roeder GV	Rogers M	Shanks D	Waddock GP	Wallace BD	Walsh MA	Wicks SJ	Woods CCE
1	Aug	18	BRISTOL ROVERS	2-0	Allen, Goddard	12652	9						2	3	11	10				5	4	7		6		8					1
2		22	Cardiff City	0-1		11577	9		4				2	3	7					5	8	11		6		10					1
3		25	LEICESTER CITY	1-4	Allen(Pen)	13091	9			11		12	2	3	10					5	4	7		6		8					1
4	Sep	1	Notts County	0-1		8745	9	11					2	3	10			12		5	4	7		6		8					1
5		8	FULHAM	3-0	Goddard, Allen, Currie	17105	9	7	11		10			3	8		12	5			4			6		2					1
6		15	Swansea City	2-1	Burke, Stephenson(og)	16931	9	7	11					3	8		10	5			4			6		2		12			1
7		22	WEST HAM UNITED	3-0	Allen 2, Goddard	24692	9	7	11	8				3	10			5			4			6		2					1
8		29	Oldham Athletic	0-0		8985	9	7		8				3	10		12	5			4			6		2				11	1
9	Oct	6	Watford	2-1	Allen, Roeder	22341	9	7	11					3	10			5			4			8		2				6	1
10		9	CARDIFF CITY	3-0	Allen 2, Roeder	12225	9	7	11					3	10			5			4			8		2			12	6	1
11		13	PRESTON NORTH END	1-1	Goddard	14316	9	7	11					3	10			5			4			8		2			12	6	1
12		20	Sunderland	0-3		25201	9	7	11					3	10			5			4			8		2			12	6	1
13		27	BURNLEY	7-0	Goddard 2, Allen 2, Roeder, Shanks, McCreery	11261	9	7	11					3	10						4			5		2	8		12	6	1
14	Nov	3	Bristol Rovers	3-1	Thomas(og), Roeder, Allen	8401	9	7			10			3	11			5			4			5		2	8			6	1
15		10	Luton Town	1-1	Allen	19619	9	7	12		10			3	11			5			4			5		2				6	1
16		17	SHREWSBURY TOWN	2-1	McCreery, Roeder	12048	9	7			10			3	11			5			4			5		2	12			6	1
17		24	CHARLTON ATHLETIC	4-0	Allen 2 (1p), Roeder, Bowles	13013	9	7	12						11			5			4			5		2	10	3		6	1
18	Dec	1	Cambridge United	1-2	Bowles	8038	9	7							10			5	11		4			8		2	12	3		6	1
19		8	WREXHAM	2-2	Goddard 2	11652	9	7		12				3	10			5	11		4			8		2				6	1
20		15	Newcastle United	2-4	Goddard, Roeder	25027	9			12	10			3	7			5	11		4			8		2				6	1
21		18	CHELSEA	2-2	Allen 2	26598	9		11	12				3	7			5			4			8		2	10			6	1
22		29	Leicester City	0-2		20743	9				10			3	7			5	11		4			8		2	12			6	1
23	Jan	1	Birmingham City	1-2	Allen	25963	9			12	6	8			8				11		4					2	10	3	7	5	1
24		12	NOTTS COUNTY	1-3	Allen	9613	9		11						8						4	12		6		2	10	3	7	5	1
25		19	Fulham	2-0	Waddock, Burke	11539	9		11		10			3	7						4			6		2	8	12		5	1
26	Feb	2	SWANSEA CITY	3-2	Allen(p), Goddard 2	11153	9		11		10			3	7						4			6		2	8	12		5	1
27		9	West Ham United	1-2	Goddard	26037	9		11		10			3	7			8			4			6		2				5	1
28		12	ORIENT	0-0		11361	9		11		8			3	10			6			4					2	7			5	1
29		16	OLDHAM ATHLETIC	4-3	Allen 2 (1p), McCreery, Goddard	8372	9		11		8			3	10			5			4			7		2	12			6	1
30		23	Preston North End	3-0	Allen, Roeder, Goddard	10351	9		11		10			3	7			5			4			8		2				6	1
31	Mar	1	SUNDERLAND	0-0		15613	9		11		10			3	7			5			4			8		2				6	1
32		8	Burnley	3-0	Gillard, Allen, Shanks	7579	9		11		10			3	7			5	12		4			8		2				6	1
33		14	WATFORD	1-1	Currie	16504	9		11		10			3	7			5	12		4			8		2				6	1
34		22	LUTON TOWN	2-2	Goddard 2	15054	9		11		10			3	7		12	5			4			8		2				6	1
35		29	Shrewsbury Town	0-3		9150			11		10			3	7			5			4	9		8		2	12			6	1
36	Apr	2	Chelsea	2-0	Busby, Burke	31401			11	9	10			3	7						4			6		2	8			5	1
37		5	BIRMINGHAM CITY	1-1	Burke	16609	9		11	8	10			3	7						4			6		2				5	1
38		8	Orient	1-1	Allen	9389	9		11	8	10			3	7						4			6		2				5	1
39		12	CAMBRIDGE UNITED	2-2	Allen, Busby	11643	9		11	8	10			3	7			12			4			6		2				5	1
40		19	Charlton Athletic	2-2	Allen 2	6975	9		11	7	10			3	8						4		1	6		2	12			5	
41		26	NEWCASTLE UNITED	2-1	Roeder, McCreery	11245			11		10			3	7		12	8	9					6	2	2	4			5	1
42	May	3	Wrexham	3-1	Currie, Hazell, Allen	6268	9				10			3				7	8		4			6	2	2				5	1
			Apps				39	16	31	10	28	1	4	38	40	1	5	29	9	4	42	6	1	40	2	41	16	7	7	35	41
			Goals				28	2	4	2	3		1		16			1			4			9		2	1				

Two own goals

F.A. Cup

		Date	Opponent	Score	Scorers	Att.	Allen CD	Bowles S	Burke SJ	Busby MG	Currie AW	Davidson PE	Elsey KW	Gillard IT	Goddard P	Hamilton WR	Harkouk RP	Hazell R	Hill GA	Howe EJ	McCreery D	Neal DJ	Pape AM	Roeder GV	Rogers M	Shanks D	Waddock GP	Wallace BD	Walsh MA	Wicks SJ	Woods CCE
R3	Jan	5	WATFORD	1-2	Hazell	19398	9			12	10							6	11		4					2	8	3	7	5	1

F.L. Cup

		Date	Opponent	Score	Scorers	Att.	Allen CD	Bowles S	Burke SJ	Busby MG	Currie AW	Davidson PE	Elsey KW	Gillard IT	Goddard P	Hamilton WR	Harkouk RP	Hazell R	Hill GA	Howe EJ	McCreery D	Neal DJ	Pape AM	Roeder GV	Rogers M	Shanks D	Waddock GP	Wallace BD	Walsh MA	Wicks SJ	Woods CCE
R2/1	Aug	28	BRADFORD CITY	2-1	McCreery, Neal	8560	9	11	4					3	10					5	8	7		6		2		12			1
R2/2	Sep	5	Bradford City	2-0	Gillard, Roeder	11372	9	7			10			3	8		11	5			4			6		2					1
R3		25	Mansfield Town	3-0	Bowles, Allen, Currie	9485	9	7	11		8			3	10			5			4			6		2					1
R4	Oct	30	WOLVERHAMPTON WAN.	1-1	Allen	20984	9	7			10			3	12			5			4			8		2			11	6	1
rep	Nov	6	Wolverhampton Wan.	0-1		26014	9	7	12		10			3	11			5			4			8		2				6	1

		P	W	D	L	F	A	W	D	L	F	A	Pts
1	Leicester City	42	12	5	4	32	19	9	8	4	26	19	55
2	Sunderland	42	16	5	0	47	13	5	7	9	22	29	54
3	Birmingham City	42	14	5	2	37	16	7	6	8	21	22	53
4	Chelsea	42	14	3	4	34	16	9	4	8	32	36	53
5	QUEEN'S PARK RGS.	42	10	9	2	46	25	8	4	9	29	28	49
6	Luton Town	42	9	10	2	36	17	7	7	7	30	28	49
7	West Ham United	42	13	2	6	37	21	7	5	9	17	22	47
8	Cambridge United	42	11	6	4	40	23	3	10	8	21	30	44
9	Newcastle United	42	13	6	2	35	19	2	8	11	18	30	44
10	Preston North End	42	8	10	3	30	23	4	9	8	26	29	43
11	Oldham Athletic	42	12	5	4	30	21	4	6	11	19	32	43
12	Swansea City	42	13	1	7	31	20	4	8	9	17	33	43
13	Shrewsbury Town	42	12	3	6	41	23	6	2	13	19	30	41
14	Orient	42	7	9	5	29	31	5	8	8	19	23	41
15	Cardiff City	42	11	4	6	21	16	5	4	12	20	32	40
16	Wrexham	42	13	2	6	26	15	3	4	14	14	34	38
17	Notts County	42	4	11	6	24	22	7	4	10	27	30	37
18	Watford	42	9	6	6	27	18	3	7	11	12	28	37
19	Bristol Rovers	42	9	8	4	33	23	2	5	14	17	41	35
20	Fulham	42	6	4	11	19	28	5	3	13	23	46	29
21	Burnley	42	5	9	7	19	23	1	6	14	20	50	27
22	Charlton Athletic	42	6	6	9	25	31	0	4	17	14	47	22

1980/81   8th in Division 2

#	Date	Opponent	Score	Scorers	Att	Burke SJ	Burridge J	Currie AW	Fenwick TW	Fereday W	Flanagan MA	Francis GCJ	Gillard IT	Hazell R	Howe EJ	Hill GA	Hucker PI	King AE	Langley TW	McCreery D	Muir IJ	Neal DJ	Neill WA	Roeder GV	Sealy AJ	Shanks D	Silkman B	Stainrod SA	Waddock GP	Walsh MA	Wicks SJ	Wilkins DM	Woods CCE
1	Aug 16	Oldham Athletic	0-1		6986	11		10					3					7		2		12		6		8			4	9	5		1
2	19	BRISTOL ROVERS	4-0	Fereday 2, Hazell, Shanks	9731	11		10		7			3	9				12		2				6		8			4		5		1
3	23	SWANSEA CITY	0-0		10854	11		10		7			3	12					9	2				6		8			4		5		1
4	30	Chelsea	1-1	Langley	23381	11		10		7			3						9	2	12	10		6		8			4		5		1
5	Sep 6	Notts County	1-2	Hill(p)	7097					7			3			12		11	9	2		10		6		8			4		5		1
6	13	NEWCASTLE UNITED	1-2	Hazell	10885	11		10		7			3	5				12	9	2				6		8			4		5		1
7	20	Sheffield Wednesday	0-1		15396	12		10					3			11		8	9	7				6		2			4		5		1
8	27	BRISTOL CITY	4-0	Neal 2, Langley, Shanks	8551	11		10					3						9	2		7		6		8			4		5		1
9	Oct 4	Blackburn Rovers	1-2	Neal	12209			10					3					7	9	2		11		6		8			4		5		1
10	7	ORIENT	0-0		9627			10					3					7	8			11		9		6			4		5		1
11	11	BOLTON WANDERERS	3-1	Langley, Burke(p), Neal	8641	11		10					3	6				7	8	4				9		2			12		5		1
12	18	Derby County	3-3	King 2, Langley	16021	11							3					8	10	7				9		6	2		4		5		1
13	22	Cardiff City	0-1		4453	11							3	12				8	10	7				9		6	2		4		5		1
14	25	WREXHAM	0-1		9050	11				12			3					8	10	7				9		6	2		4		5		1
15	Nov 1	Grimsby Town	0-0		10015								3	7				8	10					9		6	2	11	4		5	12	1
16	8	LUTON TOWN	3-2	Neal 2, King	10082								3	6				8	10	12				9		7	2	11	4		5		1
17	11	Bristol Rovers	2-1	King, Langley	6612								3	6				8	10					9		7	2	11	4		5		1
18	15	OLDHAM ATHLETIC	2-0	Silkman(p), Neal	8223								3	6				8	10					9		7	2	11	4		5		1
19	22	Preston North End	2-3	Roeder, Neal	6762								3	6				8						9		7	2	11	10		4		1
20	29	SHREWSBURY TOWN	0-0		7982								3					8	6					9		7	2	11	10		5		1
21	Dec 6	Cambridge United	0-1		6349			6					3					8						9		7	2	11	10		5		1
22	19	Bolton Wanderers	2-1	Stainrod, Flanagan	6315						6		3					8						6		2	11	9			5		1
23	26	WEST HAM UNITED	3-0	Silkman, Currie, Stainrod	23811	1		10	4			7	3											6		2	11	9	12		5		
24	27	Watford	1-1	King	23547	1			4			7	3											6		2	11	9	10		5		
25	Jan 10	PRESTON NORTH END	1-1	Stainrod	8415	1		10	4				3					8				7		6		2	11	9			5		
26	17	CHELSEA	1-0	Langley	22873	1		10	4				3					8	7					6		2	11	9			5		
27	31	Swansea City	2-1	Langley, King	12518	1		10	4				3					8	7					6		2	11	9	12		5		
28	Feb 3	CARDIFF CITY	2-0	Fenwick, Langley	9834	1		10	4				3					8	7					6		2	11	9			5		
29	7	Newcastle United	0-1		20404	1		10	4				3					8	7					6		2	11	9			5		
30	14	NOTTS COUNTY	1-1	Howe	11457	1		10	4				3	5	6			8	7							2	11	9			5		
31	21	Bristol City	1-0	Waddock	11036	1		10	4				3		6			8	7							2	11	9	12		5		
32	28	SHEFFIELD WEDNESDAY	1-2	Stainrod	15104	1		10	4		12	8	3						7					6		2	11	9			5		
33	Mar 7	BLACKBURN ROVERS	1-1	Francis	9513	1		10	4			7	8	3					12					6		2	11	9			5		
34	21	DERBY COUNTY	3-1	Francis 2, Flanagan	8905	1		10	4			7	8	3					12					6	9	2	11				5		
35	28	Wrexham	1-1	Waddock	5887	1		10	4		9	8	3						12					6	7	2		11			5		
36	31	Orient	0-4		6724	1		10	4			7	8	3										6	9	2	12	11			5		
37	Apr 4	GRIMSBY TOWN	1-0	Francis(p)	8906	1		10				7	8	3										6	9	2	4	11			5		
38	11	Luton Town	0-3		12112	12	1	10				7	8	3										6	9	2	4	11			5		
39	18	WATFORD	0-0		10571	11	1	10	4		9	8	3											2	6					7	5		
40	21	West Ham United	0-3		24599	12	1	10	4		9	8	3											2	6	11				7	5		
41	25	CAMBRIDGE UNITED	5-0	Sealy 2, Muir 2, Roeder	6668		1	10	2		9	8	3	5							11			6	7				4				
42	May 2	Shrewsbury Town	3-3	Fenwick, Waddock, Flanagan	5714			10	2		9		3	5			1				11			6	8				7			4	

Played in one game: IE Stewart (game 9, at 12), PI Hucker (game 42, at 1)

	Burke SJ	Burridge J	Currie AW	Fenwick TW	Fereday W	Flanagan MA	Francis GCJ	Gillard IT	Hazell R	Howe EJ	Hill GA	Hucker PI	King AE	Langley TW	McCreery D	Muir IJ	Neal DJ	Neill WA	Roeder GV	Sealy AJ	Shanks D	Silkman B	Stainrod SA	Waddock GP	Walsh MA	Wicks SJ	Wilkins DM	Woods CCE
Apps	14	19	31	19	6	14	10	42	8	8	5	1	26	25	15	2	16	4	39	8	38	23	15	33	1	38	2	22
Goals	1		1	2	2	3	4		2	1	1		6	8		2	8		2	2	2	2	4	3				

F.A. Cup

R	Date	Opponent	Score	Scorers	Att	Burke SJ	Burridge J	Currie AW	Fenwick TW	Fereday W	Flanagan MA	Francis GCJ	Gillard IT	King AE	McCreery D	Roeder GV	Shanks D	Silkman B	Stainrod SA	Waddock GP	Wicks SJ
R3	Jan 3	TOTTENHAM HOTSPUR	0-0		28829	1			4			7	3	8		6	2	11	9	10	5
rep	7	Tottenham Hotspur	1-3	Stainrod	36294	1		10	4			7	3	8	12	6	2	11	9		5

F.L. Cup

R	Date	Opponent	Score	Scorers	Att	Burke SJ	Currie AW	Fenwick TW	Gillard IT	Hazell R	King AE	Langley TW	McCreery D	Muir IJ	Neal DJ	Roeder GV	Shanks D	Waddock GP	Wicks SJ	Woods CCE
R2/1	Aug 26	DERBY COUNTY	0-0		11244	11	10		3	7		9	2			6	8	4	5	1
R2/2	Sep 3	Derby County	0-0		16728		10	7			11	9	2	12	6		8	4	5	1
R3	23	Notts County	1-4	Langley	6644	3	10		12			7	9	2	11	6	8	4	5	1

R2/2 won 5-3 on penalties a.e.t.

	P	W	D	L	F	A	W	D	L	F	A	Pts
1 West Ham United	42	19	1	1	53	12	9	9	3	26	17	66
2 Notts County	42	10	8	3	26	15	8	9	4	23	23	53
3 Swansea City	42	12	5	4	39	19	6	9	6	25	25	50
4 Blackburn Rovers	42	12	8	1	28	7	4	10	7	14	22	50
5 Luton Town	42	10	6	5	35	23	8	6	7	26	23	48
6 Derby County	42	9	8	4	34	26	6	7	8	23	26	45
7 Grimsby Town	42	10	8	3	21	10	5	7	9	23	32	45
8 QUEEN'S PARK RGS.	42	11	7	3	36	12	4	6	11	20	34	43
9 Watford	42	13	5	3	34	18	3	6	12	16	27	43
10 Sheffield Wed.	42	14	4	3	38	14	3	4	14	15	37	42
11 Newcastle United	42	11	7	3	22	13	3	7	11	8	32	42
12 Chelsea	42	8	6	7	27	15	6	6	9	19	26	40
13 Cambridge United	42	13	1	7	36	23	4	5	12	17	42	40
14 Shrewsbury Town	42	9	7	5	33	22	2	10	9	13	25	39
15 Oldham Athletic	42	7	9	5	19	16	5	6	10	20	32	39
16 Wrexham	42	5	8	8	22	24	7	6	8	21	21	38
17 Orient	42	9	8	4	34	20	4	4	13	18	36	38
18 Bolton Wanderers	42	10	5	6	40	27	4	5	12	21	39	38
19 Cardiff City	42	7	7	7	23	24	5	5	11	21	36	36
20 Preston North End	42	8	7	6	28	26	3	7	11	13	36	36
21 Bristol City	42	6	10	5	19	15	1	6	14	10	36	30
22 Bristol Rovers	42	4	9	8	21	24	1	4	16	13	41	23

1981/82 5th in Division 2

	Date	Opponent	Score	Scorers	Att	Allen CD	Burke SJ	Burridge J	Currie AW	Dawes IR	Fenwick TW	Fereday W	Flanagan MA	Francis GCJ	Gillard IT	Gregory JC	Hazell R	Howe EJ	Hucker PI	King PI	Micklewhite G	Neill WA	O'Connor MA	Roeder GV	Sealy AJ	Stainrod SA	Stewart IE	Waddock GP	Wicks SJ	Wilkins DM
1	Aug 29	Wrexham	3-1	King, Allen 2	4665	9		1			3		7	8	2		5			10				6		11		4		
2	Sep 1	LUTON TOWN	1-2	King	18703	9		1			3		7	8	2		5			10				6		11		4		
3	5	NEWCASTLE UNITED	3-0	King, Roeder, Stainrod	14133	9		1	4		3		7	8	12	2	5			10				6		11				
4	12	Grimsby Town	1-2	Gregory	9490	9		1	4		3		7	8	12	2	5			10				6		11				
5	19	CRYSTAL PALACE	1-0	Stainrod	17039	9		1	10		3		7		11	2	5							6		8		4		
6	22	Oldham Athletic	0-2		6421	9		1	10		3		7		11	2	5							6		8		4		
7	26	Derby County	1-3	Gregory	11246	9		1	10		3		7		11	2	5							6	12	8		4		
8	Oct 3	BLACKBURN ROVERS	2-0	Gregory, Allen	9541	9	12	1	10		3				11	2	5				7			6		8		4		
9	10	NORWICH CITY	2-0	Gregory, Stainrod	11806	9	12	1	10		3				11	2	5				7			6		8		4		
10	18	Orient	1-1	Gillard	8191	9	12	1			3			8	11	2	5				7			6		10		4		
11	24	LEICESTER CITY	2-0	Stainrod, Gregory	12419	9	12	1			3			8	7	11	2	5						6		10		4		
12	31	Charlton Athletic	2-1	Stainrod, Allen	11133	9		1			3			8	7	11	2	5						6		10		4		
13	Nov 7	ROTHERHAM UNITED	1-1	Flanagan	10949	9	9	1			3			8	7	11	2	5						6	12	10		4		
14	14	Sheffield Wednesday	3-1	Stainrod 3	17244	9		1			3				11	2	12	5			7			6		10		4		
15	21	Shrewsbury Town	1-2	Flanagan	4765	9		1			3				11	2		5			7			6		10		4		
16	24	OLDHAM ATHLETIC	0-0		9477	9		1			3				11	2		5			7			6	12	10		4		
17	28	CARDIFF CITY	2-0	Stainrod 2	10225			1			3				11	2		5			7			6	9	10		4		
18	Dec 5	Bolton Wanderers	0-1		6076		12	1			3				11	2		5			7			6	9	10		4		
19	12	BARNSLEY	1-0	Flanagan	10972			1			3	12	8		11	2		5			7			6	9			10	4	
20	26	CHELSEA	0-2		22022	12		1			3		8		11			5			7		2	6	9			10	4	
21	Jan 16	WREXHAM	1-1	Stainrod	10066	7			9		3		12		11	8		5	1			2		6		10		4		
22	30	Crystal Palace	0-0		15333	7			8		2				3	11		5	1		9			6		10		4		
23	Feb 6	GRIMSBY TOWN	1-0	Gregory	8753	7			8		2	9			3	11		5	1					6		10		4		
24	9	Cambridge United	0-1		4822	7			8		2	9			3	11		5	1		12			6		10		4		
25	16	Blackburn Rovers	1-2	Allen	6884	9					2				3	11		5	1		7	4		6		10				
26	20	DERBY COUNTY	3-0	Hazell, Fenwick, Flanagan	8890	9					2				3	11	5		1		7	4		6		10				12
27	27	Norwich City	1-0	Roeder	15216	9			7						8	3	11	5	2	1				4		6		10		
28	Mar 9	Watford	0-4		17264				7						8	3	11	5	9	1			2	6		10		4		
29	13	Leicester City	2-3	Currie, Stainrod	17812	9	12		7						8	3	11	5	2	1				6		10		4		
30	20	CHARLTON ATHLETIC	4-0	Allen 3, Fenwick	13118	9	12		7		4				8	3		5		1	11	2		6		10				
31	27	Rotherham United	0-1		10472	9	12			11	3				8			5		1	7	2				10		4	6	
32	29	SHEFFIELD WEDNESDAY	2-0	Flanagan, Stainrod	11710	9			7	3					8		11			1	4	2		6		10			5	
33	Apr 6	ORIENT	3-0	Hazell, Flanagan, Stainrod	10531	9			7				2		8	3		5		1	11			6		10	12	4		
34	10	Chelsea	1-2	Gregory	18365	9			7						8	3	11	5		1		2		6		10		4		
35	12	WATFORD	0-0		22091	9				3					8			5		1	11	2		7		10		4	6	
36	17	SHREWSBURY TOWN	2-1	Flanagan, Allen	11148	9	10			7	3	2	12	8						1	11			6				4	5	
37	24	Cardiff City	2-1	Allen, Micklewhite	5974	9					2				8	3	11			1	7			6		10		4	5	
38	May 1	BOLTON WANDERERS	7-1	* See below	9995	9	12				2				8	3	11			1	7			6		10		4	5	
39	5	Newcastle United	4-0	Gregory, Allen, Flanagan, Stainrod	10748	9	12				2			7	8	3	11			1	8			6		10		4	5	
40	8	Barnsley	0-3		10579	9	12				2				8	3		5		1	7			11		10		4	6	
41	11	Luton Town	2-3	Fenwick, Stainrod	16857	9				3	11				8					1	7	2		6		10		4	5	
42	15	CAMBRIDGE UNITED	2-1	Allen, Fenwick(p)	10467	9					7		2		8	3	11	5			12			6		10		4		
				Apps		37	12	20	20	5	36	4	37	7	35	34	24	16	22	4	26	11	1	41	7	39	3	35	9	1
				Goals		13			1		5		10		1	9	2				3	2		2		17				

Scorers in game 38: Gregory, Micklewhite, Flanagan, Fenwick (p), Allen, Stainrod.

F.A. Cup

	Date	Opponent	Score	Scorers	Att	Allen CD	Burke SJ	Burridge J	Currie AW	Dawes IR	Fenwick TW	Fereday W	Flanagan MA	Francis GCJ	Gillard IT	Gregory JC	Hazell R	Howe EJ	Hucker PI	King PI	Micklewhite G	Neill WA	O'Connor MA	Roeder GV	Sealy AJ	Stainrod SA	Stewart IE	Waddock GP	Wicks SJ	Wilkins DM
R3	Jan 2	MIDDLESBROUGH	1-1	Stainrod	12100						3			8	11			5	1		7	2		6		10	9	4		
rep	18	Middlesbrough	3-2	Stainrod 2, Neill	14819	7			8		2			9	3	11		5	1			12		6		10		4		
R4	23	Blackpool	0-0		10227	7			8		2			9	3	11		5	1					6		10		4		
rep	26	BLACKPOOL	5-1	Allen 4, Stainrod(p)	11700	7			8		2			9	3	11		5	1					6		10	12	4		
R5	Feb 13	GRIMSBY TOWN	3-1	Stainrod, Allen, Howe	13344	9					2	12		8	3	11		5	1		7			6		10		4		
R6	Mar 6	CRYSTAL PALACE	1-0	Allen	24653	9				7					8	3	11	5		1		2		6		10		4		
SF	Apr 3	West Bromwich	1-0	Allen	45015	9				7		2			8	3		5		1	11			6		10		4		
F	May 22	Tottenham Hotspur	1-1	Fenwick	100000	9				7		2			8	3	11	5		1	12			6		10		4		
rep	27	Tottenham Hotspur	0-1		92000		12			7		2			8	3	11	5		1	9	6				10		4		

R3 replay a.e.t.. SF at Highbury. Final and final replay at Wembley.

F.L. Cup (Milk Cup)

	Date	Opponent	Score	Scorers	Att	Allen CD	Burke SJ	Burridge J	Currie AW	Dawes IR	Fenwick TW	Fereday W	Flanagan MA	Francis GCJ	Gillard IT	Gregory JC	Hazell R	Howe EJ	Hucker PI	King PI	Micklewhite G	Neill WA	O'Connor MA	Roeder GV	Sealy AJ	Stainrod SA	Stewart IE	Waddock GP	Wicks SJ	Wilkins DM
R2/1	Oct 6	PORTSMOUTH	5-0	OG(Ellis), Gregory 2, Micklewhite 2	13502	9	12	1	10		3				11	2	5				7			6		8		4		
R2/2	27	Portsmouth	2-2	Flanagan, Micklewhite	7677		9	1			3		8		11	2	5				7			6		10	12	4		
R3	Nov 10	BRISTOL CITY	3-0	Flanagan, Stainrod, Allen	9215	9		1			3		8		11	2	5				7			6		10	12		4	
R4	Dec 1	Watford	1-4	Stainrod(p)	18276			1			3		8		11	2	7	5			12			6	9	10		4		

#	Date	Opponent	Score	Scorers	Att	Allen CD	Burke SJ	Currie AW	Dawes IR	Duffield MJ	Fenwick TW	Fereday W	Flanagan MA	Gregory JC	Hazell PI	Hucker PI	Micklewhite G	Neill WA	O'Connor MA	Roeder GV	Sealy AJ	Stainrod SA	Stewart IE	Waddock GP	Wicks SJ	Wilkins DM
1	Aug 28	Newcastle United	0-1		35718	12			3		6			11	5	1	7	2			9	10	8	4		
2	31	CAMBRIDGE UNITED	2-1	Sealy 2	9686				3		6			11	5	1	7	2			9	10	8	4		
3	Sep 4	DERBY COUNTY	4-1	Gregory, Fenwick (p), Stainrod 2	10217				3		6			11	5	1	7	2			9	10	8	4		12
4	7	Fulham	1-1	Stainrod	14900				3		6			11	5	1	7	2			9	10	8	4		
5	11	Oldham Athletic	1-0	Gregory	4266				3		6			11	5	1	7	2			9	10	8	4		12
6	18	SHEFFIELD WEDNESDAY	0-2		13733	12			3		6			11	5	1	7	2			9	10	8	4		
7	25	Leicester City	1-0	O'Neill (og)	10647				3		6	12		11	5	1	7	2			9	10	8	4		
8	28	CRYSTAL PALACE	0-0		12194				3		6	12		11	5	1	7	2			9	10	8	4		
9	Oct 2	BURNLEY	3-2	Neill, Allen, Micklewhite	9165	10			3		6			11	5	1	7	2			9		8	4		
10	9	Barnsley	1-0	Allen	13270	9			3		6			11	5	1	7	2				10	8	4		12
11	16	SHREWSBURY TOWN	4-0	Allen, Flanagan, Micklewhite, Gregory	9275	9			3		6	12	8	11	5	1	7	2			10			4		
12	23	Middlesbrough	1-2	Allen	7892	9			3		6	12		11	5	1	7	2			10		8	4		
13	30	BOLTON WANDERERS	1-0	Stainrod	9363	9		12	3		6			11	5	1	7	2				10	8	4		
14	Nov 6	Rotherham United	0-0		7402	9			3		6			11	5	1	7	2			12	10	8	4		
15	13	BLACKBURN ROVERS	2-2	Allen, Fenwick (p)	9149	9		10	3		6			11	5	1	7	2	12	4			8			
16	20	Cambridge United	4-1	Wicks, Sealy, Allen 2	5685	9			3		6			11	5	1	7	2			8	10	12		4	
17	27	CARLISLE UNITED	1-0	Fenwick	9397	9			3		6			11	5	1	7	2		4	8	10				
18	Dec 4	Leeds United	1-0	Allen	11528	9			3		6			11	5	1	7	2		4	8	10				
19	11	GRIMSBY TOWN	4-0	Neill, Sealy, Gregory, Micklewhite	9811	9			3		6		12	11	5	1	7	2		4	8	10				
20	18	Wolverhampton Wan.	0-4		15423	9			3		6			11	5	1	7	2		4	8	10	12			
21	27	CHELSEA	1-2	Sealy	23744	9	12		3		6			11	5	1	7		2	4	8	10				
22	29	Charlton Athletic	3-1	Micklewhite 2, Sealy	13306	9			3		6		10	11	5	1	7	2		4	8					
23	Jan 3	Derby County	0-2		14007	9			3		6		8	11	5	1	7	2		4	10	12				
24	15	NEWCASTLE UNITED	2-0	Gregory 2	13972	9			3		6		10	11	5	1	7	2			8			4		
25	22	Crystal Palace	3-0	Allen 2, Hazell	14578	9			3		6		10	11	5	1	7	2			8			4		
26	Feb 5	OLDHAM ATHLETIC	1-0		8903	9			3		6		10	11		1	7	2			8			4	5	
27	19	BARNSLEY	3-0	Gregory, Sealy, Flanagan	10271	9			3		6		10	11		1	7	2			8	12		4	5	
28	26	Shrewsbury Town	0-0		4397	9			3		6		10	11		1	7	2			8	12		4	5	
29	Mar 5	MIDDLESBROUGH	6-1	Allen 3, Micklewhite, Flanagan, Gregory	9596	9			3				10	11	5	1	7			2	8			4	6	
30	12	Bolton Wanderers	2-3	Gregory (p), Sealy	6373	9			3			12	10	11	5	1				2	8	7		4	6	
31	19	ROTHERHAM UNITED	4-0	Sealy, Flanagan, Gregory 2	9541				3		6		10	11	5	1	7	2			8	9		4		
32	22	CHARLTON ATHLETIC	5-1	Sealy 2, Hazell, Gregory, Stainrod	10776	12			3		6		10	11	5	1	7	2			8	9		4		
33	26	Blackburn Rovers	3-1	Stainrod 2, Flanagan	5317				3		6		10	11	5	1	7	2			8	9		4		
34	Apr 4	Chelsea	2-0	Gregory, Sealy	20823	12			3		6		10	11	5	1		2			8	9		4	7	
35	9	LEICESTER CITY	2-2	Gregory, Sealy	16301				3		6		10	11	5	1	7	2			8	9		4		
36	19	Sheffield Wednesday	1-0	Flanagan	11905				3		6		10	11	5	1		2			8	9		4	7	
37	23	LEEDS UNITED	1-0	Hart (og)	19573				3		6		10	11	5	1		2			8	9		4	7	
38	30	Carlisle United	0-1		5724		12		3		6		10	11	5	1		2			8	9		4	7	
39	May 2	FULHAM	3-1	Gregory, Sealy, Stainrod	24433				3		6		10	11	5	1		2			8	9		4	7	
40	7	WOLVERHAMPTON W.	2-1	Flanagan, Hazell	19854				3		6		10	11	5	1	12	2			8	9		4	7	
41	10	Burnley	1-2	Sealy	7215	10			3		6			11	5	1		2			8	9		4	7	
42	14	Grimsby Town	1-1	Stainrod	9590		6		3	12				11	5	1		2			8	9		4	7	
		Apps				25	5	2	42	1	39	5	22	42	39	42	34	39	2	9	40	31	19	33	14	3
		Goals				13					3		7	15	3		6	2			16	9			1	

Two own goals

F.A. Cup

Round	Date	Opponent	Score	Scorers	Att	Allen CD	Burke SJ	Currie AW	Dawes IR	Duffield MJ	Fenwick TW	Fereday W	Flanagan MA	Gregory JC	Hazell PI	Hucker PI	Micklewhite G	Neill WA	O'Connor MA	Roeder GV	Sealy AJ	Stainrod SA	Stewart IE	Waddock GP	Wicks SJ	Wilkins DM
R3	Jan 8	West Bromwich Albion	2-3	Fenwick (p), Micklewhite	16528	10	12		3		4		9		5		7	2		6	11			8		

Played at 1: G Benstead

F.L. Cup (Milk Cup)

Round	Date	Opponent	Score	Scorers	Att	Allen CD	Burke SJ	Currie AW	Dawes IR	Duffield MJ	Fenwick TW	Fereday W	Flanagan MA	Gregory JC	Hazell PI	Hucker PI	Micklewhite G	Neill WA	O'Connor MA	Roeder GV	Sealy AJ	Stainrod SA	Stewart IE	Waddock GP	Wicks SJ	Wilkins DM
R2/1	Oct 5	Rotherham United	1-2	Gregory	5603	8			3		6			11	5	1	7	2			9	10		4		
R2/2	26	ROTHERHAM UTD.	0-0		9653	9			3		6			11	5	1	7	2			8	10	12	4		

#	Date	Opponent	Score	Scorers	Att	Allen CD	Burke SJ	Charles JM	Dawes IR	Fenwick TW	Fereday W	Fillery MC	Flanagan MA	Gregory JC	Hazell R	Hucker PI	McDonald A	Micklewhite G	Neill WA	Roeder GV	Sealy AJ	Stainrod SA	Stewart IE	Waddock GP	Wicks SJ
1	Aug 27	Manchester United	1-3	Allen	48742	9			3			12	8	11	5	1		7	2	6		10		4	
2	29	Southampton	0-0		19522	9			3	6		8	12	11	5	1		7	2			10		4	
3	Sep 3	ASTON VILLA	2-1	Stainrod, OG(Withe)	16922	9			3	6		8		11	5	1		7	2			10	12	4	
4	6	WATFORD	1-1	Stainrod	17111	9			3	6			12	11	5	1		7	2			10	8	4	
5	10	Nottingham Forest	2-3	Dawes, Stainrod	14607				3	6				11	5	1		7	2		9	10	8	4	
6	17	SUNDERLAND	3-0	Fenwick(p), Stainrod, Allen	12929	9			3	6				11	5	1		7	2		12	10	8	4	
7	24	Wolverhampton Wan.	4-0	Allen 2, Gregory, Stainrod	11511	9			3	6				11		1	5	7	2		12	10	8	4	
8	Oct 1	ARSENAL	2-0	Gregory, Neill	26293	9			3	6				11		1	5	7	2			10	8	4	
9	15	Ipswich Town	2-0	Stainrod, Gregory	17950	9			3	6		12		11		1	5	7	2			10	8	4	
10	22	LIVERPOOL	0-1		27140	9			3	6		2		11		1	5	7				10	8	4	
11	29	Norwich City	3-0	Fenwick(2, 1Pen), Stainrod	15960	9			3	6		12		11		1		7	2			10	8	4	5
12	Nov 5	LUTON TOWN	0-1		15053	9			3	6				11		1		7	2			10	8	4	5
13	12	Coventry City	0-1		11796				3	6			12			1	5	7	2		9	10	8	4	
14	19	BIRMINGHAM CITY	2-1	Stainrod, Fenwick	10824				3	6		11				1		7	2		9	10	8	4	5
15	26	Tottenham Hotspur	2-3	Stainrod, Fenwick(p)	38789				3	6		11	12			1		7	2		9	10	8	4	5
16	Dec 3	NOTTS COUNTY	1-0	Waddock	10217				3	6		7		11		1			2		9	10	8	4	5
17	10	West Bromwich Albion	2-1	Fenwick, Stainrod	11643			12	3	6		7		11		1			2		9	10	8	4	5
18	17	EVERTON	2-0	Charles 2	11608			9	3	6		7		11		1			2			10	8	4	5
19	26	Leicester City	1-2	Fenwick(p)	17468			9	3	6		7		11		1			2			10	8	4	5
20	31	Aston Villa	1-2	Charles	19978			9	3	6		7		11		1			2			10	8	4	5
21	Jan 2	WOLVERHAMPTON W.	2-1	Wicks, Gregory	12875			9	3	6		7	12	11		1			2			10	8	4	5
22	13	MANCHESTER UNITED	1-1	Fenwick	16308			9	3	6		7		11		1			2			10	8	4	5
23	17	STOKE CITY	6-0	Charles 2, Stainrod, Gregory, Stewart, Fillery	9320			9	3	6		7		11		1		12	2			10	8	4	5
24	Feb 4	Arsenal	2-0	Stewart, Fenwick	31014			9	3	6		7	12	11		1			2			10	8	4	5
25	7	WEST HAM UNITED	1-1	Stainrod	20102			9	3	6		7		11		1		12	2			10	8	4	5
26	11	NOTTM. FOREST	0-1		16692			9	3	6		7		11		1			2			10	8	4	5
27	14	NORWICH CITY	2-0	Dawes, Waddock	9720		9		3	6		7		11		1			2			10	8	4	5
28	25	Liverpool	0-2		32206	12	9		3	6		7		11		1			2			10	8	4	5
29	Mar 3	Luton Town	0-0		11922	12		9	3	6		7		11		1			2			10	8	4	5
30	7	Sunderland	0-1		13538	9			3	6		7		11		1	12		2			10	8	4	5
31	10	COVENTRY CITY	2-1	Stainrod, Allen	10284	9			3	6		7		11		1			2			10	8	4	5
32	17	Watford	0-1		18797	9			3	6		7		11		1			2			10	8	4	5
33	24	SOUTHAMPTON	4-0	Wicks, Micklewhite, Allen, Waddock	15407	9			3	6	11	8				1		7	2			10		4	5
34	31	West Ham United	2-2	Allen 2	21099	9	12		3	6	11	8				1		7	2			10		4	5
35	Apr 7	IPSWICH TOWN	1-0	Allen	12251	9			3	6	11	8				1		7	2			10		4	5
36	14	Birmingham City	2-0	Gregory, Fenwick	10255	9			3	6	12	8		11		1		7	2			10		4	5
37	21	LEICESTER CITY	2-0	Allen, Fereday	12360	9	12		3	6	4	8		11		1		7	2			10			5
38	23	Stoke City	2-1	Allen, Fereday	13735	9			3	6	4	8		11		1		7	2			10			5
39	28	TOTTENHAM HOTSPUR	2-1	Fereday, Gregory	24937	9	12		3	6	4	8		11		1		7	2			10			5
40	May 5	Notts County	3-0	Allen(3)	7309	9			3	6	4	8		11		1		7	2			10			5
41	7	WEST BROMWICH ALB.	1-1	Fereday	14418	9			3	6	4	8		11		1		7	2			10			5
42	12	Everton	1-3	Micklewhite	20712	9		12	3	6	4	8		11		1		7	2				10		5
		Apps				25	5	12	42	41	17	30	5	37	6	42	5	30	41	1	8	41	31	36	31
		Goals				14		5	2	10	4	1		7				2	1			13	2	3	2

One own goal

F.A. Cup

Round	Date	Opponent	Score	Scorers	Att	Charles JM	Dawes IR	Fenwick TW	Fillery MC	Flanagan MA	Gregory JC	Hucker PI	Neill WA	Stainrod SA	Stewart IE	Waddock GP	Wicks SJ
R3	Jan 7	Huddersfield Town	1-2	Gregory	11924	9	3	6	7	12	11	1	2	10	8	4	5

F.L. Cup (Milk Cup)

Round	Date	Opponent	Score	Scorers	Att	Allen CD	Dawes IR	Fenwick TW	Fillery MC	Gregory JC	Hucker PI	McDonald A	Micklewhite G	Neill WA	Sealy AJ	Stainrod SA	Stewart IE	Waddock GP
R2/1	Oct 4	CREWE ALEXANDRA	8-1	*See below	8911	9	3	6	12	11	1	5	7	2		10	8	4
R2/2	25	Crewe Alexandra	0-3		3662	9	3	6	2	11	1	5	7		12	10	8	4
R3	Nov 9	Ipswich Town	2-3	Stewart, Gregory	12341	9	3	6	12	11	1	5	7	2		10	8	4

Scorers in R2/1: Stainrod 3, Waddock, Allen, Stewart, Micklewhite, McDonald.

1984/85   19th in Division 1

#	Date	Opponent	Score	Scorers	Att	Allen MJ	Bannister G	Byrne JF	Charles JM	Chivers GPS	Cooper GJ	Dawes IR	Fenwick TW	Fereday W	Fillery MC	Gregory JC	Hucker PI	James RM	Kerslake D	McDonald A	Micklewhite G	Neill WA	Robinson MJ	Stainrod SA	Stewart IE	Waddock GP	Wicks SJ
1	Aug 25	WEST BROMWICH ALB.	3-1	Stainrod 2, Fenwick	12683		9					3	6	12	8	11	1				7	2		10		4	5
2	28	Watford	1-1	Bannister	23185		9					3	6	12	8	11	1				7	2		10		4	5
3	Sep 1	Liverpool	1-1	Fereday	33982		9					3	6	4	8	11	1				7	2		10			5
4	8	NOTTM. FOREST	3-0	Fereday 2, Bannister	13507		9					3	6	4	8	11	1				7	2		10			5
5	15	Tottenham Hotspur	0-5		31655		9					3	6	4	8	11	1				7	2		10			5
6	22	NEWCASTLE UNITED	5-5	Bannister, Stainrod, Gregory, Wicks, Micklewhite	14526		9					3	6	4	8	11	1				7	2		10	12		5
7	29	Southampton	1-1	Fereday	18497		9					3	6	4	8	11	1				7	2		10	12		5
8	Oct 6	LUTON TOWN	2-3	Fillery, Bannister	12051		9					3	6	4	8	11	1				7	2		10			5
9	13	Ipswich Town	1-1	Gregory	15769		9					3	6	4	8	11	1			5	7	2		10			
10	20	COVENTRY CITY	2-1	Stainrod 2	10427		9					3	6	4	8	11	1				7	2		10	12		5
11	27	Norwich City	0-2		13817		9	12				3	6	4	8	11	1				7	2		10			5
12	Nov 3	Sunderland	0-3		16408		9	12				3	6		8	11	1				7	2		10		4	5
13	10	SHEFFIELD WEDNESDAY	0-0		13390		9	10		2		3	6	7		11	1				12				8	4	5
14	17	Arsenal	0-1		34953		9	8		2		3	6	7		11	1				12			10		4	5
15	24	ASTON VILLA	2-0	Gregory, Bannister	11689		9					3	6	7		11	1					2		10	8	4	5
16	Dec 1	Leicester City	0-4		10218		9					3	6	7		11	1					2		10	8	4	5
17	4	STOKE CITY	2-0	Bannister, Gregory	8403		9	7				3	6			11	1	8				2		10	12	4	5
18	8	EVERTON	0-0		14338		9					3	6			11	1	12			7	2		10	8	4	5
19	15	Manchester United	0-3		36134		9					3	6			11	1				7	2		10	8	4	5
20	21	LIVERPOOL	0-2		11007		9	12		5		3	6			11	1				7	2		10	8	4	
21	26	CHELSEA	2-2	Bannister, McDonald	26610		9	10				3	6		8	11	1			5	7	2				4	
22	29	Stoke City	2-0	James, Fillery	10889		9	10		5		3	6		8	11	1	12			7	2				4	
23	Jan 1	West Ham United	3-1	Byrne, Bannister, Waddock	20857		9	10		5		3	6		8	11	1				7	2				4	
24	12	TOTTENHAM HOTSPUR	2-2	Bannister 2	27404		9	10		5		3	6		8	11	1				7	2				4	
25	26	West Bromwich Albion	0-0		9194		9	10		5		3	6		8		1				7	2	11		12	4	
26	Feb 2	SOUTHAMPTON	0-4		10664		9	10		5		3	6		8	11	1				7	2				4	7
27	9	Nottingham Forest	0-2		11991		9	10		5		3	6		8	11	1				12	2				4	7
28	23	SUNDERLAND	1-0	Byrne	10063		9	10				3	6		8	11	1				7	2				4	5
29	Mar 2	NORWICH CITY	2-2	Fereday, Wicks	9475		9	10		2	8	3	6	12		11	1					7				4	5
30	9	Coventry City	0-3		8914		9	10				3	6	12	8	11	1				7	2				4	5
31	16	IPSWICH TOWN	3-0	Fereday 2, Bannister	9158		9	12		2		3	6	10	8	11	1				7					4	5
32	23	Luton Town	0-2		9373	12	9	7		2		3		10	8	11	1	6		5						4	
33	30	WATFORD	2-0	Fillery 2	12771		9	10		2		3	6	11	8		1				7				12	4	5
34	Apr 6	Chelsea	0-1		20340		9	10		2		3	6	11	8		1				7					4	5
35	8	WEST HAM UNITED	4-2	Byrne, Bannister 2, Fenwick(p)	16085		9	10		2		3	6	11	8		1				7				12	4	5
36	13	Newcastle United	0-1		21733	11	9	10		2		3	6		8		1				7				12	4	5
37	20	ARSENAL	1-0	James	20189	11	9	10		2		3	6		8	12	1			5	7					4	
38	23	Sheffield Wednesday	1-3	Fillery	22394	11	9			2		3	6	12	8	10	1			5	7					4	
39	27	Aston Villa	2-5	Bannister 2	12023		9			2		3	6	12	8	10	1				7		11			4	5
40	May 4	LEICESTER CITY	4-3	Fillery, Gregory, Bannister, Robinson	9071		9			2		3	6	12	8	11	1				7		10			4	5
41	6	Everton	0-2		50317		9			2		3	6		8	11	1				7		10		12	4	5
42	11	MANCHESTER UNITED	1-3	Bannister	20483	8	9			2		3	6	12		11	1				7		10			4	5
				Apps		5	42	23	0	23	1	42	41	26	32	37	42	20	1	16	15	18	11	19	13	31	33
				Goals			17	3					2	7	6	5		2		1	1		1	5		1	2

F.A. Cup

Rd	Date	Opponent	Score	Scorers	Att	Allen MJ	Bannister G	Byrne JF	Charles JM	Chivers GPS	Cooper GJ	Dawes IR	Fenwick TW	Fereday W	Fillery MC	Gregory JC	Hucker PI	James RM	Kerslake D	McDonald A	Micklewhite G	Neill WA	Robinson MJ	Stainrod SA	Stewart IE	Waddock GP	Wicks SJ
R3	Jan 5	Doncaster Rovers	0-1		10583		9	10		5		3	6	12	8	11	1				7	2				4	

F.L. Cup (Milk Cup)

Rd	Date	Opponent	Score	Scorers	Att	Allen MJ	Bannister G	Byrne JF	Charles JM	Chivers GPS	Cooper GJ	Dawes IR	Fenwick TW	Fereday W	Fillery MC	Gregory JC	Hucker PI	James RM	Kerslake D	McDonald A	Micklewhite G	Neill WA	Robinson MJ	Stainrod SA	Stewart IE	Waddock GP	Wicks SJ
R2/1	Sep 25	York City	4-2	Bannister 2, Fenwick(p), Fereday	10012		9					3	6	4	8	11	1				7	2		10			5
R2/2	Oct 9	YORK CITY	4-1	Bannister 2, Fereday, Micklewhite	7544		9				12	3	6	4	8	11	1				7	2		10			5
R3	30	ASTON VILLA	1-0	Gregory	12574		9	12		7		3	6	4		11	1					2		10	8		5
R4	Nov 20	Southampton	1-1	Fenwick(p)	14830		9					3	6	7		11	1					2		10	8	4	5
rep	27	SOUTHAMPTON	0-0		13754	12	9					3	6	7		11	1					2		10	8	4	5
rep2	Dec 12	SOUTHAMPTON	4-0	Waddock, Neill, Fenwick 2 (1p)	12702		9					3	6	12	8	11	1				7	2		10		4	5
R5	Jan 23	Ipswich Town	0-0		16143		9	10		5		3	6		8		1				11	2				4	7
rep	28	IPSWICH TOWN	1-2	Bannister	14653		9	10		5		3	6	12	8	11	1					2				4	7

UEFA Cup

Rd	Date	Opponent	Score	Scorers	Att	Allen MJ	Bannister G	Byrne JF	Charles JM	Chivers GPS	Cooper GJ	Dawes IR	Fenwick TW	Fereday W	Fillery MC	Gregory JC	Hucker PI	James RM	Kerslake D	McDonald A	Micklewhite G	Neill WA	Robinson MJ	Stainrod SA	Stewart IE	Waddock GP	Wicks SJ
R1/1	Sep 18	FC Reykjavik	3-0	Stainrod 2, Bannister	1600		9	12				3	6	4	8	11	1				7	2		10	14		5
R1/2	Oct 2	FC REYKJAVIK	4-0	Bannister 3, Charles	6196	14	9	10	12			3	6	4	8	11	1				7	2					5
R2/1	24	PARTIZAN BELGRADE	6-2	Gregory, Fereday, Neill, Stainrod, Bannister 2	7836		9					3	6	4	8	11	1					2		10	7		5
R2/2	Nov 7	Partizan Belgrade	0-4		45000		9			2		3	6	4	8	11	1				12			10	7		5

Home games at Highbury   Played in R2/1: SJ Burke (at 12).

1985/86   13th in Division 1

#	Date	Opponent	Score	Scorers	Att	Allen MJ	Bakholt K	Bannister G	Barron PG	Byrne JF	Chivers GPS	Dawes IR	Fenwick TW	Fereday W	Fillery MC	Gregory JC	Hucker PI	James RM	Kerslake D	McDonald A	Neill WA	Robinson MJ	Rosenior LDeG	Waddock GP	Walker C	Wicks SJ
1	Aug 17	IPSWICH TOWN	1-0	Byrne	10568			9		12	2	3	6	10		11	1	7		5		8		4		
2	20	West Ham United	1-3	Byrne	15628			9		7	2	3	6	10		11	1	12		5		8		4		
3	24	Aston Villa	2-1	Bannister 2	11896	7		9		10	2	3	6	12		11	1	8		5				4		
4	27	NOTTM. FOREST	2-1	Bannister, Fenwick(p)	9799	7		9		10	2	3	6			11	1	8		5				4		
5	31	Newcastle United	1-3	Fenwick	25219	7		9		10	2	3	6	12		11	1	8		5				4		
6	Sep 3	ARSENAL	0-1		13003	7		9		10	2	3	6	8		11	1			5			12	4		
7	7	EVERTON	3-0	Bannister 2, Byrne	14006	7		9		10	2	3	6	8		11	1			5				4		
8	14	Watford	0-2		16167	7		9		10	2	3	6	8		11	1			5			12	4		
9	21	Luton Town	0-2		9508	7		9		10	2	3	6	8		11	1			5				4		
10	28	BIRMINGHAM CITY	3-1	Rosenior, Bannister, Dawes	8411			9	1			3	6	8	11			7		2			10	4		5
11	Oct 5	LIVERPOOL	2-1	Fenwick, Bannister	21122			9	1			3	6	8	11			7		2			10	4		5
12	12	Manchester United	0-2		48845	12		9	1			3	6	8	11			7		2			10	4		5
13	19	MANCHESTER CITY	0-0		10471			9	1			3	6	8	11			7		2			10	4		5
14	26	Southampton	0-3		13645			9	1	12		3	6	11	8			7		2			10	4		5
15	Nov 2	SHEFFIELD WEDNESDAY	1-1	James	9527	7		9	1	10		3		11	8			12		2		6		4		5
16	9	West Bromwich Albion	1-0	Robinson	9018	12		9	1	10		3	6	11	8					2		7		4		5
17	16	LEICESTER CITY	2-0	Wicks, Fereday	8085	12		9	1	10		3	6	11	8					2		7		4		5
18	23	Tottenham Hotspur	1-1	Byrne	20334	12		9	1	10		3	6	11	8					2		7		4		5
19	30	COVENTRY CITY	0-2		8100	11		9	1	10		3	6		8			7		2			12	4		5
20	Dec 7	WEST HAM UNITED	0-1		20002	7		9	1	10		3	6	11	8					2			12	4		5
21	14	Ipswich Town	0-1		12166			9	1	10		3	6	11	8			7		2				4		5
22	17	ASTON VILLA	0-1		8237			9	1	10	2	3	6	11	8									4	7	5
23	28	Arsenal	1-3	Bannister	25770			9	1	10		3	6	12	8					2		7		4	11	5
24	Jan 1	OXFORD UNITED	3-1	Allen, Fereday, Byrne	13348	8		9	1	10		3	6	11						2		7		4		5
25	11	Everton	3-4	Bannister 2, Byrne	25972	8		9	1	10		3	6	11					12	2		7		4		5
26	18	NEWCASTLE UNITED	3-1	Fenwick 2 (1p), Robinson	10159			9	1	10		3	6	11	8					2		7		4		5
27	Feb 1	Nottingham Forest	0-4		11538	12		9	1	10		3	6	11	8					2		7		4		5
28	8	Manchester City	0-2		20414	5	12	9		10		3	6				1	7		2		8		4	11	
29	22	LUTON TOWN	1-1	Byrne	13252	8		9	1	10		3	6	11				7		2				4		5
30	Mar 1	Birmingham City	0-2		7093	8		9	1	10		3	6	11				7		2			12			5
31	8	Liverpool	1-4	Rosenior	26219	10			1			3	6	11				8	12	2		7	9	4		5
32	11	SOUTHAMPTON	0-2		11174				1	12		3	6	10	8					2		7	9	4	11	5
33	15	MANCHESTER UNITED	1-0	Byrne	20407	7		9	1	10		3	6	11	8					2		12		4		5
34	19	Chelsea	1-1	Kerslake	17871	7		9	1			3	6	10					8	2		11	12	4		5
35	22	WATFORD	2-1	Fenwick(p), Robinson	11069	7		9	1			3	6	10					8	2		11	12	4		5
36	29	Oxford United	3-3	Walker, Allen, Fenwick(p)	11904	8		9	1	12	5	3	6							2		7	10	4	11	
37	31	CHELSEA	6-0	Bannister 3, Byrne 2, Rosenior	18584	7		9	1	10		3	6						8	2		11	12	4		5
38	Apr 8	Sheffield Wednesday	0-0		13359	7		9	1	10		3	6						8	2		11		4		5
39	12	WEST BROMWICH ALB.	1-0	Bannister	11866	7		9	1	10		3	6						8	2		11	12	4		5
40	14	Leicester City	4-1	Allen, Bannister, Robinson, Byrne	7724	7		9	1	12	5	3	6							2	8	11	10	4		
41	26	TOTTENHAM HOTSPUR	2-5	Rosenior, Bannister	17768	7		9	1	10	5	3	6							2	8	11	12	4		
42	May 3	Coventry City	1-2	Byrne	14080				1	10	12	3	6	11	8			7		2			9	4		5
				Apps		31	1	36	31	36	14	42	37	33	17	11	11	28	14	42	16	26	18	15	5	29
				Goals		3		16		12		1	7	2				1	1			4	4		1	1

F.A. Cup

#	Date	Opponent	Score	Scorers	Att	Allen MJ	Bakholt K	Bannister G	Barron PG	Byrne JF	Chivers GPS	Dawes IR	Fenwick TW	Fereday W	Fillery MC	Gregory JC	Hucker PI	James RM	Kerslake D	McDonald A	Neill WA	Robinson MJ	Rosenior LDeG	Waddock GP	Walker C	Wicks SJ
R3	Jan 13	Carlisle United	0-1		5080	8		9	1	10		3	6					7		2		11	12	4		5

F.L. Cup (Milk Cup)

#	Date	Opponent	Score	Scorers	Att	Allen MJ	Bakholt K	Bannister G	Barron PG	Byrne JF	Chivers GPS	Dawes IR	Fenwick TW	Fereday W	Fillery MC	Gregory JC	Hucker PI	James RM	Kerslake D	McDonald A	Neill WA	Robinson MJ	Rosenior LDeG	Waddock GP	Walker C	Wicks SJ
R2/1	Sep 24	HULL CITY	3-0	Kerslake, Dawes, Bannister	7021			9		10	2	3	6	8	11		1	7					12	4		5
R2/2	Oct 8	Hull City	5-1	Kerslake 2, Rosenior 2, Fillery	4287	8		9	1	12		3	6		11			7		2			10	4		5
R3	29	Watford	1-0	Byrne	16826	7		9	1	10		3	6	11	8					2			12	4		5
R4	Nov 25	NOTTM FOREST	3-1	Fenwick(p), Bannister, Byrne	13052	12		9	1	10		3	6		8			7	11	2			4			5
R5	Jan 22	CHELSEA	1-1	Byrne	27000			9	1	10		3	6	11	8					2		7		4		5
rep	29	Chelsea	2-0	McDonald, Robinson	27937	12		9	1	10		3		11	6			8		2		4	7			5
SF1	Feb 12	LIVERPOOL	1-0	Fenwick	15051	7		9	1	10		3	6	11	8					2				4		5
SF2	Mar 5	Liverpool	2-2	Whelan(og), Gillespie(og)	23883	10		9	1			3	6	12	11			8		2		4	7			5
F	Apr 20	Oxford United	0-3		90396	7		9	1	10		3	6		8					2		4	11	12		5

Final at Wembley

69

1986/87   16th in Division 1

#		Date	Opponent	Score	Scorers	Att	Allen MJ	Bannister G	Barron PG	Brazil AB	Byrne JF	Channing JA	Chivers GPS	Dawes IR	Fenwick TW	Ferdinand L	Fereday W	Fillery MC	James RM	Kerslake D	Lee S	Maguire GT	McDonald A	Neill WA	Peacock GK	Robinson MJ	Rosenior LDeG	Seaman DA	Waddock GP	Walker C
1	Aug	23	Southampton	1-5	Allen	14711	8	9		12	10		6	3			11		4				5	2			7	1		
2		26	WATFORD	3-2	Allen, Fereday, Bannister	10700	4	9			12		6	3			11		8	7			5	2				1	10	
3		30	ASTON VILLA	1-0	Bannister	10011	4	9			10		6	3			11		8		7		5	2				1		
4	Sep	3	Newcastle United	2-0	Byrne, Bannister (p)	21417	4	9			10		6	3			11		8		7		5	2				1		
5		6	Everton	0-0		30182	4				10		6	3			11		8		7		5	2		9		1		
6		13	WEST HAM UNITED	2-3	James, Byrne	16257					10		6	3			11		8		7		5	2		12	9	1		
7		20	Manchester City	0-0		17774	4	9		12	10		6	3			11		8		7		5			2		1		
8		27	LEICESTER CITY	0-1		8306	4	9		12	10		6	3	5		2		8		7							1		11
9	Oct	4	Norwich City	0-1		15703	4	9		10			6	3			2		8				5			12		1	7	11
10		11	WIMBLEDON	2-1	Bannister, McDonald	10111	4	9			10		6	3			2		8		7		5			12		1		11
11		18	Nottingham Forest	0-1		17199	4	9			10		6	3			2		8		7		5					1	11	12
12		25	TOTTENHAM HOTSPUR	2-0	Allen, Byrne	18579	4	9			10		6	3			2		8				5					1	7	11
13	Nov	1	Luton Town	0-1		9085	4	9			10	11	6	3	5		2		8					7				1		12
14		8	LIVERPOOL	1-3	Bannister	21945	4	9			10		6	3	7		2		8				5			12		1		11
15		15	OXFORD UNITED	1-1	Byrne	9969	4	9			10		6	3	7		2		8				5			11		1		12
16		22	Manchester United	0-1		42235	4	9			10		6	3	7		2		12	8			5			11		1		
17		29	SHEFFIELD WEDNESDAY	2-2	Bannister, McDonald	8474	4	9			10		6	3	7				8				5	2		11	12	1		
18	Dec	6	Arsenal	1-3	Bannister	33806	4	9			10		6	3	7		11		8				5	2		12		1		
19		13	CHARLTON ATHLETIC	0-0		8299	4	9			10		6	3	8		11		12		7		5	2				1		
20		20	West Ham United	1-1	Fenwick (p)	17290	4	9			10				6			12	3		7		5	2		11	8	1		
21		26	COVENTRY CITY	3-1	Byrne, Bannister, Allen	8130	4	9			10			3	6				2		7		5			11	8	12	1	
22		27	Oxford United	1-0	James	11082	4	9			12		6	3					2		7	11	5			8	10	1		
23	Jan	1	Chelsea	1-3	Byrne	20982	4				10		6	3			9		2		7	11	5			8		1		12
24		3	EVERTON	0-1		16636	4				10		6		9		12		3		7		5	2		8		1		11
25		24	SOUTHAMPTON	2-1	Byrne, Bannister	8271		9			10		6		11	8	3		7				5	2			12	1		4
26	Feb	7	Aston Villa	1-0	Keown (og)	13109	7				10		6		11	8	3					2	5			9		1		4
27		14	NEWCASTLE UNITED	2-1	Byrne, Fillery	9731	7	9			10		6		11	8	3						5	2				1		4
28		28	MANCHESTER CITY	1-0	Allen	10715	7	9			10		6		11	8	3			5			2	12				1		4
29	Mar	7	Tottenham Hotspur	0-1		21071	7	9			10		6		11	8	3	12	4	5			2					1		
30		14	NOTTM. FOREST	3-1	Bannister, Fereday, McDonald	9396	7	9			10		6		11	8	3		4				5	2				1		
31		18	Liverpool	1-2	Fillery	28988	7	9			10		6		11	8	3		4				5	2				1		
32		21	Wimbledon	1-1	Rosenior	6887	7	9			10		6			8	3		4				5	2			12	1		11
33		25	Leicester City	1-4	Rosenior	7384		9			10		6			8	3		4	12			5	2			7	1		
34		28	NORWICH CITY	1-1	Rosenior	8091		9			10		6		11	8	3		4				5	2			7	1		
35	Apr	6	Watford	3-0	Bannister 3	13839		9			12				11	8	3		4	6			5	2	10		7	1		
36		11	LUTON TOWN	2-2	Byrne 2	9450		9			10				11	8	3		4	6			5	2	12		7	1		
37		18	CHELSEA	1-1	Bannister	15188		9			10				11	8	3		4	6			5	2	12		7	1		
38		20	Coventry City	1-4	Bannister	20926		9				3			12	11	8		4	6			5	2	10		7	1		
39		25	MANCHESTER UNITED	1-1	Byrne	15184	7	9			10				11	8	3		4	6			5	2	12		7	1		
40	May	2	Sheffield Wednesday	1-7	Peacock	16501		1			9			3		12	11	8	6			4	5	2	7		10			
41		4	ARSENAL	1-4	McDonald	13387					10				11	8	3	7		6		5	2	12		9		1	4	
42		9	Charlton Athletic	1-2	Rosenior	7769					10	4			11		3	12	7	6		5	2	8		9		1		
			Apps				32	34	1	4	40	2	23	23	21	2	37	18	39	3	30	14	39	29	12	11	20	41	4	15
			Goals				5	15			11			1			2	2	2				4		1		4			

One own goal

F.A. Cup

		Date	Opponent	Score	Scorers	Att	Allen MJ	Bannister G	Barron PG	Brazil AB	Byrne JF	Channing JA	Chivers GPS	Dawes IR	Fenwick TW	Ferdinand L	Fereday W	Fillery MC	James RM	Kerslake D	Lee S	Maguire GT	McDonald A	Neill WA	Peacock GK	Robinson MJ	Rosenior LDeG	Seaman DA	Waddock GP	Walker C
R3	Jan	10	LEICESTER CITY	5-2	Fenwick 2 (1p), Lee, James, Byrne	9684		9			10				6		11	8	3		7		5	2	12		14	1		4
R4		31	Luton Town	1-1	Fenwick (p)	12707	8	9			10				6		11	3			7		5	2			12	1		4
rep	Feb	4	LUTON TOWN	2-1	Fenwick, Byrne	15848	7	9			10				6		11	8	3				2	5			12	1		4
R5		21	Leeds United	1-2	Rennie (og)	31324	7	9			10	5			6		11	8	3	12	14			2				1		4

F.L. Cup (Littlewoods Challenge Cup)

		Date	Opponent	Score	Scorers	Att	Allen MJ	Bannister G	Barron PG	Brazil AB	Byrne JF	Channing JA	Chivers GPS	Dawes IR	Fenwick TW	Ferdinand L	Fereday W	Fillery MC	James RM	Kerslake D	Lee S	Maguire GT	McDonald A	Neill WA	Peacock GK	Robinson MJ	Rosenior LDeG	Seaman DA	Waddock GP	Walker C
R2/1	Sep	23	BLACKBURN ROVERS	2-1	Byrne, Brazil	6510	4	9		12	10		6	3			11		8		7					2	5	1		14
R2/2	Oct	7	Blackburn Rovers	2-2	Bannister, Walker	5100	4	9		10			6	3			2		8		7		5			12		1		11
R3		28	Charlton Athletic	0-1		6926	4	9			10		6	3	12		2		8				5			14		1	7	11

70

1987/88   5th in Division 1

League (Division 1)

#	Date	Opponent	Score	Scorers	Att	Allen MJ	Bannister G	Brock KS	Byrne JF	Channing JA	Coney DH	Dawes IR	Dennis ME	Falco MP	Fenwick TW	Ferdinand L	Fereday W	Fleming MJ	Francis TJ	Johns NP	Kerslake D	Law BJ	Maddix DS	Maguire GT	McDonald A	Neill WA	O'Neill JP	Parker PA	Peacock GK	Pizanti D	Roberts AM	Seaman DA
1	Aug 15	West Ham United	3-0	OG(Stewart), Bannister, Brock	22880	7	9	11	10		8		3		6		2								5			4				1
2	19	DERBY COUNTY	1-1	Bannister	11561	7	9	11	10		8		3		6		2								5			4				1
3	22	ARSENAL	2-0	Byrne, McDonald	18981	7	9	11	10		8		3		6		2								5			4	12			1
4	29	Southampton	1-0	Brock	15532	7	9	11	10		8		3		6		2								5			4				1
5	Sep 2	EVERTON	1-0	Allen	15380	7	9	11	10		8		3		6		2								5			4				1
6	5	Charlton Athletic	1-0	Coney	7728	7	9	11	10		8		3		6		2								5			4	12			1
7	12	CHELSEA	3-1	Bannister 3	22583	7	9	11	10		8		3		6		2								5			4				1
8	19	Oxford United	0-2		9796	7	9	11	10		8		3		6		2								5	12		4	14			1
9	26	LUTON TOWN	2-0	Coney, Fenwick(Pen)	11175	7	9	11	10		8		3		6		2								5	12		4				1
10	Oct 3	Wimbledon	2-1	Bannister, Fenwick(Pen)	8552	7	9	11	10		8		3		6										5	2		4				1
11	17	Liverpool	0-4		43735	7	9	11	10		8		3		6									14	5	2		4	12			1
12	24	PORTSMOUTH	2-1	Byrne, Fenwick	13171	7	9	11	10		8		3		6		14							12	5	2		4				1
13	31	Norwich City	1-1	Allen	14522	7			10	11	8		3		6		9									2	5	4	12			1
14	Nov 7	WATFORD	0-0		11601	7			11	10	8		3		6		14							12	5	2		4				1
15	14	Tottenham Hotspur	1-1	Coney	28113	7			11	10	9		3	8	6		2								5			4	12			1
16	21	NEWCASTLE UNITED	1-1	OG(Wharton)	11794	7	9	11	10	12	8		3		6		2								5			4	14			1
17	28	Sheffield Wednesday	1-3	Bannister	18933	7	9	11	14	10	8		3		6		2				12						5	4				1
18	Dec 5	MANCHESTER UNITED	0-2		20632	7	9	11	10		12		3	8	6		2								5			4				1
19	13	Nottingham Forest	0-4		18130	7	9	11	10		8		3		6	14	2							12	5			4				1
20	18	COVENTRY CITY	1-2	Falco	7299	7	9	11	10		12		3	8	6		2								5			4			1	
21	26	Chelsea	1-1	Kerslake	18020	7	9	11					3	8	6					1	10			12	5	2		4				
22	28	OXFORD UNITED	3-2	Falco 2, Allen	9125	7	9	11					3	8	6		12			1	10				5	2		4				
23	Jan 1	SOUTHAMPTON	3-0	Bannister, Falco, Fereday	8631	7	9	11			12	2	3	8			14			1	10		6		5			4				
24	2	Arsenal	0-0		28269	7	9	11		12		2	3	8						1	10		6		5			4				
25	16	WEST HAM UNITED	0-1		14909	7	9	11	14			2	3	8						1	10		6	12	5			4				
26	Feb 6	CHARLTON ATHLETIC	2-0	Falco, Byrne	11512	7	9	11	14			2		8						1	10		6		5			4		3		
27	13	Everton	0-2		24839	7	9	11	14			2							8	1	10		6		5			4		3		
28	27	WIMBLEDON	1-0	Byrne	9080	7			9			2		8							10	12	11	5	6			4		3		1
29	Mar 5	LIVERPOOL	0-1		23171				9		12	2		8					14		10		11	7	6			4		3		1
30	16	NOTTM. FOREST	2-1	Coney, Fereday	8316				8	12	9						7				10		11		6			4		3		1
31	19	NORWICH CITY	3-0	Channing, Coney, Fereday	9033	7				14	11			9			3				10		8	5	6			4				1
32	26	Portsmouth	1-0	Coney	13449	7					11			9			3		14		10		8	5	6			4				1
33	Apr 1	Watford	1-0	McDonald	16083	7					12			9			3		11		10		8	5	6			4				1
34	4	TOTTENHAM HOTSPUR	2-0	Kerslake 2	14866	7					14			12			3		9		10		11	5	8			4				1
35	9	Newcastle United	1-1	Kerslake(Pen)	18592	7								12			3		9		10		11	5	8	14		4				1
36	13	Derby County	2-0	Allen, Fereday	14218	7											3		9		10		11	5	8	12		4				1
37	19	Luton Town	1-2	Kerslake(Pen)	6735	7					6			12			3		9		10		11	5	8			4		14		1
38	23	SHEFFIELD WEDNESDAY	1-1	Coney	12531	7					12			9			3				10		11	5	8	14	6	4				1
39	30	Manchester United	1-2	McDonald	35733	7					12			9			3				11		8	5	10			4		6		1
40	May 7	Coventry City	0-0		15951	7					12			9			3		14		10		8	5	11			4		6		1
		Apps				38	24	26	27	14	32	33	11	19	22	1	37	2	9	7	18	1	9	18	36	23	2	40	5	6	1	32
		Goals				4	8	2	4	1	7			5	3		4				5				3							

Two own goals

F.A. Cup

#	Date	Opponent	Score	Scorers	Att	Allen MJ	Bannister G	Brock KS	Byrne JF	Channing JA	Coney DH	Dawes IR	Dennis ME	Falco MP	Fenwick TW	Ferdinand L	Fereday W	Fleming MJ	Francis TJ	Johns NP	Kerslake D	Law BJ	Maddix DS	Maguire GT	McDonald A	Neill WA	O'Neill JP	Parker PA	Peacock GK	Pizanti D	Roberts AM	Seaman DA
R3	Jan 9	Yeovil Town	3-0	Falco 2, Brock	9717	7	9	11			12	2	3	8						1	10		6		5			4				
R4	30	WEST HAM UNITED	3-1	Pizanti, Bannister, Allen	23651	7	9	11	12			2		8						1	10		6		5			4		3		
R5	Feb 20	LUTON TOWN	1-1	Neill	15356	7	9	11	12			2		8						1	10		6		5	3		4				
rep	24	Luton Town	0-1		10854	7		11	9	12		2		8							10		6		5	3		4		14		1

F.L. Cup (Littlewoods Challenge Cup)

#	Date	Opponent	Score	Scorers	Att	Allen MJ	Bannister G	Brock KS	Byrne JF	Channing JA	Coney DH	Dawes IR	Dennis ME	Falco MP	Fenwick TW	Ferdinand L	Fereday W	Fleming MJ	Francis TJ	Johns NP	Kerslake D	Law BJ	Maddix DS	Maguire GT	McDonald A	Neill WA	O'Neill JP	Parker PA	Peacock GK	Pizanti D	Roberts AM	Seaman DA
R2/1	Sep 23	MILLWALL	2-1	Bannister, McDonald	11865	7	9	11	10		8		3		6		2								5			4				1
R2/2	Oct 6	Millwall	0-0		11225	7	9	11	10		8		3		6										5	2		4				1
R3	27	Bury	0-1		5384	7	9		10	12			3		6		14	8							5	2		4		11		1

Full Members Cup (Simod Cup)

#	Date	Opponent	Score	Scorers	Att	Allen MJ	Bannister G	Brock KS	Byrne JF	Channing JA	Coney DH	Dawes IR	Dennis ME	Falco MP	Fenwick TW	Ferdinand L	Fereday W	Fleming MJ	Francis TJ	Johns NP	Kerslake D	Law BJ	Maddix DS	Maguire GT	McDonald A	Neill WA	O'Neill JP	Parker PA	Peacock GK	Pizanti D	Roberts AM	Seaman DA
R1	Dec 21	READING	1-3	Allen	4004	7		11	10	2			8	3	9	6				1	12				5			4				1

Player columns (left to right): Allen BJ, Allen MJ, Ardiles OC, Barker S, Brock KS, Channing JA, Clarke CJ, Coney DH, Dennis ME, Falco MP, Fereday W, Fleming MJ, Francis TJ, Gray AA, Herrera R, Johns NP, Kerslake D, Law BJ, Maddix DS, Maguire GT, McDonald A, Parker PA, Pizanti D, Reid P, Seaman DA, Sinton A, Spackman NJ, Stein EMS

#	Date	Opponent	Score	Scorers	Att	BJ	MJ	Ard	Bar	Bro	Cha	Cla	Con	Den	Fal	Fer	Fle	Fra	Gra	Her	Joh	Ker	Law	Mad	Mag	McD	Par	Piz	Rei	Sea	Sin	Spa	Ste
1	Aug 27	Manchester United	0-0		46377	7	6	11	8					3	9	2		10								5	4			1			12
2	Sep 3	SOUTHAMPTON	0-1		9454	7	6	11	8					3	9	2		10						12		5	4			1			14
3	10	Norwich City	0-1		11174	7	12	8	11				9	3	14	2								6		5	4			1			10
4	17	SHEFFIELD WEDNESDAY	2-0	Francis 2 (1p)	8011	7			11					3	9			8						6	2	5	4			1			10
5	24	Derby County	1-0	Stein	14008	7		11					12	3	9			8					2	6		5	4			1			10
6	Oct 1	Millwall	2-3	Allen, Francis	14103	7		12	11					3	14	9		8			1		2	6		5	4						10
7	8	NOTTM. FOREST	1-2	Stein	11205	7			11				10	3	9			8			1			6	2	5	4						12
8	15	WEST HAM UNITED	2-1	Maddix, Stein	14566	3		2	11				12		7	9		8			1		14	6		5	4						10
9	22	Arsenal	1-2	Falco	33202	3		2	11						7	9		8						12		5	4			1			10
10	29	Luton Town	0-0		8453	3		2	11				12		7	9		8						14		5	4			1			10
11	Nov 5	NEWCASTLE UNITED	3-0	Maddix, Allen, Falco	11013	3		2	12						7	9		8					14	6	11	5	4			1			10
12	12	Middlesbrough	0-1		20585	3	14	2	12						7	9		8						6	11	5	4			1			10
13	19	LIVERPOOL	0-1		20063	3	12	2	11						7	9		8					14	6		5	4	10		1			
14	26	Tottenham Hotspur	2-2	Falco, Francis	26698	3	5	2	11						7	9		8					12	6	14		4	10		1			
15	Dec 3	COVENTRY CITY	2-1	Francis, Falco	9853	3			11				2	12	7	9		8						6		5	4	10		1			
16	10	Charlton Athletic	1-1	Francis	6012	3									7	9		8					11	6	5	2	4	10		1			
17	17	EVERTON	0-0		10067			11					10	3	7	9		8						12		2	4	5		1			14
18	26	Aston Villa	1-2	Francis	25106			11					10		7	9		8						6	12	3	2	4	5	1			14
19	31	Southampton	4-1	Allen, Barker, Falco 2	15096	11	14	12					10		7			8				3		6		2	4	5		1			9
20	Jan 2	NORWICH CITY	1-1	Falco	12481	11							10		7			8						12	5	2	4	3		1			9
21	14	Wimbledon	0-1		7118	12		2	8				10		9				14			11	5	6			4	3		1			7
22	21	DERBY COUNTY	0-1		9516			8					10		9	2						12	11	5	6		4	3		1			7
23	Feb 4	MILLWALL	1-2	Falco (p)	10881			12					10		9	11		8				3	2			5	4	14		1		6	7
24	11	Nottingham Forest	0-0		19690			9		2					10			8				12		5			4	3	11	1		6	7
25	18	ARSENAL	0-0		20543			7		2				10	3	9		8				14		5			4		11	1		6	12
26	25	West Ham United	0-0		17371			7		2			14	3	9			8				10		5			4	12		1		6	11
27	Mar 11	Newcastle United	2-1	Stein, Clarke	21665					9	14	3				2		7				12				5	4	11		1		6	8
28	21	LUTON TOWN	1-1	Clarke	9072	11		12		9		3						7	2							5	4	10		1		6	8
29	25	Sheffield Wednesday	2-0	Falco, Allen	18804	11				9		3		12	2										14	5	4	10		1	7	6	8
30	27	ASTON VILLA	1-0	Sinton	11382	7				9		3		8	2										14	5	4	10		1	11	6	12
31	Apr 1	Everton	1-4	Falco (p)	23042	7				9		3		8	2											5	4	10		1	11	6	12
32	8	WIMBLEDON	4-3	Clarke, Spackman, Falco, Reid	9589	7						3	2	9	8	14										5	4	10		1	11	6	12
33	15	MIDDLESBROUGH	0-0		10347	7						3	2	9	8	14										5	4	10		1	11	6	12
34	22	Coventry City	3-0	Clarke 2, Channing	11246	12						3	2	9								7	8			5	4	10		1	11	6	
35	29	CHARLTON ATHLETIC	1-0	Sinton	13452	12						3	2	9								7	8			5	4	10		1	11	6	14
36	May 8	MANCHESTER UNITED	3-2	Sinton, Gray 2	10010							3	2	9					14			7	8			5	4	10		1	11	6	12
37	13	TOTTENHAM HOTSPUR	1-0	Falco	21873	3		10					2	9		14						7	8		12	5	4			1	11	6	
38	16	Liverpool	0-2		38387	3		2						9		14						7	8		12	5	4	10		1	11	6	

	BJ	MJ	Ard	Bar	Bro	Cha	Cla	Con	Den	Fal	Fer	Fle	Fra	Gra	Her	Joh	Ker	Law	Mad	Mag	McD	Par	Piz	Rei	Sea	Sin	Spa	Ste
Apps	1	28	8	25	14	9	12	16	17	27	31	1	19	11	2	3	21	6	33	8	30	36	15	14	35	10	16	31
Goals		4		1		1	5			12			7	2			2						1			3	1	4

F.A. Cup

Rd	Date	Opponent	Score	Scorers	Att	BJ	MJ	Ard	Bar	Bro	Con	Den	Fal	Fer	Fra	Ker	Law	Mad	Mag	McD	Par	Piz	Rei	Sea	Ste
R3	Jan 7	Manchester United	0-0		36222	11		12			10		7	9	8			5	6	2	4	3		1	14
rep	11	MANCHESTER UTD.	2-2	Stein, McDonald	22236		14	8			10	12	9			11	5	6		2	4	3		1	7
rep2	23	Manchester United	0-3		47257	14		8	11		10		9		12			5	6	2	4	3		1	7

First replay a.e.t.

F.L. Cup (Littlewoods Challenge Cup)

Rd	Date	Opponent	Score	Scorers	Att	BJ	MJ	Ard	Bar	Con	Den	Fal	Fer	Fra	Gra	Joh	Ker	Law	Mad	Mag	McD	Par	Piz	Rei	Sea	Ste
R2/1	Sep 28	CARDIFF CITY	3-0	Francis, Fereday, Allen	6078	7		12	11		3	9		8		1		2	6	14	5	4				10
R2/2	Oct 12	Cardiff City	4-1	Falco 2, Maddix, Stein	2692			2	11	12		7	9	8		1		14	6	3	5	4				10
R3	Nov 2	CHARLTON ATHLETIC	2-1	Francis 2	8701	3		2	11			7	9	8				12	6		5	4			1	10
R4	30	WIMBLEDON	0-0		10504	3	5		11	2		7	9	8					6	12		4	10		1	
rep	Dec 14	Wimbledon	1-0	Falco	6585	3				10	5	7	9	8				11	6		2	4	12		1	
R5	Jan 18	Nottingham Forest	2-5	Stein, Kerslake	24065	12		2	8	10		9			14		11	5	6			4	3		1	7

Full Members Cup (Simod Cup)

Rd	Date	Opponent	Score	Scorers	Att	Ard	Bro	Con	Den	Fal	Fer	Fra	Ker	Law	Mad	Mag	McD	Par	Piz	Rei	Sea	Spa	Ste
R3	Feb 1	Sheffield Wednesday	1-0	Coney	3957	8	2	10	11	9	6				12	14	5	4	3		1		7
R4	14	Watford	1-1	Coney	8103	9	2	10			12		11		8		5		3		1	6	7
SF	27	Everton	0-1		7472	7	2	10	3			8	14			12	5	4		11	1	6	9

R4 won on penalties a.e.t.   Played in R4: AJ McCarthy (at 4, substituted)

Mercantile Credit Centenary Trophy

Rd	Date	Opponent	Score	Scorers	Att	BJ	MJ	Ard	Bar	Den	Fal	Fer	Fra	Mad	McD	Par	Sea	Ste
QF	Aug 31	ARSENAL	0-2		10019	7	6	11	8	3	9	2	10	12	5	4	1	14

1989/90   11th in Division 1

#	Date	Opponent	Score	Scorers	Att	Allen MJ	Bardsley DJ	Barker S	Channing JA	Clarke CJ	Falco MP	Ferdinand L	Francis TJ	Herrera R	Iorfa D	Kerslake D	Law BJ	Maddix DS	McDonald A	Parker PA	Reid P	Roberts AM	Rutherford MA	Sansom KG	Seaman DA	Sinton A	Spackman NJ	Stein EMS	Wegerle RC	Wilkins RC	Wright PH
1	Aug 19	CRYSTAL PALACE	2-0	Wright 2 (1p)	16161	7			2	9	12							14	5	4	8			3	1	11	6				10
2	22 Chelsea		1-1	Clarke	24354	7			2	9	12							14	5	4	8			3	1	11	6				10
3	26 Norwich City		0-0		14021			7	2	9	12					14			5	4	8			3	1	11	6				10
4	30 LUTON TOWN		0-0		10565		14		2	9	12								5	4	8			3	1	11	6		7		10
5	Sep 9 Manchester City		0-1		23420	7			2	9								14	5	4	8			3	1	11	6	12			10
6	16 DERBY COUNTY		0-1		10697	7	14		2	9			12						5	4	8			3	1	11	6				10
7	23 Aston Villa		3-1	Francis 3	14170	7			2	9			10					12	5	4	8			3	1	11	6				14
8	30 Tottenham Hotspur		2-3	Bardsley, Francis	23781	7	8		2	9	12		10						5	4				3	1	11	6				
9	Oct 14 SOUTHAMPTON		1-4	Francis	10022	7	14		2	9			10					3	5	4	8				1	11	6				12
10	21 CHARLTON ATHLETIC		0-1		10608	7	8		2	9								4	5				12	3	1	11	6				10
11	28 Nottingham Forest		2-2	Sinton, Wright	19442	7	6		2	9									5	4	8		10	3	1	11					12
12	Nov 4 Wimbledon		0-0		5984	7			2	9			12					10	5	4	8			3	1	11	6				
13	11 LIVERPOOL		3-2	Wright 2 (1p), Falco	18804			7	2	12	9							6	5	4	8			3	1	11					10
14	18 Arsenal		0-3		38236			7	2	12	9						6		5	4	8	1		3		11		14			10
15	25 MILLWALL		0-0		9141	2		7		9			10					6	5	4	8	1		3		11		14			12
16	Dec 2 Crystal Palace		3-0	Maddix, Sinton 2	12784	2				12	9	10						6	5	4	8	1		3		11				7	
17	9 CHELSEA		4-2	Ferdinand 2, Falco, Clarke	17835	2	12			14	9	10						6	5	4	8	1		3		11				7	
18	16 Sheffield Wednesday		0-2		14569	2	8	12			9	10						6	5	4		1		3		11			14	7	
19	26 COVENTRY CITY		1-1	Falco	9889	2	8				9							6	5	4				3	1	11			10	7	
20	30 EVERTON		1-0	Sinton	11683	2	8				9						4	6	5					3	1	11			10	7	12
21	Jan 1 Manchester United		0-0		34824	2	8				9						4	6	5					3	1	11			10	7	12
22	13 NORWICH CITY		2-1	Falco, Clarke	11439	2	8			12	9							6	5	4				3	1	11			10	7	
23	20 Luton Town		1-1	Falco	9703	2	8			12	9							6	5	4				3	1	11			10	7	
24	Feb 10 Derby County		0-2		14445	2	8		12	9								6	5	4				3	1	11			10	7	14
25	24 Millwall		2-1	Barker, Wegerle	11505	2	8			9							4	6	5					3	1	11			10	7	
26	Mar 3 ARSENAL		2-0	Wilkins, Wegerle	18693	2	8			9								6	5	4				3	1	11			10	7	
27	17 TOTTENHAM HOTSPUR		3-1	Clarke, Sinton, Barker	16691	2	8			9	12							6	5	4				3	1	11			10	7	
28	20 ASTON VILLA		1-1	Clarke	15856	2	8			9	12							6	5	4				3	1	11			10	7	
29	24 NOTTM. FOREST		2-0	Sinton, Barker	14853	2	8			9	12							6	5	4				3	1	11			10	7	
30	31 Charlton Athletic		0-1		8768	2	8			9	12						5	6		4				3	1	11			10	7	
31	Apr 3 Southampton		2-0	Maddix, Wegerle	14757	2	8			9							5	6		4				3	1	11			10	7	
32	7 Everton		0-1		19418	2	8		12	9							5	6		4				3	1	11			10	7	
33	11 MANCHESTER CITY		1-3	Wegerle	8437	2	8		12	9							5	6		4				3	1	11			10	7	
34	14 MANCHESTER UNITED		1-2	Channing	19887	2		8	12	9	10							6	5	4				3	1	11				7	
35	16 Coventry City		1-1	Maddix	10012	2		8		9	12	10						6	5	4				3	1	11				7	
36	21 SHEFFIELD WEDNESDAY		1-0	Clarke	10448	2		8		9								6	5	4				3	1	11			10	7	
37	28 Liverpool		1-2	Wegerle	37758	2		8		9			12		3		4	6	5						1	11			10	7	
38	May 5 WIMBLEDON		2-3	Wegerle, Channing	9676	2		8	9				12	14			4	6	5					3	1	11			10	7	
Apps						2	31	28	23	34	21	9	4	1	1	1	10	32	34	32	15	5	2	36	33	38	13	2	19	23	15
Goals							1	3	2	6	5	2	5					3								6			6	1	5

F.A. Cup

Rd	Date	Opponent	Score	Scorers	Att	Allen MJ	Bardsley DJ	Barker S	Channing JA	Clarke CJ	Falco MP	Ferdinand L	Francis TJ	Herrera R	Iorfa D	Kerslake D	Law BJ	Maddix DS	McDonald A	Parker PA	Reid P	Roberts AM	Rutherford MA	Sansom KG	Seaman DA	Sinton A	Spackman NJ	Stein EMS	Wegerle RC	Wilkins RC	Wright PH
R3	Jan 6 Cardiff City		0-0		13834	2	8			9								6	5	4				3	1	11			10	7	
rep	10 CARDIFF CITY		2-0	Wilkins, Wegerle	12228	2	8			9								6	5	4				3	1	11			10	7	
R4	27 Arsenal		0-0		43483	2	8			9								6	5	4				3	1	11			10	7	12
rep	31 ARSENAL		2-0	Sansom, Sinton	21547	2	8			9								6	5	4				3	1	11			10	7	
R5	Feb 18 Blackpool		2-2	Clarke 2	9641	2	8			9								6	5	4				3	1	11			10	7	
rep	21 BLACKPOOL		0-0		15323	2	8			9								6	5	4				3	1	11			10	7	12
rep2	26 BLACKPOOL		3-0	Sinton, Sansom, Barker	12775	2	8			9								6	5	4				3	1	11			10	7	
R6	Mar 11 LIVERPOOL		2-2	Wilkins, Barker	21057	2	8			9	12							6	5	4				3	1	11			10	7	
rep	14 Liverpool		0-1		30090	2	8			9	12							6	5	4				3	1	11			10	7	

R5 replay a.e.t.

F.L. Cup (Littlewoods Challenge Cup)

Rd	Date	Opponent	Score	Scorers	Att	Allen MJ	Bardsley DJ	Barker S	Channing JA	Clarke CJ	Falco MP	Ferdinand L	Francis TJ	Herrera R	Iorfa D	Kerslake D	Law BJ	Maddix DS	McDonald A	Parker PA	Reid P	Roberts AM	Rutherford MA	Sansom KG	Seaman DA	Sinton A	Spackman NJ	Stein EMS	Wegerle RC	Wilkins RC	Wright PH
R2/1	Sep 20 STOCKPORT COUNTY		2-1	Spackman, Clarke	6745			8	2	9	12		7						5	4	14			3	1	11	6				10
R2/2	Oct 2 Stockport County		0-0		5997			7	2	9			10						5	4	8			3	1	11	6				10
R3	25 COVENTRY CITY		1-2	Wright (p)	9277			6	2	9			10				4	5		7			12	3	1	11					8

1990/91   12th in Division 1

	Date		Opponent	Score	Scorers	Att	Allen BJ	Bardsley DJ	Barker S	Brevett RE	Caeser GC	Channing JA	Falco MP	Ferdinand L	Herrera R	Iorfa D	Law BJ	Maddix DS	McCarthy AJ	McDonald A	Meaker MJ	Parker PA	Peacock D	Roberts AM	Sansom KG	Sinton A	Stejskal J	Tilson A	Wegerle RC	Wilkins RC	Wilson CA
1	Aug	25	Nottingham Forest	1-1	Wegerle	21619		2	12			4	9	14				6		5				1	3	11			10	7	8
2		29	WIMBLEDON	0-1		9782		2	12			4	9	14				6		5				1	3	11			10	7	8
3	Sep	1	CHELSEA	1-0	Wegerle (p)	19813		2				6	9							5		4		1	3	11			10	7	8
4		8	Manchester United	1-3	Wegerle (p)	43428		2	12				9					6		5		4		1	3	11			10	7	8
5		15	LUTON TOWN	6-1	Wegerle 2, Sinton, Wilkins, Falco, Parker	10196		2					9	12				6		5		4		1	3	11			10	7	8
6		22	Aston Villa	2-2	Wegerle (p), Sinton	23301		2					9					6		5		4		1	3	11			10	7	8
7		29	Coventry City	1-3	Ferdinand	9897		2	14			12		9				6		5		4		1	3	11			10	7	8
8	Oct	6	TOTTENHAM HOTSPUR	0-0		21405		2	8				12	9				6		5		4		1	3	11			10	7	
9		20	Leeds United	3-2	Wegerle 2, Wilkins	27443		2	8				12	9				6		5		4			3	11	1		10	7	
10		27	NORWICH CITY	1-3	Wegerle (p)	11103		2	8			12	14	9				6		5		4			3	11	1		10	7	
11	Nov	3	Everton	0-3		22358		2	8				9					6		5		4			3	11	1		10	7	12
12		10	Southampton	1-3	Falco	14970	12	2	8				9					6		5		4			3	11	1		10	7	
13		17	CRYSTAL PALACE	1-2	Falco	14360		2	8				9			6				5		4		1	3	11			10	7	
14		24	ARSENAL	1-3	Wegerle (p)	18555		2	8						4	12	6		5					1	3	11			10	7	9
15	Dec	1	Manchester City	1-2	Sinton	25080		2	8	5					4	9	6				12			1	3	11			10	7	
16		8	Wimbledon	0-3		5432		2	8	5			9		4					12				1	3	11			10	7	6
17		15	NOTTM. FOREST	1-2	Wegerle (p)	10156		2	8	5			9					6			12				3	11	1		10	7	4
18		23	Derby County	1-1	Wegerle	16429		2	8				9					6					5		3	11	1	4	10	7	
19		26	LIVERPOOL	1-1	Falco	17848		2	8	5			9					6							3	11	1	4	10	7	
20		29	SUNDERLAND	3-2	Maddix, Wegerle (p), Falco	11072		2	8	5			9					6			12				3	11	1	4	10	7	
21	Jan	1	Sheffield United	0-1		21158		2	8				9					6			12		5		3	11	1	4	10	7	
22		12	Chelsea	0-2		19255		2	8				9					6			14		5		3	11	1	12	10	7	4
23		19	MANCHESTER UNITED	1-1	Falco	18544		2	8				9	10				6			12		5		3	11	1	4		7	
24	Feb	2	Luton Town	2-1	Ferdinand 2	8479	9	2	8					10				6			12		5		3	11	1	4		7	
25		16	Crystal Palace	0-0		16006	12	2	8				9	10				6					5		3	11	1	4		7	
26		23	SOUTHAMPTON	2-1	Ferdinand 2	11009		2	8					9				6					5		3	11	1	4	10	7	
27	Mar	2	MANCHESTER CITY	1-0	Ferdinand	12746		2	8				9			12		6					5		3	11	1	4	10	7	
28		16	COVENTRY CITY	1-0	Ferdinand	9510		2	8				9			12		6					5		3	11	1	4	10	7	
29		23	Tottenham Hotspur	0-0		30860		2	8	3			9					6					5			11	1	4	10	7	
30		30	Liverpool	3-1	Ferdinand, Wegerle, Wilson	37251	12	2	8	3			9					6					5			11	1	4	10	7	14
31	Apr	1	DERBY COUNTY	1-1	Wegerle (p)	12036	9	2	8	3						14		6					12	5		11	1	4	10	7	
32		6	Sunderland	1-0	Tilson	17899		2	8	3			9					6					5			11	1	4	10	7	
33		10	ASTON VILLA	2-1	Allen, Tilson	11539	14	2	8	3			9					6					12	5		11	1	4	10	7	
34		13	SHEFFIELD UNITED	1-2	Allen	13801	9	2	8	3								6			14		12	5		11	1	4	10	7	
35		17	LEEDS UNITED	2-0	Wegerle, Barker	10998		2	8	3								6		9				5		11	1	4	10	7	
36		23	Arsenal	0-2		42395	12	2	8	3								6		9			14	5		11	1	4	10	7	
37	May	4	Norwich City	0-1		13469	9	2	8	3						12				9			8	4	5		11	1		10	7	
38		11	EVERTON	1-1	Wegerle	12508	12	2	8	3								6		9			4	5		11	1		10	7	

Apps	10	38	35	10	5	5	20	18	3	6	3	32	2	17	8	17	19	12	28	38	26	19	35	38	13
Goals	2		1				5	8				1				1				3		2	18	2	1

F.A. Cup

	Date		Opponent	Score	Scorers	Att	Allen BJ	Bardsley DJ	Barker S	Brevett RE	Caeser GC	Channing JA	Falco MP	Ferdinand L	Herrera R	Iorfa D	Law BJ	Maddix DS	McCarthy AJ	McDonald A	Meaker MJ	Parker PA	Peacock D	Roberts AM	Sansom KG	Sinton A	Stejskal J	Tilson A	Wegerle RC	Wilkins RC	Wilson CA
R3	Jan	7	Manchester United	1-2	Maddix	35065		2	8			5	9	14				6	12						3	11	1		10	7	4

F.L. Cup (Rumbelows Cup)

	Date		Opponent	Score	Scorers	Att	Allen BJ	Bardsley DJ	Barker S	Brevett RE	Caeser GC	Channing JA	Falco MP	Ferdinand L	Herrera R	Iorfa D	Law BJ	Maddix DS	McCarthy AJ	McDonald A	Meaker MJ	Parker PA	Peacock D	Roberts AM	Sansom KG	Sinton A	Stejskal J	Tilson A	Wegerle RC	Wilkins RC	Wilson CA
R2/1	Sep	26	PETERBOROUGH UTD.	3-1	Ferdinand, Maddix, Wegerle	8714		2	12					9				6		5		4		1	3	11			10	7	8
R2/2	Oct	9	Peterborough United	1-1	Ferdinand	7545		2	8					9				6		5		4		1	3	11			10	7	
R3		31	BLACKBURN ROVERS	2-1	Falco, Barker	8398		2	8				9				12	6		5		4			3	11	1		10	7	
R4	Nov	27	LEEDS UNITED	0-3		15832		2	8				9		4	9	6							1	3	11			10	7	5

Full Members Cup (Zenith Data Systems Cup)

	Date		Opponent	Score	Scorers	Att	Allen BJ	Bardsley DJ	Barker S	Brevett RE	Caeser GC	Channing JA	Falco MP	Ferdinand L	Herrera R	Iorfa D	Law BJ	Maddix DS	McCarthy AJ	McDonald A	Meaker MJ	Parker PA	Peacock D	Roberts AM	Sansom KG	Sinton A	Stejskal J	Tilson A	Wegerle RC	Wilkins RC	Wilson CA
R2	Nov	20	Southampton	0-4		5071	9	2	8								5		6		14	4		1	3	11			10	7	12

#	Date	Opponent	Score	Scorers	Att	Allen BJ	Bailey DL	Bardsley DJ	Barker S	Brevett RE	Ferdinand L	Holloway IS	Impey AR	Iorfa D	McCarthy AJ	McDonald A	Maddix DS	Meaker MJ	Peacock D	Penrice GK	Ready K	Roberts AM	Sinton A	Stejskal J	Thompson GL	Tilson A	Walsh PAM	Wegerle RC	Wilkins RC	Wilson CA
1	Aug 17	Arsenal	1-1	Bailey	38099		7	2	8	3	9	12				6			5				11	1				10	4	
2	21	NORWICH CITY	0-2		10626		7	2	8	3	9	4				6			5				11	1	12			10		
3	24	COVENTRY CITY	1-1	Wegerle	9393		7	2	8	12	9	4				6			5				11	1	14			10		3
4	27	Liverpool	0-1		32700		7	2	8		9	4				6			5				11	1	12			10		3
5	31	Sheffield Wednesday	1-4	Bailey	25022	11	7	2	8		9	4				6			5					1	12			10		3
6	Sep 4	WEST HAM UNITED	0-0		16816		7	2	8	3	12	4				6			5					1	9			10		11
7	7	SOUTHAMPTON	2-2	Barker, Thompson	9237		7	2	8	3						12	6		5				4	1	9			10		11
8	14	Tottenham Hotspur	0-2		30059			2	8	3		12			14	5	6					1	11		9	4				7
9	17	Luton Town	1-0	Barker	9185		14	2	8	3		12				5	6						11	1	10	4	9			7
10	21	CHELSEA	2-2	Wilson, Peacock	19579			2	8			4				5	6		3				11	1	9			10		7
11	28	Crystal Palace	2-2	Barker, Wegerle	15372	12		2	8			4				5	6		3				11	1	9			10		7
12	Oct 5	NOTTM. FOREST	0-2		13058	12		2	8		9	7					6		5				11	1	4			10		3
13	19	Wimbledon	1-0	Bailey	4133		10	2	8			7					6		5				11	1	9	4				3
14	26	EVERTON	3-1	Bailey, Barker 2	10002		10	2	8			7					6		5				11	1	9	4				3
15	Nov 2	ASTON VILLA	0-1		10642		10	2	8			7					6		5	12			11	1	9	4				3
16	16	Leeds United	0-2		27087		10	2	8		12	7					6		5	10			11	1	9	4			14	3
17	23	OLDHAM ATHLETIC	1-3	Ferdinand	8947		7	2	8		9	12					6		5	10			11	1					4	3
18	30	Notts County	1-0	Ferdinand	7891			2	8		9					7	6		5	10			11	1					4	3
19	Dec 7	SHEFFIELD UNITED	1-0	Wegerle	10106			2	8			12				7	6		5	9			11	1				10	4	3
20	14	Manchester City	2-2	Wegerle, Bailey	21437		14	2	8			12				7	6		5	9			11	1				10	4	3
21	21	Norwich City	1-0	Bailey	11436		9	2	8			7					6		5				11	1				10	4	3
22	26	LIVERPOOL	0-0		21693		9	2	8			7					6		5				11	1				10	4	3
23	28	SHEFFIELD WEDNESDAY	1-1	Wilkins	12990		9	2	8			7					6		5				11	1	12			10	4	3
24	Jan 1	Manchester United	4-1	Sinton, Bailey 3	38554		9	2	8			7					6		5				11	1				10	4	3
25	11	Coventry City	2-2	Penrice 2	12003		9	2	8			7	11				6		5	12				1				10	4	3
26	18	ARSENAL	0-0		20497		9	2	8			7					6		5	10			11	1				12	4	3
27	Feb 1	WIMBLEDON	1-1	Penrice	9194		9		8			7					6		5	10	2		11	1				12	4	3
28	8	Everton	0-0		18049		9	2	8			7					6		5	10			11	1			14	12	4	3
29	15	Oldham Athletic	1-2	Wegerle	13092			2	8			7					6	12	5	9			11	1				10	4	3
30	22	NOTTS COUNTY	1-1	Ferdinand	8495			2			9	8	7				6		5	10			11	1					4	3
31	29	Sheffield United	0-0		17958			2			9	8					6		5	10			11	1	4				7	3
32	Mar 7	MANCHESTER CITY	4-0	Ferdinand 2, Wilson (p), Barker	10791			2	12		9	8	4				6		5	10			11	1					7	3
33	11	LEEDS UNITED	4-1	Ferdinand, Allen, Sinton, Wilson (p)	14641	10		2	12		9	8	4				6		5				11	1					7	3
34	14	Aston Villa	1-0	Ferdinand	19630	10		2			9	8	4				6		5				11	1					7	3
35	21	West Ham United	2-2	Allen 2	21401	10		2	12		9	8	4				6		5				11	1					7	3
36	28	MANCHESTER UNITED	0-0		22603	10		2			9	8	4				6		5				11	1					7	3
37	Apr 4	Southampton	1-2	Ferdinand	13849	10		2	7		9	8	4			6	5			12			11	1						3
38	11	TOTTENHAM HOTSPUR	1-2	Sinton	20678	10		2			9	8	4				6		5	12			11	1					7	3
39	18	Chelsea	1-2	Allen	16951	12		2			9	8	4				6		5	10			11	1					7	3
40	20	LUTON TOWN	2-1	Ferdinand 2	10749	10		2			9	8	4				6		5	12			11	1					7	3
41	25	Nottingham Forest	1-1	Allen	22228	10		2			9	8	4			6			5	12			11	1					7	3
42	May 2	CRYSTAL PALACE	1-0	Humphrey (og)	14903	10	12	2	11		9	8	4				6		5					1					7	3
		Apps				11	24	41	34	7	23	40	13	1	3	28	19	1	39	19	1	1	38	41	15	10	2	21	27	40
		Goals				5	9		6		10								1	3			3		1			5	1	3

One own goal

F.A. Cup

R	Date	Opponent	Score	Att	Bailey	Bardsley	Barker	Holloway	Maddix	Peacock	Penrice	Sinton	Stejskal	Wegerle	Wilkins	Wilson
R3	Jan 4	Southampton	0-2	13710	9	2	8	7	6	5	12	11	1	10	4	3

F.L. Cup (Rumbelows Cup)

R	Date	Opponent	Score	Scorers	Att	Bailey	Bardsley	Barker	Brevett	Ferdinand	Holloway	Impey	McDonald	Maddix	Peacock	Penrice	Roberts	Sinton	Stejskal	Thompson	Tilson	Wegerle	Wilkins	Wilson
R2/1	Sep 24	Hull City	3-0	Thompson, Barker 2	4979		2	8		12	4		5	6	3			11	1	9		10		7
R2/2	Oct 9	HULL CITY	5-1	Bardsley, Thompson 2, Bailey 2	5251	10	2	8			7	14		6	5	12		11	1	9	4			3
R3	29	Manchester City	0-0		15512	10	2	8			7			6	5			11	1	9	4			3
rep	Nov 20	MANCHESTER CITY	1-3	Penrice	11033	7	2	8	3	9				6	5	10			1				4	11

Played in R2/2: R Herrera (at 14)

Full Members Cup (Zenith Data Systems Cup)

R	Date	Opponent	Score	Scorers	Att	Bailey	Bardsley	Barker	Ferdinand	Holloway	Impey	Maddix	Peacock	Penrice	Sinton	Stejskal	Thompson	Tilson	Wilkins	Wilson
R2	Oct 23	Norwich City	2-1	Sinton, Impey	4436	10	2	8		7	12	6	5		11	1	9	4		3
R3	Nov 26	CRYSTAL PALACE	2-3	Bardsley, Wilkins	4492		2	8	9	12	14	6	5	10	11	1			4	3

Played in R3: JA Channing (at 7 - substituted)

#	Date	Opponent	Res	Scorers	Att	Allen BJ	Bailey DL	Bardsley DJ	Barker S	Brevett RE	Channing JA	Doyle M	Ferdinand L	Holloway IS	Impey AR	Maddix DS	McDonald A	Meaker MJ	Peacock D	Penrice GK	Ready K	Roberts AM	Sinton A	Stejskal J	Thompson GL	White DW	Wilkins RC	Wilson CA
1	Aug 17	Manchester City	1-1	Sinton	24471		10	2					9	8	7		5		6				11	1	12		4	3
2	19	SOUTHAMPTON	3-1	Ferdinand 2, Bardsley	10925		10	2					9	8	7		5		6				11	1	12		4	3
3	22	SHEFFIELD UNITED	3-2	Barker, Ferdinand, Bailey	10932		10	2	7				9	8			5		6				11	1	12		4	3
4	26	Coventry City	1-0	Impey	13437		10	2	8				9		7		5		6	12			11	1			4	3
5	29	Chelsea	0-1		22910		10	2	8				9		7		5		6	12			11	1			4	3
6	Sep 2	ARSENAL	0-0		20861		10	2	8				9		7		5		6	12			11	1			4	3
7	5	IPSWICH TOWN	0-0		12806		10	2	8				9		7		5		6	12			11	1			4	3
8	12	Southampton	2-1	Sinton, Channing	14125				8		2		9		7	12	5		6	10			11	1			4	3
9	19	MIDDLESBROUGH	3-3	Ferdinand, Penrice, Sinton (p)	12272				8		2		9	14	7	12	5		6	10			11	1			4	3
10	26	Manchester United	0-0		33287			2	12	3			9	8	7	6	5			10			11	1			4	
11	Oct 3	TOTTENHAM HOTSPUR	4-1	Holloway, Wilkins, Penrice 2	19845		9	2						8	7		5		6	10			11	1			4	3
12	17	Norwich City	1-2	Allen	16009	12	9	2						8	7		5		6	10			11	1			4	3
13	24	LEEDS UNITED	2-1	Bardsley, Ferdinand	18326	10		2	12				9	8	7		5		6				11	1			4	3
14	Nov 1	Aston Villa	0-2		20140	10	12	2	11				9	8	7		5		6			1					4	3
15	7	Wimbledon	2-0	Wilkins, Allen	6771	10		2					9	8	7		5		6			1	11				4	3
16	23	LIVERPOOL	0-1		21056	10		2					9	8	7		5		6			1	11				4	3
17	28	Blackburn Rovers	0-1		15850	10		2					9	8	7		5		6	12		1	11				4	3
18	Dec 5	OLDHAM ATHLETIC	3-2	Ferdinand 2, Penrice	11804	12		2					9	8	7		5		6	10		1	11				4	3
19	12	CRYSTAL PALACE	1-3	Penrice	14571			2					9	8	7		5		6	10		1	11				4	3
20	19	Sheffield Wednesday	0-1		23164			2	12				9	8	7		5		6			1	11				4	3
21	28	EVERTON	4-2	Sinton 3, Penrice	14802			2	7				9	8			5		6	10		1	11				4	3
22	Jan 9	Middlesbrough	1-0	Ferdinand	15616	12		2	8	3			9		7		5		6			1	11				4	
23	18	MANCHESTER UNITED	1-3	Allen	20142	10	9	2	4					8	7		5		6			1	11		12			3
24	27	CHELSEA	1-1	Allen	15806	10		2	4	3			9	8		11	5		6			1				12		7
25	30	Sheffield United	2-1	Allen, Holloway	16386	10		2	4	3			9	8	7		5		6	12		1	11					
26	Feb 6	MANCHESTER CITY	1-1	Wilson	13003	10		2	4	3			9	8			5		6			1	11					7
27	9	Ipswich Town	1-1	White	17426	10		2		3		4	9	8			5		6	12		1	11			14		7
28	20	COVENTRY CITY	2-0	Peacock, Pearce (og)	12453	10		2	4	3			9	8			5		6			1	11					7
29	24	Nottingham Forest	0-1		22436	10	12	2	4	3			9	8			5		6			1	11					7
30	27	Tottenham Hotspur	2-3	Peacock, White	32341			2	4	3			9	8	12				6			1	11			10		7
31	Mar 6	NORWICH CITY	3-1	Ferdinand 2, Wilson	13892	12		2		3		4	9		7		5	6			11	1				10		8
32	10	Liverpool	0-1		30370			2		3		4	9		7		5	6			11	1				10	12	8
33	13	WIMBLEDON	1-2	Ferdinand	12270	10		2		3		4	9		7		5	6			11	1	13			12		8
34	20	Oldham Athletic	2-2	Allen, Sinton	10946	10		2				4	9	8	7				6	14		1	11					3
35	24	BLACKBURN ROVERS	0-3		10677	10	9	2		3				8	7		5		6			1	11				4	
36	Apr 3	Crystal Palace	1-1	Allen	14705	10	9	2		3				8	7				6			1	11			12		
37	10	NOTTM. FOREST	4-3	Ferdinand 3, Wilson (p)	16782	10		2					9	8	7		5		6			1	11				4	3
38	12	Everton	5-3	Impey, Ferdinand 3, Bardsley	19026	10		2	12				9	8	7		5		6			1	11				4	3
39	May 1	Leeds United	1-1	Ferdinand	31408	10		2	8				9		7		5		6			1	11				4	3
40	4	Arsenal	0-0		18817	10		2	8	12			9		7		5		6			1	11				4	3
41	9	ASTON VILLA	2-1	Ferdinand, Allen	18904	10		2	8				9		7		5		6			1	11				4	3
42	11	SHEFFIELD WEDNESDAY	3-1	Allen 2, Ferdinand	12177	10		2	8				9		7		5		6			1	11				4	3
		Apps				25	15	40	25	15	2	5	37	24	40	14	39	3	38	15	3	28	38	15	4	7	27	41
		Goals				10	1	3	1		1		20	2	2				2	6			7			2	2	3

One own goal

F.A. Cup

#	Date	Opponent	Res	Scorers	Att	Allen BJ	Bailey DL	Bardsley DJ	Barker S	Brevett RE	Channing JA	Doyle M	Ferdinand L	Holloway IS	Impey AR	Maddix DS	McDonald A	Meaker MJ	Peacock D	Penrice GK	Ready K	Roberts AM	Sinton A	Stejskal J	Thompson GL	White DW	Wilkins RC	Wilson CA
R3	Jan 4	SWINDON TOWN	3-0	Ferdinand 2, Penrice	12106			2	7				9	8	12		5		6	10		1	11				4	3
R4	23	MANCHESTER CITY	1-2	Holloway	18652	10	12	2	4	3			9	8			5		6			1	11					7

F.L. Cup (Coca Cola Cup)

#	Date	Opponent	Res	Scorers	Att	Allen BJ	Bailey DL	Bardsley DJ	Barker S	Brevett RE	Channing JA	Doyle M	Ferdinand L	Holloway IS	Impey AR	Maddix DS	McDonald A	Meaker MJ	Peacock D	Penrice GK	Ready K	Roberts AM	Sinton A	Stejskal J	Thompson GL	White DW	Wilkins RC	Wilson CA
R2/1	Sep 23	GRIMSBY TOWN	2-1	Ferdinand 2	7275		10			3	2		9	8	7	6			5	12		1	11				4	
R2/2	Oct 6	Grimsby Town	1-2	Bailey	8443		9	2						8	7		5		6	10			11	1	12		4	3
R3	27	Bury	2-0	Allen, Peacock	4680	10		2	7				9	8			5		6	12			11	1			4	3
R4	Dec 2	Sheffield Wednesday	0-4		17161	12		2					9	8	7		5		6				11	1			4	3

R2/2 won on penalties 6-5 a.e.t.

#	Mon	Date	Opponent	Score	Scorers	Att	Allen BJ	Bardsley DJ	Barker S	Brevett RE	Doyle M	Ferdinand L	Holloway IS	Impey AR	McCarthy AJ	McDonald A	Meaker MJ	Peacock D	Penrice GK	Ready K	Roberts AM	Sinclair TL	Stejskal J	White DW	Wilkins RC	Wilson CA	Witter AJ	Yates S
1	Aug	14	Aston Villa	1-4	Ferdinand	32944	10		11			9	8	7				5		2	1			12	4	3		6
2		18	LIVERPOOL	1-3	Wilkins	19625			8			9		7				5	10	2	1	11		12	4	3		6
3		21	SOUTHAMPTON	2-1	Penrice, Wilson(p)	10613			8	12		9		7				5	10	2	1	11		14	4	3		8
4		25	Chelsea	0-2		20191			8	3		9		7				5	10	2	1			12	4	11		8
5		28	West Ham United	4-0	Ferdinand 2, Peacock, Penrice	18084	14	2	8			9		7		6		5	10	12	1	11			4	3		
6	Sep	1	SHEFFIELD UNITED	2-1	Sinclair, Wilson(p)	11113		2	8			9		7		6		5	10	12	1	11			4	3		
7		11	Manchester City	0-3		24445	12	2			8	9		7		6		5	10		1	11			4	3		
8		18	NORWICH CITY	2-2	Sinclair, Ferdinand	13359		2	8			9		7		6		5	10			11	1		4	3		
9		27	Wimbledon	1-1	McDonald	9478		2	8			9		7		6		5	10	14		11	1	12	4	3		
10	Oct	2	IPSWICH TOWN	3-0	White 2, Barker	12292	10	2	8	12				7		6		5				11	1	9	4	3		
11		16	Newcastle United	2-1	Ferdinand, Allen	33801	10	2	8					7		6		5				11	1	9	4	3		12
12		23	COVENTRY CITY	5-1	Ferdinand, Allen 2, Impey, Barker	12979	10	2	8			9	12	7		6		5				11	1		4	3		
13		30	Manchester United	1-2	Allen	44663	10	2	8			9	12	7		6		5				11	1		4	3		
14	Nov	6	BLACKBURN ROVERS	1-0	OG	17636	10	2	8			9	12	7		6		5				11	1		4	3		
15		20	Everton	3-0	Allen(3)	17326	10	2	8			9		7				5				11	1		4	3		6
16		24	Swindon Town	0-1		14674	10	2	8			9	4	7				5				11	1			3		6
17		27	TOTTENHAM HOTSPUR	1-1	Ferdinand	17694	10	2	8			9	4	7		6	11	5					1			3		
18	Dec	4	ASTON VILLA	2-2	Penrice, OG	14915	10	2	8				12	7		6	11		9	5			1		4	3		
19		8	Liverpool	2-3	Barker, Ferdinand	24561	10	2	8			9		7			11	5	12	6			1		4	3		
20		11	Southampton	1-0		11946	10	2	8			9	12	7				5		6			1		4	3		14
21		27	OLDHAM ATHLETIC	2-0	White, Penrice	13218		2		12			8	7				5	9			11	1	10	4	3		6
22		29	Leeds United	1-1	Meaker	39124		2				9	8	12			7	5	10			11	1		4	3		6
23	Jan	1	SHEFFIELD WEDNESDAY	1-2	Ferdinand	16858		2	8			9					7	5	10			11	1		4	3		6
24		3	Arsenal	0-0		34935		2	8			9					7	5	10			11	1		4	3		6
25		16	NEWCASTLE UNITED	1-2	Penrice	15774		2	8			9		7			12	5	10		1	11			4	3		6
26		22	Coventry City	1-0	White	12065		2	8					7			12	5	10			11	1	9	4	3		6
27	Feb	5	MANCHESTER UNITED	2-3	Wilson(p), Ferdinand	21267		2	8			9		7			12	5	10			11	1		4	3		6
28	Mar	5	MANCHESTER CITY	1-1	Penrice	13474		2	8			9		7				5	10			11	1		4	3		6
29		12	Norwich City	4-3	Barker, Peacock, White, Penrice	16499		2	8					12			7	5	10			11	1	9	4	3		6
30		16	Sheffield United	1-1	Barker	14183		2	8				12				7	5	10			11	1	9	4	3		6
31		19	WIMBLEDON	1-0	Peacock	11368						9	8				7	5		2		11	1	10	4	3		6
32		26	Ipswich Town	3-1	Impey 2, Ferdinand	14653	12		11			9	8	7	5				14	2	1			10	4	3		6
33	Apr	2	Oldham Athletic	1-4	Ferdinand	10440			11			9	8	7	5				12	2	1			10	4	3		6
34		4	LEEDS UNITED	0-4		15365	12	2	11			9	8	7					10	5	1				4	3		6
35		9	Sheffield Wednesday	1-3	White	22437	10	2	4			9	8	7			11	5					1	12		3		6
36		13	CHELSEA	1-1	Ferdinand	15735		2	11			9	8	7								5	1	12	10	3		6
37		16	EVERTON	2-1	White, Ferdinand	13330		2	12			9	8	7								5	1	11	10	3		6
38		24	Blackburn Rovers	1-1	Ready	19193		2	12			9	8	7								5	1	11	10	3		6
39		27	ARSENAL	1-1	Penrice	11442	12	2	11				8	7					9	5	1			10		3		6
40		30	SWINDON TOWN	1-3	Ferdinand	9875	12		11			9	8	7	2				10	5	1				4	3		6
41	May	3	WEST HAM UNITED	0-0		10850	14		11	12		9	8		2				10	5	1	7			4	3		6
42		7	Tottenham Hotspur	2-1	Sinclair 2	26105	10		11	2		9	8	14						5	1	7			4	3		6
Apps							21	32	37	7	1	35	25	33	4	12	14	30	26	22	16	32	26	19	39	42	1	29
Goals							7		5			16		3		1	1	3	8	1		4		7	1	3		

Two own goals

F.A. Cup

R	Mon	Date	Opponent	Score	Scorers	Att	Allen BJ	Bardsley DJ	Barker S	Brevett RE	Doyle M	Ferdinand L	Holloway IS	Impey AR	McCarthy AJ	McDonald A	Meaker MJ	Peacock D	Penrice GK	Ready K	Roberts AM	Sinclair TL	Stejskal J	White DW	Wilkins RC	Wilson CA	Witter AJ	Yates S
R3	Jan	8	Stockport County	1-2	Barker	7569		2	8			9		12			7	5	10			11	1	13	4	3		6

F.L. Cup (Coca Cola Cup)

R	Mon	Date	Opponent	Score	Scorers	Att	Allen BJ	Bardsley DJ	Barker S	Brevett RE	Doyle M	Ferdinand L	Holloway IS	Impey AR	McCarthy AJ	McDonald A	Meaker MJ	Peacock D	Penrice GK	Ready K	Roberts AM	Sinclair TL	Stejskal J	White DW	Wilkins RC	Wilson CA	Witter AJ	Yates S
R2/1	Sep	21	Barnet	2-1	Ferdinand, Barker	3569		2	8			9		7		6		5	10			11	1		4	3		
R2/2	Oct	6	BARNET	4-0	Allen 3, Impey	6314	10	2	8	12				7		6		5				11	1	9	4	3		
R3		27	MILLWALL	3-0	Sinclair, Barker, Ferdinand	14190	10	2	8			9	12	7		6		5				11	1		4	3		
R4	Dec	1	SHEFFIELD WEDNESDAY	1-2	Meaker	13253	10	2	8			9		7		6	11	5					1	12	4	3		

1994/95 — 8th in the Premier League

No	Date	Opponent	Score	Scorers	Att	Allen BJ	Bardsley DJ	Barker S	Brevett RE	Dichio DS	Dykstra S	Ferdinand L	Gallen KA	Hodge SB	Holloway IS	Impey AR	Maddix DS	McCarthy AJ	McDonald A	Meaker MJ	Penrice GK	Ready K	Roberts AM	Sinclair TL	White DW	Wilkins RC	Wilson CA	Yates S
1	Aug 20	Manchester United	0-2		43214		2	4				9	10		8	7	14		5		12		1	11			3	6
2	24	SHEFFIELD WEDNESDAY	3-2	Ferdinand, Sinclair, Gallen	12788		2	4				9	10		8	7	12		5				1	11			3	6
3	27	IPSWICH TOWN	1-2	Ferdinand	12456		2	4				9	10		8	7			5		12		1	11			3	6
4	31	Leicester City	1-1	Willis (og)	18695		2	4				9	12		8	7			5		10		1	11			3	6
5	Sep 10	COVENTRY CITY	2-2	Penrice 2	11398		2	4	3			9	12		8	7			5		10		1	11				6
6	17	Everton	2-2	Ferdinand 2	27291		2	4	3			9			8	7			5		10	12	1				11	6
7	24	WIMBLEDON	0-1		11061		2	4	3			9	12			7			5	11	10		1				8	6
8	Oct 2	Nottingham Forest	2-3	Ferdinand, Allen	21449	12	2	4	3			9			8	7	10		5				1	11				6
9	8	Tottenham Hotspur	1-1	Impey	25799	10	2	4				9			8	7	12		5				1	11			3	6
10	15	MANCHESTER CITY	1-2	Wilson	13631	10	2	4				9	12		8	7			5				1	11			3	6
11	22	Norwich City	2-4	Barker, Gallen	19431	12	2	4			1		10		8				5		7			11	9		3	6
12	29	ASTON VILLA	2-0	Dichio, Penrice	16073		2	4		9	1		10	7	8		12		5		14			11			3	6
13	31	LIVERPOOL	2-1	Sinclair, Ferdinand	18295		2	4			1	9	10	8		7			5					11			3	6
14	Nov 5	Newcastle United	1-2	Dichio	34278		2	4		12	1	9	10	8		7			5					11			3	6
15	19	LEEDS UNITED	3-2	Ferdinand 2, Gallen	17416			4			1	9	10	8	12	7			5			2		11			3	6
16	26	Blackburn Rovers	0-4		21302			4			1	9	10	8		7			5			2		11			3	6
17	Dec 4	WEST HAM UNITED	2-1	Ferdinand, Sinclair	12780			4			1	9	10	8	12	7	6		5					11			3	2
18	10	MANCHESTER UNITED	2-3	Ferdinand 2	18948		2	4			1	9	10	8		7	6		5					11			3	
19	17	Sheffield Wednesday	2-0	Ferdinand, Maddix	23288		2	4			1	9	10	8	12	7	6		5					11			3	
20	26	Crystal Palace	0-0		16699			4			1	9	10	8		7	6		5		12			11			3	2
21	28	SOUTHAMPTON	2-2	Barker, Gallen	16078			4	12		1	9	10	8		7	6		5		11						3	2
22	31	Arsenal	3-1	Gallen, Allen, Impey	32393	12	2	4				9	10	8		7	6		5		11		1				3	
23	Jan 14	Aston Villa	1-2	Yates	26578		2					9	10	8	4	7	6	12			11		1				3	5
24	24	Leeds United	0-4		28750		2		3			9	10	8	4	7	6	14			11		1	12				5
25	Feb 4	NEWCASTLE UNITED	3-0	Ferdinand 2, Barker	16576		2	4	3	12		9	10	8		7	6		5				1	11				
26	11	Liverpool	1-1	Gallen	35996		2	4	11			9	10	8		7	6		5				1				3	
27	26	NOTTM. FOREST	1-1	Barker	13383			4				9	10	8		7	6		5	11	12	14	1				3	2
28	Mar 4	Wimbledon	3-1	Ferdinand 2, Holloway	9176			4	11			9	10	8		7	6		5		12	2	1				3	
29	8	LEICESTER CITY	2-0	McDonald, Wilson	10189			4		9			10	8		7	6		5		12	2	1	11			3	
30	15	NORWICH CITY	2-0	Ferdinand, Gallen	10519		2	4				9	10	8		7	6		5				1	11			3	
31	18	EVERTON	2-3	Ferdinand, Gallen	14488		2	4				9	10	8		7	6		5		12		1	11			3	
32	22	CHELSEA	1-0	Gallen	15103		2	4		9			10	8		7			5			6	1	11			3	
33	Apr 1	Coventry City	1-0	Sinclair	15751			4	3	9			10	8		7			5			6	1	11			2	
34	4	BLACKBURN ROVERS	0-1		16508			4	3	9	12		10	8		7			5			6	1	11			2	
35	8	ARSENAL	3-1	Impey, Gallen, Ready	16341			4	3			9	10	8		7			5		12	6	1	11			2	
36	11	Ipswich Town	1-0	Ferdinand	11736			4	3			9	10	8		7	14		5		12	6	1	11			2	
37	15	Southampton	1-2	Ferdinand	15210		2		3			9	10	8		7			5		12	6	1	11		14	4	
38	17	CRYSTAL PALACE	0-1		14227		2		3	14		9	12		8	7	6		5		10	6	1	11			4	
39	29	Chelsea	0-1		21704		2		3			9	12	11		7	6		5		10		1				8	4
40	May 3	West Ham United	0-0		22923		2	4	12			9	14		8	7	6		5		10		1	11			3	
41	6	TOTTENHAM HOTSPUR	2-1	Ferdinand 2	18637		2	4	3			9			8	7	6		5		10		1	11			3	
42	14	Manchester City	3-2	Ferdinand 2, Dichio	27850		2	4	3	14		9	10			7	6		5		8		1	11				12
	Apps					5	30	37	19	9	11	37	37	15	31	40	27	2	39	8	19	13	31	33	1	2	36	23
	Goals					2		4		3		24	10		1	3	1		1		3	1		4			2	1

One own goal

F.A. Cup

Rd	Date	Opponent	Score	Scorers	Att	Allen BJ	Bardsley DJ	Barker S	Brevett RE	Dichio DS	Dykstra S	Ferdinand L	Gallen KA	Hodge SB	Holloway IS	Impey AR	Maddix DS	McCarthy AJ	McDonald A	Meaker MJ	Penrice GK	Ready K	Roberts AM	Sinclair TL	White DW	Wilkins RC	Wilson CA	Yates S
R3	Jan 7	AYLESBURY UNITED	4-0	Maddix, Ferdinand, Gallen, Meaker	15417	12	2	4				9	10	8	14	7	6		5	11			1				3	
R4	28	WEST HAM UNITED	1-0	Impey	17694		2	4		9			10	8		7	6		5				1	11			3	
R5	Feb 18	MILLWALL	1-0	Wilson (p)	16457		2	4				9	10	8		7	6		5	11			1				3	
R6	Mar 12	Manchester United	0-2		42830		2	4	11			9	10	8		7	6		5		12		1				3	

R1 played at home by arrangement.

F.L. Cup (Coca Cola Cup)

Rd	Date	Opponent	Score	Scorers	Att	Allen BJ	Bardsley DJ	Barker S	Brevett RE	Dichio DS	Dykstra S	Ferdinand L	Gallen KA	Hodge SB	Holloway IS	Impey AR	Maddix DS	McCarthy AJ	McDonald A	Meaker MJ	Penrice GK	Ready K	Roberts AM	Sinclair TL	White DW	Wilkins RC	Wilson CA	Yates S
R2/1	Sep 20	Carlisle United	1-0	Ferdinand	9570		2	4				9			8	7			5		10	12	1	11			3	6
R2/2	Oct 5	CARLISLE UNITED	2-0	Allen, Wilson (p)	6561	10	2	4				9	12		8	7			5				1	11			3	6
R3	25	MANCHESTER CITY	3-4	Gallen, Sinclair, Penrice	11701		2	4		9	1		10		8				5	7	12			11			3	6

1995/96

19th in the Premier League: Relegated

#	Mon	Date	Opponent	Res	Scorers	Att	Allen BJ	Bardsley DJ	Barker S	Brazier MR	Brevett RE	Challis TM	Charles L	Dichio DS	Gallen KA	Goodridge GRS	Hateley MW	Holloway IS	Impey AR	Maddix DS	McDonald A	Murray P	Osborn SE	Penrice GK	Plummer C	Quashie N	Ready K	Roberts AM	Sinclair TL	Sommer JP	Wilkins RC	Yates S	Zelic N
1	Aug	19	Blackburn Rovers	0-1		25932		2	7		5			11	10			8	6	4	3		12					1	9				
2		23	WIMBLEDON	0-3		11837		2	7		5			11	10			8	6	4	3							1	9			13	12
3		26	MANCHESTER CITY	1-0	Barker	14212		2	7		5			11	10			8	6	4	3			12				1	9				
4		30	Liverpool	0-1		37548		2	7		5			11	10				6	4	3			12				1	9			8	
5	Sep	9	SHEFFIELD WEDNESDAY	0-3		12659		2	7		5			11	10			8	6	4	3			12				1	9				
6		16	Leeds United	3-1	Dichio(2), Sinclair	31505		2	7		5			10				8		6	3		11				4		9	1			
7		25	TOTTENHAM HOTSPUR	2-3	Dichio, Impey	15859	12		7		5			10				8	2	6	3		11				4		9	1			
8		30	Bolton Wanderers	1-0	Dichio	17362			7		5			10				8	2	6	3		11				4		9	1	12		
9	Oct	14	NEWCASTLE UNITED	2-3	Dichio(2)	18254			7		5			10		12		8	2	6			11				4		9	1			3
10		21	Middlesbrough	0-1		29283		2	7		5			10	12			8	11	6							4		9	1			3
11		28	NOTTM. FOREST	1-1	Sinclair	17549		2	7	12	5			10		13		11		6			14				4		9	1	8	3	
12	Nov	4	Southampton	0-2		15137		2	7		5			10	12					6							4		9	1	8	3	
13		19	COVENTRY CITY	1-1	Barker	11189			7		5		12	10	11				2	6							4		9	1	13	3	8
14		22	Everton	0-2		30009			7	9	5			12	11			6	4		13						2		10	1	8	3	
15		25	West Ham United	0-1		21504			7	6				12	10	9		8	2	13	3						4			1	11	5	
16	Dec	2	MIDDLESBROUGH	1-1	McDonald	17546			7		2			12	10		11	6	8		3						4		9	1		5	
17		9	Tottenham Hotspur	0-1		28851		2	7		4		13	10			11	6	8		3		12						9	1		5	
18		16	BOLTON WANDERERS	2-1	Osborn, Impey	11456		2	7		4			12			11	6	8		3		10				13		9	1		5	
19		23	ASTON VILLA	1-0	Gallen	14778	13	2	7	12	5				10		11		8		3						14		9	1	6	4	
20		26	Arsenal	0-3		38259		2	7		5			12	10		11	13	8		3								9	1	6	4	
21		30	Manchester United	1-2	Dichio	41890	10	2	6		5			12				7	8	3						11	13		9	1		4	
22	Jan	2	CHELSEA	1-2	Allen	14904	10	12	6		3			13				7	8	2						11	4		9	1		5	
23		13	BLACKBURN ROVERS	0-1		13957	10	2	6		4				13	12		8	14		3					11			9	1	7	5	
24		20	Wimbledon	1-2	Hateley	9123	10	2	7	6	4			12	13	11					3					8			9	1		5	
25	Feb	3	Manchester City	0-2		27509	10		7	14	4			13	12		11	6	2		3					8			9	1		5	
26		11	LIVERPOOL	1-2	Dichio	18405		2	7		3			11	10			6		4						8			9	1		5	
27		17	Sheffield Wednesday	3-1	Barker(2), Goodridge	22442	13	2	7		3				10	12		6	11	4						8			9	1		5	
28	Mar	2	ARSENAL	1-1	Gallen	17970		2	7		3			12	10			6	11							8			9	1		5	
29		6	LEEDS UNITED	1-2	Gallen	13991		2	7	12	3			11	10	13		6								8			9	1		5	
30		9	Aston Villa	2-4	Gallen, Dichio	28221		2	7		3			11	10	12		6								8			9	1		5	
31		16	MANCHESTER UNITED	1-1	OG(Irwin)	18817		2	7		3			11	10		13	6	12	4						8	14		9	1		5	
32		23	Chelsea	1-1	Barker	25590		2	7	14	3			11	10		13	8	6	4							12		9	1		5	
33		30	SOUTHAMPTON	3-0	Brevett, Dichio, Gallen	17615		2	7		3			11	10			6	8	4									9	1		5	
34	Apr	6	Newcastle United	1-2	Holloway	36583		2			3			11	10		12	6	8	4									9	1	7	5	
35		8	EVERTON	3-1	Impey, Hateley, Gallen	18349		2			3				10		11	6	8	4									9	1	7	5	
36		13	Coventry City	0-1		22906		2	7		3			11	10		11	6	8	4									9	1	12	5	
37		27	WEST HAM UNITED	3-0	Ready, Gallen(2)	18828			6		3		12	11	10		7			4							2		9	1	8	5	
38	May	5	Nottingham Forest	0-3		22910		2	6		3		13	11	10					4		7			12	14			9	1	8	5	
			Apps				8	29	33	11	27	11	4	30	30	7	14	27	29	22	26	1	8	3	1	11	22	5	37	33	15	30	4
			Goals				1		5		1			10	8	1	2	1	3		1		1			1	1		2				

One own goal

F.A. Cup

Rd	Mon	Date	Opponent	Res	Scorers	Att	Allen BJ	Bardsley DJ	Barker S	Brevett RE	Dichio DS	Gallen KA	Hateley MW	Holloway IS	Impey AR	Maddix DS	McDonald A	Quashie N	Ready K	Roberts AM	Sinclair TL	Sommer JP	Wilkins RC	Yates S
R3	Jan	6	Tranmere Rovers	2-0	Sinclair, Quashie	10230	10		6	2	14	13		8	12		3	11	4		9	1	7	5
R4		29	CHELSEA	1-2	Quashie	18542	10	2		4			11	6	8	12	3	7			9	1		5

F.L. Cup (Coca Cola Cup)

Rd	Mon	Date	Opponent	Res	Scorers	Att	Bardsley DJ	Barker S	Brazier MR	Brevett RE	Dichio DS	Gallen KA	Goodridge GRS	Hateley MW	Holloway IS	Impey AR	Maddix DS	McDonald A	Osborn SE	Ready K	Roberts AM	Sinclair TL	Wilkins RC	Yates S
R2/1	Sep	19	Oxford United	1-1	Dichio	7477		7		5	10				8	2	6	3	11	4	1	9		
R2/2	Oct	3	OXFORD UNITED	2-1	Ready, Gallen	9207		7	12	5	10	9	13		8	2	6	3	11	4	1		14	
R3		25	YORK CITY	3-1	Sinclair, Impey, Dichio	12972	2	7		5	10				11	6				4	1	9	8	3
R4	Nov	29	Aston Villa	0-1		24951	2	7	6		10			12	8			3		4	1	9	11	5

R2/2 a.e.t.

1976/77 Division 1

1	Liverpool	42	18	3	0	47	11	5	8	8	15	22	57
2	Manchester City	42	15	5	1	38	13	6	9	6	22	21	56
3	Ipswich Town	42	15	4	2	41	11	7	4	10	25	28	52
4	Aston Villa	42	17	3	1	55	17	5	4	12	21	33	51
5	Newcastle United	42	14	6	1	40	15	4	7	10	24	34	49
6	Manchester United	42	12	6	3	41	22	6	5	10	30	40	47
7	West Bromwich Alb.	42	10	6	5	38	22	6	7	8	24	34	45
8	Arsenal	42	11	6	4	37	20	5	5	11	27	39	43
9	Everton	42	9	7	5	35	24	5	7	9	27	40	42
10	Leeds United	42	8	8	5	28	26	7	4	10	20	25	42
11	Leicester City	42	8	9	4	30	28	4	9	8	17	32	42
12	Middlesbrough	42	11	6	4	25	14	3	7	11	15	31	41
13	Birmingham City	42	10	6	5	38	25	3	6	12	25	36	38
14	QUEEN'S PARK RGS.	42	10	7	4	31	21	3	5	13	16	31	38
15	Derby County	42	9	9	3	36	18	0	10	11	14	37	37
16	Norwich City	42	12	4	5	30	23	2	5	14	17	41	37
17	West Ham United	42	9	6	6	28	23	2	8	11	18	42	36
18	Bristol City	42	8	7	6	25	19	3	6	12	13	29	35
19	Coventry City	42	7	9	5	34	26	3	6	12	14	33	35
20	Sunderland	42	9	5	7	29	16	2	7	12	17	38	34
21	Stoke City	42	9	8	4	21	16	1	6	14	7	35	34
22	Tottenham Hotspur	42	9	7	5	26	20	3	2	16	22	52	33

1981/82 Division 2

1	Luton Town	42	16	3	2	48	19	9	10	2	38	27	88
2	Watford	42	13	6	2	46	16	10	5	6	30	26	80
3	Norwich City	42	14	3	4	41	19	8	2	11	23	31	71
4	Sheffield Wed.	42	10	8	3	31	23	10	2	9	24	28	70
5	QUEEN'S PARK RGS.	42	15	4	2	40	9	6	2	13	25	34	69
6	Barnsley	42	13	4	4	33	14	6	6	9	26	27	67
7	Rotherham United	42	13	5	3	42	19	7	2	12	24	35	67
8	Leicester City	42	12	5	4	31	19	6	7	8	25	29	66
9	Newcastle United	42	14	4	3	30	14	4	4	13	22	36	62
10	Blackburn Rovers	42	11	4	6	26	15	5	7	9	21	28	59
11	Oldham Athletic	42	9	9	3	28	23	6	5	10	22	28	59
12	Chelsea	42	10	5	6	37	30	5	7	9	23	30	57
13	Charlton Athletic	42	11	5	5	33	22	2	7	12	17	43	51
14	Cambridge United	42	11	4	6	31	19	2	5	14	17	34	48
15	Crystal Palace	42	9	2	10	25	26	4	7	10	9	19	48
16	Derby County	42	9	8	4	32	23	3	4	14	21	45	48
17	Grimsby Town	42	5	8	8	29	30	6	5	10	24	35	46
18	Shrewsbury Town	42	10	6	5	26	19	1	7	13	11	38	46
19	Bolton Wanderers	42	10	4	7	28	24	3	3	15	11	37	46
20	Cardiff City	42	9	2	10	28	32	3	6	12	17	29	44
21	Wrexham	42	9	4	8	22	22	2	7	12	18	34	44
22	Orient	42	6	8	7	23	24	4	1	16	13	37	39

1982/83 Division 2

1	QUEEN'S PARK RGS.	42	16	3	2	51	16	10	4	7	26	20	85
2	Wolverhampton Wan.	42	14	5	2	42	16	6	10	5	26	28	75
3	Leicester City	42	11	4	6	36	15	9	6	6	36	29	70
4	Fulham	42	13	5	3	36	20	7	4	10	28	27	69
5	Newcastle United	42	13	6	2	43	21	5	7	9	32	32	67
6	Sheffield Wed.	42	9	8	4	33	23	7	7	7	27	24	63
7	Oldham Athletic	42	8	10	3	38	24	6	9	6	26	23	61
8	Leeds United	42	7	11	3	28	22	6	10	5	23	24	60
9	Shrewsbury Town	42	8	9	4	20	15	7	5	9	28	33	59
10	Barnsley	42	9	8	4	37	28	5	7	9	20	27	57
11	Blackburn Rovers	42	11	7	3	38	21	4	5	12	20	37	57
12	Cambridge United	42	11	7	3	26	17	2	5	14	16	43	51
13	Derby County	42	7	10	4	27	24	3	9	9	22	34	49
14	Carlisle United	42	10	6	5	44	28	2	6	13	24	42	48
15	Crystal Palace	42	11	7	3	31	17	1	5	15	12	35	48
16	Middlesbrough	42	8	7	6	27	29	3	8	10	19	38	48
17	Charlton Athletic	42	11	3	7	40	31	2	6	13	23	55	48
18	Chelsea	42	8	8	5	31	22	3	6	12	20	39	47
19	Grimsby Town	42	9	7	5	32	26	3	4	14	13	44	47
20	Rotherham United	42	6	7	8	22	29	4	8	9	23	39	45
21	Burnley	42	10	4	7	38	24	2	4	15	18	42	44
22	Bolton Wanderers	42	10	2	9	30	26	1	9	11	12	35	44

1983/84 Division 1

1	Liverpool	42	14	5	2	50	12	8	9	4	23	20	80
2	Southampton	42	15	4	2	44	17	7	7	7	22	21	77
3	Nottingham Forest	42	14	4	3	47	17	8	4	9	29	28	74
4	Manchester United	42	14	3	4	43	18	6	11	4	28	23	74
5	QUEEN'S PARK RGS.	42	14	4	3	37	12	8	3	10	30	25	73
6	Arsenal	42	10	5	6	41	29	8	4	9	33	31	63
7	Everton	42	9	9	3	21	12	7	5	9	23	30	62
8	Tottenham Hotspur	42	11	4	6	31	24	6	6	9	33	41	61
9	West Ham United	42	10	4	7	39	24	7	5	9	21	31	60
10	Aston Villa	42	14	3	4	34	22	3	6	12	25	39	60
11	Watford	42	9	7	5	36	31	7	2	12	32	46	57
12	Ipswich Town	42	11	4	6	34	23	4	4	13	21	34	53
13	Sunderland	42	8	9	4	26	18	5	4	12	16	35	52
14	Norwich City	42	9	8	4	34	20	3	7	11	14	29	51
15	Leicester City	42	11	5	5	40	30	2	7	12	25	38	51
16	Luton Town	42	7	5	9	30	33	7	4	10	23	33	51
17	West Bromwich Alb.	42	10	4	7	30	25	4	5	12	18	37	51
18	Stoke City	42	11	4	6	30	23	2	7	12	14	40	50
19	Coventry City	42	8	5	8	33	33	5	6	10	24	44	50
20	Birmingham City	42	7	7	7	19	18	5	5	11	20	32	48
21	Notts County	42	6	7	8	31	36	4	4	13	19	36	41
22	Wolverhampton Wan.	42	4	8	9	15	28	2	3	16	12	52	29

1984/85 Division 1

1	Everton	42	16	3	2	58	17	12	3	6	30	26	90
2	Liverpool	42	12	4	5	36	19	10	7	4	32	16	77
3	Tottenham Hotspur	42	11	3	7	46	31	12	5	4	32	20	77
4	Manchester United	42	13	6	2	47	13	9	4	8	30	34	76
5	Southampton	42	13	4	4	29	18	6	7	8	27	29	68
6	Chelsea	42	13	3	5	38	20	5	9	7	25	28	66
7	Arsenal	42	14	5	2	37	14	5	4	12	24	35	66
8	Sheffield Wed.	42	12	7	2	39	21	5	7	9	19	24	65
9	Nottingham Forest	42	13	4	4	35	18	6	3	12	21	30	64
10	Aston Villa	42	10	7	4	34	20	5	4	12	26	40	56
11	Watford	42	10	5	6	48	30	4	8	9	33	41	55
12	West Bromwich Alb.	42	11	4	6	36	23	5	3	13	22	39	55
13	Luton Town	42	12	5	4	40	22	3	4	14	17	39	54
14	Newcastle United	42	11	4	6	33	26	2	9	10	22	44	52
15	Leicester City	42	10	4	7	39	25	5	2	14	26	48	51
16	West Ham United	42	7	8	6	27	23	6	4	11	24	45	51
17	Ipswich Town	42	8	7	6	27	20	5	4	12	19	37	50
18	Coventry City	42	11	3	7	29	22	4	2	15	18	42	50
19	QUEEN'S PARK RGS.	42	11	6	4	41	30	2	5	14	12	42	50
20	Norwich City	42	9	6	6	28	24	4	4	13	18	40	49
21	Sunderland	42	7	6	8	20	26	3	4	14	20	36	40
22	Stoke City	42	3	3	15	18	41	0	5	16	6	50	17

1985/86 Division 1

1	Liverpool	42	16	4	1	58	14	10	6	5	31	23	88
2	Everton	42	16	3	2	54	18	10	5	6	33	23	86
3	West Ham United	42	17	2	2	48	16	9	4	8	26	24	84
4	Manchester United	42	12	5	4	35	12	10	5	6	35	24	76
5	Sheffield Wed.	42	13	6	2	36	23	8	4	9	27	31	73
6	Chelsea	42	12	4	5	32	27	8	7	6	25	29	71
7	Arsenal	42	13	5	3	29	15	7	4	10	20	32	69
8	Nottingham Forest	42	11	5	5	38	25	8	6	7	31	28	68
9	Luton Town	42	12	6	3	37	15	6	6	9	24	29	66
10	Tottenham Hotspur	42	12	2	7	47	25	7	6	8	27	27	65
11	Newcastle United	42	12	5	4	46	31	5	7	9	21	41	63
12	Watford	42	11	6	4	40	22	5	5	11	29	40	59
13	QUEEN'S PARK RGS.	42	12	3	6	33	20	3	4	14	20	44	52
14	Southampton	42	10	6	5	32	18	2	4	15	19	44	46
15	Manchester City	42	7	7	7	25	26	4	5	12	18	31	45
16	Aston Villa	42	7	6	8	27	28	3	8	10	24	39	44
17	Coventry City	42	6	5	10	31	35	5	5	11	17	36	43
18	Oxford United	42	7	7	7	34	27	3	5	13	28	53	42
19	Leicester City	42	7	8	6	35	35	3	4	14	19	41	42
20	Ipswich Town	42	8	5	8	20	24	3	3	15	12	31	41
21	Birmingham City	42	5	2	14	13	25	3	3	15	17	48	29
22	West Bromwich Alb.	42	3	8	10	21	36	1	4	16	14	53	24

1986/87 Division 1

1	Everton	42	16	4	1	49	11	10	4	7	27	20	86
2	Liverpool	42	15	3	3	43	16	8	5	8	29	26	77
3	Tottenham Hotspur	42	14	3	4	40	14	7	5	9	28	29	71
4	Arsenal	42	12	5	4	31	12	8	5	8	27	23	70
5	Norwich City	42	9	10	2	27	20	8	7	6	26	31	68
6	Wimbledon	42	11	5	5	32	22	8	4	9	25	28	66
7	Luton Town	42	14	5	2	29	13	4	7	10	18	32	66
8	Nottingham Forest	42	12	8	1	36	14	6	3	12	28	37	65
9	Watford	42	12	5	4	38	20	6	4	11	29	34	63
10	Coventry City	42	14	4	3	35	17	3	8	10	15	28	63
11	Manchester United	42	13	3	5	38	18	1	11	9	14	27	56
12	Southampton	42	11	5	5	44	24	3	5	13	25	44	52
13	Sheffield Wed.	42	9	7	5	39	24	4	6	11	19	35	52
14	Chelsea	42	8	6	7	30	30	5	7	9	23	34	52
15	West Ham United	42	10	4	7	33	28	4	6	11	19	39	52
16	QUEEN'S PARK RGS.	42	9	7	5	31	27	4	4	13	17	37	50
17	Newcastle United	42	10	4	7	33	29	2	7	12	14	36	47
18	Oxford United	42	8	8	5	30	25	3	5	13	14	44	46
19	Charlton Athletic	42	7	7	7	26	22	4	4	13	19	33	44
20	Leicester City	42	9	7	5	39	24	2	2	17	15	52	42
21	Manchester City	42	8	6	7	28	24	0	9	12	8	33	39
22	Aston Villa	42	7	7	7	25	25	1	5	15	20	54	36

1987/88 Division 1

1	Liverpool	40	15	5	0	49	9	11	7	2	38	15	90
2	Manchester United	40	14	5	1	41	17	9	7	4	30	21	81
3	Nottingham Forest	40	11	7	2	40	17	9	6	5	27	22	73
4	Everton	40	14	4	2	34	11	5	9	6	19	16	70
5	QUEEN'S PARK RGS.	40	12	4	4	30	14	7	6	7	18	24	67
6	Arsenal	40	11	4	5	35	16	7	8	5	23	23	66
7	Wimbledon	40	8	9	3	32	20	6	6	8	26	27	57
8	Newcastle United	40	9	6	5	32	23	5	8	7	23	30	56
9	Luton Town	40	11	6	3	40	21	3	5	12	17	37	53
10	Coventry City	40	6	8	6	23	25	7	6	7	23	28	53
11	Sheffield Wed.	40	10	2	8	27	30	5	6	9	25	36	53
12	Southampton	40	6	8	6	27	26	6	6	8	22	27	50
13	Tottenham Hotspur	40	9	5	6	26	23	3	6	11	12	25	47
14	Norwich City	40	7	5	8	26	26	5	4	11	14	26	45
15	Derby County	40	6	7	7	18	17	4	6	10	17	28	43
16	West Ham United	40	6	9	5	23	21	3	6	11	17	31	42
17	Charlton Athletic	40	7	7	6	23	21	2	8	10	15	31	42
18	Chelsea	40	7	11	2	24	17	2	4	14	26	51	42
19	Portsmouth	40	4	8	8	21	27	3	6	11	15	39	35
20	Watford	40	4	5	11	15	24	3	6	11	12	27	32
21	Oxford United	40	5	7	8	24	34	1	6	13	20	46	31

1988/89 Division 1

1	Arsenal	38	10	6	3	35	19	12	4	3	38	17	76
2	Liverpool	38	11	5	3	33	11	11	5	3	32	17	76
3	Nottingham Forest	38	8	7	4	31	16	9	6	4	33	27	64
4	Norwich City	38	8	7	4	23	20	9	4	6	25	25	62
5	Derby County	38	9	3	7	23	18	8	4	7	17	20	58
6	Tottenham Hotspur	38	8	6	5	31	24	7	6	6	29	22	57
7	Coventry City	38	9	4	6	28	23	5	9	5	19	19	55
8	Everton	38	10	7	2	33	18	4	5	10	17	27	54
9	QUEEN'S PARK RGS.	38	9	5	5	23	16	5	6	8	20	21	53
10	Millwall	38	10	3	6	27	21	4	8	7	20	31	53
11	Manchester United	38	10	5	4	27	13	3	7	9	18	22	51
12	Wimbledon	38	10	3	6	30	19	4	6	9	20	27	51
13	Southampton	38	6	7	6	25	26	4	8	7	27	40	45
14	Charlton Athletic	38	6	7	6	25	24	4	5	10	19	34	42
15	Sheffield Wed.	38	6	6	7	21	25	4	6	9	13	26	42
16	Luton Town	38	8	6	5	32	21	2	5	12	10	31	41
17	Aston Villa	38	7	6	6	25	22	2	7	10	20	34	40
18	Middlesbrough	38	6	7	6	28	30	3	5	11	16	31	39
19	West Ham United	38	3	6	10	19	30	7	2	10	18	32	38
20	Newcastle United	38	3	6	10	19	28	4	4	11	13	35	31

1989/90 Division 1

1	Liverpool	38	13	5	1	38	15	10	5	4	40	22	79
2	Aston Villa	38	13	3	3	36	20	8	4	7	21	18	70
3	Tottenham Hotspur	38	12	1	6	35	24	7	5	7	24	23	63
4	Arsenal	38	14	3	2	38	11	4	5	10	16	27	62
5	Chelsea	38	8	7	4	31	24	8	5	6	27	26	60
6	Everton	38	14	3	2	40	16	3	5	11	17	30	59
7	Southampton	38	10	5	4	40	27	5	5	9	31	36	55
8	Wimbledon	38	5	8	6	22	23	8	8	3	25	17	55
9	Nottingham Forest	38	9	4	6	31	21	6	5	8	24	26	54
10	Norwich City	38	7	10	2	24	14	6	4	9	20	28	53
11	QUEEN'S PARK RGS.	38	9	4	6	27	22	4	7	8	18	22	50
12	Coventry City	38	11	2	6	24	25	3	5	11	15	34	49
13	Manchester United	38	8	6	5	26	14	5	3	11	20	33	48
14	Manchester City	38	9	4	6	26	21	3	8	8	17	31	48
15	Crystal Palace	38	8	7	4	27	23	5	2	12	15	43	48
16	Derby County	38	9	1	9	29	21	4	6	9	14	19	46
17	Luton Town	38	8	8	3	24	18	2	5	12	19	39	43
18	Sheffield Wed.	38	8	6	5	21	17	3	4	12	14	34	43
19	Charlton Athletic	38	4	6	9	18	25	3	3	13	13	32	30
20	Millwall	38	4	6	9	23	25	1	5	13	16	40	26

1990/91 Division 1

1	Arsenal	38	15	4	0	51	10	9	9	1	23	8	83
2	Liverpool	38	14	3	2	42	13	9	4	6	35	27	76
3	Crystal Palace	38	11	6	2	26	17	9	3	7	24	24	69
4	Leeds United	38	12	2	5	46	23	7	5	7	19	24	64
5	Manchester City	38	12	3	4	35	25	5	8	6	29	28	62
6	Manchester United	38	11	4	4	34	17	5	8	6	24	28	59
7	Wimbledon	38	8	6	5	28	22	6	8	5	25	24	56
8	Nottingham Forest	38	11	4	4	42	21	3	8	8	23	29	54
9	Everton	38	9	5	5	26	15	4	7	8	24	31	51
10	Tottenham Hotspur	38	8	9	2	35	22	3	7	9	16	28	49
11	Chelsea	38	10	6	3	33	25	3	4	12	25	44	49
12	QUEEN'S PARK RGS.	38	8	5	6	27	22	4	5	10	17	31	46
13	Sheffield United	38	9	3	7	23	23	4	4	11	13	32	46
14	Southampton	38	9	6	4	33	22	3	3	13	25	47	45
15	Norwich City	38	9	3	7	27	32	4	3	12	14	32	45
16	Coventry City	38	10	6	3	30	16	1	5	13	12	33	44
17	Aston Villa	38	7	9	3	29	25	2	5	12	17	33	41
18	Luton Town	38	7	5	7	22	18	3	2	14	20	43	37
19	Sunderland	38	6	6	7	15	16	2	4	13	23	44	34
20	Derby County	38	3	8	8	25	36	2	1	16	12	39	24

1991/92 Division 1

1	Leeds United	42	13	8	0	38	13	9	8	4	36	24	82
2	Manchester United	42	12	7	2	34	13	9	8	4	29	20	78
3	Sheffield Wed.	42	13	5	3	39	24	8	7	6	23	25	75
4	Arsenal	42	12	7	2	51	22	7	8	6	30	24	72
5	Manchester City	42	13	4	4	32	14	7	6	8	29	34	70
6	Liverpool	42	13	5	3	34	17	3	11	7	13	23	64
7	Aston Villa	42	13	3	5	31	16	4	6	11	17	28	60
8	Nottingham Forest	42	10	7	4	36	27	6	4	11	24	31	59
9	Sheffield United	42	9	6	6	29	23	7	3	11	36	40	57
10	Crystal Palace	42	7	8	6	24	25	7	7	7	29	36	57
11	QUEEN'S PARK RGS.	42	6	10	5	25	21	6	8	7	23	26	54
12	Everton	42	8	8	5	28	19	5	6	10	24	32	53
13	Wimbledon	42	10	5	6	32	20	3	9	9	21	33	53
14	Chelsea	42	7	8	6	31	30	6	6	9	19	30	53
15	Tottenham Hotspur	42	7	3	11	33	35	8	4	9	25	28	52
16	Southampton	42	7	5	9	17	28	7	5	9	22	27	52
17	Oldham Athletic	42	11	5	5	46	36	3	4	14	17	31	51
18	Norwich City	42	8	6	7	29	28	3	6	12	18	35	45
19	Coventry City	42	6	7	8	18	15	5	4	12	17	29	44
20	Luton Town	42	10	7	4	25	17	0	5	16	13	54	42
21	Notts County	42	7	5	9	24	29	3	5	13	16	33	40
22	West Ham United	42	6	6	9	22	24	3	5	13	15	35	38

1992/93 Premier Division

1	Manchester United	42	14	5	2	39	14	10	7	4	28	17	84
2	Aston Villa	42	13	5	3	36	16	8	6	7	21	24	74
3	Norwich City	42	13	6	2	31	19	8	3	10	30	46	72
4	Blackburn Rovers	42	13	4	4	38	18	7	7	7	30	28	71
5	QUEEN'S PARK RGS.	42	11	5	5	41	32	6	7	8	22	23	63
6	Liverpool	42	13	4	4	41	18	3	7	11	21	37	59
7	Sheffield Wed.	42	9	8	4	34	26	6	6	9	21	25	59
8	Tottenham Hotspur	42	11	5	5	40	25	5	6	10	20	41	59
9	Manchester City	42	7	8	6	30	25	8	4	9	26	26	57
10	Arsenal	42	8	6	7	25	20	7	5	9	15	18	56
11	Chelsea	42	9	7	5	29	22	5	7	9	22	32	56
12	Wimbledon	42	9	4	8	32	23	5	8	8	24	32	54
13	Everton	42	7	6	8	26	27	8	2	11	27	28	53
14	Sheffield United	42	10	6	5	33	19	4	4	13	21	34	52
15	Coventry City	42	7	4	10	29	28	6	9	6	23	29	52
16	Ipswich Town	42	8	9	4	29	22	4	7	10	21	33	52
17	Leeds United	42	12	8	1	40	17	0	7	14	17	45	51
18	Southampton	42	10	6	5	30	21	3	5	13	24	40	50
19	Oldham Athletic	42	10	6	5	43	30	3	4	14	20	44	49
20	Crystal Palace	42	6	9	6	27	25	5	7	9	21	36	49
21	Middlesbrough	42	8	5	8	33	27	3	6	12	21	48	44
22	Nottingham Forest	42	6	4	11	17	25	4	6	11	24	37	40

1993/94 Premier Division

1	Manchester United	42	14	6	1	39	13	13	5	3	41	25	92
2	Blackburn Rovers	42	14	5	2	31	11	11	4	6	32	25	84
3	Newcastle United	42	14	4	3	51	14	9	4	8	31	27	77
4	Arsenal	42	10	8	3	25	15	8	9	4	28	13	71
5	Leeds United	42	13	6	2	37	18	5	10	6	28	21	70
6	Wimbledon	42	12	5	4	35	21	6	6	9	21	32	65
7	Sheffield Wed.	42	10	7	4	48	24	6	9	6	28	30	64
8	Liverpool	42	12	4	5	33	23	5	5	11	26	32	60
9	QUEEN'S PARK RGS.	42	8	7	6	32	29	8	5	8	30	32	60
10	Aston Villa	42	8	5	8	23	18	7	7	7	23	32	57
11	Coventry City	42	9	7	5	23	17	5	7	9	20	28	56
12	Norwich City	42	4	9	8	26	29	8	8	5	39	32	53
13	West Ham United	42	6	7	8	26	31	7	6	8	21	27	52
14	Chelsea	42	11	5	5	31	20	2	7	12	18	33	51
15	Tottenham Hotspur	42	4	8	9	29	33	7	4	10	25	26	45
16	Manchester City	42	6	10	5	24	22	3	8	10	14	27	45
17	Everton	42	8	4	9	26	30	4	4	13	16	33	44
18	Southampton	42	9	2	10	30	31	3	5	13	19	35	43
19	Ipswich Town	42	5	8	8	21	32	4	8	9	14	26	43
20	Sheffield United	42	6	10	5	24	23	2	8	11	18	37	42
21	Oldham Athletic	42	5	8	8	24	33	4	5	12	18	35	40
22	Swindon Town	42	4	7	10	25	45	1	8	12	22	55	30

1994/95 Premier Division

1	Blackburn Rovers	42	17	2	2	54	21	10	6	5	26	18	89
2	Manchester United	42	16	4	1	42	4	10	6	5	35	24	88
3	Nottingham Forest	42	12	6	3	36	18	10	5	6	36	25	77
4	Liverpool	42	13	5	3	38	13	8	6	7	27	24	74
5	Leeds United	42	13	5	3	35	15	7	8	6	24	23	73
6	Newcastle United	42	14	6	1	46	20	6	6	9	21	27	72
7	Tottenham Hotspur	42	10	5	6	32	25	6	9	6	34	33	62
8	QUEEN'S PARK RGS.	42	11	3	7	36	26	6	6	9	25	33	60
9	Wimbledon	42	9	5	7	26	26	6	6	9	22	39	56
10	Southampton	42	8	9	4	33	27	4	9	8	28	36	54
11	Chelsea	42	7	7	7	25	22	6	8	7	25	33	54
12	Arsenal	42	6	9	6	27	21	7	3	11	25	28	51
13	Sheffield Wed.	42	7	7	7	26	26	6	5	10	23	31	51
14	West Ham United	42	9	6	6	28	19	4	5	12	16	29	50
15	Everton	42	8	9	4	31	23	3	8	10	13	28	50
16	Coventry City	42	7	7	7	23	25	5	7	9	21	37	50
17	Manchester City	42	8	7	6	37	28	4	6	11	16	36	49
18	Aston Villa	42	6	9	6	27	24	5	6	10	24	32	48
19	Crystal Palace	42	6	6	9	16	23	5	6	10	18	26	45
20	Norwich City	42	8	8	5	27	21	2	5	14	10	33	43
21	Leicester City	42	5	6	10	28	37	1	5	15	17	43	29
22	Ipswich Town	42	5	3	13	24	34	2	3	16	12	59	27

1995/96 Premier Division

1	Manchester United	38	15	4	0	36	9	10	3	6	37	26	82
2	Newcastle United	38	17	1	1	38	9	7	5	7	28	28	78
3	Liverpool	38	14	4	1	46	13	6	7	6	24	21	71
4	Aston Villa	38	11	5	3	32	15	7	4	8	20	20	63
5	Arsenal	38	10	7	2	30	16	7	5	7	19	16	63
6	Everton	38	10	5	4	35	19	7	5	7	29	25	61
7	Blackburn Rovers	38	14	2	3	44	19	4	5	10	17	28	61
8	Tottenham Hotspur	38	9	5	5	26	19	7	8	4	24	19	61
9	Nottingham Forest	38	11	6	2	29	17	4	7	8	21	37	58
10	West Ham United	38	9	5	5	25	21	5	4	10	18	31	51
11	Chelsea	38	7	7	5	30	22	5	7	7	16	22	50
12	Middlesbrough	38	8	3	8	27	27	3	7	9	8	23	43
13	Leeds United	38	8	3	8	21	21	4	4	11	19	36	43
14	Wimbledon	38	5	6	8	27	33	5	5	9	28	37	41
15	Sheffield Wed.	38	7	5	7	30	31	3	5	11	18	30	40
16	Coventry City	38	6	7	6	21	23	2	7	10	21	37	38
17	Southampton	38	7	7	5	21	18	2	4	13	13	34	38
16	Manchester City	38	7	7	5	21	19	2	4	13	12	39	38
19	QUEEN'S PARK RGS.	38	6	5	8	25	26	3	1	15	13	31	33
20	Bolton Wanderers	38	5	4	10	16	31	3	1	15	23	40	29

QPR'S RECORD AGAINST OTHER LEAGUE CLUBS

Present day names used throughout

	Home:					Away:					Total Goals:			
	P	W	D	L	F	A	W	D	L	F	A	F	A	% won
Aberdare Athletic	12	5	0	1	16	5	1	3	2	6	7	22	12	50.00
Accrington Stanley	4	2	0	0	8	2	2	0	0	6	3	14	5	100.00
Aldershot	30	7	4	4	37	15	5	2	8	20	25	57	40	40.00
Arsenal	40	9	6	5	23	17	2	6	12	16	35	39	52	27.50
Aston Villa	38	13	3	3	29	14	7	4	8	26	32	55	46	52.63
Barnsley	24	8	3	1	24	16	2	3	7	12	30	36	46	41.67
Birmingham C	30	8	4	3	25	17	1	3	11	10	29	35	46	30.00
Blackburn Rovers	28	7	2	5	24	19	4	2	8	13	20	37	39	39.29
Blackpool	8	3	0	1	12	2	1	2	1	3	4	15	6	50.00
Bolton Wanderers	16	6	0	2	19	10	2	2	4	13	16	32	26	50.00
Bournemouth	66	20	6	7	56	28	8	7	18	37	61	93	89	42.42
Bradford C	6	3	0	0	9	0	0	1	2	2	5	11	5	50.00
Bradford Park Ave.	8	1	0	3	3	5	1	2	1	6	4	9	9	25.00
Brentford	56	10	12	6	43	36	9	6	13	37	49	80	85	33.93
Brighton & Hove Alb.	62	19	6	6	64	31	7	6	18	38	64	102	95	41.94
Bristol C	60	17	6	7	56	28	7	8	15	35	54	91	82	40.00
Bristol Rovers	58	19	3	7	62	33	6	8	15	28	53	90	86	43.10
Burnley	16	6	0	2	18	7	1	2	5	8	12	26	19	43.75
Bury	14	7	0	0	17	7	1	2	4	3	9	20	16	57.14
Cambridge U	8	3	1	0	11	4	1	0	3	5	5	16	9	50.00
Cardiff C	42	14	3	4	53	17	3	4	14	24	40	77	57	40.48
Carlisle U	18	5	3	1	15	6	4	0	5	17	17	32	23	50.00
Charlton Athletic	42	10	7	4	37	23	5	8	8	26	31	63	54	35.71
Chelsea	40	7	9	4	30	24	4	6	10	23	28	53	52	27.50
Chesterfield	12	1	4	1	11	11	3	0	3	11	9	22	20	33.33
Colchester U	26	9	3	1	31	12	3	2	8	11	25	42	37	46.15
Coventry C	90	22	11	12	81	65	8	13	24	38	92	119	157	33.33
Crewe Alexandra	2	1	0	0	2	0	0	0	1	0	2	2	2	50.00
Crystal Palace	68	18	6	10	59	42	10	13	11	39	40	98	82	41.18
Darlington	2	1	0	0	4	0	0	1	0	0	0	4	0	50.00
Derby County	28	4	7	3	20	12	4	2	8	18	28	38	40	28.57
Doncaster Rov.	8	2	0	2	10	5	1	1	2	3	7	13	12	37.50
Everton	42	10	6	5	36	27	4	4	13	25	42	61	69	33.33
Exeter C	58	18	7	4	56	23	9	10	10	30	40	86	63	46.55
Fulham	18	6	2	1	14	5	6	1	2	15	12	29	17	66.67
Gillingham	54	14	9	4	54	24	8	10	9	34	38	88	62	40.74
Grimsby T	26	9	2	2	31	9	0	7	6	13	24	44	33	34.62
Halifax T	10	5	0	0	22	4	1	2	2	8	8	30	12	60.00
Huddersfield T	6	3	0	0	10	3	0	1	2	2	5	12	8	50.00
Hull City	30	6	7	2	26	20	2	3	10	15	37	41	57	26.67
Ipswich T	42	11	5	5	29	21	4	6	11	21	33	50	54	35.71
Leeds U	36	8	5	5	23	18	6	5	7	23	33	46	51	38.89
Leicester C	40	13	4	3	39	20	4	4	12	22	43	61	63	42.50
Leyton Orient	46	16	4	3	51	21	4	10	9	26	47	77	68	43.48
Lincoln C	4	1	0	1	3	3	1	1	0	5	0	8	3	50.00
Liverpool	40	5	4	11	20	28	1	2	17	14	40	34	68	15.00
Luton T	78	23	10	6	73	36	6	11	22	32	70	105	106	37.18
Manchester City	34	8	6	3	22	12	1	5	11	12	30	34	42	26.47
Manchester Utd.	38	5	7	7	28	28	1	3	15	13	39	41	67	15.79
Mansfield T	20	5	4	1	16	6	3	2	5	25	26	41	32	40.00
Merthyr Town	20	5	5	0	25	6	5	0	5	15	16	40	22	50.00
Middlesbrough	30	7	8	0	32	12	4	4	7	17	21	49	33	36.67
Millwall	56	11	7	10	50	31	4	7	17	17	53	67	84	26.79
Newcastle U	36	9	3	6	35	24	7	2	9	28	27	63	51	44.44

	p	w	d	l	f	a	w	d	l	f	a	tf	ta	
Newport County	58	19	8	2	72	27	12	5	12	49	53	121	80	53.45
Northampton T	58	19	4	6	55	36	6	3	20	39	62	94	98	43.10
Norwich C	90	24	12	9	82	45	7	13	25	35	76	117	121	34.44
Nottm Forest	36	10	3	5	31	22	0	7	11	9	30	40	52	27.78
Notts County	36	10	3	5	31	22	5	7	6	21	23	52	45	41.67
Oldham Ath.	22	6	3	2	18	13	3	2	6	12	18	30	31	40.91
Oxford U	18	5	2	2	19	12	3	2	4	12	14	31	26	44.44
Peterborough U	12	3	3	0	11	6	2	1	3	8	15	19	21	41.67
Plymouth Argyle	32	10	0	6	30	20	4	0	12	12	33	42	53	43.75
Port Vale	20	8	2	0	22	9	4	3	3	13	12	35	21	60.00
Portsmouth	22	5	3	3	15	7	3	3	5	8	18	23	25	36.36
Preston North End	16	3	4	1	10	7	2	3	3	11	9	21	16	31.25
Reading	62	17	6	8	53	36	5	6	20	31	62	84	98	35.48
Rochdale	2	1	0	0	3	0	0	1	0	2	2	5	2	50.00
Rotherham U	8	2	1	1	13	4	1	1	2	3	3	16	7	37.50
Scunthorpe U	6	3	0	0	8	2	2	0	1	5	3	13	5	83.33
Sheffield Utd.	24	8	2	2	20	14	2	7	3	9	12	29	26	41.67
Sheffield Wednesday	42	9	7	5	32	26	5	2	14	18	39	50	65	33.33
Shrewsbury T	36	10	7	1	31	15	4	8	6	21	23	52	38	38.89
Southampton	58	12	8	9	46	38	7	9	13	34	54	80	92	32.76
Southend U	70	23	7	5	75	43	11	5	19	40	65	115	108	48.57
Stockport County	2	0	1	0	0	0	1	0	0	3	2	3	2	50.00
Stoke C	14	5	1	1	18	7	3	1	3	7	8	25	15	57.14
Sunderland	18	7	2	0	18	7	3	1	5	6	11	24	18	55.56
Swansea	26	5	8	0	21	12	6	0	7	17	22	38	34	42.31
Swindon T	78	24	7	8	89	42	7	13	19	37	62	126	104	39.74
Thames	4	2	0	0	9	0	0	0	2	2	4	11	4	50.00
Torquay U	46	12	7	4	59	29	6	8	9	38	50	97	79	39.13
Tottenham Hotspur	42	9	7	5	32	25	3	7	11	21	36	53	61	28.57
Tranmere Rovers	6	2	1	0	12	4	2	0	1	5	3	17	7	66.67
Walsall	40	15	5	0	38	13	10	3	7	31	31	69	44	62.50
Watford	90	23	15	7	79	53	20	11	14	68	57	147	110	47.78
West Bromwich Albion	16	4	1	3	8	10	2	3	3	7	10	15	20	37.50
West Ham Utd.	44	9	8	5	31	20	4	7	11	30	38	61	58	29.55
Wimbledon	20	4	1	5	12	15	4	3	3	11	10	23	25	40.00
Wolves	16	4	2	2	14	11	3	1	4	13	14	27	25	43.75
Workington	6	3	0	0	10	3	1	2	0	3	1	13	4	66.67
Wrexham	14	3	2	2	12	7	3	2	2	10	8	22	15	42.86
York City	4	1	1	0	7	2	0	1	1	3	4	10	6	25.00

OVERALL TOTALS TO THE END OF 1995/96

	p	w	d	l	f	a	w	d	l	f	a	tf	ta	pts
	2940	804	368	298	2750	1558	360	370	740	1650	2517	4400	4075	3305

Made up of:

	p	w	d	l	f	a	w	d	l	f	a	tf	ta	pts
Prem/Div. 1	822	187	117	107	607	457	90	106	215	421	654	1028	1111	969
Div. 2	546	164	65	44	531	255	69	76	128	278	416	809	671	654
Div. 3	414	132	42	33	484	235	56	56	95	298	366	782	601	474
Div. 3 (South)	1158	321	144	114	1128	611	145	132	302	653	1081	1781	1692	1208

Prem/Div.1 totals include the "new" Premiership and the old Division 1.

F.A. Cup Record in non-League Seasons

Players appearances and goals are included in the A-Z section only if they also made a League appearance.

1895/96

Rnd	Date	Opponent	Score	Scorers	Att											
Q1	Oct 12	OLD ST. STEPHEN'S	1-1	Ward	3000	Hiscox W	Teagle	Harvey	Knight	Hiscox H	MacKenzie	Davis	Handford	Burge	Ward	Wallington E
rep	Oct 15	Old St. Stephen's	0-1		1500	Hiscox W	Teagle	Harvey	Knight	Spurr	MacKenzie	Davis	Handford	Burge	Ward	Wallington E

1896/97

Rnd	Date	Opponent	Score	Scorers	Att											
Q1	Oct 10	MARLOW	1-3	Ward	3000	Hunt	Teagle	Todd	Knight	Musslewhite	MacKenzie	Davis	Lee	Galley	Ward	Wallington E

1897/98

Rnd	Date	Opponent	Score	Scorers	Att											
PR	Sep 18	WINDSOR & ETON	3-0	Evans 2, A Wallington	2000	Hunt	Tyler	Hughes F	Walburton	Musslewhite	Blyth	MacKenzie	Evans	Hughes R	Wallington A	Wallington E
Q1	Sep 25	WOLVERTON LNWR	2-1	Evans, E Wallington	5000	Hunt	Teagle	Hughes F	Walburton	Musslewhite	Blyth	MacKenzie	Evans	Hughes R	Wallington A	Wallington E
Q2	Oct 16	CHESHAM GENERALS	4-0	E Wallington 2,A Wallington, Musslewhite	6000	Hunt	Teagle	Hughes F	Walburton	Musslewhite	Blyth	Davis	Evans	Hughes R	Wallington A	Wallington E
Q3	Oct 30	Clapton	0-3			Hunt	Teagle	Hughes F	Walburton	Musslewhite	Blyth	Hardwick	Evans	Hughes R	Wallington A	Wallington E

Q1 played at home, by arrangement.

1898/99

Rnd	Date	Opponent	Score	Scorers	Att											
PR	Sep 24	Richmond Association	0-3			Leather	Allen	Hughes F	Knight	Musslewhite	Blyth	Wallington A	Evans	Brooks	Jones	Wallington E

1899/1900

Rnd	Date	Opponent	Score	Scorers	Att											
PR	Sep 23	LONDON WELSH	4-2	Bedingfield, Smith, Turnbull 2	4987	Clutterbuck	Knowles	McConnell	Crawford	Tennant	Keech	Smith	Heywood	Bedingfield	Turnbull	Cowie
Q1	Sep 30	FULHAM	3-0	Haywood, Bedingfield, Turnbull	5000	Clutterbuck	Gaylard	McConnell	Crawford	Tennant	Keech	Smith	Heywood	Bedingfield	Turnbull	Cowie
Q2	Oct 14	WEST HAMPSTEAD	5-0	Turnbull 3 (1p), Smith, Haywood	6000	Clutterbuck	Knowles	McConnell	Crawford	Hitch	Keech	Smith	Heywood	Keech	Turnbull	Evans
Q3	Oct 28	Wandsworth	7-1	Keech 3, Evans 2, Hitch, Haywood	1000	Clutterbuck	Knowles	McConnell	Smith	Hitch	Tennant	Jordan	Heywood	Evans	Cowie	Cowie
Q4	Nov 18	CIVIL SERVICE	3-0	Haywood, Hitch, Turnbull	3000	Clutterbuck	Knowles	McConnell	Crawford	Hitch	Skinner	Smith	Heywood	Bedingfield	Turnbull	Cowie
Q5	Dec 9	Luton Town	1-1	Evans	3000	Clutterbuck	Gaylard	McConnell	Crawford	Hitch	Skinner	Smith	Heywood	Bedingfield	White	Evans
rep	Dec 13	LUTON TOWN	4-1	Haywood, Bedingfield, White, Smith	2000	Clutterbuck	Gaylard	McConnell	Crawford	Hitch	Keech	Smith	Heywood	Bedingfield	White	Evans
R1	Jan 27	WOLVERHAMPTON WAN.	1-1	Haywood	10000	Clutterbuck	Knowles	McConnell	Crawford	Hitch	Turnbull	Turnbull	Heywood	Bedingfield	White	Hannah
rep	Jan 31	Wolverhampton Wan.	1-0	Bedingfield, Smith, Turnbull 2	7000	Clutterbuck	Knowles	McConnell	Crawford	Hitch	Turnbull	Turnbull	Heywood	Bedingfield	White	Hannah
R2	Feb 17	MILLWALL	0-2		12000	Clutterbuck	Knowles	McConnell	Crawford	Hitch	Keech	Smith	Heywood	Bedingfield	White	Hannah

1900/01

Rnd	Date	Opponent	Score	Scorers	Att											
Q3	Nov 3	FULHAM	7-0	Goldie 2, Foxall 2, Downing, Gray, Hitch	4000	Clutterbuck	Bellingham	Newlands	Keetch	Hitch	Skinner	Gray	Downing	Goldie	Humphries	Foxall
Q4	Nov 17	Watford	1-1	Gray	4000	Clutterbuck	Newlands	McConnell	Keetch	Hitch	Skinner	Gray	Newbigging	Goldie	Humphries	Foxall
rep	Nov 21	WATFORD	4-1	Humphries 3, Newbigging	2000	Clutterbuck	Bellingham	McConnell	Newlands	Hitch	Skinner	Gray	Newbigging	Goldie	Humphries	Foxall
Q5	Dec 8	Luton Town			5000	Clutterbuck	Newlands	McConnell	Keetch	Hitch	Skinner	Gray	Downing	Goldie	Humphries	Foxall

1901/02

Rnd	Date	Opponent	Score	Scorers	Att											
Q3	Nov 2	COUCH END	2-0	Stewart, Millar	1500	Collins	Newlands	Aston	Bowman	Freeman	Keech	Stewart	Pryce	Millar	McQueen	Seeley
Q4	Nov 20	WEST NORWOOD	4-0	Millar 4	3000	Collins	Newlands	Aston	Bowman	Freeman	Keech	Stewart	Pryce	Millar	McQueen	Seeley
Q5	Nov 30	Luton Town	0-2		5000	Collins	Newlands	Aston	Bowman	White	Keech	Stewart	Pryce	Millar	McQueen	Seeley

1902/03

Rnd	Date	Opponent	Score	Scorers	Att											
Q3	Nov 1	LUTON TOWN	0-3		8000	Collins	White	Edwards J	Bowman	Clipsham	Skinner	Hamilton	King	Abbott	Wilson	Busby

1903/04

Rnd	Date	Opponent	Score	Scorers	Att											
Q3	Oct 31	FULHAM	1-1	Murphy	12000	Collins	Lyon	Newlands	Bowman	Hitch	Bull	Hamilton	McCairns	Murphy	McGowan	Wilson
rep	Nov 4	Fulham	1-3	Brown	18000	Collins	Lyon	Newlands	Bowman	Hitch	Bull	Hamilton	McCairns	Brown	McGowan	Wilson

Season	Rd	Date	Opponent	Score	Scorers	Att	GK										
1904/05	06	Dec 10	BRENTFORD	1-2	Ryder	10000	Howes	Archer	Lyon	Bowman	Hitch	Cross J	Cross W	Ronaldson	Bevan	Ryder	Stewart
1905/06	R1	Jan 13	Fulham	0-1		7000	Howes	White	Newlands	Yenson	Hitch	Downing	Thompson	Fletcher	Murphy	Ryder	Lyon
1906/07	R1	Jan 12	Bristol Rovers	0-0		6000	Howes	White	Newlands	Yenson	McLean	Downing	O'Donnell	Fletcher	Green	Sugden	Ryder
	rep	14	BRISTOL ROVERS	0-1		8000	Howes	White	Newlands	Yenson	McLean	Downing	O'Donnell	Fletcher	Green	Sugden	Ryder
1907/08	R1	Jan 11	READING	1-0	Barnes	28000	Shaw	White	McDonald	Yenson	Lintott	Downing	Pentland	Sugden	Walker	Gittens	Barnes
	R2	Feb 1	Swindon Town	1-2	Walker	9771	Shaw	White	Fidler	Lintott	McLean	Downing	Pentland	Sugden	Walker	Gittens	Barnes
1908/09	R1	Jan 16	WEST HAM UTD.	0-0		17000	Shaw	McDonald	Fidler	Duff	Morris	Downing	MacDonald	Rogers	Greer	Drake	Barnes
	R2	20	West Ham United	0-1		10000	Shaw	McDonald	Fidler	Duff	Mitchell	Downing	MacDonald	Rogers	Greer	Barnes	Law
1909/10	R1	Jan 15	Norwich City	0-0		10000	Shaw	McDonald	Fidler	Mitchell	Hartwell	Wake	McNaught	Travers	Steer	Whyman	Barnes
	rep	19	NORWICH CITY	3-0	Steer, McNaught, Whyman	5000	Shaw	McDonald	Fidler	Mitchell	Hartwell	Wake	McNaught	Travers	Steer	Whyman	Barnes
	R2	Feb 5	Southend United	0-0	Donald	5000	Shaw	McDonald	Fidler	Mitchell	Hartwell	Wake	McNaught	Travers	Steer	Whyman	Barnes
	rep	9	SOUTHEND UNITED	3-2	Steer 2, Travers	11000	Shaw	McDonald	Fidler	Mitchell	Hartwell	Wake	McNaught	Travers	Steer	Whyman	Barnes
	R3	19	West Ham United	1-1	Steer	31000	Shaw	McDonald	Fidler	Mitchell	Hartwell	Wake	Ferguson	Travers	Steer	Whyman	Barnes
	rep	24	WEST HAM UNITED	1-0	Steer	18500	Shaw	McDonald	Fidler	Mitchell	Hartwell	Wake	Ferguson	Travers	Steer	Whyman	Barnes
	R4	Mar 5	Barnsley	0-1		23500	Shaw	McDonald	Fidler	Mitchell	Hartwell	Wake	McNaught	Travers	Steer	Whyman	Barnes
	R3 replay a.e.t.																
1910/11	R1	Jan 14	Bradford Park Ave.	3-5	McKie 2, Steer	25000	Shaw	McDonald	Fidler	Mitchell	Morris	Butterworth	Whyman	Steer	McKie	Browning	Brindley
1911/12	R1	Jan 13	BRADFORD CITY	0-0		18000	Shaw	McDonald	Pullen	Ovens	Mitchell	Wake	Smith	Revill	Thornton	Browning	Barnes
	rep	18	Bradford City	0-4		10000	Shaw	McDonald	Pullen	Ovens	Mitchell	Wake	Whyman	Revill	King	Browning	Barnes
1912/13	R1	Jan 11	HALIFAX TOWN	4-2	Revill, Birch, Whyman, Ovens	11000	Fidler	Fidler	Pullen	Ovens	Mitchell	Wake	Thompson W	Birch	Whyman	Revill	Barnes
	R2	Feb 1	Middlesbrough	2-3	Birch 2	25000	Shaw	Fidler	Pullen	Ovens	Mitchell	Wake	Thompson W	Birch	Whyman	Revill	Barnes
1913/14	R1	Jan 10	BRISTOL CITY	2-2	Miller, Birch	18000	Nicholls	Higgins	Pullen	Ovens	Mitchell	Wake	Thompson W	Birch	Miller	Gregory	Fortune
	rep	15	Bristol City	2-0	Birch, Gregory	14000	Nicholls	Higgins	Pullen	Ovens	Mitchell	Wake	Thompson W	Birch	Miller	Gregory	Fortune
	R2	31	Swansea Town	2-1	Birch 2	15000	Nicholls	Higgins	Pullen	Ovens	Mitchell	Wake	Thompson W	Birch	Miller	Gregory	Fortune
	R3	Feb 21	Birmingham	2-1	Gregory, Miller	33000	Nicholls	Higgins	Pullen	Ovens	Mitchell	Wake	Thompson W	Birch	Miller	Gregory	Fortune
	R4	Mar 7	Liverpool	1-2	Mitchell (p)	36500	Nicholls	Ovens	Pullen	Whyman	Mitchell	Wake	Thompson W	Birch	Miller	Gregory	Fortune

1914/15

R	Date	Opponent	Score	Scorers	Att	1	2	3	4	5	6	7	8	9	10	11
R1	Jan 5	GLOSSOP	2-1	Birch, Miller	7000	McLeod	Millington	Pullen	Broster	Mitchell	Whyman	Thompson W	Birch	Miller	Simons	Donald
R2	30	LEEDS CITY	1-0	Simons	10000	McLeod	Millington	Pullen	Broster	Mitchell	Whyman	Thompson W	Birch	Miller	Simons	Donald
R3	Feb 20	Everton	1-2	Birch	33000	McLeod	Millington	Pullen	Broster	Mitchell	Whyman	Thompson W	Birch	Miller	Simons	Donald

R3 played at Stamford Bridge

1919/20

R	Date	Opponent	Score	Scorers	Att	1	2	3	4	5	6	7	8	9	10	11
R1	Jan 10	Aston Villa	1-2	Birch	33000	Merrick	Wingrove	Pullen	Broster	Mitchell	Blackman FE	Thompson W	Birch	Smith JW	Gregory	Donald

1945/46

R	Date	Opponent	Score	Scorers	Att	1	2	3	4	5	6	7	8	9	10	11
R1/1	Nov 17	Barnet	6-2	Heathcote, Mallett 2, Neary 3	6800	Allen AR	Rose	Swinfen	Daniels	Ridyard	Farrow	Neary	Mallett	Heathcote	Blizzard	Whitehead
R1/2	24	BARNET	2-1	Swinfen, Neary	11600	Allen AR	Rose	Jefferson	Daniels	Ridyard	Farrow	Neary	Mallett	Heathcote	Swinfen	Whitehead
R2/1	Dec 8	IPSWICH TOWN	4-0	Neary, Stock, Addinall 2	12000	Allen AR	Rose	Jefferson	Daniels	Ridyard	Farrow	Blizzard	Mallett	Addinall	Stock	Whitehead
R2/2	15	Ipswich Town	2-0	Daniels, Addinall	12000	Allen AR	Rose	Jefferson	Daniels	Ridyard	Farrow	Neary	Mallett	Addinall	Stock	Whitehead
R3/1	Jan 5	CRYSTAL PALACE	0-0		20080	Allen AR	Rose	Jefferson	Daniels	Ridyard	Heath	Neary	Mallett	Heathcote	Stock	Pattison
R3/2	9	Crystal Palace	0-0		26400	Allen AR	Rose	Jefferson	Daniels	Ridyard	Heath	Whitehead	Mallett	Neary	Stock	Pattison
rep	16	Crystal Palace	1-0	Addinall	23000	Brown,Harry	Rose	Jefferson	Daniels	Ridyard	Farrow	Blizzard	Mallett	Addinall	Stock	Whitehead
R4/1	26	Southampton	1-0	Addinall	19000	Allen AR	Rose	Jefferson	Daniels	Ridyard	Farrow	Neary	Mallett	Addinall	Stock	Pattison
R4/2	30	SOUTHAMPTON	4-3	Addinall 3, Stock	16000	Allen AR	Rose	Jefferson	Daniels	Ridyard	Farrow	Neary	Mallett	Addinall	Stock	Whitehead
R5/1	Feb 9	BRENTFORD	1-3	Pattison	19885	Allen AR	Rose	Jefferson	Daniels	Ridyard	Farrow	Swinfen	Mallett	Addinall	Stock	Pattison
R5/2	14	Brentford	0-0		20000	Reay	Rose	Jefferson	Daniels	Ridyard	Farrow	Swinfen	Mallett	Addinall	Heath	Pattison

R3/2 abandoned in extra time. R3 replay at Craven Cottage.

MISCELLANEOUS GAMES

1907/08 Charity Shield

	Date	Opponent	Score	Scorers	Att	1	2	3	4	5	6	7	8	9	10	11
	Apr 27	Manchester United	1-1	Cannon	12000	Shaw	McDonald	Fidler	Lintott	McLean	Downing	Pentand	Cannon	Skitton	Gittens	Barnes
rep	Aug 29	Manchester United	0-4		10000	Shaw	McDonald	Fidler	Lintott	McLean	Downing	McNaught	Cannon	Skitton	Gittens	Barnes

Both games at Stamford Bridge. Replay played at start of 1908/09 season.

1911/12 Charity Shield

	Date	Opponent	Score	Scorers	Att	1	2	3	4	5	6	7	8	9	10	11
	May 4	Blackburn Rovers	1-2	Revill	10000	Shaw	McDonald	Ovens	Whyman	Mitchell	Wake	Smith	Revill	McKie	Thornton	Barnes

Played at White Hart Lane

1939/40 Season abandoned on outbreak of war.

	Date	Opponent	Score	Scorers	Att	1	2	3	4	5	6	7	8	9	10	11
1	Aug 26	WATFORD	2-2	Mangnall 2	8000	Allen	Reay	Jefferson	Lowe	Ridyard	March	McEwan	Mallett	Mangnall	Fitzgerald	Bonass
2	30	Bournemouth	2-2	Mangnall, Swinfen	4000	Allen	Reay	Jefferson	Lowe	Ridyard	March	Stock	Swinfen	Mangnall	Fitzgerald	Bonass
3	Sep 2	Walsall	0-1		5000	Allen	Reay	Jefferson	Lowe	Ridyard	Farmer	Stock	Swinfen	Mangnall	Fitzgerald	Bonass

QUEEN'S PARK RANGERS MANAGERS

James Cowan	1907-14	Dave Sexton	1974-77
James Howie	1914-20	Frank Sibley	1977-78
Ned Liddell	1920-25	Steve Burtenshaw	1978-79
Bob Hewison	1925-31	Tommy Docherty	1979-80
John Bowman	1931	Terry Venables	1980-84
Archie Mitchell	1931-33	Alan Mullery	1984
Mick O'Brien	1933-35	Frank Sibley (caretaker)	1984-85
Billy Birrell	1935-39	Jim Smith	1985-88
Ted Vizard	1939-44	Peter Shreeve (caretaker)	1988
Dave Mangnall	1944-52	Trevor Francis	1988-89
Jack Taylor	1952-59	Don Howe	1989-91
Alex Stock	1959-68	Gerry Francis	1991-94
Tommy Docherty	1968	Ray Wilkins	1994-96
Les Allen	1968-71	Stewart Houston	1996 on
Gordon Jago	1971-74		

1967/68, with the League Cup and Third Division Trophy. Back; Sanderson, I Morgan, Harris, Wilks, R Morgan, Lazarus, Turpie. Centre; Moughton, Clement, Kelly, Springett, Leach, Hazell. Front; Hunt, Watson, Langley, Keen, Allen, Marsh, Keetch.

Player			D.O.B	Place of Birth	Died	First Lge Season	Last Lge Season	Previous Club	Next Club	Appearances				Goals			
										League	FAC	FLC	Other	League	FAC	FLC	Oth.
Abbott	RF	Ron	02/08/53	Lambeth		1973	1978	App.	Drogheda	46	5	3	0	4	0	0	0
Abbott	SW	Shirley	19/02/1889	Alfreton	1947	1923		Portsmouth	Chesterfield	12	0	0	0	0	0	0	0
Abel	SC	Sam	30/12/10	Neston		1934	1938	Fulham	Retired	36	1	0	5	6	0	0	0
Adams	EW	Ernie	03/04/22	Willesden		1947	1949	Preston NE		5	0	0	0	0	0	0	0
Addinall	AW	Bert	30/01/21	Paddington		1946	1952	British Oxygen	Brighton & Hove A.	150	13	0	0	59	10	0	0
Adlam	LW	Les	24/06/06	Guildford		1931	1932	Oldham Athletic	Cardiff City	56	8	0	0	0	0	0	0
Allen	AR	Reg	03/05/19	Marylebone		1938	1949	Corona	Manchester Utd.	183	28	0	2	0	0	0	0
Allen	BJ	Bradley	13/09/71	Harold Wood		1988	1995	Jnrs.	Charlton Athletic	81	5	7	1	27	0	5	0
Allen	CD	Clive	20/05/61	Stepney		1978	1979	App.	Arsenal	136	9	12	0	72	7	4	0
						1981	1983	Crystal Palace	Tottenham Hotspur								
Allen	J	Joe	30/12/09	Bilsthorpe	1978	1933	1934	Tottenham H	Mansfield Town	51	3	0	4	6	1	0	0
Allen	J	Jimmy	1913	Amble		1935	1936	Huddersfield T	Clapton Orient	44	1	0	2	1	0	0	0
Allen	JC	Ian	27/01/32	Paisley		1953		Beith Juniors	Bournemouth	1	0	0	0	0	0	0	0
Allen	LW	Les	04/09/37	Dagenham		1965	1968	Tottenham H	Woodford Town	128	8	15	0	55	3	4	0
Allen	MJ	Martin	14/08/65	Reading		1984	1989	App.	West Ham Utd.	136	9	18	3	16	1	1	1
Allum	A	Bert	15/10/30	Notting Hill		1957		Dover	Dover	1	0	0	0	0	0	0	0
Anderson	TC	Tommy	24/09/34	Edinburgh		1958		Bournemouth	Torquay United	10	0	0	0	3	0	0	0
Anderton	SJ	Sylvan	23/11/34	Reading		1961		Chelsea	Dover	4	0	0	0	0	0	0	0
Andrews	CJ	Cecil'Archie'	01/11/30	Alton		1956	1957	Crystal Palace	Sittingbourne	58	4	0	3	1	0	0	0
Andrews	JP	Jimmy	01/02/27	Invergordon		1959	1961	Leyton Orient	Coaching staff	82	4	1	1	16	1	0	0
Angell	PF	Peter	11/01/32	Slough	1979	1953	1964	Slough Town	Charlton (coach)	417	27	6	7	37	1	2	0
Ardiles	OC	Ossie	03/08/52	Cordoba, Argentina		1988		Tottenham H	Swindon Town	8	1	2	1	0	0	0	0
Armitage	S	Stan	05/06/19	Woolwich		1946			Gravesend & Nthfleet	2	0	0	0	0	0	0	0
Armstrong	JH	Jimmy		Lymington		1928	1932	Clapton Orient	Watford	122	11	0	0	5	0	0	0
Ashford	HE	Herbert		Southall		1920	1921	Brentford	Ayr United	10	0	0	0	0	0	0	0
Ashman	D	Don	09/10/02	Staindrop	1984	1932	1934	Middlesbrough	Darlington	78	5	0	4	0	0	0	0
Bailey	DL	Dennis	13/11/65	Lambeth		1991	1992	Birmingham City	Gillingham	39	2	5	1	10	0	3	0
Bailey	S	Sid		London		1921				1	0	0	0	0	0	0	0
Bain	K	Ken		Scotland		1921	1923	Mid Rhondda		91	7	0	0	0	0	0	0
Baker	PR	Peter	24/08/34	Walthamstow		1960	1962	Sheffield Wed.	Romford	27	0	1	0	0	0	0	0
Bakholt	K	Kurt	12/08/63	Odense, Denmark		1985		Vejie		1	0	0	0	0	0	0	0
Baldock	JWN	John		London		1920				1	0	0	0	0	0	0	0
Ballantyne	J	Johnny		Glasgow		1935	1936	Partick Thistle		25	1	0	1	3	0	0	0
Balogun	T	Tesi	27/03/31	Nigeria		1956		Skegness Town	Holbeach United	13	2	0	1	3	2	0	2
Banks	R	Reg				1935	1936	West Bromwich A.	Tunbridge Wells	12	0	0	0	3	0	0	0
Bannister	G	Gary	22/07/60	Warrington		1984	1987	Sheffield Wed.	Coventry City	136	9	23	4	56	1	9	6
Barber	MJ	Mike	24/08/41	Kensington		1960	1962	Arsenal	Notts County	63	2	4	0	11	2	0	0
Bardsley	DJ	David	11/09/64	Manchester		1989	1995	Oxford United		241	19	20	3	4	0	1	1
Barker	S	Simon	04/11/64	Farnworth		1988	1995	Blackburn Rovers		254	21	27	7	26	3	5	0
Barley	DC	Derek 'Jack'	20/03/32	Highbury		1953		Arsenal	Aldershot	4	0	0	0	0	0	0	0
Barr	JM	John	09/09/17	Bridge of Weir		1946		Third Lanark		4	0	0	0	0	0	0	0
Barr	W	William				1925				2	0	0	0	0	0	0	0
Barrie	WB	Walter	09/08/09	Kirkcaldy		1932	1937	West Ham Utd.	Carlisle Utd.	157	12	0	5	1	0	0	0
Barron	PG	Paul	16/09/53	Woolwich		1985	1986	West Bromwich A.	Reading	32	1	9	0	0	0	0	0
Bartlett	FL	Fred	05/03/13	Reading		1934	1936		Clapton Orient	48	2	0	1	0	0	0	0
Beats	E	Edwin		Bristol		1927		Aston Villa		1	0	0	0	1	0	0	0
Beck	JA	John	25/05/54	Edmonton		1972	1975	App.	Coventry City	40	4	2	0	1	0	0	0
Bedford	NB	Brian	24/12/33	Ferndale		1959	1965	Bournemouth	Scunthorpe Utd.	258	16	9	1	161	13	6	0
Beecham	EC	Ernie	23/08/1896	Hertford	1985	1932	1934	Fulham	Brighton & Hove A.	86	9	0	0	0	0	0	0
Bennett	EE	Edward	22/08/25	Kilburn		1948		Southall	Southall	2	0	0	0	0	0	0	0
Benson	GH	George		Burnley		1923		Stalybridge Celtic	Port Vale	17	0	0	0	0	0	0	0
Bentley	RTF	Roy	17/05/24	Bristol		1961	1962	Fulham	Reading (mgr.)	45	6	1	0	0	0	0	0
Best	TH	Tommy	23/12/20	Milford Haven		1949		Cardiff City	Hereford United	13	1	0	0	3	0	0	0
Birch	J	Jimmy	1888	Blackwell	1940	1920	1925	Aston Villa	Brentford	183	29	0	0	60	19	0	0
Black	S	Sammy	18/11/05	Motherwell	1977	1938		Plymouth Argyle		5	0	0	0	0	0	0	0
Blackman	FE	Fred	01/01/1889	Brixton		1920	1921	Leeds City	Retired	42	2	0	0	0	0	0	0
Blackman	JJ	Jack	1911	Bermondsey		1931	1935	Weston United	Crystal Palace	108	8	0	4	62	7	0	2
Blake	AG	Albert	1900	Fulham		1933	1935	Watford	Tunbridge Wells	81	5	0	3	9	0	0	1
Blizzard	LWB	Les	13/03/23	Acton		1946			Bournemouth	5	3	0	0	0	0	0	0
Bolam	RC	Robert		Birtley		1924		South Shields		2	0	0	0	0	0	0	0
Bott	WE	Wilf	25/04/07	Featherstone		1936	1938	Newcastle United	Lancaster	75	9	0	4	34	3	0	1
Bottoms	MC	Mike	11/01/39	Harrow		1960		Harrow Town	Oxford United	2	0	1	0	0	0	0	0
Bowers	AGW	Alf	1895	Bow		1926		Bristol Rovers		1	0	0	0	0	0	0	0
Bowles	S	Stan	24/12/48	Manchester		1972	1979	Carlisle Utd.	Nottm. Forest	255	25	27	8	70	8	7	11
Boxshall	D	Danny	02/04/20	Bradford		1946	1947	Salem Athletic	Bristol City	29	8	0	0	14	3	0	0
Bradshaw	JH	John	1892	Burnley		1921		Aberdare Ath.	Burnley	5	0	0	0	0	0	0	0
Brady	PJ	Pat	11/03/36	Dublin		1963	1964	Millwall	Gravesend & Nrtfleet	62	5	3	0	0	0	0	0
Brady	TR	Ray	03/06/37	Dublin		1963	1965	Millwall	Hastings United	88	6	3	0	0	1	0	0
Brazier	MR	Matthew	02/07/76	Whipps Cross		1995		Jnrs.		11	1	2	0	0	0	0	0
Brazil	AB	Alan	15/06/59	Glasgow		1986		Coventry City	Witham Town	4	0	2	0	0	0	1	0
Brevett	RE	Rufus	24/09/69	Derby		1990	1995	Doncaster Rovers		85	2	6	0	1	0	0	0
Bridges	BJ	Barry	29/04/41	Horsford		1968	1970	Birmingham City	Millwall	72	4	6	0	31	1	3	0
Brock	KS	Kevin	09/09/62	Middleton Stoney		1987	1988	Oxford United	Newcastle United	40	4	6	2	2	1	0	0
Brown	AR	Dick	14/02/11	Pegswood		1932	1933	Blyth Spartans	Northampton Town	60	9	0	1	20	1	0	2
Brown	C	Charlie	14/01/1898	Stakeford	1979	1924	1925	Southampton	Poole	67	6	0	0	3	0	0	0
Brown	HA	Harry	1898	Durham		1924		Shildon		13	1	0	0	3	0	0	0
Brown	HT	Harry	09/04/24	Kingsbury	1982	1951	1955	Derby County	Plymouth Argyle	189	11	0	1	0	0	0	0
Burgess	D	Daniel 'Dick'		Goldenhill		1925	1926	Aberdare Ath.	Sittingbourne	46	4	0	0	9	0	0	0
Burke	SJ	Steve	29/09/60	Nottingham		1979	1984	Nottm. Forest	Doncaster Rovers	67	3	6	1	5	0	0	0

Player			D.O.B	Place of Birth	Died	First Lge Season	Last Lge Season	Previous Club	Next Club	Appearances				Goals			
										League	FAC	FLC	Other	Leagu	FAC	FLC	Oth.
Burnham	J	Jack		Sunderland		1921	1922	Brighton & Hove A.	Durham City	31	2	0	0	0	0	0	0
Burns	JC	Jack	27/11/06	Fulham		1927	1930	Crypto	Brentford	117	8	0	0	29	5	0	0
Burridge	J	John	03/12/51	Workington		1980	1981	Crystal Palace	Wolves	39	2	4	0	0	0	0	0
Busby	MG	Martyn	24/03/53	Slough		1969	1976	App.	Notts County	145	8	13	1	17	3	0	0
						1977	1979	Notts County	Retired								
Butler	E	Ernie		Stillington		1922	1923	Ebbw Vale	Hartlepools Utd.	34	1	0	0	0	0	0	0
Byrne	JF	John	01/02/61	Manchester		1984	1987	York City	Le Harve	126	9	13	1	30	2	4	0
Cable	TH	Tommy	27/11/00	Barking	1986	1925	1926	Leyton	Tottenham H	18	0	0	0	2	0	0	0
Caesar	GC	Gus	05/03/66	Tottenham		1990		Arsenal (loan)		5	0	0	0	0	0	0	0
Cameron	J	James		Inverness		1923		Hearts		24	1	0	0	0	0	0	0
Cameron	K	Ken	1905	Hamilton		1936		Hull City	Rotherham Utd.	8	0	0	0	1	0	0	0
Cameron	R	Bobby	23/11/32	Greenock		1950	1958	Port Glashow	Leeds United	256	19	0	4	59	3	0	0
Campbell	CJ	Charles		Blackburn		1925		Pembroke Dock	Reading	4	0	0	0	1	0	0	0
Cape	JP	Jackie	16/11/10	Carlisle	1994	1937	1938	Manchester Utd.	Carlisle Utd.	61	3	0	1	12	1	0	0
Carey	PR	Peter	14/04/33	Barking		1960		Leyton Orient	Colchester Utd.	15	1	1	0	1	0	0	0
Carr	WP	Billy	06/11/01	Cambois		1935	1936	Derby County	Barrow	28	0	0	0	0	0	0	0
Challis	TM	Trevor	23/10/75	Paddington		1995		Jnrs.		11	2	0	0	0	0	0	0
Chandler	ACH	Arthur	27/11/1895	Paddington	1984	1920	1922	Hampstead	Leicester City	78	8	0	0	16	2	0	0
Channing	JA	Justin	19/11/68	Reading		1986	1992	App.	Bristol Rovers	55	1	5	5	5	0	0	0
Chapman	RFJ	Reg	07/09/21	Shepherds Bush	1992	1946	1952			97	4	0	0	2	0	0	0
Charles	JM	Jeremy	26/09/59	Swansea		1983	1984	Swansea City	Oxford United	12	1	1	2	5	0	0	1
Charles	L	Lee	20/8/71	Hillingdon		1995		Chertsey Town		4	0	0	0	0	0	0	0
Charlesworth	GW	George	29/11/01	Bristol	1965	1926		Bristol Rovers	Crystal Palace	23	0	0	0	3	0	0	0
Charlton	W	William	04/06/12	South Stoneham		1936	1937	Wimbledon	Barnet	20	1	0	0	10	0	0	0
Cheetham	TM	Tommy	11/10/10	Newcastle		1935	1938	Army	Brentford	115	10	0	4	81	10	0	1
Chivers	GPS	Gary	15/05/60	Stockwell		1984	1986	Swansea City	Watford	60	2	6	1	0	0	0	0
Cini	J	Joe		Malta		1959		Floriana	(Malta)	7	0	0	0	1	0	0	0
Clark	C	Clive	14/12/40	Roundhay		1958	1960	Leeds United	West Bromwich A.	66	3	4	0	8	0	0	0
						1969		West Bromwich A.	Preston NE								
Clark	W	Willie	25/02/32	Larkhall		1953	1955	Petershill		95	1	0	1	32	0	0	0
Clarke	C	Charlie		Fleet	1943	1935	1937		Luton Town	6	0	0	0	0	0	0	0
Clarke	CJ	Colin	30/10/62	Newry		1988	1989	Southampton	Portsmouth	46	7	3	0	11	2	1	0
Clarke	FJ	Frank	15/07/42	Willenhall		1967	1969	Shrewsbury Town	Ipswich Town	67	4	5	0	17	2	5	0
Clarke	GB	George	24/07/00	Bolsover	1977	1933		Crystal Palace	Folkstone	15	0	0	1	6	0	0	0
Clayton	HL	Horace		Holland Park		1920	1921			6	0	0	0	1	0	0	0
Clayton	L	Lew	07/06/24	Royston		1950	1953	Barnsley	Bournemouth	91	2	0	0	5	0	0	0
Clement	DT	Dave	02/02/48	Battersea	1982	1966	1978	Jnrs.	Bolton Wanderers	407	29	34	6	21	3	3	1
Cockburn	WO	Bill	1899	Willington Quay	1958	1928	1929	Liverpool	Swindon Town	57	5	0	0	0	0	0	0
Cockell	DJ	Dave	01/02/39	Ashford		1960	1961	Hounslow	Crawley Town	9	1	1	0	0	0	0	0
Coggins	WH	Billy	16/09/01	Bristol	1958	1935		Everton	Bath City	6	0	0	0	0	0	0	0
Colgan	W	Wally	03/04/37	Castleford		1957	1958	Ashley Road		3	0	0	0	0	0	0	0
Collier	JC	Jock	01/02/1897	Dysart	1940	1926	1927	Hull City	York City	36	1	0	0	1	0	0	0
Collins	JH	Jimmy	30/01/11	Bermondsey	1983	1931	1932	Tooting	Tunbridge Wells	22	0	0	0	4	0	0	0
Collins	JW	John	10/08/42	Chiswick		1959	1966	Jnrs.	Oldham Athletic	172	15	6	0	46	6	4	0
Coney	DH	Dean	18/09/63	Dagenham		1987	1988	Fulham	Norwich City	48	5	6	3	7	0	0	2
Connor	R	Robert	1913	Newcastle		1934			Yeovil & Petters	5	0	0	1	0	0	0	0
Cooper	GJ	Gary	20/11/65	Edgware		1984			Fisher Athletic	1	0	2	1	0	0	0	0
Coward	WC	Billy		Windsor		1927	1931	Windsor & Eton	Walsall	126	12	0	0	24	4	0	0
Crawford	JF	Jackie	26/09/1896	Jarrow	1975	1934	1936	Chelsea	Retired	53	2	0	4	15	1	0	2
Cribb	SR	Stan	11/05/05	Gosport	1989	1931		West Ham Utd.	Cardiff City	28	4	0	0	12	6	0	0
Crickson	GE	Gerry	21/09/34	Dover		1952	1955	Jnrs.	Dover	5	1	0	0	0	0	0	0
Crompton	N	Norman	1905	Farnworth		1927		Oldham Athletic	Horwich RMI	1	0	0	0	0	0	0	0
Cunningham	J	Joey	1905	Lochie		1926	1931	Newport County	Walsall	168	6	0	0	0	0	0	0
Cunningham	TE	Tommy	07/12/55	Bethnal Green		1976	1978	Chelsea	Wimbledon	30	3	2	0	2	0	0	0
Currie	AW	Tony	01/01/50	Edgware		1979	1982	Leeds United	Vancouver W'caps	81	9	8	0	5	0	1	0
Dand	R	Robert		Ilford		1924		Reading	Margate	1	0	0	0	0	0	0	0
Daniels	AWC	Arthur		Mossley		1930		Watford		14	0	0	0	3	0	0	0
Daniels	HAG	Harry	25/06/20	Kensington		1946	1947		Brighton & Hove A.	14	16	0	0	0	1	0	0
Davidson	PE	Peter	31/10/56	Newcastle		1979		Berwick Rangers	Berwick Rangers	1	0	0	0	0	0	0	0
Davies	E	Eddie	05/06/27	Oswestry		1950		Arsenal	Crewe Alexandra	1	0	0	0	1	0	0	0
Davis	AG	Arthur	1892	Birmingham	1955	1922	1923	Aston Villa	Notts County	62	5	0	0	21	1	0	0
Dawes	IR	Ian	22/02/63	Croydon		1981	1987	App.	Millwall	229	8	28	5	3	0	1	0
Dawson	A	Alec	23/10/33	Glasgow		1956	1958	Gourock Jnrs.	Sittingbourne	59	5	0	3	5	2	0	0
Dawson	G	George	13/09/30	Glasgow		1955		Motherwell		1	0	0	0	0	0	0	0
Dean	J	Joby	25/11/34	Chesterfield		1955	1956	Thoresby Col.	Sutton Town	16	1	0	0	0	0	0	0
Delve	JF	John	27/09/53	Isleworth		1972	1973	App.	Plymouth Argyle	15	1	1	0	0	0	0	0
Dennis	ME	Mark	02/05/61	Streatham		1987	1988	Southampton	Crystal Palace	28	2	2	4	0	0	0	0
Devine	J	Joe	08/09/05	Motherwell	1980	1933	1934	Sunderland	Birmingham	57	6	0	2	9	1	0	0
Devine	J	John		Aberdeen		1938				7	0	0	1	3	0	0	0
Dichio	DS	Danny	19/10/74	London		1994	1995			39	2	4	0	13	0	2	0
Dobinson	H	Harry	02/03/1898	Darlington		1923		Burnley		2	0	0	0	0	0	0	0
Donald	DM	Davie	29/12/1878	Coatbridge	1932	1920		Watford	Hamilton	22	4	0	0	0	0	0	0
Doyle	M	Maurice	17/10/69	Ellesmere Port		1992	1993	Crewe Alexandra	Millwall	6	0	0	0	0	0	0	0
Drabble	F	Frank	08/07/1888	Southport	1964	1923		Southport	Retired	2	0	0	0	0	0	0	0
Drew	WA	William				1926		Barnet		1	0	0	0	0	0	0	0
Drinkwater	R	Ray	18/05/31	Jarrow		1957	1962	Portsmouth	Bath City	199	12	3	1	0	0	0	0
Dudley	RA	Reg	03/02/15	Hemel Hempstead		1946	1949	Millwall	Watford	58	4	0	0	0	0	0	0
Duffield	MJ	Martin	28/02/64	Park Royal		1982		App.	Enfield	1	0	0	0	0	0	0	0
Dugdale	JR	Jimmy	15/01/32	Liverpool		1962		Aston Villa	Retired	10	3	0	0	0	0	0	0th.

Player			D.O.B	Place of Birth	Died	First Lge Season	Last Lge Season	Previous Club	Next Club	Appearances				Goals			
										League	FAC	FLC	Other	League	FAC	FLC	Oth.
Duggan	EJ	Ted	27/07/22	West Ham		1948	1950	Luton Town	Worcester City	47	1	0	0	5	0	0	0
Durrant	FH	Fred	19/06/21	Dover		1946	1948	Brentford	Exeter City	51	2	0	0	26	0	0	0
Duthie	JF	John	07/01/03	Fraserburgh		1927		Norwich City	York City	11	0	0	0	0	0	0	0
Dutton	T	Tommy	11/11/06	Southport	1982	1934		Leicester City	Doncaster Rovers	23	1	0	2	6	0	0	0
Dykstra	S	Sieb	20/10/66	Kerkrade, Holland		1994		Motherwell		11	0	1	0	0	0	0	0
Eastoe	PR	Peter	02/08/53	Tamworth		1976	1978	Swindon Town	Everton	72	3	8	2	15	0	5	0
Eaton	F	Frank	12/11/02	Stockport	1979	1933		Reading		15	2	0	2	2	0	0	0
Edgley	HH	Harold	1892	Crewe	1966	1921	1922	Aston Villa	Stockport Co.	69	6	0	0	6	0	0	0
Edwards	JH	Joseph				1925				3	0	0	0	0	0	0	0
Eggleton	JAE	Jimmy	29/08/1897	Heston	1963	1926	1928	Watford	(Trainer)	42	1	0	0	0	0	0	0
Elsey	KW	Karl	20/11/58	Swansea		1978	1979	Pembroke Borough	Newport County	7	0	0	0	0	0	0	0
Embleton	SW	Sid	1906	Poplar		1930			Walthamstow Ave.	2	0	0	0	0	0	0	0
Emmerson	GAH	George	15/05/06	Bishop Auckland	1966	1933	1934	Cardiff City	Rochdale	52	5	0	3	13	3	0	0
Evans	B	Bernard	04/01/37	Chester		1960	1962	Wrexham	Oxford United	78	4	2	0	35	4	0	0
Evans	C	Charles		Luton		1929				1	0	0	0	0	0	0	0
Evans	IP	Ian	30/01/52	Egham		1970	1973	App.	Crystal Palace	39	0	3	0	2	0	0	0
Evans	WB	Billy		Llanglos		1924			Southend Utd.	17	0	0	0	0	0	0	0
Falco	MP	Mark	22/10/60	Hackney		1987	1990	Glasgow Rangers	Millwall	87	10	6	3	27	2	4	0
Fallon	PD	Peter	19/10/22	Dublin		1953		Exeter City	Retired	1	0	0	0	0	0	0	0
Farmer	A	Alec	09/10/09	Lochgelly		1933	1937	Yeovil & Petters	Ass. trainer	79	4	0	8	10	0	0	0
Farrow	DA	Des	11/02/26	Peterborough		1948	1952	Leicester City	Stoke City	118	12	0	0	7	0	0	0
Faulkner	R	Robert		Glasgow		1920	1921	Blackburn Rovers	South Shields	50	2	0	0	1	0	0	0
Fenwick	H	Harrison		Ashington		1924			Shildon	19	0	0	0	0	0	0	0
Fenwick	TW	Terry	17/11/59	Camden, Co Durham		1980	1987	Crystal Palace	Tottenham H	256	18	29	5	33	6	6	0
Ferdinand	L	Les	18/12/66	Paddington		1986	1994	Hayes	Newcastle United	162	7	13	1	80	3	7	0
Fereday	W	Wayne	16/06/63	Warley		1980	1988	App.	Newcastle United	196	13	27	6	21	0	3	1
Ferguson	C	Chris		Kirkconnel		1930		Chelsea	Wrexham	15	0	0	0	1	0	0	0
Ferguson	MK	Mike	09/03/43	Burnley		1969	1972	Aston Villa	Cambridge Utd.	68	6	3	0	2	1	0	0
Fidler	TG	Tommy	04/09/33	Hounslow		1954		Hounslow	Dover	12	2	0	0	2	2	0	0
Field	WH	William		Oxford		1923	1925	Oxford City		29	0	0	0	0	0	0	0
Fillery	MC	Mike	17/09/60	Mitcham		1983	1986	Chelsea	Portsmouth	97	5	11	4	9	0	1	0
Finch	RJ	Bobby	24/08/48	Camberwell	1978	1967	1968	App.	Durban City(SA)	5	0	1	0	0	0	0	0
Finney	CW	Bill	05/09/31	Stoke-on-Trent		1957		Birmingham City	Crewe Alexandra	10	0	0	0	1	0	0	0
Fitzgerald	AM	Alf	25/01/11	Conisbrough	1981	1936	1938	Reading	Aldershot	94	5	0	4	43	7	0	2
Flanagan	MA	Mike	09/11/52	Ilford		1980	1983	Crystal Palace	Charlton Ath.	78	12	3	0	20	0	2	0
Fleming	MJ	Mark	11/08/69	Hammersmith		1987	1988	YTS	Brentford	3	1	0	1	0	0	0	0
Fletcher	J	Jack	1910	Tyne Dock		1935		Bournemouth	Clapton Orient	21	0	0	0	0	0	0	0
Ford	E	Ewart		Bedworth		1924	1925	Hinckley United	Merthyr Town	55	9	0	0	4	0	0	0
Foster	CJ	Cyril		Aylesbury		1928	1929	Watford		5	0	0	0	0	0	0	0
Francis	GCJ	Gerry	06/12/51	Chiswick		1968	1978	App.	Crystal Palace	312	18	21	1	57	1	5	2
						1980	1981	Crystal Palace	Coventry City								
Francis	GE	George	04/02/34	Acton		1961		Brentford	Brentford	2	0	1	0	1	0	2	0
Francis	TJ	Trevor	19/04/54	Plymouth		1987	1989	Glasgow Rangers	Sheffield Wed.	32	1	8	1	12	0	3	0
Fry	RP	Bob	29/06/35	Pontypridd		1957		Bath City	Bexleyheath & W.	1	0	0	1	0	0	0	0
Gallen	KA	Kevin	21/09/75	Chiswick		1994	1995	Jnrs.		67	4	4	0	18	1	2	0
Gardner	W	Wally	07/06/1893	Langley Moor		1922		Spennymoor U	Ashington	2	0	0	0	0	0	0	0
Gibbons	JR	John	08/04/25	Charlton		1948		Dartford	Ipswich Town	8	0	0	0	2	0	0	0
Gibbs	DW	Derek	22/12/34	Fulham		1963	1964	Leyton Orient	Romford	27	2	0	0	0	0	0	0
Gilberg	H	Harry	27/06/23	Tottenham		1951	1952	Tottenham H	Brighton & Hove A.	66	4	0	0	12	0	0	0
Gilfillan	JE	John	29/9/1898	Townhill		1937		Portsmouth		21	2	0	1	0	0	0	0
Gilhooley	M	Mike	26/11/1896	Glencraig		1927		Bradford City		9	0	0	0	0	0	0	0
Gillard	IT	Ian	09/10/50	Hammersmith		1968	1981	App.	Aldershot	408	36	32	8	9	1	1	0
Gilmore	HP	Patrick 'Mike'				1938		Bournemouth	Hull City	6	1	0	3	0	0	0	0
Givens	DJ	Don	09/08/49	Limerick		1972	1977	Luton Town	Birmingham City	242	24	20	8	77	10	7	7
Glover	AR	Alan	21/10/50	Laleham		1968		App.	West Bromwich A.	6	1	0	0	0	0	0	0
Goddard	G	George	20/12/03	Gomshall	1987	1926	1933	Redhill	Brentford	243	16	0	0	174	12	0	0
Goddard	P	Paul	12/10/59	Harlington		1977	1979	App.	West Ham Utd.	70	0	5	0	23	0	0	0
Gofton	G	George	28/02/12	Hartlepool	1990	1932		Newcastle United		7	4	0	0	8	0	0	0
Golding	NJ	Jimmy	23/01/37	Southwark		1959	1960	Tonbridge	Kettering Town	30	1	0	1	6	0	0	0
Goodier	E	Ted	15/10/02	Farnworth	1967	1931	1934	Oldham Athletic	Watford	139	13	0	4	2	0	0	0
Goodman	WR	William	1894	Islington		1923				1	0	0	0	0	0	0	0
Goodridge	GRS	Gregory	10/7/1971	Barbados		1995		Torquay United	Bristol City	7	1	1	0	1	0	0	0
Gough	CWM	Claude		Llandrindod Wells		1926		Clapton Orient	Torquay United	19	0	0	0	0	0	0	0
Gould	HL	Harry		London		1920		Met. Police		2	0	0	0	0	0	0	0
Graham	M	Malcolm	26/01/34	Wakefield		1963		Leyton Orient	Barnsley	21	1	1	0	7	1	0	0
Grant	GM	George	1891	Plumstead		1920	1921	Millwall		69	3	0	0	1	0	0	0
Gray	AA	Andy	22/02/64	Lambeth		1988		Aston Villa	Crystal Palace	11	0	0	0	2	0	0	0
Gregory	C	Clarence		Birmingham		1922		Sunderland	Yeovil & Petters	24	0	0	0	1	0	0	0
Gregory	J	Jack		Birmingham		1920	1922	Willenhall Swifts	Yeovil & Petters(p/m)	112	12	0	0	21	4	0	0
Gregory	JC	John	11/05/54	Scunthorpe		1981	1985	Brighton & Hove A.	Derby County	161	9	16	4	36	1	5	1
Gretton	T	Tommy		Walsall		1929		Wolves	Walsall	4	0	0	0	0	0	0	0
Grimsdell	EF	Ernie	1892	Watford	1947	1920		Watford	Guildford Utd.	22	1	0	0	0	0	0	0
						1922		Guildford Utd.	Dartford								
Gullan	SK	Stan	26/01/26	Edinburgh		1950	1954	Clyde	Tunbridge Wells	48	0	0	0	0	0	0	0
Haley	WT	Bill	16/02/04	Bexleyheath	1960	1931		Fulham	Dartford	17	0	0	0	5	0	0	0
Hall	EW	Ernie		Barndale, Coventry		1931	1932	Bedworth Town	Chester	62	9	0	0	0	0	0	0
Hamilton	JE	John		Nottingham		1926		Blackpool		10	0	0	0	0	0	0	0
Hamilton	WR	Billy	09/05/57	Belfast		1978	1979	Linfield	Burnley	12	1	0	0	2	0	0	0
Hammond	JH	Joe	1909	West Ham		1933	1935	London P.M.		18	1	0	2	6	0	0	1

90

Player			D.O.B	Place of Birth	Died	First Lge Season	Last Lge Season	Previous Club	Next Club	Appearances				Goals			
										League	FAC	FLC	Other	League	FAC	FLC	Oth.
Harkouk	RP	Rachid	19/05/56	Chelsea		1978	1979	Crystal Palace	Notts County	20	1	3	0	3	0	0	0
Harris	AJ	Allan	28/12/42	Hackney		1967	1970	Chelsea	Plymouth Argyle	94	1	3	0	0	0	0	0
Harris	B	Bernie	14/3/1899	Sheffield		1929	1931	Luton Town	Swindon Town	60	7	0	0	0	0	0	0
Harris	GT	George	1898	High Wycombe		1924	1925	Notts County	Fulham	38	5	0	0	0	0	0	0
Harris	N	Neil	09/02/20	Glasgow		1946			Swansea Town	1	1	0	0	1	1	0	0
Harrison	JH	Jim	31/07/28	Hammersmith		1952				6	0	0	0	1	0	0	0
Hart	E	Ernie		Huddersfield		1922		Folkestone	Guildford United	5	0	0	0	2	0	0	0
Hart	G	George		Gosforth		1923	1924	Bedlington Col.	Durham City	8	0	0	0	1	0	0	0
Hartburn	J	Johnny	20/12/20	Houghton-le-Spring		1947	1948	Yeovil Town	Watford	58	6	0	0	11	2	0	0
Hasty	PJ	Paddy	17/03/32	Belfast		1959		Leyton Orient	Tooting & Mitcham	1	0	0	0	0	0	0	0
Hateley	MW	Mark	07/11/61	Liverpool		1995		Glasgow Rangers		14	1	1	0	2	0	0	0
Hatton	C	Cyril	14/09/18	Grantham	1987	1946	1952	Notts County	Chesterfield	162	15	0	0	64	7	0	0
Hawkins	BW	Bert	29/09/23	Bristol		1953		West Ham Utd.	Cheltenham Town	8	0	0	0	3	0	0	0
Hawley	FW	Fred	28/7/1890	Derby	1954	1926	1927	Brighton & Hove A.	Loughboro Corin.	29	0	0	0	1	0	0	0
Hazell	AP	Tony	19/09/47	High Wycombe		1964	1974	Jnrs.	Millwall	369	18	28	0	4	0	1	0
Hazell	R	Bob	14/06/59	Kingston, Jamaica		1979	1983	Wolves	Leicester City	106	6	12	0	8	1	0	0
Heath	WJ	Bill	26/06/20	Stepney		1946	1952		Dover	96	8	0	0	3	0	0	0
Heathcote	W	Wilf	29/06/11	Hemsworth		1946			Millwall	5	3	0	0	1	1	0	0
Hebden	GHR	George	02/06/00	West Ham	1973	1925	1929	Leicester City	Gillingham	60	4	0	0	0	0	0	0
Hellawell	MS	Mike	30/06/38	Keighley		1955	1956	Salts	Birmingham City	45	3	0	2	7	1	0	0
Herrera	R	Roberto	12/06/70	Torquay		1988	1991	YTS	Fulham	8	0	3	2	0	0	0	0
Higgins	RV	Ron	14/02/23	Silvertown		1952		Brighton & Hove A.	Sittingbourne	3	0	0	0	1	0	0	0
Hill	CJ	Charlie'Midge'	06/09/18	Cardiff		1948	1949	Torquay United	Swindon Town	21	0	0	0	1	0	0	0
Hill	GA	Gordon	01/04/54	Sunbury		1979	1980	Derby County	Montreal Manic	14	1	1	0	1	0	0	0
Hill	J	Joe	1906	Sheffield		1932		Barnsley	Stockport Co.	15	1	0	0	1	0	0	0
Hill	LG	Len	15/2/1899	Islington	1979	1920	1924	Southend United	Southampton	162	14	0	0	0	0	0	0
Hill	WL	William	09/06/30	Uxbridge		1951		Uxbridge	Ramsgate	10	1	0	0	1	0	0	0
Hirst	H	Henry	24/10/1899	Horbury	1925			Preston NE	Charlton Ath.	26	4	0	0	0	1	0	0
Hodge	SB	Steve	25/10/62	Nottingham		1994		Leeds United	Watford	6	0	0	0	0	0	0	0
Hold	O	Oscar	19/10/18	Carlton, West Yorks		1951	1952	Everton	March Town (p/m)	5	0	0	0	1	0	0	0
Hollins	JW	John	16/07/46	Guildford		1975	1978	Chelsea	Arsenal	151	11	13	8	6	1	0	0
Holloway	IS	Ian	12/03/63	Kingswood		1991	1995	Bristol Rovers	Bristol Rovers	147	8	13	2	4	1	0	0
Hooper	H	Harry	1900	Brierley Hill		1926		Leicester City		16	0	0	0	0	0	0	0
Hoten	RV	Ralph	27/12/1896	Pinxton	1978	1930		Northampton Town		9	0	0	0	4	0	0	0
Howe	EJ	Ernie	15/02/53	Chiswick		1977	1981	Fulham	Portsmouth	89	12	5	0	3	3	0	0
Howe	HG	Harold	09/04/06	Hemel Hempstead	1976	1929	1932	Watford	Crystal Palace	69	6	0	0	13	1	0	0
Hucker	PI	Peter	28/10/59	Hampstead		1980	1985	App.	Oxford United	160	11	13	4	0	0	0	0
Hudson	SR	Stan	10/02/23	Fulham	1951	1948	1949			22	1	0	0	7	0	0	0
Hunt	RG	Ron	19/12/45	Paddington		1964	1972	App.	Retired	219	15	22	0	1	0	0	0
Hurrell	WP	Willie	28/01/20	Dundee		1953		Millwall	Tunbridge Wells	6	3	0	0	1	2	0	0
Hurst	W	Bill		Newcastle		1923	1924	Derby County		10	0	0	0	4	0	0	0
Impey	AR	Andy	30/09/71	Hammersmith		1991	1995	Yeading		155	8	13	2	11	1	2	1
Ingham	A	Tony	18/02/25	Harrogate		1950	1962	Leeds United	(comm. mgr.)	514	30	4	7	3	0	0	0
Iorfa	D	Dominic	01/10/68	Lagos, Nigeria		1989	1991	Standard Liege	Galatasary	8	0	1	0	0	0	0	0
Jacks	GC	George	14/03/46	Stepney		1964		App.	Millwall	1	0	0	0	0	0	0	0
James	L	Leighton	16/02/53	Loughor		1977	1978	Derby County	Burnley	28	5	0	0	4	2	0	0
James	NL	Norman	25/03/08	Bootle	1985	1936	1938	Bradford City		68	5	0	3	1	0	0	0
James	RM	Robbie	23/03/57	Gorseinon		1984	1986	Stoke City	Leicester City	87	5	9	0	5	1	0	0
Jefferson	A	Arthur	14/12/16	Goldthorpe		1936	1949	Peterborough U	Aldershot	211	33	0	5	1	0	0	0
Jobson	JT	Jack	08/08/03	Washington		1932		Stockport Co.	Gateshead	4	0	0	0	0	0	0	0
John	R	Reg	22/8/1899	Aberdare		1920	1925	Aberdare Ath.	Charlton Ath.	131	14	0	0	1	0	0	0
Johns	NP	Nicky	08/06/57	Bristol		1987	1988	Charlton Ath.	Maidstone Utd.	10	3	2	1	0	0	0	0
Johnson	HE	Harry	1901	Birmingham		1923	1925	Southampton	Cradley Heath	50	5	0	0	15	0	0	0
Johnson	JH	Jack	28/5/1897	Bristol	1974	1927	1928	Swindon Town	Cradley Heath	18	1	0	0	7	1	0	0
Jones	CH	Charlie	1911	Swansea		1932	1933	Southend		16	0	0	0	1	0	0	0
Keen	JF	James	25/11/1897	Walker	1980	1923		Newcastle United	Hull City	31	1	0	0	0	0	0	0
Keen	MT	Mike	19/03/40	High Wycombe		1959	1968	Jnrs.	Luton Town	393	25	22	0	39	2	4	0
Keetch	RD	Bobby	25/10/41	Tottenham		1966	1968	Fulham	Durban City	52	2	2	0	0	0	0	0
Kellard	T	Tom	1905	Oldham		1927	1928	Oldham Athletic	Burton Town	5	0	0	0	1	0	0	0
Kelly	EP	Eddie	07/02/51	Glasgow		1976		Arsenal	Leicester City	28	0	3	2	1	0	0	0
Kelly	MJ	Mike	18/10/42	Northampton		1966	1969	Wimbledon	Birmingham City	54	5	5	0	0	0	0	0
Kelly	WB	Brian	25/09/37	Isleworth		1958		Dover	Bexleyheath & W.	6	0	0	0	0	0	0	0
Kerr	A	Andy		Falkirk		1925		Reading		2	0	0	0	0	0	0	0
Kerrins	PM	Pat	13/09/30	Fulham		1953	1959	Jnrs.	Crystal Palace	146	9	0	3	30	0	0	1
Kerslake	D	David	19/06/66	Stepney		1984	1989	App.	Swindon Town	58	4	8	4	6	0	4	0
King	AE	Andy	14/08/56	Luton		1980	1981	Everton	West Bromwich A.	30	2	1	0	9	0	0	0
Knight	FC	Fred				1921				2	0	0	0	1	0	0	0
Knowles	F	Frank	1891	Hyde		1923	1924	Newport County		35	5	0	0	0	0	0	0
Lane	HW	Harry	23/10/1894	Stoney Stanton		1922		Charlton Ath.		5	0	0	0	0	0	0	0
Langford	W	Walter		Wolverhampton		1933	1934	Leicester City	Wellington T	11	1	0	1	0	0	0	0
Langley	EJ	Jimmy	07/02/29	Kilburn		1965	1966	Fulham	Hillingdon Boro(p/m)	87	8	10	0	9	1	1	0
Langley	TW	Tommy	08/02/58	Lambeth		1980		Chelsea	Crystal Palace	25	0	3	0	8	0	1	0
Large	F	Frank	26/01/40	Leeds		1962		Halifax Town	Northampton Town	18	3	1	0	5	2	0	0
Law	BJ	Brian	01/01/70	Merthyr Tydfil		1987	1990	YTS	Wolves	20	3	3	1	0	0	0	0
Lay	PJ	Peter	04/12/31	Stratford		1956		Nottm. Forest	King's Lynn	1	0	0	0	0	0	0	0
Lazarus	M	Mark	05/12/38	Stepney		1960	1961	Leyton Orient	Wolves	206	14	15	0	76	3	5	0
						1961	1963	Wolves	Brentford								
						1965	1967	Brentford	Crystal Palace								
Leach	JM	Jimmy	1898	Spennymoor	1951	1922		Aston Villa		1	0	0	0	0	0	0	0

Player			D.O.B	Place of Birth	Died	First Lge Season	Last Lge Season	Previous Club	Next Club	Appearances				Goals			
										League	FAC	FLC	Other	League	FAC	FLC	Oth.
Leach	MJC	Mick	16/01/47	Clapton	1992	1964	1977	App.	Detroit Express	313	23	19	6	61	3	6	0
Leary	SE	Stuart	30/04/33	Cape Town, SA	1988	1962	1965	Charlton Ath.	Retired	94	7	3	0	29	3	0	0
Lee	S	Sammy	07/02/59	Liverpool		1986		Liverpool	Osasuna	30	3	2	0	0	1	0	0
Legge	AE	Albert	19/06/01	Hednesford		1930		Charlton Ath.		9	0	0	0	1	0	0	0
Lennon	AV	Alex	23/10/25	Glasgow		1948		Rotherham Utd.	Mansfield Town	1	0	0	0	0	0	0	0
Lewis	JW	Jim		Hammersmith		1930	1931	Walthamstow Ave.	Walthamstow Ave.	12	0	0	0	4	0	0	0
Lillie	J	John		Newcastle		1924		Liverpool	Clapton Orient	3	0	0	0	0	0	0	0
Lock	H	Herbert	22/1/1887	Southampton	1957	1921		Glasgow Rangers	Bournemouth	6	0	0	0	0	0	0	0
Locke	LC	Les	24/01/34	Perth		1958	1959	Bromley	Guildford City	76	3	0	3	24	2	0	3
Lofthouse	J	Jimmy	24/03/1894	St Helens		1926	1927	Bristol Rovers	Aldershot	80	1	0	0	27	0	0	0
Longbottom	A	Arthur	30/01/33	Leeds		1954	1960	Methley United	Port Vale	201	11	0	4	62	5	0	1
Lowe	HP	Harry		Kingskettle		1935	1938	Watford	Guildford City	158	10	0	4	40	0	0	1
Lumsden	FL	Frank		Sunderland		1935	1936	Huddersfield T	Burnley	38	1	0	1	8	0	0	0
Maddix	DS	Danny	11/10/67	Ashford		1987	1995	Tottenham H.		188	20	17	5	7	2	2	0
Maguire	GT	Gavin	24/11/67	Hammersmith		1986	1988	App.	Portsmouth	40	6	3	0	0	0	0	0
Malcolm	A	Andy	04/05/33	West Ham		1962	1964	Chelsea	Port Elizabeth	84	8	2	0	5	1	0	0
Mallett	J	Joe	08/01/16	Gateshead		1937	1946	Charlton Ath.	Southampton	70	18	0	3	11	4	0	0
Mancini	TJ	Terry	04/10/42	St Pancras		1971	1974	Orient	Arsenal	94	12	5	0	3	2	0	0
Manning	JT	Jack	1886	Boston	1946	1920		Rotherham Utd.	Boston	22	2	0	0	5	0	0	0
March	R	Dickie	09/10/08	Washington	1987	1932	1938	Crawcrook Alb.	(catering mgr.)	220	14	0	7	3	0	0	0
Marcroft	EH	Ted	1910	Rochdale		1932		Middlesbrough	Cardiff City	29	4	0	0	8	1	0	0
Marsden	B	Ben		Hanley		1920	1924	Port Vale	Reading	126	6	0	0	6	0	0	0
Marsh	RW	Rodney	11/10/44	Hatfield		1965	1971	Fulham	Manchester City	211	11	20	0	106	8	20	0
Mason	WS	Bill	31/10/08	Earlsfield	1995	1933	1938	Fulham	Retired	154	6	0	10	0	0	0	0
Masson	DS	Don	26/08/46	Banchory		1974	1977	Notts County	Derby County	116	8	12	8	18	1	3	2
McAdams	WJ	Billy	20/01/34	Belfast		1964	1965	Brentford	Barrow	33	3	2	0	11	1	0	0
McAllister	W	Billy		Glasgow		1926		Middlesbrough	Raith Rovers	26	0	0	0	1	0	0	0
McCarthy	AJ	Alan	11/01/72	Wandsworth		1988	1994	YTS	Leyton Orient	11	1	0	2	0	0	0	0
McCarthy	LD	Len		Caerau		1937	1938	Portsmouth		22	4	0	1	9	1	0	1
McClelland	JB	John	05/03/35	Bradford		1961	1962	Lincoln City	Portsmouth	71	7	1	0	22	2	0	0
McCreery	D	David	16/09/57	Belfast		1979	1980	Manchester Utd.	Tulsa Roughnecks	57	2	8	0	4	0	1	0
McCulloch	A	Andy	03/01/50	Northampton		1970	1972	Walton & Hersham	Cardiff City	42	1	4	0	10	0	1	0
McDonald	A	Alan	12/10/63	Belfast		1983	1995	App.		363	30	40	5	11	1	3	0
McEwan	W	Billy	29/08/14	Glasgow	1991	1938	1949	Petershill	Leyton Orient	96	12	0	2	17	3	0	0
McGee	PG	Paul	19/06/54	Dublin		1977	1978	Sligo Rovers	Preston NE	39	2	3	0	7	0	1	0
McGovern	MJ	Mick	15/02/51	Hayes		1967	1971	App.	Swindon Town	12	1	0	0	0	0	0	0
McGovern	T	Tom		Glasgow		1920		Brentford		2	0	0	0	0	0	0	0
McKay	J	Johnny	27/06/27	Port Glasgow		1949	1951	Irvine	Yeovil Town	17	0	0	0	1	0	0	0
McKay	W	Billy	10/03/27	Rothesay		1955		Deal Town	Dover	6	0	0	0	0	0	0	0
McLeod	GJ	George	30/11/32	Inverness		1963	1964	Brentford	South Africa	41	0	1	0	4	0	0	0
McLintock	F	Frank	28/12/39	Glasgow		1973	1976	Arsenal	Leicester City(mgr.)	127	14	14	8	5	0	1	0
McMahon	HJ	Hugh	24/09/09	Grangetown	1986	1936	1937	Reading	Sunderland	41	3	0	1	3	1	0	1
McNab	JS	Jock	17//4/1895	Cleland	1949	1928	1929	Liverpool	Retired	54	5	0	0	2	0	0	0
McQuade	TJ	Terry	24/02/41	Hackney		1963	1964	Millwall	Leyton Orient	20	3	2	0	2	0	0	0
Meaker	MJ	Michael	18/08/71	Greenford		1990	1994	YTS	Reading	34	3	2	1	1	1	1	0
Metchick	DJ	Dave	14/08/43	Bakewell		1968	1969	Peterborough Utd.	Arsenal	3	0	1	0	1	0	0	0
Micklewhite	G	Gary	21/03/61	Southwark		1981	1984	Manchester Utd.	Derby County	106	6	13	2	11	1	5	0
Middlemiss	H	Bert	19/12/1888	Newcastle	1941	1920		Tottenham H	Retired	16	0	0	0	1	0	0	0
Middleton	J	Jack	19/4/1898	Sunderland	1974	1925	1926	Leicester City	Aldershot	54	0	0	0	9	0	0	0
Millbank	JH	Joe	30/09/19	Edmonton		1948		Crystal Palace	Bedford Town	1	0	0	0	0	0	0	0
Mills	DG	Don	17/08/26	Rotherham	1994	1946	1948		Torquay United	76	3	0	0	9	3	0	0
						1949	1950	Torquay United	Cardiff City								
Mitchell	AP	Archie	15/12/1885	Smethwick	1949	1920		Aston Villa	Brentford	35	24	0	1	3	1	0	0
Mobley	VJ	Vic	11/10/43	Oxford		1969	1970	Sheffield Wed.	(youth coach)	25	3	3	0	0	0	0	0
Moffatt	H	Hugh	1900	Camerton		1929		Walsall		15	0	0	0	3	0	0	0
Molloy	P	Peter 'Paddy'	1909	Haslingden	1993	1935		Cardiff City	Stockport Co.	3	0	0	0	0	0	0	0
Moore	J	Jimmy	01/09/1891	Felling		1924		Halifax Town	Crewe Alexandra	26	0	0	0	5	0	0	0
Moralee	WE	Bill	03/05/06	Crook	1967	1936	1937	Bournemouth		22	0	0	1	0	0	0	0
Morgan	IA	Ian	14/11/46	Walthamstow		1964	1972	App.	Watford	173	6	11	0	26	1	1	0
Morgan	RE	Roger	14/11/46	Walthamstow		1964	1968	App.	Tottenham H	180	13	13	0	39	1	4	0
Mortimore	JH	John	23/09/34	Farnborough		1965		Chelsea	Sunderland	10	0	0	0	0	0	0	0
Moughton	CE	Colin	30/12/47	Harrow		1965	1966	App.	Colchester Utd.	6	0	0	0	0	0	0	0
Mountford	GF	George	30/03/21	Stoke-on-Trent		1952	1953	Stoke City	Hereford United	35	3	0	0	2	0	0	0
Muir	IJ	Ian	05/05/63	Coventry		1980		App.	Birmingham C	2	0	0	0	2	0	0	0
Muir	WM	Billy	27/08/25	Ayr		1948	1952	Irvine	Torquay United	17	0	0	0	4	0	0	0
Murdin	SH	Steve				1925				1	0	0	0	0	0	0	0
Murray	P	Paul	31/8/1976	Carlisle		1995		Carlisle United		1	0	0	0	0	0	0	0
Mustard	J	Jack	1905	Boldon		1926	1927	Crawcrook Albion	South Shields	37	1	0	0	4	0	0	0
Myers	EC	Colin	1901	Chapeltown		1924		Northampton Town	Exeter City	17	5	0	0	3	7	0	0
Nash	RG	Bobby	08/02/46	Hammersmith		1964		Jnrs.	Exeter City	17	1	0	0	0	0	0	0
Neal	DJ	Dean	05/01/61	Edmonton		1979	1980	App.	Tulsa Roughnecks	22	0	2	0	8	0	1	0
Neary	HF	Frank	06/03/21	Aldershot		1946		Finchley	West Ham Utd.	27	8	0	0	11	5	0	0
						1949		Leyton Orient	Millwall								
Needham	DW	Dave	21/05/49	Leicester		1977		Notts County	Nottm. Forest	18	0	2	0	3	0	0	0
Neil	A	Andy	1896	Kilmarnock		1927	1929	Brighton & Hove A.	Retired	106	6	0	0	1	0	0	0
Neill	WA	Warren	21/11/62	Acton		1980	1987	App.	Portsmouth	181	12	19	3	3	2	1	1
Nelson	D	Dave	03/02/18	Douglas Water	1988	1949	1950	Brentford	Crystal Palace	31	0	0	0	0	0	0	0
Nelson	WE	Bill	20/09/29	Silvertown		1955		West Ham Utd.	Ramsgate Ath.	9	0	0	0	0	0	0	0
Nicholas	CB	Brian	20/04/33	Aberdare		1948	1954	Jnrs.	Chelsea	113	7	0	0	2	0	0	0

Player			D.O.B	Place of Birth	Died	First Lge Season	Last Lge Season	Previous Club	Next Club	Appearances League	FAC	FLC	Other	Goals League	FAC	FLC	Oth.
Nixon	T	Tom		Newcastle		1928	1932	Crawcrook Albion	Crystal Palace	58	0	0	0	1	0	0	0
Nutt	PJ	Phil	18/05/58	Westminster		1975	1976	App.	Hounslow	4	0	0	0	1	0	0	0
O'Brien	MT	Mick	10/8/1893	Kilcock	1940	1920	1921	South Shields	Leicester City	66	4	0	0	3	1	0	0
O'Connor	MA	Mark	10/03/63	Southend-on-Sea		1981	1982	App.	Bristol Rovers	3	0	0	0	0	0	0	0
O'Neill	JP	John	11/03/58	Derry		1987		Leicester City	Norwich City	2	0	0	0	0	0	0	0
O'Rourke	J	John	11/02/45	Northampton		1971	1972	Coventry City	Bournemouth	34	2	1	0	12	0	0	0
Ogley	W	Bill	1896	Rotherham		1924			Newport County	Castleford	36	5	0	0	2	0	0	0
Orr	DM	Doug	08/11/37	Glasgow		1957		Hendon	Hendon	5	0	0	0	0	0	0	0
Osborn	SE	Simon	19/1/72	New Addington		1995		Reading	Wolves	8	0	2	0	1	0	0	0
Ovenstone	DG	Davie	17/06/13	St Monance	1983	1935		Raith Rovers	Cardiff City	15	1	0	0	3	0	0	0
Oxley	RL	Dick	10/4/1893	Barrow	1950	1923		Southport	Northampton Town	18	0	0	0	0	0	0	0
Pape	AM	Andy	22/03/62	Hammersmith		1979		Jnrs.	Ikast (Denmark)	1	0	0	0	0	0	0	0
Parker	PA	Paul	04/04/64	West Ham		1987	1990	Fulham	Manchester Utd.	125	16	14	5	1	0	0	0
Parker	RR	Dick	14/9/1894	Stockton	1969	1922	1923	South Shields	Millwall	61	5	0	0	30	4	0	0
Parkes	PBF	Phil	08/08/50	Sedgley		1970	1978	Walsall	West Ham Utd.	344	27	27	8	0	0	0	0
Parkinson	AA	Alf	30/04/22	Camden Town		1946	1950		Retired	76	3	0	0	5	2	0	0
Parsons	DJ	Derek	24/10/29	Hammersmith		1952			Ashford Town	2	1	0	0	1	0	0	0
Paterson	J	Jock	1904	Fife		1925	1927	Mid Rhondda	Wellesley Jnrs.	36	0	0	0	6	0	0	0
Pattison	JM	Johnny	19/12/18	Glasgow		1937	1949	Motherwell	Leyton Orient	92	15	0	2	26	6	0	0
Peacock	D	Darren	03/02/68	Bristol		1990	1993	Hereford Utd.	Newcastle United	126	3	12	2	6	0	1	0
Peacock	GK	Gavin	18/11/67	Eltham		1986	1987	App.	Gillingham	17	1	0	0	1	0	0	0
Peacock	T	Terry	18/04/35	Hull		1956	1957	Hull City	Sittingbourne	16	1	0	0	4	0	0	0
Pearson	H	Harry	1911	Birkenhead		1938		Coventry City	Barrow	11	3	0	1	1	0	0	0
Pearson	JA	John	23/04/35	Isleworth		1958	1959	Brentford	Kettering Town	21	0	0	0	9	0	0	0
Penrice	GK	Gary	23/03/64	Bristol		1991	1995	Aston Villa	Watford	82	4	7	1	20	1	2	0
Perkins	SA	Steve	03/10/54	Stepney		1977		Chelsea	Wimbledon	2	0	0	0	0	0	0	0
Petchey	GW	George	24/06/31	Whitechapel		1953	1959	West Ham Utd.	Crystal Palace	255	16	0	7	22	2	0	0
Pickett	TR	Tommy	05/02/09	Merthyr Tydfil		1929	1931	Kentish Town	Bristol City	46	6	0	0	0	0	0	0
Pierce	W	Bill	29/10/07	Ashington	1976	1923	1930	Bedlington Col.	Carlisle Utd.	179	14	0	0	2	1	0	0
Pigg	W	Bill	1897	High Spen		1924	1925	Ashington	Carlisle Utd.	21	4	0	0	0	0	0	0
Pinner	MJ	Mike	16/02/34	Boston		1959	1960	Sheffield Wed.	Manchester Utd.	19	2	1	1	0	0	0	0
Pizanti	D	David	27/05/62	Israel		1987	1988	FC Koln		21	4	4	3	0	1	0	0
Plummer	C	Chris	12/10/76	Isleworth		1995		Jnrs.		1	0	0	0	0	0	0	0
Plunkett	AETB	Adam	16/03/03	Blantyre	1992	1925		Bury	Guildford City	15	0	0	0	0	0	0	0
Pointon	WJ	Bill	25/11/20	Hanley		1948	1949	Port Vale	Brentford	26	0	0	0	6	0	0	0
Pollard	R	Bob	25/8/1899	Wigan		1929	1931	Exeter City	Cardiff City	66	7	0	0	0	0	0	0
Poppitt	J	Johnny	20/01/23	West Sleekburn		1950	1953	Derby County	Chelmsford City	106	5	0	0	0	0	0	0
Pounder	AW	Albert	27/07/31	Charlton		1953	1955	Charlton Ath.	Sittingbourne	53	2	0	0	6	0	0	0
Powell	GR	George	11/10/24	Fulham	1989	1947	1952	Fulham	Snowdown Col.	145	10	0	0	0	0	0	0
Powell	IV	Ivor	05/07/16	Bargoed		1938	1948	Bargoed	Aston Villa	110	12	0	2	2	0	0	0
Powell	MP	Mike	18/04/33	Slough		1952	1958	Jnrs.	Yiewsley	105	3	0	0	0	0	0	0
Price	E	Ted		Walsall		1920			Brentford	7	0	0	0	0	0	0	0
Price	LP	Lew	12/8/1896	Caersws	1969	1928		Notts County	Grantham	3	0	0	0	0	0	0	0
Prior	SJ	Stan	20/12/10	Swindon		1937		Charlton Ath.	Cheltenham Town	6	0	0	0	3	0	0	0
Pritchett	KB	Keith	08/11/53	Glasgow		1974		Doncaster Rovers	Brentford	4	0	0	0	0	0	0	0
Quashie	N	Nigel	20/7/78	Nunhead		1995		Jnrs.		11	2	0	0	0	2	0	0
Quigley	T	Tommy	26/03/32	Mid Calder		1956		Portsmouth	Worcester City	16	0	0	1	7	0	0	0
Quinn	GP	Gordon	11/05/32	Hammersmith		1952	1956	Eastcote B.C.	Plymouth Argyle	22	1	0	0	1	0	0	0
Ramscar	FT	Fred	24/01/19	Salford		1947	1949	Wolves	Preston NE	51	6	0	0	4	1	0	0
Ramsey	AP	Alex		Gateshead		1921		Newcastle United	Aberaman Ath.	6	0	0	0	0	0	0	0
Rance	CS	Charlie	28/2/1889	Bow	1966	1922		Tottenham H		13	0	0	0	0	0	0	0
Ready	K	Karl	14/08/72	Neath		1991	1995	YTS		61	1	6	0	3	0	1	0
Reay	EP	Ted	05/08/14	Tynemouth		1937	1949	Sheffield Utd.	(ass. trainer)	34	2	0	3	0	0	0	0
Reed	A	Arthur		Ealing		1921		Tufnell Park	Reading	21	0	0	0	0	0	0	0
Reed	G	Gordon	06/05/13	Spennymoor		1934		Newport County	Darlington	9	0	0	0	4	0	0	0
Reid	P	Peter	20/06/56	Huyton		1988	1989	Everton	Manchester City	29	0	3	0	1	0	0	0
Rhodes	A	Albert	29/04/36	Dinnington		1955	1956	Worksop Town	Tonbridge	5	0	0	0	0	0	0	0
Richardson	AJ	Tony	07/01/32	Southwark		1951		Slough S.C.		2	0	0	0	0	0	0	0
Richardson	DW	Derek	13/07/56	Hackney		1976	1978	Chelsea	Sheffield Utd.	31	0	1	0	0	0	0	0
Richardson	S	Stuart	12/06/38	Leeds		1958		Methley United	Oldham Athletic	1	0	0	0	0	0	0	0
Richmond	H	Hugh		Kilmarnock		1925		Coventry City	Blyth Spartans	10	0	0	0	0	0	0	0
Ridley	JG	John	19/1/03	Mickley		1934		Reading	North Shields	17	1	0	3	0	0	0	0
Ridyard	A	Alf	05/05/08	Cudworth		1937	1947	West Bromwich A.	(trainer)	28	15	0	1	0	0	0	0
Rivers	W	Walter	08/01/09	Throckley		1933		Crystal Palace	Gateshead	3	0	0	1	0	0	0	0
Roberts	AM	Tony	04/08/69	Bangor		1987	1995	YTS		99	7	11	2	0	0	0	0
Roberts	J	Joe	02/10/00	Tranmere	1984	1927		Watford	York City	4	0	0	0	0	0	0	0
Robinson	JW	John		Grangetown		1923		Guildford City		5	0	0	0	1	0	0	0
Robinson	MJ	Michael	12/07/58	Leicester		1984	1986	Liverpool	Osasuna	48	2	8	0	5	0	1	0
Roeder	GV	Glenn	13/12/55	Woodford		1978	1983	Orient	Newcastle United	157	11	13	0	17	0	1	0
Rogers	A	Albert		Manchester		1928	1929	Southall		12	0	0	0	4	0	0	0
Rogers	DE	Don	25/10/45	Paulton		1974		Crystal Palace	Swindon Town	18	1	0	0	5	0	0	0
Rogers	M	Martyn	26/01/60	Nottingham	1992	1979		Manchester Utd.	(Australia)	2	0	0	0	0	0	0	0
Rose	J	Jack	26/10/21	Sheffield		1946	1947	Peterborough U	Retired	17	11	0	0	0	0	0	0
Rosenior	LDeG	Leroy	24/03/64	Clapton		1985	1986	Fulham	Fulham	38	4	5	0	8	0	2	0
Rounce	GA	George	1905	Grays	1936	1927	1932	Uxbridge	Fulham	171	17	0	0	59	12	0	0
Rowe	AJ	Alf		Poplar		1925		Plymouth Argyle		4	0	0	0	1	0	0	0
Rowe	J	Jonty		Packmoor		1935	1936	Reading	Port Vale	52	4	0	0	0	0	0	0
Russell	SEJ	Sid	1911	Feltham		1932	1935	Tunbridge Wells	Northampton Town	42	1	0	2	0	0	0	0
Rutherford	MA	Michael	06/06/72	Sidcup		1989		YTS		2	0	1	0	0	0	0	0

Player			D.O.B	Place of Birth	Died	First Lge Season	Last Lge Season	Previous Club	Next Club	Appearances				Goals			
										League	FAC	FLC	Other	League	FAC	FLC	Oth.
Rutter	KG	Keith	10/09/31	Leeds		1954	1962	Methley United	Colchester Utd.	339	18	5	7	1	0	1	0
Sales	A	Arthur	04/03/00	Lewes	1977	1930	1931	Chelsea	Bournemouth	35	3	0	0	0	0	0	0
Salt	H	Harry		Sheffield		1926		Peterborough U	Grays United	5	0	0	0	0	0	0	0
Salvage	BJ	Barry	21/12/47	Bristol	1986	1970	1972	Millwall	Brentford	21	1	1	0	1	0	0	0
Samuel	DJ	Dan	1911	Swansea		1935		Reading	Barrow	9	0	0	0	3	0	0	0
Sanderson	K	Keith	09/10/40	Hull		1965	1968	Plymouth Argyle	Goole Town	104	9	11	0	10	2	0	0
Sansom	KG	Kenny	26/09/58	Camberwell		1989	1990	Newcastle United	Coventry City	64	10	7	1	0	2	0	0
Saphin	RFE	Reg	08/08/16	Kilburn		1946	1950	Walthamstow Ave.	Watford	30	2	0	0	0	0	0	0
Saul	FL	Frank	23/08/43	Canvey Island		1970	1971	Southampton	Millwall	43	2	5	0	4	0	2	0
Sealy	AJ	Tony	07/05/59	Hackney		1980	1983	Crystal Palace	Fulham	63	1	4	0	18	0	0	0
Seaman	DA	David	19/09/63	Rotherham		1986	1989	Birmingham City	Arsenal	141	17	13	4	0	0	0	0
Seary	RM	Ray	18/09/52	Slough		1971		App.	Cambridge Utd.	1	0	0	0	0	0	0	0
Shanks	D	Don	02/10/52	Hammersmith		1974	1980	Luton Town	Brighton & Hove A.	180	11	14	1	10	1	0	0
Shepherd	E	Ernie	14/08/19	Wombwell		1950	1955	Hull City	Hastings United	219	12	0	1	51	2	0	0
Sheppard	W	Bill	1907	Ferryhill		1930		Watford	Coventry City	13	0	0	0	4	0	0	0
Sibley	FP	Frank	04/12/47	Uxbridge		1963	1970	App.	(coaching staff)	143	10	15	0	3	1	1	0
Silkman	B	Barry	29/06/52	Stepney		1980		Brentford	Orient	23	2	0	0	2	0	0	0
Sinclair	TL	Trevor	02/03/73	Dulwich		1993	1995	Blackpool		102	4	9	0	10	1	3	0
Sinton	A	Andy	19/03/66	Newcastle		1988	1992	Brentford	Sheffield Wed.	160	13	14	3	22	2	0	1
Slack	RG	Rodney	11/04/40	Farcet		1961		Leicester City	Cambridge Utd.	1	0	0	0	0	0	0	0
Smith	AW	Albert	27/08/18	Stoke-on-Trent	1992	1946	1948	Shirley Jnrs.	Sittingbourne	61	7	0	0	2	0	0	0
Smith	EWA	Eddie	23/03/29	London		1957		Colchester Utd.	Chelmsford City	17	1	0	2	1	1	0	0
Smith	FA	Frank	30/04/36	Colchester		1962	1965	Tottenham H	Wimbledon	66	3	2	0	0	0	0	0
Smith	GC	George	23/04/15	Bromley-by-Bow	1983	1947	1948	Brentford	Ipswich Town	75	8	0	0	1	0	0	0
Smith	JW	Jack		Derby		1920	1921	Third Lanark	Swansea Town	75	5	0	0	28	2	0	0
Smith	N(2)	Norman				1937	1938	Charlton Ath.	Chelsea	68	3	0	0	2	0	0	0
Smith	N	Norman	15/12/1897	Newburn	1978	1930	1931	Sheffield Wed.	Retired	26	1	0	0	0	0	0	0
Smith	SC	Steve	27/3/1896	Hednesford	1980	1928		Clapton Orient		24	1	0	0	1	0	0	0
Smith	SR	Stephen				1925		Guildford United	Mansfield Town	2	0	0	0	0	0	0	0
Smith	WC	Conway	13/07/26	Huddersfield		1950	1955	Huddersfield T	Halifax Town	174	6	0	1	81	3	0	0
Sommer	JP	Juergen	22/2/64	New York		1995		Luton Town		33	2	0	0	0	0	0	0
Spackman	NJ	Nigel	02/12/60	Romsey		1988	1989	Liverpool	Glasgow Rangers	29	0	2	2	1	0	1	0
Spence	WJ	Bill	10/01/26	Hartlepool		1951	1953	Portsmouth	Retired	58	4	0	0	0	0	0	0
Spottiswood	J	Joe		Carlisle		1925		Swansea Town		22	0	0	0	2	0	0	0
Spratley	AS	Alan	05/06/49	Maidenhead		1968	1972	App.	Swindon Town	29	2	1	0	0	0	0	0
Springett	PJ	Peter	08/05/46	Fulham		1962	1966	App.	Sheffield Wed.	137	10	13	0	0	0	0	0
Springett	RDG	Ron	22/07/35	Fulham		1955	1957	Victoria	Sheffield Wed.	133	7	3	3	0	0	0	0
						1967	1968	Sheffield Wed.	Retired								
Stainrod	SA	Simon	01/02/59	Sheffield		1980	1984	Oldham Athletic	Sheffield Wed.	145	12	17	3	48	6	5	3
Standley	TL	Tommy	23/12/32	Poplar		1957		Basildon	Bournemouth	15	0	0	0	2	0	0	0
Stein	EMS	Mark	28/01/66	Cape Town, SA		1988	1989	Luton Town	Oxford United	33	3	4	4	4	1	2	0
Stejskal	J	Jan	15/01/62	Czechoslavakia		1990	1993	Sparta Prague	Slavia Prague	108	3	11	1	0	0	0	0
Stephenson	H			London		1930				2	0	0	0	0	0	0	0
Stephenson	J	Jimmy	1895	New Delaval	1958	1927		Watford	Norwich City	18	0	0	0	0	0	0	0
Stewart	G	George	18/10/20	Chimside		1947	1952	Brentford	Shrewsbury Town	38	2	0	0	5	0	0	0
Stewart	IE	Ian	10/09/61	Belfast		1980	1984	Jnrs.	Newcastle Utd.	67	3	9	3	2	0	2	0
Stock	AWA	Alec	30/03/17	Peasedown St John		1937	1938	Charlton Ath.	Yeovil T (p/m)	16	8	0	1	3	2	0	2
Swan	J	Jack	10/7/1893	Easington		1926	1927	Watford		28	0	0	0	5	0	0	0
Sweetman	SC	Sid		London		1924	1928	Hampstead T	Millwall	100	2	0	0	0	0	0	0
Swinfen	R	Reg	04/05/15	Battersea		1936	1946	Civil Service	Yeovil Town	26	7	0	4	5	1	0	0
Symes	HC	Ernest		Acton		1924	1925	Aberdare Ath.		26	4	0	0	0	0	0	0
Tagg	AP	Tony	10/04/57	Epsom		1975		App.	Millwall	4	0	0	0	0	0	0	0
Taylor	B	Brian	02/07/44	Hammersmith		1962	1965	Jnrs.	Romford	50	0	2	0	0	0	0	0
Taylor	GA	Geoff	22/01/23	Henstead		1953		Bristol Rovers	Guildford City	2	0	0	0	0	0	0	0
Taylor	JG	Jim	05/11/17	Hillingdon		1953		Fulham	Tunbridge Wells (p/m)	41	3	0	0	0	0	0	0
Teale	RG	Richard	27/02/52	Millom		1974		Walton & Hersham	Fulham	1	0	1	0	0	0	0	0
Temby	W	Bill	16/09/34	Dover		1955	1956	Rhyl	Dover	7	0	0	0	3	0	0	0
Thomas	D	Dave	05/10/50	Kirkby-in-Ashfield		1972	1976	Burnley	Everton	182	14	17	7	28	2	3	1
Thompson	C			Bighton Banks		1921		Newcastle United		1	0	0	0	0	0	0	0
Thompson	GL	Garry	07/10/59	Birmingham		1991	1992	Crystal Palace	Cardiff City	19	0	5	1	1	0	3	0
Thompson	J			Willesden		1924	1925	Yeovil & Petters		22	4	0	0	0	0	0	0
Thompson	O	Oliver	1902	Gateshead		1928		Chesterfield	York City	18	0	0	0	0	0	0	0
Tillson	A	Andy	30/06/66	Huntingdon		1990	1991	Grimsby Town	Bristol Rovers	29	0	2	1	2	0	0	0
Tomkys	MG	Mike	14/12/32	Kensington		1951	1958	Fulham	Yiewsley	86	8	0	2	16	2	0	0
Towers	EJ	Jim	15/04/33	Shepherds Bush		1961		Brentford	Millwall	28	3	2	0	15	0	1	0
Trodd	W					1934			Leyton	6	0	0	1	0	0	0	0
Turner	W	Bill	1896	South Moor		1927		Bury		38	1	0	0	0	0	0	0
Turpie	RP	Bob	13/11/49	Hampstead		1969		App.	Peterborough Utd.	2	0	0	0	0	0	0	0
Tutt	W					1930	1931	Canterbury W.		7	0	0	0	3	0	0	0
Underwood	ED	Dave	15/03/28	St Pancras	1989	1951		Edgware Town	Watford	2	0	0	0	0	0	0	0
Vafiadis	O	Seth	08/09/45	Hammersmith		1963		Chelsea	Millwall	15	0	0	0	4	0	0	0
Vallance	H	Hugh		Edgbaston		1928		Aston Villa	Brighton & Hove A.	1	0	0	0	0	0	0	0
Vango	AJ	Alf		Walthamstow		1930	1931	Gillingham	Clapton Orient	12	0	0	0	0	0	0	0
Varco	PS	Percy	17/04/04	Fowey	1982	1926		Aston Villa	Norwich City	16	0	0	0	4	0	0	0
Venables	TF	Terry	06/01/43	Bethnal Green		1969	1974	Tottenham H	Crystal Palace	177	14	15	0	19	1	2	0
Vigrass	J	John		Leek		1921	1923	Leek Alex.	Macclesfield T	66	5	0	0	1	0	0	0
Vincent	E	Ernie	28/10/07	Washington	1978	1935	1936	Manchester Utd.	Doncaster Rovers	28	2	0	1	0	0	0	0
Waddock	GP	Gary	17/03/62	Kingsbury		1979	1986	App.	Charleroi	203	14	22	1	8	0	2	0
Walker	C	Clive	26/05/57	Oxford		1985	1986	Sunderland	Fulham	20	4	3	0	1	0	1	0

Player			D.O.B	Place of Birth	Died	First Lge Season	Last Lge Season	Previous Club	Next Club	Appearances				Goals			
										League	FAC	FLC	Other	League	FAC	FLC	Oth.
Wallace	BD	Barry	17/04/59	Plaistow		1977	1979	Jnrs	Tulsa Roughnecks	25	2	1	0	0	0	0	0
Waller	W	William		Bolton		1923		Chorley		2	0	0	0	0	0	0	0
Walsh	MA	Mickey	13/08/54	Chorley		1978	1980	Everton	FC Porto	18	1	1	0	3	0	0	0
Walsh	PAM	Paul	01/10/62	Plumstead		1991		Tottenham H (loan)		2	0	0	0	0	0	0	0
Warburton	A	Arthur	10/09/08	Bury	1978	1938		Fulham	Retired	17	4	0	0	0	0	0	0
Wardle	G	George	24/09/19	Kimblesworth		1948	1950	Cardiff City	Darlington	53	1	0	0	4	0	0	0
Waterall	A	Albert	01/03/1887	Nottingham	1963	1926		Stockport Co.	Clapton Orient	2	0	0	0	0	0	0	0
Watson	E	Edward	1899	Shotton		1922		Sunderland	Rochdale	8	0	0	0	0	0	0	0
Watson	G	George	1914	Shotton Colliery		1934		Durham City		8	0	0	0	1	0	0	0
Watson	IL	Ian	07/01/44	Hammersmith		1965	1973	Chelsea	Retired	202	16	14	0	1	0	1	0
Watts	TF			London		1920	1922		Yeovil & Petters	4	0	0	0	0	0	0	0
Waugh	LS			Newcastle		1923		Bedlington Col.		5	0	0	0	0	0	0	0
Waugh	WL	Billy	27/11/21	Edinburgh		1950	1952	Luton Town	Bournemouth	77	2	0	0	6	0	0	0
Webb	DJ	David	09/04/46	Stratford		1974	1977	Chelsea	Leicester City	116	8	15	8	7	0	2	2
Wegerle	RC	Roy	19/03/64	Johannesburg, SA		1989	1991	Luton Town	Blackburn Rovers	75	11	5	1	29	1	1	0
Welton	RP	Pat	03/05/28	Eltham		1958		Leyton Orient	St. Albans C (mgr.)	3	0	0	0	0	0	0	0
Westwood	D	Danny	25/07/53	Dagenham		1974		Billericay T	Gillingham	1	0	1	0	1	0	0	0
Whatmore	EL	Ernie	25/04/00	Kidderminster	1991	1928	1931	Bristol Rovers		78	4	0	0	3	0	0	0
Whitaker	C	Colin	14/06/32	Leeds		1960		Shrewsbury Town	Rochdale	8	0	0	0	0	0	0	0
White	DW	Devon	02/03/64	Nottingham		1992	1994	Cambridge Utd.	Notts County	27	0	2	0	9	0	0	0
Whitehead	WT			Saffron Walden		1925		Swansea Town	Preston NE	24	4	0	0	5	0	0	0
Whitelaw	G	George	01/01/37	Paisley		1958	1959	Sunderland	Halifax Town	26	0	0	1	10	0	0	0
Whitfield	K	Ken	24/03/30	Bishop Auckland		1959	1960	Brighton & Hove A.	Bideford (p/m)	19	4	0	0	3	0	0	0
Whittaker	R	Dick	10/10/34	Dublin		1963		Peterborough Utd.	King's Lynn	17	0	1	0	0	0	0	0
Wicks	JR	Jim		Reading		1924		Reading		5	0	0	0	0	0	0	0
Wicks	SJ	Steve	03/10/56	Reading		1979	1980	Derby County	Crystal Palace	189	5	23	4	6	0	0	0
						1981	1985	Crystal Palace	Chelsea								
Wilcox	JC	Joe	19/01/1894	Coleford	1956	1926		Bristol Rovers	Gillingham	9	0	0	0	2	0	0	0
Wiles	GH	George	1905	East Ham		1929	1931	Sittingbourne	Walsall	18	0	0	0	0	0	0	0
Wiles	HS	Harry		East Ham		1929	1932	Sittingbourne	Walsall	42	1	0	0	25	0	0	0
Wilkins	DM	Dean	12/07/62	Hillingdon		1980	1982	App.	Brighton & Hove A.	6	0	1	0	0	0	0	0
Wilkins	RC	Ray	14/09/56	Hillingdon		1989	1993	Glasgow Rangers	Crystal Palace	171	14	16	2	7	2	0	1
						1994	1995	Crystal Palace									
Wilks	A	Alan	05/10/46	Slough		1966	1970	Chelsea	Gillingham	50	1	3	0	14	0	5	0
Williams	B	Brian	05/11/55	Salford		1977		Bury	Swindon Town	19	2	2	0	0	0	0	0
Williams	WT	Bill	23/08/42	Esher		1961	1962	Portsmouth	West Bromwich A.	45	2	1	0	0	0	0	0
Wilson	AN	Andy	14/02/1896	Newmains	1973	1931		Chelsea	Nimes	20	3	0	0	3	0	0	0
Wilson	CA	Clive	13/11/61	Manchester		1990	1994	Chelsea	Tottenham H	172	8	16	3	12	1	1	0
Wingrove	J					1920		Uxbridge		24	3	0	0	0	0	0	0
Witter	AJ	Tony	12/08/65	London		1993		Crystal Palace	Millwall	1	0	0	0	0	0	0	0
Wood	AB	Arthur	08/05/1890	Southampton	1977	1923	1924	Newport County	Retired	20	0	0	0	0	0	0	0
Woods	CCE	Chris	14/11/59	Swineshead		1979	1980	Nottm. Forest	Norwich City	63	1	8	0	0	0	0	0
Woods	PJ	Pat	29/04/33	Islington		1952	1960	Jnrs.	Hellenic (Aust.)	304	20	2	7	15	0	0	1
Woodward	HJ	Horace	16/01/24	Islington		1949	1950	Tottenham H	Walsall	57	1	0	0	0	0	0	0
Woodward	JH			Catford		1927	1928	Watford	Merthyr Town	10	1	0	0	0	0	0	0
Wright	E	Ernie	1912	Middleton		1934			Crewe Alexandra	1	0	0	0	0	0	0	0
Wright	PH	Paul	17/08/67	East Kilbride		1989		Aberdeen	Hibernian	15	2	2	0	5	0	1	0
Wyper	HTH	Tommy	08/10/00	Calton		1931		Charlton Ath.	Bristol Rovers	11	0	0	0	0	0	0	0
Yates	J	John	1903	Manchester		1929		Aston Villa		10	0	0	0	0	0	0	0
Yates	S	Steve	29/01/70	Bristol		1993	1995	Bristol Rovers		82	4	5	0	1	0	0	0
Young	H	Bert	04/09/1899	Liverpool	1976	1929		Newport County	Bristol Rovers	14	1	0	0	1	0	0	0
Young	J	Jack	1895	Whitburn	1952	1926	1928	West Ham Utd.	Accrington Stanley	89	2	0	0	12	0	0	0
Young	W	William		South Shields		1924	1925	Tyneside District	Gillingham	8	0	0	0	2	0	0	0
Zelic	N	Ned	04/07/71	Sydney		1995		Borussia Dortmond	Eintract Frankfurt	4	0	0	0	0	0	0	0

Played in FA Cup Only

Player			D.O.B	Place of Birth	Died	First Lge Season	Last Lge Season	Previous Club	Next Club	Appearances				Goals			
Benstead	G	Graham	20/08/63	Aldershot		1982		App.	Norwich City	0	1	0	0	0	0	0	0
Campbell	D	Dougold	14/12/22	Kirkintilloch		1948			Crewe Alexandra	0	1	0	0	0	0	0	0
Silver	A	Alan				1954			Tunbridge Wells	0	1	0	0	0	0	0	0

Played in 1939 only

Player			D.O.B	Place of Birth	Died	First Lge Season	Last Lge Season	Previous Club	Next Club								
Bonass	AE	Albert	1912	York		1945	1939	Chesterfield									
Mangnall	D	Dave	21/09/05	Wigan		1962	1939	Millwall									

Played in Division 3(S) Cup only

Player			D.O.B	Place of Birth	Died	First Lge Season	Last Lge Season	Previous Club	Next Club	Appearances				Goals			
Ives	GH	George		Barton, Lincs		1937		Brentford		0	0	0	1	0	0	0	0
Stevens	RF	Ronald				1938		Luton Town		0	0	0	1	0	0	0	0